P9-CMB-186

THE IRWIN SERIES IN ECONOMICS

EDITORIAL COMMITTEE

MALCOLM M. DAVISSON, *Chairman*
University of California

W. ALLEN WALLIS
University of Chicago

EDWARD S. SHAW
Stanford University

LLOYD G. REYNOLDS
Yale University

COLLECTIVE BARGAINING

PRINCIPLES AND CASES

COLLECTIVE BARGAINING

PRINCIPLES AND CASES

JOHN T. DUNLOP

HARVARD UNIVERSITY

1951

RICHARD D. IRWIN, INC.

Chicago, Illinois

COPYRIGHT 1949 BY RICHARD D. IRWIN, INC.

ALL RIGHTS RESERVED · THIS BOOK OR ANY PART THEREOF MAY NOT BE
REPRODUCED WITHOUT THE WRITTEN PERMISSION OF THE PUBLISHER

First Printing, January 1949

Second Printing, July 1949

Third Printing, May 1950

Fourth Printing, August 1951

PRINTED IN THE UNITED STATES OF AMERICA

HD
6483
D8

PREFACE

THIS book has grown out of the teaching of an undergraduate course, "Trade Unionism and Collective Bargaining," a one-semester introduction to labor economics. As a result of this teaching experience, another introduction to collective bargaining—along less conventional textbook lines —is offered. Many aspects of collective bargaining cannot readily be understood in the absence of specific illustration— promotion, layoff, discharge, and discipline problems are illustrative—and few students have had the experience necessary to visualize concretely the issues of the work community. "Collective bargaining" remains an empty phrase, tinged with favorable emotional reactions but devoid of substance or content. Moreover, the operation of collective bargaining cannot be depicted in terms of the day-to-day problems of employees, unions, and managements. The student is likewise frequently unable to make one world of the formal principles of economics and the facts of actual wage-fixing. The teacher must constantly struggle against simple generalizations in a field in which students normally bring strong prejudices to the classroom. The discriminating mind cannot be cultivated readily simply by lectures and reading; some other means is required to elicit reaction from students and to challenge them with significant problems and issues.

The cases in this volume constitute an attempt to meet some of these limitations of the conventional introduction to collective bargaining and to supplement the standard readings. They have been built from arbitration awards and proceedings, from umpire decisions, from records of negotiations, and from interviews and field trips. A great many different

vii

56808

officials of labor organizations, management representatives, arbitrators and umpires, and state and federal government officials have assisted in the collection of the basic materials from which these cases have been developed. A great deal of sifting, rewriting, and substitution of cases has been necessary in the light of actual teaching experience. The experiment has proceeded far enough, however, to warrant a preliminary judgment. These cases have very materially improved the understanding of my students, and it is hoped that others may have the same experience with them.

The cases may be used in a variety of ways: they may provide assigned reading in a lecture course, the students may be asked to submit a series of short papers in the form of "decisions" on the cases presented; ideally, however, the specific situations provide the basis for discussion in the classroom. Questions at the end of each case have been developed to facilitate the understar.ling and framing of principles. A discussion section on these cases has been substituted for a third lecture each week in my own course. While sections usually number twenty-five to thirty-five students, it is well to remember that instruction in many law schools follows the same method with classes of several hundred students.

The experience with these cases during the last three years suggests that students have come to have a better understanding of collective bargaining and labor economics in the following respects:

1. There are at least two sides, and frequently many more, to most issues in this field. It is a healthy discovery to some students to learn that managements can be wrong, and to others that unions make mistakes.

2. The clear statement of contending positions is an education in itself. The student can be lead to identify the premises from which such positions develop.

3. The process of industrial jurisprudence involved in collective bargaining is illustrated in rich detail.

4. A number of different conceptions of labor relations can be illustrated by the various ways in which students will handle a case: there are certain to be legalists and strict constructionists in the interpretation of an agreement; the approach of the social worker or clinician will emerge, concentrating upon the human or personal aspects of the case; and the view will be illustrated that emphasizes the problems of accommodating two organizations.

5. The hard discovery is made that one can never know all the facts about a situation. While cases which hinge narrowly on issues of fact have been excluded, there will be many occasions when ideally more information could be desired. In the world of action and behavior, the decisions of labor leaders, business executives, and arbitrators must be made on partial information.

6. The collective agreement can never cover all contingencies. A great many problems arise which were not envisaged by the parties, and perhaps could not have been. The importance of the spirit or tone of a collective bargaining relationship is recognized in this fashion.

7. The arbitration process is illuminated. Particular attention can be directed to the tactics and policies which lie behind each side in the arbitration of disputes.

8. The union and the company both emerge as organizations whose leaders have internal problems of reconciling conflicting views and interests.

9. The handling of wage cases requires the utilization of economic theory as a tool of analysis rather than as an end in itself. Particular situations cannot be solved by the mouthing of formulas or the duplication of diagrams from textbooks. The richness and complexity of wage issues can lead the student to make economic theory less a formal exercise and more a method of analysis of vexing issues.

10. The process of problem-solving is the chief virtue of the method. The compulsion that the student make up his

own mind about a particular situation stimulates debate and reflection.

There are no "right" answers to the cases presented, in the sense that there are right answers to typical mathematical problems. No key of correct solutions has been provided in the back of the book. In each case presented, there was a historical answer, in that an arbitrator or a union leader or business executive rendered a decision, or joint negotiations achieved agreement, before or after a work stoppage. In some few instances, these decisions have been presented in the write-up of the cases. The problem has then centered around the wisdom of the decision. In most cases, no answer is provided. The primary emphasis should be placed upon the rationale of an answer, for the understanding of the problem is more important than any answer. The beginning of wisdom in labor relations and collective bargaining is the recognition of problems.

The introductory chapters in Part I are intended to provide for the general reader a survey of the more prominent aspects of collective bargaining. They constitute both a general setting to the cases in Part II and a survey of some of the more significant problems of public policy in the field. If collective bargaining is the accepted national policy, it is imperative that its characteristics and limitations be widely understood.

The author gratefully acknowledges in the preparation of this volume the suggestions and critical comments of colleagues at Harvard University. Professor Sumner H. Slichter reviewed some of the cases in the early phases of this experiment; Professor James J. Healy provided many a complex problem for stimulating discussion from his rich experience as an arbitrator; and Professor Walter Galenson and Mr. Lloyd Ulman have made many helpful suggestions from their experience in teaching the cases in sections.

In the early stages of this endeavor, Mr. Lloyd Ulman and Mr. M. Goodman were helpful in selecting and preparing cases. As research assistant over a two-year period, Miss Esther Ross very materially advanced the project by the effective preparation of additional cases; and the imaginative work of Mr. and Mrs. John Armstrong, as librarians of the Industrial Relations Library, helped to provide much of the basic source materials. Mrs. Lillian Hagg faithfully performed the arduous task of typing the manuscript. In addition, the comments and critical suggestions of numerous students have been indispensable.

This volume is dedicated to D. S., who demonstrated that the handling of individuals is the greatest of the arts and from whom the author learned that an awareness of the real place of men in organizations is the basis for influencing groups.

JOHN T. DUNLOP

HARVARD UNIVERSITY
January 1949

TABLE OF CONTENTS

INDEX

Part One

An Introduction to Collective
Bargaining

Chapter I

~~~~~~

THE EMERGENCE OF COLLECTIVE
BARGAINING

LABOR unions and large-scale business enterprises are both a product of modern industrial society. While each has roots which extend far into the past, they have acquired their distinctive current features during the last hundred years. Both organizations are part of the transformation of an agricultural and commercial community into an industrial society. Both organizations will be decisive, it is widely conceded, in the shaping of the economic destiny—indeed, the total life—of the nation in the next generation.

Collective bargaining has no place in an agricultural society of self-employed farmers. During the past century a predominantly rural society has given way gradually to urban communities. The farm as the principal place of work has been displaced by the factory and the office. The local and regional orientation of affairs has yielded to the dominance of a common national life. The emergence of collective bargaining is one manifestation of this fundamental change in the society, the growth of an industrial nation.

Structural Changes in the American Economy

In 1850 there were 7.4 million men and women in the country who worked for a living. Today the labor force aggregates more than 60 million. In 1850 more than 55 per cent of the community earned its livelihood in agriculture. Today agriculture employs less than 15 per cent of the labor force. While there are more people working in agriculture today than a century ago, its relative share of all workers has

3

steadily declined. The industrial sectors of the economy have rapidly expanded—manufacturing, mining, transportation, communications, and construction.

But the industrial community creates other types of employment than factory jobs. The services of wholesale and retail trade, finance, and banking are required. Professional services, clerical occupations, and government employment have been among the most rapidly growing sectors. In 1948 the industrial sectors included 21.7 million, distributed as follows: manufacturing, 15.4 million; construction, 1.6 million; mining, 0.9 million; and transportation and public utilities, 3.8 million. In addition there were 8.6 million in trade, 4.6 million in service industries, and 5.4 million in government service. Agriculture had 7.9 million. This diversity of employment is one of the more important structural changes in the economy. The industrialization process has created much more than a "proletariat," to restrict the term to factory employees.

The relative decline of agricultural employment and the expansion in industry, wholesale and retail trade, service trades, and government has created an economy of wage- and salary-earners. While there may be 6 or 7 million proprietors and self-employed business and professional men and women outside of agriculture, the great majority of our citizens earn their livelihood as wage- and salary-earners. More than two-thirds of the national income is distributed in the form of wages and salaries.

The expansion of other sections of the economy relative to agriculture is related to the rapid increase in the standard of living over the past century. On the average an employee in industry has tended to produce a greater value of output than an employee in agriculture. This statement does not imply that the industrial worker works harder nor that he is necessarily more skilled. Since his energies and skills are typically combined with more capital equipment and machinery and a high order of management, the product of industry per hour of labor services has typically been greater than in agriculture. The gradual shifting of the work force out of agriculture and into industry has consequently been a means of increasing total output. An employee spared from agriculture typically increased production by a great amount elsewhere when re-employed.

The gradual transposition of the work force from agriculture to industry has had other consequences. Since rural areas have had the larger natural rates of increase in population, a relative increase in industrial employment has required a continuing large movement of workers from farms to cities. The rural and farm origins of the industrial work force, except for those who immigrated from cities abroad, has had important consequences on the ideas, beliefs, and habits of industrial workers. Thus, much of the independence of Detroit workers is to be understood only in terms of the migrations of large numbers from Kentucky, Tennessee, and rural areas of the Middle West. Our industrial work force is not yet composed predominantly of second and third generations of city-dwellers. When that day arrives the industrial worker may be expected to have dropped many of his agricultural antecedents.

In 1850 the national income was almost $5 billion (in 1940 prices). Today national income approximates $127 billion (also in 1940 prices). This enormous expansion in goods and services is partly the consequence of an increase in population and the simple duplication of facilities. However, the national income today would be only $37 billion (in 1940 prices) if the only changes since 1850 had been the extension of existing methods of production with the increase in population.

The largest part of the increased income, $85 billion, out of the $122 billion increase, must be ascribed to an increase in the productiveness of the economy.

It has already been noted that a rearrangement of the work force by a transfer of workers from agriculture to industry has tended to increase total output. These reallocations of the man power of the community, it is estimated, account for 40 per cent of the improvement in productiveness of the system.[1] (This factor would account for an increase of $35 billion since 1850.) The most important single factor responsible for the increase in the national income over the century has been the improvement in the productivity of labor within industries and in the growth of new industries. (This factor would account for an increase of $52 billion since 1850.)

Although these figures are necessarily only rough estimates, the accompanying tabular presentation may help to visualize the fundamental forces at work over the past century:

National income in 1850 (1940 prices)......................	$5 billion
Duplication of facilities with population increases............................	$37 billion
Reallocation of labor force among industries	34 "
Increase in productivity within industries...	51 "
National income in 1948 (1940 prices).....................	127 billion

The increase in productivity of a man-hour of work is basically to be attributed to the enormous technical revolution of the period. It is not merely that more capital investment in plant and equipment are combined with labor services. More capital equipment of the 1850 vintage would not have accounted for the expansion in production. The quality of equipment, the technical knowledge of management, the layout and arrangement of industry, and the skill of workers have been so improved that, when combined, they have

[1] Simon Kuznets, *National Income: A Summary of Findings* (New York: National Bureau of Economic Research, 1946), p. 48.

yielded enormously greater value of output per unit of labor input.

In 1850 a worker typically had the help of only 0.5 horsepower of energy from animals and from minerals. By 1940 the community used 27 horsepower hours for each hour of human effort. In 1850 for each worker in manufacturing, it is estimated there was $557 (in 1850 prices) worth of capital equipment. In 1940 the figure approximated $6,000 (in 1940 prices).[2] These statistics provide some indication of the quantity of capital goods combined with labor services to account for the expansion in productivity. But they do not measure the most significant changes which were in the technical knowledge and in the quality of the combination of labor services, capital goods, and management. The revolution in technique and the rearrangements in the productive process yielded the striking improvements in the standard of living of the last century.

The gains in productivity were distributed in a variety of forms:

a) The hours of work were gradually reduced. The scheduled hours of work per week approximated sixty-nine hours for nonagricultural employment in 1850. That schedule was slightly less than six days of twelve hours each. Today, scheduled hours per week are in the neighborhood of forty, five days of eight hours each.

b) The level of money wages and salaries has increased sharply, even relative to prices. In 1850 the wages of nonagricultural workers probably averaged in the vicinity of 9 cents per hour. In 1940 they averaged somewhat over 60 cents, and today they exceed $1.30 per hour. The level of money wages and salaries has been a rising plane, and, perhaps, even an increasingly rising plane.

c) Since prices have increased over the period, these money values do not indicate the increase in the real purchasing

[2] Prices had roughly doubled.

power of an hour's work. Roughly speaking, living costs doubled in the period 1850–1940; they have since increased another 70 per cent. The real wage per hour today of industrial workers would appear to be over four times that of a century ago. But these figures underestimate the improvement in the real wage rate since they cannot reflect adequately the improvements in quality and the development of new commodities and gadgets. For any single product, the improvement in productivity typically has been reflected both in an improvement in quality and in at least an initial period of reduction in price.

d) A part of the benefits of increasing productivity has no doubt gone, at least in the first instance, as higher or excess profits to the enterprise introducing the change. Such returns might be designated as the rewards of innovation and are a part of the price the community pays for a dynamic system. In pure theory these excess profits are removed by competition. They can be restored only by more innovation. In this type of a world, where monopoly elements are not significant, profits are said to be the engine which keeps the system dynamic. One of the central problems of the modern economy—with monopoly elements in business and with unions in the labor markets—is the struggle over the initial division of the gains of increasing productivity.

The basic technological and market changes in the economy, which are at once adaptations to and a prime mover of the industrial economy, produced a revolution within the business community. The corporate form of organization became dominant. Ownership and management were separated. Large groups of employees were brought together in a single workplace. An internal management organization suitable to large-scale operations developed. A business bureaucracy of various departments is organized—production, sales, engineering, finances, etc. The personnel or industrial relations department is among the latest additions to the business organization.

These same basic technological and market changes in the structure of the economy have produced a change in the labor market. Factory employment and the growth of cities made the work community the decisive focus of the life of the worker. Not only is he dependent for employment upon the level of industrial activity, but the larger family and the small community cease to be such important instruments of social control and security to the individual. The job determines not only economic destiny but frequently the social and larger aspects of life.

The development of the industrial economy has depersonalized relations in the labor market. The large-scale enterprise must operate by rule and regulation. Consequently, the working boss of the small shop becomes the inanimate corporation, the familiarity of the first name gives way to the badge number, and the attention to individual and unique problems becomes remote.

The dynamic industrial economy involves threats to the skill of the individual worker. Changes in tastes and methods of production may eliminate a job or drastically change its content. These changes are requisite to the growth of the system; the essence of the increase in productiveness already observed is just such change. It must not be inferred that the net effect of these changes is to produce a less-skilled work force on the whole. The evidence is quite to the contrary. But for individual workers there must be change with greater or less cost of movement and with greater or less sense of insecurity.

The industrial system, whose spectacular achievements over a century have been noted, has not grown smoothly. The system time and again has been raked with depression. In fact, there were only a few years of full employment in the whole century, and these were mainly wartime periods. These depression periods, particularly when prolonged as in 1873–79 and 1929–33, created great hardship for industrial workers. They raised doubts in the minds of workers, as in the rest of the community, over the basic institutions of the economy. The question could not be escaped at such times whether the notable achievement of the economy had been purchased at too high a price. It is no accident that the periods of greatest labor organization in the century follow these worst depression periods—the upsurgence of the Knights of Labor (1881–86) and the New Deal period (1933–37).

The organization of wage-earners into labor unions and the growth of management organization—in a word, the emergence of collective bargaining—is basically a facet of these structural changes in the economy over the past century. Only a broad brush has been used to outline the main contours of the impact of the growth of an industrial economy on the work force and the business organization. The details are written in the history of the growth of each enterprise and the emergence of each local and national union. The emergence of collective bargaining was inherent in the development of an industrial economy, at least in a society in which governmental authority does not make all significant decisions.

Structural Changes in Community Values and Institutions

The ideas and beliefs of an agricultural society are not appropriate to an industrial community. The institutions of the agricultural community—courts and local governments— are likely to be inadequate in an industrial age. The century of rapid technological and market changes, which altered the economic structure, also witnessed a related transformation in the values of the community and in the public institutions of the society.

The American community of 1850 was a testimony to its long apprenticeship to the soil. Emerson observed in 1844 that "the vast majority of the people of this country live by the land, and carry its qualities in their manners and opinions." These qualities included a hostility to the rising industrial world. Thomas Jefferson had extolled the agricultural community: "Generally speaking the proportion which the aggregate of the other classes of citizens bears in any state to that of its husbandmen, is the proportion of the unsound to its healthy parts, and is a good enough barometer whereby to measure its degree of corruption. While we have land to labour then, let us never wish to see our citizens occupied at a workbench. . . ."

The "manners and opinions" which Emerson regarded as derived from the soil might be summarized as follows: Individual advancement was to be achieved solely by hard work; leisure was regarded as a vice; the economic destiny of an individual depended solely upon his ability to work and save; poverty was regarded as the reward for sloth; the poor deserved their fate; and the public care of the impoverished was treated as the encouragement of idleness. These values did not spring from the soil in any literal sense. They had their antecedents in the philosophic preconceptions of the Age of Enlightenment. But the significant point is that these ideas and beliefs were congenial to the agricultural and frontier economy of the first half of the nineteenth century. They were consistent with the objective facts of the society.

The system of values of the American community of 1850 was also congenial to the emerging industrialists. They thrived on the spirit of individualism. The accent on thrift and saving facilitated the requisite accumulation of capital.

No strong government was envisaged to curb or direct the great outbursts of industrial energy.

But the community values of 1850 could not persist in a mature industrial society. The technological and market changes, referred to in the last section, were creating an economy incompatible with these values rooted in the soil (and in the philosophy of Enlightenment). Economic prosperity of the individual depended upon the availability of jobs rather than merely upon the willingness to work. The rising productivity made increased leisure possible; it was not necessarily an evil in an economy which permitted an increasing margin over subsistence or which steadily revised upward the content of subsistence. Individuals in the community, particularly wage-earners, came to question the costs of the rapid expansion in living standards. The quest for security developed both out of the insecurities of the industrial society and the increasing proportion of older age groups in the population. Thus, the older order of community values began to change under the impact of the industrial economy. Ideas themselves as advocated by reformers and new social classes played a distinctive role in the creation of a new set of community values. The community has yet to develop a full and complete set of values consistent with the objective facts of the industrial economy.

The labor union was not envisaged in the community values of 1850. A labor union in many ways is the negation of the idea that economic status depends on individual effort. The status of the individual worker depends to a large extent on collective action. The union strives for shorter hours and more leisure. It is an instrument to legislate in the economic or political field the security of wage-earners. The union stresses higher wages through collective action rather than individual thrift as a means of economic advancement. The intellectual life of the country could envisage little place for a labor union in 1850. The wages-fund doctrine was a "demonstration" that the artificial increase in wage rates, by union action, could not improve the lot of the wage-earners of the community. There was no economic rationale for a union. As the industrial community has grown and the values of the community have changed to provide a role for the union, so too has economic analysis developed a place for the labor organization.

The dominant community values of 1850 with their accent on individualism were to have a decisive impact on the labor movement itself which developed in America with the spread of industrialization. The class-conscious characteristics of many European labor movements did not take deep root. These antecedent community values have created many of the most serious internal problems of the American labor movement. The individual worker was difficult to organize. Union growth was slow. The closed shop and similar forms of union security were developed to hold any ground won. Unions had to contend not only with hostile employers and a hostile community but frequently with hostile wage-earners. The unorganized workers would not respect picket lines as would have been the case among European class-conscious wage-earners. These community values also help to explain the essential economic or "bread-and-butter" character of American unions.

Despite the dominance of economic objectives in the American unions, it must be recognized that a labor movement always has other activities. The labor organization is broader than collective bargaining. These other activities of a labor movement are primarily beyond the scope of this volume. In some environments the labor union may become, in effect, an instrument of political action. It may become a force in a variety of community activities—public education and health and welfare activities. It is clear that a labor movement cannot become significant in the area of collective bargaining without affecting the whole structure of the community in a variety of other ways.

At no point was the influence of the dominant community values more decisive than in the views of the courts. At the outset the common law, built upon commercial and agricultural antecedents, could find no place for a union. It was a conspiracy against trade. Here, as in all other facets of the life of the community, the impact of industrialization has finally wrought its change. The courts came to tolerate labor organizations if their objectives and purposes were held to be legal. Public policy has since reached the point of declaring it to be in the public interest to encourage the practices and procedures of collective bargaining.[3]

The Extent of Collective Bargaining

The oldest existing international union, the International Typographical Union, is less than a hundred years old. It was founded in 1852. By the end of 1948, 15.5 million workers were members of labor organizations in the United States. They were organized into more than 60,000 local unions which for the most part were constituent parts of 145 international[4] and national unions affiliated with the American Federation of Labor (AFL) and the Congress of Industrial Organization (CIO). The ten largest unions, each with a membership of over 300,000, comprised 37 per cent of all organized workers. The terms and conditions of employment for these union members were set forth in some 75,000 written agreements negotiated with employers or their associations.

While 42 million workers were employed in nonagricultural pursuits in 1948, collective bargaining was far more significant for setting the terms of labor bargains than a

[3] Chapter II constitutes a discussion of recent public policy toward collective bargaining.

[4] The difference between an international and a national union in practice is that the international union has local unions in Canada and occasionally in Mexico.

simple comparison with the 15.5 million union members might suggest. The percentage of employees organized in various sectors of the economy were as shown in Table 1. Beyond a certain point in an industry or a locality, collective bargaining becomes so significant that it effectively conditions, at least within narrow limits, all labor bargains. The influence of collective bargaining is far greater than the area of union membership.

TABLE 1

	Number of Employees (in Millions)	Estimated Percentage under Union Agreement
Manufacturing	15.4	70
Mining	0.9	80–100
Construction	1.6	80–100
Transportation	2.7	80–100
Public utilities	1.1	40–60
Trade	8.6	Below 20
Finance	1.6	Below 20
Service	4.6	20–40
Government	5.4	Below 20
Agriculture	7.9	Below 20

The industrial community which has emerged in the past century has produced the institution of collective bargaining —labor unions and management organization. It is a fair inference that labor unions will include a larger proportion of the work force in a generation than even at present. Collective bargaining may be expected to become even more extensive. The operation of collective bargaining consequently becomes decisive for the performance of the economy and for the structure of the society.

SUGGESTIONS FOR FURTHER READING

CLARK, JOHN MAURICE. *Alternative to Serfdom*, pp. 61–90. New York: Alfred A. Knopf, 1948.

DEWHURST, J. F., and ASSOCIATES. *America's Needs and Resources*, pp. 17–51. New York: Twentieth Century Fund, 1947.

LESTER, RICHARD A., and SHISTER, JOSEPH (eds.). *Insights into Labor Issues*, pp. 163–93. New York: Macmillan Co., 1948.

SIMONS, HENRY. *Economic Policy for a Free Society*, pp. 121–59. Chicago: University of Chicago Press, 1948.

SLICHTER, SUMNER H. *The Challenge of Industrial Relations*, pp. 1–28. Ithaca: Cornell University Press, 1947.

Chapter II

COLLECTIVE BARGAINING:
A NATIONAL POLICY

THE encouragement of collective bargaining is the announced policy of the country. Section 1 of the Wagner Act, and the same language was carried over into the Taft-Hartley Law, declared it to be the policy of the United States "to eliminate the causes of certain substantial obstructions to the free flow of commerce and to mitigate and eliminate these obstructions when they have occurred by encouraging the practice and procedures of collective bargaining and by protecting the exercise by workers of full freedom of association, self-organization, and designation of representatives of their own choosing, for the purpose of negotiating the terms and conditions of their employment or other mutual aid or protection."

This policy had its antecedents in the Norris-La Guardia Act (1932), the Railway Labor Act (1926), the experience of the War Labor Board in World War I, and in the reports and recommendations of numerous commissions that had investigated prominent strikes and labor unrest over the previous half-century. A distinguished line of special commissions had found that the flagrant denial by employers of the right to organize had been a frequent issue in industrial disputes.

The Wagner Act

The Wagner Act established for the United States the public policy of encouraging collective bargaining as the means of adjusting the relations between managements and their employees. The statute proceeded from explicit premises which may be identified as follows:

1. The inequality in bargaining power between individual employees and large-scale business concerns tends to depress wage rates. The statement of "Findings and Policies" at the outset of the Wagner Act holds that this inequality of bargaining power depresses "the purchasing power of wage earners in industry and prevents [*sic*] the stabilization of competitive wage rates and working conditions within and between industries." The organization of workers results in wage-rate levels which are better, using the test of aggregate national income, for the economy as a whole and which eliminate "unfair competition" between firms based solely on their power to depress wage rates.

2. The denial of the right to organize—the Wagner Act says by "employers," and the Taft-Hartley Law says by "some employers"—creates industrial strife. The public protection of the right to organize eliminates this type of dispute. Since interference by management with the rights of organization of workers may take a variety of forms, the Wagner Act designated a series of "unfair practices," including discrimination for union membership or activity, the establishment or support of a company-dominated union, and the refusal to bargain collectively.

3. The Wagner Act was formulated on the implied premise that, if the obstructions to organization of workers imposed by managements were eliminated, workers would "naturally" join labor unions. Industrial workers if freed from employer influence could be expected, almost inevitably, to become union members. A union organization would emerge either within the enterprise spontaneously or as a result of the assistance of outside labor unions. The term "self-organization" was applied to both processes.

From the vantage point of a decade, these explicit premises

of the Wagner Act were substantially influenced by the great depression following 1929. The reference to the effect of inequality of bargaining upon purchasing power reflects the impact of the depression on the economic thinking of the country. The notion that organization of the workers would prevent "unfair wage-cutting" and stabilize competitive conditions within and among industries was a result of the experience with creeping wage cuts during the depression. It might even be said that the Wagner Act was a product of the depression. There is much to support such a statement even beyond the premises and language of the Act. The prolonged failure of the economic system during the depression created distrust in existing institutions and led to interest in labor organizations on the part of millions of workers. But the Wagner Act was not purely a product of the great depression following 1929. It has been noted that labor organizations, and public policies to encourage collective bargaining, were also the result of long-run forces at work in a society gradually adapting itself to industrialization.

The Taft-Hartley Law

The Taft-Hartley Act will be more readily understood if it also is approached both as a product of certain immediately antecedent events and as in part a reflection of basic forces at work in the community. Union membership rose from approximately 5 million in 1935 to over 15 million at the end of World War II. The end of hostilities evoked the largest work stoppages in January, 1946, that the country had ever seen. There were nation-wide strikes during the first half of 1946 in the steel, meat packing, railroad, and coal industries. These stoppages alienated large sections of public opinion, some on the grounds that the unavailability of peacetime goods must be due to these strikes, and others through fear that the closing down of vital industries was a threat to society itself which could not be tolerated. These judgments were formed without close attention to the merits of the particular stoppages.

The inflationary postwar period with high employment displaced the emphasis on union organization to prevent wage cuts. In the postwar inflation, individual wage-earners had at times considerable bargaining power and did exact wage rates materially above even the union scale. Fixed-income sections of the work force came to believe that the unions were in some way partly responsible for their plight created by rapidly rising prices. It might be said that just as the Wagner Act was partly a product of the depression, so the Taft-Hartley Act reflects a postwar inflationary period.

Longer-run forces were also at work in bringing about the Taft-Hartley Act. The Wagner Act had never pretended to be a comprehensive labor code. Many problems were not considered, such as emergency disputes, boycotts, and jurisdictional disputes. It would have been surprising, indeed, if ten years of experience on a new policy would not have revealed some modifications at the legislative level. The growth of the labor movement to a more influential position in the community created more concern and interest in the internal operations of unions. The isolated cases of abuse of union office or the arbitrary action by a union officer toward a member took on new status in view of the widespread nature of organization. Many union officers and members were new and had not the discipline, training, and experience of the "old timers."

As a consequence of these longer-run forces and the special postwar inflationary setting and strike record, large sections of public opinion were convinced that "something had to be done" about labor organizations. Mr. George Meany, Secretary-Treasurer of the American Federation of Labor, recognized in a forthright manner this basis of the Taft-Hartley

Law when he said in October, 1947: "We have built up our organizations and we have raised the wages of the people we represent, but we have failed somewhere, because we haven't got public opinion with labor in this country, and we might just as well admit it. Labor unions are not in good with the public generally, or the N.A.M. [National Association of Manufacturers], and all the reactionary forces couldn't have passed this legislation." The specific provisions of the law are far too technical and detailed to be related to public opinion other than in this general way.

The basic premises which underlay the Taft-Hartley Law may be identified. How accurately these premises reflect the true character of workers, unions, and managements will emerge from an understanding of collective bargaining in operation in particular cases.

1. The Act reflected the belief that the individual worker should be protected by public policy, not alone in his right to join a labor organization, but also in his choice to refrain from being a member if he so elects. To Section 7 of the Wagner Act, which sets worth the "right to self-organization," the Taft-Hartley Law added, "and shall also have the right to refrain from any or all of such activity. . . ." It became an unfair practice for a labor union to interfere with this right of the individual employee to refrain from joining a union (except as union membership may be a condition of employment when required in a contract in accordance with the election and other procedures of the Taft-Hartley Law). The Taft-Hartley Law in effect denied a premise of the Wagner Act noted above, namely, that freed of employer domination industrial workers will "naturally" join labor organizations.

The protection of the right to refrain from union membership qualified the announced policy of encouraging the practices and policies of collective bargaining. Because of the practical possibilities open to an employer to utilize the procedures of the Taft-Hartley Law to delay or frustrate labor organization, the basic policy of encouraging collective bargaining may have been altered. Professor Cox has concluded that "the Taft-Hartley amendments represent an abandonment of the policy of affirmatively encouraging the spread of union organization and collective bargaining."[1]

2. The interests of labor organizations and their individual members are not to be regarded as identical, according to the Taft-Hartley Law. Public policy cannot be restricted to considering labor organizations as an entity; it must push on into the relations between union members and union officers and between members and the union organization. The Act presumed that many union members are captives; they are persistently trying to get out of the union organization. The Act presumed that union leaders do not reflect, in a significant number of cases or in important cases, the true wishes and opinions of the rank and file of members. On these grounds public policy should go behind the actions of union leaders to determine more directly the members' views or to permit them to escape the organization.

It is this assumption of the Taft-Hartley Law, perhaps more than any other, which is responsible for the intensity of the reaction of labor organizations to the law. Labor leaders believe they know and understand their members. They identify themselves and their organizations with the members. They believe their interests are mutual and inseparable. They deeply resent the allegations that they do not really represent their members and that the rank and file of union members would in any way be disloyal to the common interests of the union.

3. The right to strike in certain industries particularly affected with the public interest should be qualified at least

---

[1] Archibald Cox, "Some Aspects of the Labor Management Relations Act, 1947," *Harvard Law Review*, Vol. LXI (November, 1947), p. 44.

for a limited period, by resort to fact-finding boards and injunctions. These special procedures may be invoked in "emergency disputes."

On the basis of these assumptions, the Taft-Hartley Law developed a detailed and jumbled regulation of the relations between unions and managements. It is easy to get lost in the complexities of this legislation. There are certain fundamental respects, however, in which the Taft-Hartley Law sought to introduce major changes in the public policy toward collective bargaining. They will be noted briefly.

1. The Act introduced the principle of the public regulation of the *contents or provisions* of the labor agreement. The Congress had not previously provided any extensive or explicit limitations on the substantive terms of the agreements concluded under free collective bargaining. The Taft-Hartley Law provided a series of limitations. (*a*) The closed-shop form of union security is illegal. (*b*) The checkoff clause must provide for the individual member to authorize the deduction of union dues. (*c*) The termination or reopening clauses of the agreement must provide for sixty days' notice to the other party and thirty days' notice to the Federal Mediation and Conciliation Service. (*d*) Welfare funds must conform to specified standards.

The significant point is not so much the wisdom of the particular regulations of the provisions of labor agreements as it is the innovation in policy itself. Is the public prepared to insist upon a particular contract provision when unions and managements may otherwise agree? What are the mechanics for the enforcement of the public policy when the parties are otherwise agreed? What provisions of the agreement are susceptible to public regulation, and which are to be left exclusively to the parties for collective bargaining? The Congress embarked on a program of regulating the union security provisions of agreements. Should the same policy be extended to seniority provisions, to wage clauses, and to the scope of the grievance procedure? If the Congress is to embark on the policy of regulating the terms of agreements, the question arises as to the method to be used in reaching such decisions and the role which unions and managements are to have in formulating the specific regulations.

2. The Taft-Hartley Law also constituted the first attempt to regulate on a national basis the internal processes of labor organizations. In treating the relation between the union and its members, the Act provided that, in order to use the facilities of the National Labor Relations Board, a union must conform to specified standards: (a) The union must distribute financial reports or make them available to members. (b) The union must file anticommunist affidavits for each officer. (c) Initiation fees that are "excessive or discriminatory" constitute the basis for an unfair labor practice. (d) The Act made it an unfair labor practice on the part of the *employer* to discriminate against an employee for nonmembership in a labor organization for other grounds than nonpayment of dues. These regulations on the internal life of the union are indirect and roundabout. They are made a condition to access to the National Labor Relations Board or are imposed indirectly upon the employer.

3. The Taft-Hartley Law adopted the principle that some interruptions of work are of such a vital nature to the public interest that special procedures are established to be invoked by the President of the United States. These disputes must involve a substantial part or all of an industry where a stoppage will imperil the national health or safety.

The Bargaining Unit and the Scope of Bargaining

There must be a union organization and management and a defined group of employees represented by the union in order for there to be collective bargaining. The public policy of encouraging collective bargaining practices accordingly requires that a public body be prepared to designate the appropriate unit for bargaining and the organization that represents the employees.

The National Labor Relations Board holds elections among employees to determine which labor organization, if any, a majority desire to select as their bargaining representative. Before any election can be held, however, it is necessary to determine the election district, that is, the group of eligible voters. The appropriate unit may be a craft, an industrial unit of all employees in a plant or company, or some other grouping of employees. Just as the choice of the election district in the political arena may have decisive effects on the outcome of an election, so also in the collective bargaining field. The introduction of the election process into the organization of unions and the public determination of the bargaining unit—both introduced by the Wagner Act and altered in minor respects only by the Taft-Hartley amendments—have had major consequences for collective bargaining and the labor movement that were not foreseen in 1935.

Prior to the Wagner Act, unions were organized by a variety of informal methods. Perhaps the most general method was for a nucleus of strategic workers to go on strike when an employer had refused to recognize the union. The remainder of the workers were organized on the picket line. Some workers joined unions readily because they had been members of a labor organization in the old country. In other cases, a strong union might approach an employer and secure recognition for his employees on the threat of withdrawal of transportation for supplies or finished goods. In other instances, an employer might be induced to sign an agreement by the threat of refusal of another union, or the same union, to handle the product at the consumer or some intermediate stage. Prior to the Wagner Act, organization was a test of strength. It is not surprising then that labor unions were prominent primarily among groups of strategic workers who were in a position to put considerable pressure upon a company to secure recognition.

Organization by election is quite a different process. The collective bargaining election takes on much of the character of a political election. There are slogans and name-calling. The union makes campaign promises. There is resort to means of mass communication and mass appeal. Workers are not asked to go on the picket line, although that may have to come later; they are simply asked to *vote* for the union. Election methods can be applied to large groups of employees to displace or to supplement traditional organizing tactics that are directed to small groups of strategic workers. The election process is especially adapted for the organization of large industrial units. It facilitates the organization of workers who possess little individual bargaining power, that is, the relatively unskilled worker.

The introduction of the election, with the employer required to recognize the victor, has had a major impact on the labor movement. The strategy of organizing has become quasi-political. The organization of larger units and less strategic groups of employees is encouraged. The individual union member may be expected to have a different relation to the union when he has simply voted for the organization than when he has joined it via the picket line.

Even more far-reaching effects for the labor movement and collective bargaining have developed from the public determination of the appropriate bargaining unit. Prior to the Wagner Act, the range of employees to be covered by an agreement was left to the bargaining process. Competition between two unions for employees was not supposed to take place. The American Federation of Labor itself was supposed to resolve questions of conflicting claims between unions.

The principle of exclusive jurisdiction prescribed for each union an allotted jurisdiction, recognized in a charter. If each union lived within this jurisdiction, serious problems concerning the appropriate unit for collective bargaining could not arise. The public determination of the bargaining unit was made difficult and highly controversial by the split within the labor movement and the emergence of the Congress of Industrial Organization soon after the Wagner Act was passed. A bargaining-unit determination by the government can vitally affect the survival of a union in competition with rival organizations. An industrial unit may swallow up a craft union, leaving only an unrecognized minority in a larger group, and, conversely, a series of craft-unit determinations may take from an industrial union many of the strategic workers it had relied upon for strength in bargaining.

From the point of view of management, the public determination of the bargaining unit when a number of rival unions are involved may result in highly unsatisfactory bargaining arrangements. A company may find itself in a situation that requires negotiation of separate agreements with a variety of unions. Rivalries among these groups will be reflected in a struggle in bargaining for more favorable contract provisions. The introduction of company-wide policies, an understandable desire on the part of management, may be made impossible in negotiating the diverse demands of a variety of bargaining units.

From the importance of the bargaining unit to unions and managements, it follows that determination of the bargaining unit is the most significant responsibility exercised by the National Labor Relations Board for the future of collective bargaining. But public policy has not alone affected the results of bargaining by the administrative determination of the unit; the Congress in the Taft-Hartley Law excluded particular groups of employees, such as foremen, from the law. Public policy has shaped collective bargaining by these determinations of the employees to be included in the bargaining unit.

The public policy of encouraging collective bargaining has had still another effect on the bargaining process that was not anticipated at the time of the passage of the Wagner Act. That law provided that it was an unfair labor practice for an employer to refuse to bargain collectively. The Taft-Hartley Law added a correlate unfair labor practice for labor unions. These requirements appear reasonable enough on their face. But what do they mean?

The requirement to bargain may be interpreted in procedural terms. The parties are required to take certain steps, that is, to confer, to discuss, to consider proposals, to make counteroffers, and so on. To bargain in good faith is at best an elusive concept, and one party may go through the motions without any intention of reaching an agreement. The requirement to bargain, viewed procedurally, injects a government agency into all the intimate details of the bargaining process when a charge of refusal to bargain has been filed.

The requirement to bargain may be interpreted in substantive terms. The government may decide what is, and what is not, an appropriate subject of collective bargaining. The scope of bargaining comes to be defined by public regulation. The following types of questions must be faced: Is a pension plan a subject for bargaining? What about demands or counterdemands regarding the members of the board of directors or union officers? And what about a plan to increase production or improve quality? Until the Wagner Act, the scope of collective bargaining was determined by the bargaining process itself. The policy of encouraging collective bargaining has been extended to determine by public agency the demarcation between subjects that are appropriate for bargaining and those that are not. The future of collective bargaining will be very significantly shaped by the way in which public policy defines the scope of bargaining and the range of topics treated in an agreement.

The Functions of Collective Bargaining in the Community

The public policy to encourage collective bargaining requires a scrutiny of the role which collective bargaining plays in the industrial community. What can be expected of it? What does it purport to do? For what purposes is it ill-adapted? Only when these questions have been faced is it possible to appraise the operation of collective bargaining.

Collective bargaining seeks to fulfill three purposes in an industrial community with the traditions of a political democracy. (1) It fixes the price of labor services. (2) It provides a system of industrial jurisprudence, establishing and administering the conditions, other than wages, under which wage-earners render their services. (3) It provides a mechanism by which employees may be represented in decisions affecting their individual and group interests. Collective bargaining represents the extension of the democratic idea into the work community. These purposes may not be achieved, but such are the claims of collective bargaining. Each of these facets of collective bargaining may be examined briefly.

1. A number of methods could be invoked to determine the price of labor services in a community. Public authorities could fix all wages. A minimum wage is an instance of public wage-fixing. During the war period 1942–45, all wage changes were subject to the approval of the stabilization authorities. Or, wages might be left to the play of market forces. Competition between wage-earners for jobs and between firms for employees would govern the price of labor services. Collective bargaining involves the formal organization of buyers and sellers in the labor market. The action of government and

the impact of market forces, however, are not without effect on wages under collective bargaining; rather do these various forces affect wage rates through unions and managements. Changes in the competitive positions of firms and industries and in the demand and supply for various types of labor do affect the price of labor under collective bargaining. The chain of effect is through the decision-making processes of unions and managements, and their bargaining, rather than in any automatic or mechanical manner. The market and collective bargaining methods of fixing wages are not to be treated as unrelated. Market forces characteristically influence the collective bargain, although collective bargaining introduces a new element, the union as an organization, into wage-fixing.

Collective bargaining has the advantage over government wage-fixing in that the persons most familiar with the type of work, the special problems of the company and the employees, the surrounding locality and industry influences, make the decision. Collective bargaining permits a flexibility that more centralized wage-fixing could not tolerate. This flexibility and adaptability of collective bargaining is superior in many cases to the market determination of wages. The parties may also experiment with one type of wage payment rather than another. They may develop new forms of compensation, such as vacation payment or health and insurance plans, to meet particular problems. Such individuals also may give fair consideration to many job classifications unique to plants for which no market rate ordinarily would be established.

The determination of wages by collective bargaining may involve problems that other methods of fixing wages in the community would avoid. The parties to the bargain may be able to increase wages and prices at the expense of the rest of the community. Critics of collective bargaining are fearful that strong unions and their employers will act in the labor market like any monopolist in the sale of goods. Wages will be higher in these instances, and employment less. In this way, the wage structure of the community will be distorted and employment distributed among firms and industries in less than an ideal fashion. It is also feared that collective bargaining may push the whole level of wage rates up faster than the long-term gains in productivity. Prices must rise in continual inflation to the detriment of fixed-income groups in the community.

It would be futile to deny that such potential dangers exist in the fixing of the price of labor services by collective bargaining. Every method of wage-fixing has its limitations. The crucial question of public policy would be rather to appraise how serious these dangers have been in fact. Can the institutions of collective bargaining be shaped from within or from without to yield a wage structure and a wage level more responsive to the needs of the community as a whole? The issue is a challenge to the unions and managements of the country.

2. Collective bargaining seeks to serve the dual function of, first, creating in a legislative fashion the terms and conditions, in addition to wages, under which wage-earners perform services and, second, administering in a judicial way the agreements which incorporate these terms and conditions of employment. The process of negotiating and administering agreements establishes the common law of the work community. It is difficult for the outsider to appreciate the diversity and complexity of problems which arise in the workplace. One of the purposes of this volume of cases is to introduce the general reader to some of these problems.

As a system of industrial jurisprudence, collective bargaining recognizes certain rights and duties of management and establishes rights and duties *applicable to all workers*. Call-in payment, for instance, is provided for all employees required to report to work. All workers are protected from arbitrary discharge. Then, collective bargaining establishes the *relative rights of particular individual workers in particular jobs*. A contract and its administration will determine the relative rights of two workers in a particular job in the event of a transfer, the possibility of a promotion, a temporary layoff in the work force, or a permanent reduction in the staff. These determinations are among the most important in any contract. They pertain not so much to the rights of management relative to the employees as a whole but rather to the relative rights among different classes of employees or among particular individuals. Finally, as a system of industrial jurisprudence, collective bargaining establishes a *procedure for the redress of grievance*. The grievance procedure, including arbitration as a final step, is in many ways at the heart of the operation of collective bargaining. This procedure will be examined in its various aspects in the next two chapters.

As a system of industrial jurisprudence, collective bargaining seeks to settle disputes short of industrial warfare, without resort to strikes and lockouts. It seeks to maintain *industrial peace*. A distinction should be recognized between a work stoppage arising under a contract and one resulting from a dispute over the provisions of a new agreement. While each new collective bargaining relationship tends to be plagued with stoppages under a contract for a limited period, the record of peace under agreements has not ordinarily been criticized if measured by the absence of stoppages. It is stoppages arising over the terms of new agreements that have caused greatest concern. This observation suggests that it is the legislative function of creating new agreements, rather than the administrative and judicial function of interpreting agreements, that requires most attention as a matter of public policy. The creative processes of collective bargaining have yet to be applied seriously to this problem.

3. Collective bargaining seeks to introduce a measure of democracy into industry. Through their representatives, wage-earners have come to have a voice in the decisions which so vitally affect their economic status and the life of their work community from day to day. Collective bargaining is supposed to provide the individual worker with a sense of participation in the affairs of the immediate department, and the company, and so on into the affairs of the industry, the community, and the nation. It attempts to provide a significant outlet for the energies and creative ideas of workmen, which can be so easily lost in the hierarchies of any organization. It seeks to harness the latent energy and productiveness of workers who tend to produce most when they are secure in their jobs and convinced of the worthwhileness of their endeavor.

These objectives are sometimes lost because of conflict between unions and management organizations. At other times, the goal of a sense of participation in the affairs of the industry is lost within the union itself. The rank and file may have little opportunity, or may choose to exert little influence, on the decisions of the union organization.

These objectives are high standards by which to judge the performance of any social institution. At times, these objectives may be internally inconsistent. Industrial peace may require stronger and more disciplined organizations, reducing in some degree the democratic element of the influence of the individual members. Wage rates that will bring industrial peace may produce unfortunate economic consequences. The parties at bargaining may have to choose between developing details of the system of industrial jurisprudence and wage increases. In any event, collective bargaining is to be viewed in its many facets. Any over-all judgment of the performance of collective bargaining must be shaped by attention to the three aspects of the relations between unions and managements, which have been discussed in this section.

The Formulation of Public Policy

Collective bargaining is a relatively new institution. The term itself is less than sixty years old. Many of its features are in the experimental stage as labor unions and managements try various policies within their organizations and various means of conducting their relations. Collective bargaining need take no final form as it adapts slowly to the changes in the total environment in which the parties live. Nonetheless, as judged by the history of the experience of unions and managements in western European countries, collective bargaining in the United States is young.

If the experience of other countries and the tendencies inherent in union and management organizations are studied, they suggest that during the next generation particular patterns of growth in collective bargaining are to be expected. A larger proportion of the work force will be organized and covered by agreements. There will be an extension of multiple-firm bargaining as the employers of the country organize themselves into formal and informal associations for purposes of bargaining. The employers of the country have been as difficult to organize effectively for bargaining as were wage-earners themselves for many years. The scope of bargaining can be expected to be broadened to include a larger range of problems affecting the security and economic status of wage-earners.

An even more significant range of problems for the next generation concerns the relation of collective bargaining to public regulation. The Wagner Act involved some extension

of governmental supervision over collective bargaining, as in
the bargaining-unit determination, which even the labor
movement did not generally foresee. The Taft-Hartley Law,
passed by a Congress opposed in principle to the extension of
governmental regulation, involved a radical expansion of the
authority of government in the collective bargaining process.
The terms of agreements were made subject to public policy as
noted; the internal affairs of labor organizations were prescribed in some detail; special procedures may be involved in
emergency disputes. These remarks are not intended to pass
judgment on the wisdom of the particular extensions of public regulations. They do suggest the need for reflection on the
implications of these policies. To what extent are the terms of
agreements to be the subject of public regulation? How far can
governmental determination be extended without excluding
from collective bargaining the significant problems? What
standards should prescribe the limits of public regulation of
the internal government of a labor union? To what extent
will the determination of key contracts by fact-finding or
other emergency procedures in effect determine contract provisions for other management and labor organizations?

The last decade should have clearly indicated to the parties
to collective bargaining that they must learn to solve their
problems or the public will insist that public agencies do the
job. The failure of labor organizations (and managements,
too) to develop their own procedures for settling jurisdictional disputes resulted in legislation on the point. The failure
of critical industries, coal for instance, to develop by collective bargaining machinery to settle disputes over the terms of
new agreements led to the emergency disputes and injunction
provisions of the Taft-Hartley Law. The internal government
practices of some unions have led to the beginnings of public
regulation of union operations.

A critical range of problems confronts the country in the question of just how much public regulation of collective bargaining there shall be. The free collective bargaining process has many advantages. It has flexibility. It is relatively decentralized. It can operate close to the particular problem. It provides balance of power in a community in which public decision-making becomes more and more important. The further extension of public regulation of collective bargaining can only shift to the political arena more and more of the activities and energies of labor organizations and managements.

The most significant point to be noted in appraising the Taft-Hartley Law is not the provisions of the law, significant as were the changes in public policy which the statute sought to establish. Greater importance must be attached to the legislative process by which the law was enacted. It was unfortunate, indeed, for the community that believes in self-government to have had the public regulation of collective bargaining shaped hardly at all by the labor and management representatives most familiar with its operations.

The time has arrived to establish the principle that the legal framework of collective bargaining shall represent largely the consensus of labor and management. The time has passed for more "get-even" labor legislation. There will be some issues on which the public interest will require limitations and regulations of collective bargaining. In such instances, it is important that the proposed regulations be filtered through the experience and thinking of the representatives of both sides in collective bargaining.

If the problems of the division of responsibility between collective bargaining and public regulation in the field of industrial relations are to be understood, there is need for widespread knowledge of the processes, procedures, and institutions of collective bargaining. The cases which comprise this volume are intended to contribute to this end.

SUGGESTIONS FOR FURTHER READING

CLARK, JOHN MAURICE. *Alternative to Serfdom*, pp. 118–53. New York: Alfred A. Knopf, 1948.

COX, ARCHIBALD. "Some Aspects of the Labor Management Relations Act, 1947," *Harvard Law Review*, Vol. LXI, pp. 1–49, 274–315.

SLICHTER, SUMNER H. *Trade Unions in a Free Society*. Cambridge, Mass.: Harvard University Press, 1947.

TAYLOR, GEORGE W. *Government Regulation of Industrial Relations*. New York: Prentice-Hall, Inc., 1948.

WRIGHT, DAVID McCORD. *Democracy and Progress*. New York: Macmillan Co., 1948.

Chapter III

UNION AND MANAGEMENT ORGANIZATION FOR COLLECTIVE BARGAINING

THE parties to collective bargaining are *organizations*. It is a relationship between formally constituted groups. Any study of collective bargaining, consequently, requires insight into the internal structure and operation of unions and managements, as well as into their interrelations. If the group character of collective bargaining is understood at the outset, two pitfalls can be avoided.

First, there are many good people who have treated labor-management issues as problems primarily of personal relations, the rapport between a foreman and an operator, or between a business executive and a labor leader. From this viewpoint the improvement of industrial relations is a feature of "how to win friends and influence people." A pious version contends that industrial peace is to be achieved primarily through personal morality; better industrial relations await more moral individuals.

Second, there are many sophisticated people who envisage problems of collective bargaining primarily as questions of managerial administration, the operation of a plant or a department. The existence of a labor organization is viewed as the result of inefficient management and the poor "handling of men." The improvement of industrial relations, from this perspective, requires the development of more efficient administration. When pieces of paper flow more promptly and "lines of communication" are securely established, industrial peace will have been achieved.

There can be little doubt that a sensitivity to human relations and an understanding of administrative techniques both have much to contribute to collective bargaining. The primary fact must be firmly grasped, however, that collective bargaining involves the relations between two organizations. Representatives of labor and management in the collective bargaining process do not act as autonomous individuals or administrators. They have a role to fulfill within their organizations, and their relations involve the dealings between two complex institutions.

Like any continuing organization, unions and companies point with pride to founding fathers. In the histories of both there have been periods of crises and difficulty. Frequently, both have grown from humble beginnings in the face of real difficulties. Slogans and principles come to be formulated. An elaborate folklore is developed on the place of the organization in the industry and the community and its contribution to them. There are varying degrees of authority and responsibility among the individuals associated with companies and unions. Some are leaders and others followers. In both organizations there is designation of responsibility for policy decisions and for administration of the affairs of the body. In brief, each organization is a distinct entity with a life of its own. Collective bargaining is the process by which unions and managements accommodate each other at points where the two organizations come into contact.

Both unions and managements normally perform a variety of activities outside of the collective bargaining relationship. Companies require an organization, for instance, to produce and distribute their output, to handle the requisite financial transactions, and to deal with governmental and community agencies. Unions similarly require an organization to handle relations with other unions, to undertake political activity in some cases, to represent the union before the community and government agencies, and to "educate" members. Some management organizations are created solely for purposes of collective bargaining; thus, some associations are restricted to handling virtually all problems of a group of firms pertaining to union relations. Likewise, there are some unions whose activities seldom extend beyond a narrow construction of collective bargaining. Unions and managements, however, usually perform a variety of functions not closely related to collective bargaining; their internal structure and organization must be understood, consequently, in terms of the full range of their activities.

Contrast between Unions and Managements

While unions and companies share the common features of continuing groups, striking contrasts between them are frequently noted. These contrasts are actually the differences between the *ideas* about, or the conception of, unions and managements which are generally entertained. These are differences between the organizations as they are supposed to operate. Companies are primarily economic institutions; unions are said to be characteristically political. The one is supposed to be controlled by stockholders; the other by members voting as individuals rather than in accordance with relative financial interests. Companies are said to maximize profits; it is not clear what is the analogous prime objective of unions. Some unions have been interested in maximizing the income of their members; others have been interested mainly in furthering the power of the union, in some instances even against the economic interests of the members; still some few others have been interested primarily in political power or revolutionary objectives. Thus it is said that, while each union partakes of some elements of a business, every union is a part of a social *movement*. Although the proportions vary, each labor leader is part business executive or administrator, part politician, and part high priest. The business executive in contrast is seldom characterized as a politician or leader of a movement.

The hierarchy of offices in a business is supposedly filled by appointments in which merit and ability are the basis of selection. The company is supposed to be managed efficiently with responsibility centered at the top. The union, in contrast, is expected to meet the test of a democracy. Efficiency is subordinate in principle to the civil rights of the members within the union. Leaders are chosen by ballot in the atmosphere of elections in which demagoguery inevitably finds a place. While administrative responsibility may be centered at the top of the union, approval of many detailed policies may be required by the rank and file. The labor executive or administrator on even routine matters is ever conscious of a constituency and an electorate.

These contrasts between unions and companies are in accordance with idealized pictures of the two organizations; they follow from the way unions and companies are supposed to behave. In actual practice the contrast is normally not so sharp. A great many unions function as highly integrated organizations primarily concerned with negotiating and administering agreements. Most companies, in turn, have certain political elements in their operation. It would be dangerous indeed to approach a study of collective bargaining with a highly stereotyped model of the operation of unions or companies. Their fundamental differences emerge in particular situations, many of which will be noted in the cases that will be presented in Part II.

The Decision-Making Process

Since collective bargaining is a relationship between organizations, the internal procedures which unions and managements adopt to formulate decisions are a vital part of the total bargaining process. An understanding of the anatomy and the functioning of labor and business organizations is indispensable to any study of collective bargaining. The representatives of each side at the conference table must be placed in the context of the organizational wheels and connections of which each is a part.

This conception of the bargaining process suggests the following types of questions. Who really makes decisions in a complex hierarchy? Are the decisions typically made by one man or by a committee? What is the division of responsibility within the organization for various types of problems? What information is available when decisions are made? Are there any procedures to insure that various points of view within the organization receive careful attention? What steps are available for the review and appeal of decisions? Only when such questions have been explored for a union and a management organization is it possible to begin to comprehend a particular collective bargaining relationship. These questions provide clues to what makes an organization tick.

A fundamental distinction is to be drawn between policy decisions and administrative decisions in the operation of an organization. Policy decisions establish general rules and guideposts, while administrative decisions apply such policies to particular situations.

The distinction is a relative matter, and many different levels of policy-making and administration may exist in a single organization with each administrator establishing some policies for those below him. Thus, the top policy group or individual in a company may decide upon the introduction of a job evaluation plan involving a specified cost increase, leaving to an executive considerable discretion as to the features of the plan. This officer may in turn establish the policy of increasing the differentials for skilled workers, leaving to subordinates the administration of this policy including the selection of the particular jobs to receive the greater increase. A whole series of policy-making administration relationships may exist in a single organization as one moves from top officers to minor supervisory personnel, each with a narrower range of problems and each with less discretionary powers. In the functioning of unions or managements, it frequently is important to ascertain the point or points in the organizational hierarchy at which decisions have been formulated.

The decision-making process requires further scrutiny. Any decision would seem to involve at least these four aspects: (*a*) the recognition of a problem, difficulty, or situation; (*b*) a survey of some possible solutions; (*c*) the exploration of the consequences, both immediate and remote, of some of the possible solutions; and (*d*) the choice among the alternatives. A decision must not be presumed to imply a change from present practice. Thus, the considered judgment to make no change is to be treated as a decision.

Consider the illustration of a company officer who has had called to his attention a problem concerning smoking during work hours in a plant. There may be frequent infractions of existing rules. Typically, a number of complaints and reports, or a dramatic incident, are required to compel recognition that the problem requires a decision. A series of alternatives may be considered: no smoking anywhere; clearly designated smoking areas; the existing practice; specified time periods for smoking; leave the problem to the union; departmental rules; etc. The implications of these various alternatives are explored including a consideration of the experience of other firms. Finally, a decision is made—in this case, a policy decision.

The four aspects of the decision-making process may involve different levels of the organizational hierarchy. The initiation of a problem may come from "above" or from "below" or from outside the organization. The boss may have a suggestion or an idea (above), or subordinates may require direction (below). The research arm of an organization may initiate a matter for decision. Differences of opinion arise between parts of the organization; these conflicts must be resolved. Decisions of a policy character in most organizations, no doubt, arise through particular cases in which subordinates seek instruction from those above them in the hierarchy. It is impossible to anticipate all the diverse types of situations that will arise, and policy-making typically is initiated by problem cases. Policy-making starts with the recognition that a case has implications of a general sort. A problem broader than the case is posed for decision. The recognition and formulation of problems is one of the most significant aspects of decision-making in any organization.

The discovery of alternative solutions to the problem and the exploration of the consequences of these alternatives may involve many different levels of an organization. In fact, most top-level decision-making involves the choice among alternative plans which have been formulated in detail by many sections of the organization. If a single plan is presented, the choice is between approval and disapproval. Many decisions involve the approval of actions proposed by subordinates.

The decisions made by an organization—whether administrative or policy-making—will be significantly shaped by the information available to decision-makers. This information reflects the procedures and lines of communication that have been established within the organization. Frequently these arrangements restrict a decision-maker to the information as presented by immediate subordinates. A subordinate is understandably anxious to appear in the best possible light, and an account of a problem or situation is accordingly colored. Such bias is normally not deliberate.

It is a basic problem of every organization to provide channels of information, an intelligence system, which presents to a decision-maker an account of situations that has been carefully checked for partiality. It may be possible to get reports from different sources. Written statements may facilitate accurate reporting. The "facts of the case" do not normally pre-exist for the decision-maker. A number of different bits of information, each with a tag indicating its source, is the raw material for the decision-maker. He must come to some judgment from these as to "the facts" of the situation.

When two organizations deal with each other in collective bargaining, the representative of each must have a degree of confidence in his own internal information-gathering system. A company official handling a grievance will wish to feel that he knows exactly what went on in the department in which the grievance arose. Similarly, the union representative does not care to be shown to be ignorant of the facts. Each may not disclose the full extent of his knowledge, particularly if it appears to be advantageous not to do so, but each will desire confidence in the reliability of his own information system. In order to make decisions in the interest of the organization, the internal channels of information must be orderly and reliable.

The growth of collective bargaining has centered considerable attention on the internal communication system of managements. Where there was no labor organization in a plant, there was little basis for top decision-makers to question the information that was filtered up to them through layers of supervision. It made little real difference whether a foreman's report of a discharge, to be filed in the personnel records, was entirely accurate. Similarly, there would be no one to question a report as to the basis for promotion of an employee. When a union enters the picture, however, management representatives require a new confidence in the reliability of information. Not only must they know a great many things that previously did not concern them, but they must be prepared to defend management action before a union representative and frequently before an arbitrator. An extensive and reliable information system is indispensable for these "foreign relations" of an organization.

The Impact of Unions on Management Organization

Among the most prominent consequences of the organization of wage-earners is the reorganization and change required in the internal management of companies. The administrative and policy-making machinery of the company must be oriented to confront a labor organization. The change in internal management is no less conspicuous in "well-managed concerns" than in less well-run firms. The task of treating with a union compels these changes. Some of the more prominent features of this management revolution may be noted.

1. The necessity for a reliable information system has already been noted. The top management is compelled, not only to ascertain the behavior of its representatives, but also to develop intelligence on the conduct of the union in various parts of the bargaining unit.

2. The existence of a union impels management to establish internal organization in order to insure uniform standards of administration of policies throughout the departments or plants organized by the union. The union will be quick to call to management's attention that a more favorable practice is followed in one place than in another, contending that the more favorable practice should be extended. In the absence of a union, such differences may escape the attention of top management. They may be sources of discontent, but these differences ordinarily do not have much leverage. Under union conditions such differences serve as excellent arguments for a concession to the union.

The union is usually organized, either formally or informally, so that small differences in handling wage payment, layoffs, promotions, leaves of absence, or a thousand other matters are quickly noticed. Before the introduction of unions when foremen had extensive responsibilities, such minor differences were certain to develop. Under union conditions, managements develop administrative practices to secure a higher degree of uniformity to escape whipsaw tactics. Among these devices are detailed, written administrative rules; conferences of management representatives; and review of departmental action.

3. The introduction of a union tends to centralize the process of policy-making in management organizations on labor relations problems. Management cannot afford to have a variety of policies determined on the same problem when the union maintains a vigilant watch to detect such inconsistencies. Centralization of policy-making is intended to prevent undesirable precedents. If management deals with an organization whose policy decisions are centralized, it too must be prepared to act in a highly centralized fashion.

4. The growth of a collective bargaining relation tends to require management to develop a staff organization concerned with affairs and problems dealing with the union. There is need to compile information on the activities of the same or other unions in similar circumstances. The operating management must be serviced with all relevant information on problems that touch the union. The staff functions of the labor relations department emerge.

The introduction of a union affects the operation of a company in many other ways. Unions tend to provide an incentive for managements to use their work force more efficiently; they may compel attention to human problems otherwise neglected; they have been instrumental in some cases in improving the technical processes of production. But attention has been directed above to ways in which the introduction of a union contributes to the internal reorganization of the decision-making process within management. The administrative and policy-making arrangements are themselves altered. Those changes are among the most far-reaching in the community associated with the introduction of collective bargaining.

Management Organization

No two companies have the same management organization for collective bargaining. Formal arrangements will vary with the size of the concern and its operating units, the geographical range of operations, the general management organization, the number of unions with which the management bargains, the contents of its policies, and the personalities on both sides. A national chain store in the retail field, for example, has different problems than a company with a single manufacturing plant. The general dispersion in operations and the employment of young girls with a high turnover rate in the chain store typically will require unique features of organization. It would be ridiculous to expect a single form of management organization for collective bargaining. Each management hierarchy is likely to be shaped to deal with its distinctive internal and external problems. Each management system is also likely to be changed from time to time as these problems alter.

Despite these differences, there are at least three persistent aspects of management organization related to collective bargaining. In any given situation, the student of collective bargaining, or the practitioner, will seek out these relationships in order to understand the operation of the management side of the table.

a) Top-Management Organization.—The organization of top management for decision-making directly affecting collective bargaining is a salient feature of management organization. What is the status within the management hierarchy of the officer directly responsible for industrial relations? What is his delegation of authority? Does he contribute his viewpoint in the councils of the company on broad questions of policy? Does he know what is "going on" in the company? What are the procedures whereby legal considerations, the financial position of the company, operating and production views, and public relations find their impact on collective bargaining decisions of the company? The final decisions of the company will be significantly affected by the mechanism within top management to balance or to weigh the influence of the legal, production, sales, financial, and industrial relations departments of the company on collective bargaining problems.

In some few companies, the chief spokesman in contract negotiations is the chief executive. In other cases, the company may be represented primarily by an operations man, by the industrial relations officers, or by legal counsel. These differences may reflect simply the accidents of personalities, or they may reflect fundamental views of the management organization toward collective bargaining. The use of the chief executive of the company may symbolize a belief in the critical importance of industrial relations in the company. A production vice-president may reflect the conception of bargaining primarily as a continuing relationship with the main chain of operating authority in the company, from the top down to each foreman. The use of counsel may reflect a legalistic approach to labor relations in the company. The choice of representative will also have been influenced by the practices and policies of the union.

The significant point is that the procedures and division of responsibility within the top-management organization will be a critical factor in most collective bargaining relationships. In small companies with one-man managements, these issues of balance among departments become problems of analyzing the thought processes and emotions of that one man. In larger enterprises the decision process is more institutionalized. The procedures within top management attract the attention of every student of a particular case.

b) Management Hierarchy in the Grievance Procedure.—Although no two companies may have the same internal organization, the grievance procedure hierarchy is a feature common to all managements under collective bargaining. A chain of management command is recognized in the steps of the grievance procedure. This chain is one of the innovations in management organization accompanying the introduction of a union. A typical procedure would provide for appeal to the foreman as step one, the superintendent of the department as step two, the plant manager as step three, and the vice-president in charge of operations or the industrial relations officer as step four.

A consequence of the grievance procedure is to identify points of decision-making within the company affecting relations with the union. Responsibility which may have been diffused or not clearly defined is concentrated in the grievance chain of command within the company.

The top step in this chain of command within management, before the arbitration step, has important consequences for the whole organization. The top appeal may be to the head of the industrial relations department or to the vice-president in charge of production, or to the chief executive of the company. In choosing among these alternatives, top management must establish procedures to define the relative responsibilities of the industrial relations department and the main operating departments of the company. Both departments have real interest in the policy implications of the settlement of any grievance. In fact, the administration of the management side of a grievance procedure requires at each step the clearest possible designation of responsibility and the closest co-operation between the operating and industrial relations departments of the company. Even then top management may have to decide differences in views between these two departments.

In the collective bargaining process, the grievance-procedure steps are points in union and management organizations where representatives meet to consider cases in behalf of their whole organizations. Behind the management representative, foreman to top step, there must be procedures for reconciling or choosing between the views of the operating and industrial relations departments. The industrial relations department may wish to replace a foreman because he handles workers badly; the operating department finds him technically proficient. The industrial relations department may believe that no case has been established for the discipline or discharge of a worker that would stand up before an arbitrator, whereas the operating department may believe the worker is so "objectionable" as to warrant risking a reversal with possible award of back pay by an arbitrator.

The grievance procedure steps are points at which management deals with the union. Necessarily, they are also points at which management must present a single position, and hence procedures must be established to reconcile or resolve internal conflicts within the management organization.

c) *Industrial Relations Administration.*—A management organization must have machinery to make many decisions within the framework of its agreement with the union organization. The decisions do not involve top management directly, but they are requisite to the daily operation of a business. Thus, the contract may provide that new employees must join the union, but the company must establish machinery to select particular new employees. The contract may provide for "reasonable leaves of absence," but more administrable standards must be formulated for the instruction of supervisors and for the choice among applicants for leave. The contract may allow a union to question a piece rate on a particular operation, but a whole system of setting rates must be administered by the company. A contract may require that seniority be the basis for promotion where ability is equal. If this clause is to be meaningful, the company will have to establish seniority lists and tests of the performance of each worker. In brief, there is a substantial administrative organization required within a management to direct a labor force under the terms of a labor agreement. The industrial relations department typically co-ordinates this responsibility.

Personnel Administration

A great many of management's activities that are directly related to employees fall outside the scope of the typical agreement. Organizational arrangements must be provided for these activities. Terms of the agreement usually do not apply to some employees, such as foremen, technicians, and clerical employees. Policies comparable to those established for employees under an agreement must be made for employees within the management hierarchy or for employees outside the bargaining unit for other reasons. A company may elect to establish many programs not required or covered by contract such as pensions, recreation, and medical care. All of these programs require administrative machinery. In any specific situation there will be difficulty in distinguishing industrial relations and personnel activities. The same organizational arrangements within the company may handle both. The machinery for the administration of industrial relations and personnel policies must be closely integrated.

Despite the diverse forms of management organization, the student of collective bargaining will in any particular situation concentrate upon the top-management organization, the management machinery related to the grievance procedure, and the administration of personnel and industrial relations policies.

These formal features of management organization need to be illustrated. Some indication of the organization within the modern business for dealing with labor relations is apparent from an outline of the activities of a particular industrial relations department. Even such an outline neglects the organization within top management and the details of the grievance machinery. The organization of the industrial relations and personnel department of a particular company[1] has been outlined as follows:

A. INDUSTRIAL RELATIONS DEPARTMENT—Industrial Relations Manager

    I. Personnel Division—Personnel Director

        a) Employment Section—Employment Supervisor
            1. Interviewing
            2. Testing
            3. Investigation
            4. Hiring
            5. Transferring
            6. Military returns

        b) Personnel Office Section—Personnel Office Manager—Personnel Office Supervisor
            1. Records and reports
            2. Employee services
            3. Absentee control
            4. Transportation
            5. Employee identification
            6. Service problems
            7. Employee correspondence
            8. Induction program coordination

    II. Safety and Sanitation Division—Safety and Sanitation Engineer

        a) Safety Section—Safety Supervisor
            1. Accident preventions
            2. Accident investigation
            3. Safety store

[1] Caterpillar Tractor Company (for March 1, 1946) as reported in the *Management Almanac, 1946* (New York: National Industrial Conference Board), pp. 283–84.

    4. Safety education

    5. Records and reports

  b) Sanitation Section—Sanitation Supervisor—
Shift Foreman

    1. Rest rooms

    2. Shower and locker rooms

    3. Office areas

    4. Designated shop areas

    5. Machine tool cleaning

  c) Industrial Hygiene Section—Industrial Hygienist

    1. Analysis of:

      (a) Vapors

      (b) Fumes

      (c) Water

      (d) Liquids

    2. Control of toxic substances

    3. Bacteriology

III. Medical Division—Medical Director

                   Assistant Medical Director

                   Personnel Consultant

                   Plant Surgeon

                   Plant Physician

  a) Preemployment medical examinations and reexaminations

  b) First aid stations

  c) Technician service

    1. Medical laboratory

    2. X-ray laboratory

    3. Physiotherapy treatments

  d) Medical records and reports

  e) Rehabilitation program

  f) Consultations

    1. Employees

    2. Supervisory

    3. Veterans

IV. Insurance Division—Insurance Manager

  a) Group Insurance Section—Group Insurance Supervisor
—Insurance Supervisor

1. Claims
2. Records and reports
3. Insurance explanations to employees

b) Workmen's Compensation Section—Compensation Insurance Supervisor
1. Investigation
2. Temporary disability claim payments
3. Permanent disability settlements
4. Industrial Commission contacts

V. Job Analysis Division—Job Analysis Manager
   a) Evaluation of office positions
   b) Wage and salary structure recommendations based on—
   1. Area studies
   2. Industry studies
   3. Job evaluation
   c) Audit of recommended changes
   d) Coordination of job evaluation and job analysis
   e) Statistical information

VI. Restaurant Division—Restaurant Manager
   a) Food Preparation Section—Kitchen Supervisor—Shift Supervisor
   1. Kitchen and bakery
   2. Quality control
   3. Inventory control
   b) Food Serving Section—Service Supervisor
   1. Serving of food
      (a) Dining rooms
      (b) Shop Restaurants
      (c) Candy stands
   2. Quality control

VII. Employee Publication Division—Employee Publication Manager
   a) Employees' bi-weekly magazine
   b) Printed notification to employees
   1. Annual report to employees

      2. Booklets—Industrial relations topics
      3. Miscellaneous printed matter
    c) Bulletin board notices and control

VIII. General Industrial Relations
    a) Employee Activities—Activities Director
      1. Coordination of sports and hobbies program
      2. Counselor to employee groups
      3. Employee induction conferences
      4. Employee group entertainment
    b) Employee Retirement—Retirement Manager
      1. Administration of retirement plan

B. LABOR RELATIONS DEPARTMENT—Labor Relations Manager—Labor Relations Staff
      1. Collective bargaining
      2. Arbitration
      3. Two-way communication with plant supervision
      4. Relations with government agencies
      5. Research

Union Organization

No two unions, just as has been observed in the instance of companies, have identical internal arrangements for reaching decisions in the collective bargaining relationship. The level within the union at which a decision is achieved varies with the type of problem. Such observations may seem to preclude any attempts to generalize about the decision-making process within unions. It is true that far too few facts are known (and even fewer can be documented) to generalize with confidence on the many aspects of the internal life of the labor organization. But the careful observer or the practitioner will concentrate upon three important aspects of union organization for collective bargaining.

a) *The Elected Hierarchy.*—In the international union, top policy-making may be made at one of three levels: the convention of elected delegates, the executive board frequently composed of vice-presidents and other elected officers, and the chief executive of the organization. The convention is almost always the body of final policy-making authority, short of appeal to the rank and file of members through a referendum (in some few cases) or through the delegates elected to the next convention. The division of authority between council and chief executive differs widely among unions. In some few unions the president and secretary are not even members of the council; they are directed to carry out policies adopted by the council. At the other extreme are unions in which the chief executive alone formulates all major decisions.

Just as title does not infallibly indicate the chief executive of a corporation—it may be the chairman of the board or the president—so likewise in a union. In a few instances in which the influence of the older German trade unionists was strong, the secretary-treasurer is the chief executive. The Amalgamated Butcher Workers and Meat Cutters of America is an example. In most international unions the president is the chief executive, although old age or sickness may result in the unofficial delegation of active responsibility to another officer.

Over the years, the centralization of top-level decision-making in the chief executive of the labor organization no doubt has increased. The council may approve or advise in varying degrees in different unions. The national rather than local character of many problems no doubt has been most significant in creating the centralization tendency. The interdependence of wage rates in one locality upon those in others, the influence of national legislation, and the growth of the large-scale enterprise with activities throughout the country are indicative of the national scope of many decisions in the labor unions.

In the local union, there are levels of policy-making roughly analogous to those that have just been indicated for the international union: the local union meeting, the local executive board, and the business agent and the stewards. Here again, the division of the decision-making responsibility at different levels will vary considerably even among local unions that are a part of the same international union.

While local unions elect a president and other officers, the business agent typically is a full-time union employee. In the usual case, he is elected. The steward is the elected representative of the union in a department or other unit of operation of management. The steward typically is an employee working at his trade or in the shop; he is usually compensated by the union only for such part time as he spends on union business involving a loss of earnings from his regular employment.

b) *The Union Representative.*—In order to operate on a national basis, the chief executives of the unions have created, largely in the last twenty-five years, two devices of internal union organization. The first is the national office staff, comparable to staff employees of other organizations, to advise the chief executive and carry on the routine business of the national office. Thus, many unions have established research, legal, financial, contract files, technical and engineering, welfare, and public relations departments. The second, and more important, creation in organization has been the international representative or organizer, to use the most common designation. These officers are normally appointed by the chief executive, although approval of the council may be necessary. They supervise and service the local unions in an assigned territory or branch of the industry. They may take part in local negotiations in which their role may be anything from adviser to active chief negotiator. They may direct the conduct of strikes. They may represent the union in arbitration and in relations with government agencies. These positions in the labor union would be called "bureaucracy" by the student of government. The international representative and the organizer constitute the emergence in the labor movement of a professional group. Their livelihood depends upon the union as an organization.

The ordinary local union does not employ comparable full-time representatives; the elected full-time business agent normally is sufficient. In some large local unions, however, there are appointed assistant business agents, full-time employees of the union, who correspond to the international representatives in the national union.

c) Union Organization in the Grievance Procedure.—The grievance procedure in the union, just as in management organization, represents a chain of command or a hierarchy of decision-making extending from the steward at the bottom, through the business agent, to an international representative, and in rare instances to the international chief executive. The steps in the procedure identify in the union organization points of decision-making in its relation to a management organization.

Some indication of the range of activities of an international union organization is evident from the following outline of the work of various departments of the United Steelworkers of America, CIO. The summary has been prepared from the report of the officers to the annual convention, 1947.

A. Executive Branch—International Officers
   1. Preside at all International Conventions and sessions of International Executive Board
   2. Interpret meaning of Constitutions
   3. Direct affairs of International Union
   4. Advise, assist, and instruct local unions or districts
   5. Appoint, direct, suspend, or remove organizers, representatives, agents, and employees—also committees to conduct Union affairs
   6. Reorganization of locals and districts

B. RESEARCH DEPARTMENT—Fact-finding and analysis of economic data hearing on Union welfare

1. Financial and operation information for contract negotiation and for organizing purposes
2. Rate information—wage rate questionnaires and research on current rates and earnings
3. Special studies
   a) Wages, prices, profits in industry
   b) Extent and nature of specific contract provisions
   c) Extent of organizations
4. Servicing local unions
   a) In arbitration proceedings
   b) Contract negotiations
   c) Grievances

5. Government agencies
   a) Testimony setting forth Union position on various vital issues to Congressional committees and governmental bodies
   b) Participation in governmental programs such as ERP

C. FINANCIAL DEPARTMENT
1. Installation of accounting procedures
2. Auditing of local union accounts
3. Publication of Union financial statements
4. Program of fund investment, particularly investment in government bonds
5. Conduct of strike relief fund

D. ORGANIZATIONAL DEPARTMENT
1. Formalities of policy for recruiting of new members—areas of concentration, class of workers, etc.
2. Forming new locals
3. Training organizers
4. Instruction and advice to local; financial aid
5. Public relations work with community and civic leaders

E. ENGINEERING DEPARTMENT
1. Conduct of wage inequity investigation
2. Description and classification of jobs
3. Conduct of training school for staff representatives

4. Development of principles for determining fair day's work—basis for measurement

5. Establishment of incentive levels to yield fair returns on new or changed jobs

F. Publicity and Education Department

1. Publicity
   a) Conducting press conferences
   b) Newspaper releases
   c) Radio talks
   d) Information to membership of Union activity
      (1) Publication of monthly *Steel Labor*
      (2) Pamphlets for specialized Union departments
      (3) Official communications from officers and executive board
   e) Information to college students and faculties

2. Education
   a) Conducting special summer institutes at various colleges
   b) Extension courses
   c) Publication of manuals and pamphlets, a guide to specialized Union problems

3. Athletic activities
   a) Development of long range sports program for organizing of district and regional leagues and tournaments—baseball, basket ball, soft ball, bowling

4. Co-operatives
   a) Encourage consumer co-operative organizations among Union members
   b) Organize special food sales to protest high prices

G. Legislation and Political Action

1. Legislation
   a) Present Union position to individual Congressmen
   b) Testimony before Congressional committees
   c) Support of "every type of legislation beneficial to the mass of Americans" and "opposition to bills not in the public interest"

2. Political Action
   a) Establishment of Political Action Committee to direct affairs of political action within the organization
   b) Encourage registration and voting

H. LEGAL DEPARTMENT

1. Analysis of proposed, pending, and enacted labor legislation and interpretation and study of its application to Union operations
2. Preparation of pamphlets, bulletins, letters, etc.
3. Drafting testimony for legislative committees
4. Assistance to Union representatives in preparation of cases for arbitrations, briefs, etc.
5. Representing Union in courts and before executive and legislative governmental agencies

I. WORKMEN'S COMPENSATION

1. Preparation of booklets to provide information on essential information of various State compensation acts
2. Digest of State and Federal Compensation Act—interpretation—distribution to members
3. Accident and exposure information forms

The rank and file of union members, the constituency of the elected officers, play a decisive, though variable, role in the decision-making process within labor organizations. Members in mass cannot make decisions as the term is ordinarily understood. The individual members of a labor organization, however, do influence the decisions of the organization in a variety of ways—election of officers, votes on proposals submitted for ratification, expression of views and opinions at meetings, withholding of dues payments where no checkoff exists, interest in rival organizations, etc. One of the chief tasks of an elected or appointed union officer is to maintain contact with the pulse of the union membership. This relation of decision-making to constituency is a reflection of the political character of labor organizations. The union has many of the features and consequently the problems of a political democracy.

The decisions which the hierarchy of a labor organization make frequently involve a choice among the interests of different members or groups of members. One member rather than another is entitled to a promotion or must be laid off. The officers must choose between the long-run and the short-run interests of the members. This choice may take the form of a decision favorable to the organization as against the members as individuals. Such a question may be involved in the decision between a wage increase and improved union security or in discussion of the level of union dues. A decision may be required as to the form of concessions to be sought from managements. Vacations and pensions may be preferred by senior employees, while a particular department or group may prefer larger wage increases. In the process of making these decisions, the officer of the labor organization acts as a politician, in the best sense of the word. He seeks a working compromise among the conflicting interests of the individuals who compose the organization.

It may be contended that this political element of the decision-making process is not absent in management organization. The stockholders are analogous to the rank and file. In some cases the relationship of management to the stockholders may resemble that of union officers to members. Managements have real problems of reconciling conflicting interests of different types of stockholders and bondholders. But, in the ordinary case, the economic destiny of the stockholder is not so completely dependent upon the one management as the employee is upon the single job. The members of the union are more frequently in contact with the union officers than most stockholders with the company. These differences in degree yield a labor hierarchy much more sensitive to the membership than most managements are to stockholders.

The relationships of a union officer to the constituency and to the rest of the union hierarchy is frequently the most important aspect of a decision. It is a commonplace that most political representatives attempt to avoid alienating groups of their constituency. In the same way, union officers may seek to avoid unpopular decisions. In relationships with management, for instance, a union representative may elect not to settle a questionable grievance on account of the internal hostility such a settlement would produce. The decision of the union representative is not to be narrowly interpreted in terms of the technical merits of the particular grievance but rather in terms of the political context of the representative in his relations with the rank and file and with management. To understand decision-making within the labor organization is, not only to grasp the workings of the union hierarchy, but also to be sensitive to the subtle relations between the officers and their representatives and the rank and file of union members.

The Question of Prerogatives

The preceding sketch of decision-making in managements and labor organizations can help to clarify the discussion of "prerogatives." Managements have frequently regarded unions as an encroachment upon a given territory of management "rights." The union is pictured as continuously engaged in expanding its activities at the expense of these prerogatives of management. From this viewpoint all decision-making within the area of collective bargaining originally "belonged" to management. The unions secured a beach head which they have been seeking to enlarge. The union is said to be motivated by an irresistible urge to "share" in all the decision-making processes within a management. Collective bargaining is even depicted as a form or method of management. Managements which have approached the collective bargaining relationship with a central emphasis upon prerogatives have devoted great energy to containing the union and the scope of its activities. The National Labor Relations Board, as was noted in Chapter II, in defining the content of bargaining has been drawn into the prerogatives controversy.

Some managements have contended that pension plans, for instance, are not a required subject for collective bargaining; they are the exclusive prerogatives of management.

There is no doubt that labor organizations constitute a challenge to the dominent influence of business in the community over the past century. Unions also provide limitations on the range of possible decisions within a management. But the problems involved in the discussion of prerogatives will be more clearly understood if the collective bargaining process be depicted as that of accommodating two organizations—a union and a management.

a) The two organizations each face certain intimate questions of internal operations. Officers and leaders must be selected. The structure and internal government of each must be established. Lines of authority and a communications and "intelligence" system free from external domination are imperative. Such activities are indispensable to the existence of an independent organization.

b) The collective bargaining contract explicitly defines an area of the respective rights and duties of the union and management. In general terms, the management is guaranteed the right of administrative initiative,[2] that is, the right to make initial decisions and to put these decisions into effect. The union in turn is provided the right of protest and redress from a decision usually with the explicit understanding that, if the management is found to be in error, under the grievance procedure, full restitution (retroactively) will be made to the union. But the management is provided in the right of administrative initiative the authority to proceed to undertake operations to get the job done. The agreement also typically provides that these decisions may be carried out without stoppage of work on the part of the union.

c) The scope of the collective bargaining relationship is

[2] Thomas Kennedy, *Effective Labor Arbitration* (Philadelphia: University of Pennsylvania Press, 1948), pp. 90–127.

never static. The agreement cannot anticipate all problems and contingencies which arise under its provisions. Furthermore, at renewal dates the parties in negotiating a new agreement continually reshape the prescribed rights and obligations of each organization. The quest for prerogatives in the sense of a final definition of these rights and duties is certain to fail in a dynamic world.

d) A great deal of confusion in practice over prerogatives can be eliminated when both organizations recognize the difference between the authority for a decision and the consultative process. There are large areas of the relationship between the organizations where consultation in advance of final decision will be found to be highly useful. Managements will receive many useful suggestions from union representatives, and unions in turn will be assisted by comments and information from management representatives. The consultative process in advance of decision need not prejudice the formal authority for decision-making. In the accommodation of union and management organizations, which is the collective bargaining process, advanced consultation has a decisive role to play.

SUGGESTIONS FOR FURTHER READING

BAKKE, E. WIGHT. *Mutual Survival: The Goal of Unions and Management.* New Haven, Conn.: Labor and Management Center, Yale University, 1946.

FRIEDRICH, C. J. "Responsible Government Service under the American Constitution," *Problems of the American Public Service,* pp. 3–74. New York: McGraw-Hill Book Co., 1935.

GORDON, R. A. *Business Leadership in the Large Corporation.* Washington, D.C.: The Brookings Institution, 1945.

HERBERG, WILL. "Bureaucracy and Democracy in Labor Unions," *Antioch Review,* Fall, 1943, pp. 405–17.

ROSS, ARTHUR M. *Trade Union Wage Policy,* pp. 21–74. Berkeley: University of California Press, 1948.

Chapter IV

THE LABOR AGREEMENT

THE terms and conditions of a labor agreement are designated to govern the relations between a union organization and a management. The negotiation of such an agreement is akin to the creation of a constitution. The labor contract, however, is typically limited to a specific period, such as a year, although sections of the agreement may have a longer or shorter or even an indefinite term.

The phrase "collective bargaining" is sometimes restricted to the legislative act of the creation of the charter of the relations between the parties. At other times, the term is used to include the discussions between management and union representatives under an agreement. These discussions may be of a mixed character; they may constitute the administration and interpretation of the agreement or they may consist of the creation of supplemental agreements. The administration of a contract involves judicial elements, interpreting the meaning of particular sections of the agreement. The creation of supplemental agreements is a return to legislative action. In actual practice it is frequently impossible to separate these elements in discussions between the parties under an agreement. As a consequence, general usage loosely applies the term "collective bargaining" to all discussions between representatives of unions and managements. It is desirable for many purposes, however, to distinguish the general process of creating an agreement or supplemental agreements and the process of interpreting and administering an agreement on a day-to-day basis.

The Total Contractual Relationship

The initial contract between a union and a management is likely to be a very brief document, particularly when neither organization has had extensive collective bargaining experience. As the relationship extends over time, through successive contract negotiations, the agreement typically becomes longer and more complex. The initial contract, for instance, between the Carnegie-Illinois Steel Corporation and the Steelworkers Organizing Committee, negotiated in March, 1937, was confined to a single page. In a decade the agreement grew to a small booklet of over seventy pages of fine type. This agreement even today is a relatively simple contract if account is taken of the number of plants and employees covered.

An examination of labor agreements suggests a twofold classification: (a) simple agreements which are confined to a few fundamentals and procedural steps for disposing of problems as they arise, and (b) detailed agreements which seek to specify the rights and duties of the parties in a great variety of circumstances. These two types of agreements symbolize different conceptions of the labor-management relation. The first seeks to designate a few fundamental rights and duties and specifies procedures which the parties will employ as problems arise from day to day. This conception of the agreement is derived from the fact that it is really impossible to anticipate all the types of problems which will arise under a contract during a year. The second view may recognize the difficulties of anticipating problems, but it contends that it is better to have as many contingencies as possible reduced to writing. It is felt that this method involves less misunderstanding.

These differences in the conception of the agreement are

reflected not only in its length and detail but also in the operation of the grievance procedure. The procedural type of agreement will ordinarily provide for a broader definition of problems which can be taken up as grievances. Virtually any question may be raised in some cases. The more detailed agreement is likely to limit grievances strictly to questions of interpretation of the contract. In actual practice, it may be difficult to classify particular agreements as examples of these two extreme types.

The choice between these two types of agreements will be a distinctive feature of each labor-management relation. It is doubtful that either type is to be preferred on general grounds. The internal requirements of a union and management, the custom in the industry, and the types of problems that confront collective bargaining in the industry, will be among the factors which dictate the choice between the two types. In the railroad and transit industries, for instance, where there are enormously complex questions of scheduling operations, the agreements contain many detailed rules covering this problem. In the construction industry, on the other hand, in which a particular craft performs fairly standard operations, the agreements are usually quite simple.

The total relationship between a union and a management is normally considerably broader in a number of respects than the text of the signed agreement. The contract is to be viewed as the skeleton of the relation. The parties, in a variety of ways, from day to day, build the flesh and blood of a relationship between the two organizations. The total charter of rights and duties, or the constitution, of a labor-management relationship must be broadly conceived to encompass the following items:

a) Many agreements provide for a series of supplemental agreements, or they incorporate by reference existing conditions, practices, and conditions of employment. An agreement may provide, for instance, that each plant establish a seniority agreement specifying appropriate districts and lists. Many agreements append a list of job classifications, specifying the rate for each job. Other contracts provide that the existing wage scales shall be maintained throughout the contract period, including any general wage increase or decrease provided in the agreement. Still other contract provisions may specify that the company will maintain existing benefit plans through the contract period. The actual content of the agreement thus may be very extensive by resort to incorporating existing conditions and practices.

b) The total relation must be conceived to include the interpretations of the contract that the parties have developed in the settlement of grievances or that have been established through arbitration when the parties themselves did not reach agreement on a grievance. In this fashion the words of a contract come to have specific meaning in a variety of circumstances. In many relationships careful records are kept of the grievances handled and the understandings achieved in particular cases. These constitute an intricate system of precedents, filling in the necessarily general provisions of a contract. In some instances only oral understandings are made. One of the real problems of both labor and management organizations is to be certain that oral understandings between lower levels of the hierarchy do not later embarrass the policy-making levels.

c) In some relations there is a practice to exchange letters setting forth agreement on problems discussed between representatives of the union and management organization during the contract period. These letters frequently concern problems that were not explicitly covered in the contract; they are to be regarded as a series of minor supplemental agreements.

The file of these letters constitutes a significant aspect of the total relationship between the parties.

d) In some cases the constitution and the bylaws of a union may come to have the status of a facet of the total contractual relationship. The agreement may explicitly provide, as has been the case in certain unions in the printing industry, that no union member will be required to perform any act in violation of the union constitution or bylaws. The same result may be achieved by prolonged practice and oral understanding. Under these circumstances the union may seek unilaterally to change the terms of the relationship by altering its constitution or bylaws.

e) Many managements have extensive rules and written policies requisite to their operations. At times, parts of these rules may become formally a part of the written definition of rights and duties between the parties. Thus, the agreement may provide that the company shall establish reasonable rules of discipline. Such written rules which have been unchallenged and accepted for a long period or which have been tested through the grievance procedure can be conceived as a part of the total relationship. A unilateral change by management in these rules may be challenged by the union as an unwarranted change in the relationship.

The relationship between a labor and a management organization thus consists of an agreement which may be the skeleton of the formal definition of rights and duties. There may be a variety of other formal documents comprising the total relationship—supplemental agreements, minutes of negotiations, codified practices, settled grievances, and arbitration awards. In addition, there may be a variety of practices and oral understandings. All of the factors of this relationship between the parties are meshed into the rules, regulations, and bylaws of each organization requisite to its own purely internal operation. Such is the nature of the constitution at any one time defining the total relationship between the two organizations.

Provisions of the Agreement

The provisions of agreements between various unions and managements differ widely. The reasons for these differences deserve brief attention. The effect of the length of time the parties have been dealing with each other on the detail and complexity of the agreement has already been noted. Other influences may be grouped under two headings: first, the internal requirements of the union and management organizations and, second, the objective problems with which collective bargaining must deal.

Illustrative of the first heading is the fact that some unions are impelled to bargain for a checkoff and other unions prefer the individual collection of dues as a result of tradition and policy. The steps in the grievance machinery will be adapted to the internal organization of both parties. Illustrative of the second heading is the fact that the problems of the sequence of layoffs will be different in a seasonal industry, such as clothing, from one with steady employment, such as a public utility. There are many problems unique to a piecework operation. The significance of these environmental factors on the provisions of agreements will be elaborated briefly in the next section.

Although contract terms do vary widely, a listing of the captions of the provisions of a single agreement may help to visualize the relationship of particular clauses to the total agreement. The following headings have been adapted from a current agreement in the woolen and worsted industry. The agreement tends to be simple and procedural rather than detailed.

PREAMBLE AND STATEMENT OF PURPOSE

ARTICLE

I. Bargaining unit, or definition of employees covered by the agreement
   Form of union security and checkoff

II. Powers and duties of the employer

III. Wages
   Provisions for a general increase
   Wage reopening during contract period
   Revision of rates on particular jobs when there is a change in method or work load
   Reporting time
   Shift premiums
   Equal pay for women when performing the same work as men
   Rates applicable when employees transferred
   Waiting time under piece rates

IV. Hours of work
   Overtime pay schedules
   Holiday pay

V. Vacation pay

VI. Group life, accident, and health insurance

VII. Bulletin boards

VIII. Grievance procedure

IX. Discharge cases

X. Arbitration

XI. Seniority
   Seniority districts
   Seniority lists
   Probationary periods
   Layoff and recalls
   Promotions

Transfers
Top seniority
Leave of absence
Termination of seniority and employment

XII. Military service

XIII. Term of the agreement

A brief examination of the above captions will indicate that these provisions may be grouped under a more limited number of headings: the bargaining unit (I), the rights of the management and union organizations (I and II), compensation of employees (III, IV, V, VI), the grievance procedure (VIII, IX, X), the relative rights of different employees to particular jobs (XI), and the term of the agreement (XIII). These headings in variant forms appear in the great majority of agreements.

The Influence of Environment on Contract Provisions

It is easy to overemphasize the role of personal and accidental factors in collective bargaining. It is difficult to discern the persistent and underlying forces at work in the bargaining process. Yet the provisions of agreements—the policies agreed upon by unions and managements—fundamentally reflect the more enduring features of the environment of the collective bargaining relationship. This fundamental fact must be perceived or collective bargaining will appear capricious.

Some agreements provide for the closed shop; other parties seem satisfied with a union shop or a maintenance of membership. Some agreements provide for piece rates; in other cases neither party would accept a piecework system. Some agreements provide for layoffs by seniority; others require that a reduction in work be spread evenly among all employees. Some agreements permit any disagreement or difference between the parties to be raised as a grievance, while other contracts explicitly limit the grievance machinery to questions of interpretation. Some agreements provide that the wage rate for a particular job classification may be re-examined at any time; others provide for a fixed wage scale during the life of the agreement except for changes in job content. If these types of differences are to be understood, the influence of the environment in which the parties negotiate and operate must be discerned.

The term "environment" is used in this discussion to signify a number of influences exterior to the union and the management which shape and mold the problems with which negotiators must grapple. These factors characteristically limit the range of discretion of the parties. It is convenient to think of these environmental factors under three headings.

a) The technological and physical characteristics of the industry and its operation will decisively affect the problems posed for collective bargaining and the range of answers that can be found. The intermittent and casual nature of employment in the longshore and construction industries helps to account for the emergence of the closed shop with the union-controlled hiring hall to allocate the employment opportunities. The physical necessity for peak loads in the morning and evening rush hours in the transit industry creates problems that are the subject of extended rules in the agreement. The fact of increasing speeds of airplanes created a divergence of views on methods of wage payment, with the union favoring pay per mile and the companies pay per hour. The method of payment finally accepted involves a compromise, with the wage rate including both hourly and mileage elements. The variation in the quality of yarn and the unevenness in the flow of work in the textile industries create the necessity for guarantees and other features of piece-rate systems. These illustrations could be multiplied endlessly, yet they should indicate that the keen observer of collective bargaining will seek out the technological and physical factors that create problems for the parties and fashion the particular labor-management relationship.

b) The market and competitive features of the firm and industry will decisively shape the collective bargaining relationship. The uniformity in timing of wage changes among companies in the basic steel industry is to be attributed to pricing arrangements and practice within the industry. The prevalence of arbitration in the transit industry is largely the result of the practice of setting fares by a public regulatory body. The great world-wide shortage of coal after 1940 is probably basically responsible for the fact that the wage rates in the coal industry in most countries have risen relatively from one of the lowest to one of the highest in the structure of wage rates. The large number of small firms in such industries as women's clothing and millinery, combined with their weak competitive position in dealing with buyers of their products, accounts for the fact that the unions in these fields have used the collective bargaining mechanism to affect competitive conditions in the industries. The competitive relations among a group of firms will account frequently for the timing of expiration dates of contracts.

c) The relations of a union to other unions and a management to other managements is a decisive feature of the environment in which collective bargaining operates. The idea can be generalized to encompass all industrial relations ties. Thus, if Mr. Murray and Mr. Lewis are rival leaders of American labor, the contract developments in the coal industry will be a very significant facet of the total environment and climate of basic steel negotiations. Or, a machine tool company located in a predominantly textile or steel community may be compelled to follow the wage patterns of these industries by virtue of the overwhelming influence of this feature of its environment. A collective bargaining relationship may have developed into following the leadership of another bargaining relationship. Or, a rival and factional condition within a local union may compel concessions to a particular group of employees, or a larger wage increase, simply to secure a settlement.

The relative importance of these industrial relations dependencies to contract provisions varies considerably. These factors are likely to be most decisive where rival unionism and internal factionalism is most keen. These rivalries and factions are temporary in many cases, although some have persisted for many years. The technological and competitive features of the environment in which collective bargaining takes place are likely to be most decisive in contract provisions where factionalism and rivalries are relatively insignificant.

The recognition of these external or environmental factors in a collective bargaining relation will guard against the fallacy that negotiators have almost limitless discretion and that relative "bargaining power" is the final arbiter in all negotiations. If bargaining power is understood to include a reflection of these environmental factors, there may be little basis for quarrel. But at times the term implies arbitrary and capricious results in the bargaining process. The fundamental point is that both the problems of collective bargaining and the resulting contract provisions are decisively shaped by the total environment, regarded as the technological, competitive, and industrial relations context in which the parties bargain.

One illustration of the necessity of recognizing the influence of these environmental factors is provided by an examination of the action of the Congress in seeking to eliminate the closed shop in the Labor-Management Relations Act (1947). The Congress appeared to find the closed shop in conflict with certain individual rights which it regarded as fundamental. On the level of moral principle it seemed to contend that no man should have to join a union in order to secure a job, although it would be all right for him to have to join in thirty days' time under an authorized union shop. The Congress appeared to believe that the distinction between a closed shop and a union shop was arbitrary and followed from the greater bargaining power, or abuse of that power, on the part of a union.

The simple fact is, however, that the collective bargaining process over the years had developed closed shops in those sectors of the economy where special problems existed which could not be handled under union-shop provisions. Thus, the fact that unions in the building and construction industry were characteristically used as a source of supply of skilled labor by itinerant contractors, frequently engaged on projects of a short duration, accounts for the existence of the closed shop. The closed shop is thus deeply rooted in the characteristics and environment of the industry. It serves a particular purpose. It is already apparent that the law would not be likely to alter such deeply rooted institutions.

The moral of the story is not that the closed shop is above abuse or beyond the scope of legislation. Rather, the point is that the attempt to draw a line between a closed shop and a union shop without regard to the environmental factors which basically produced the closed shop was doomed to failure. The influence of the total environment will claim the attention of the person seeking to explain collective bargaining contract provisions.

The Grievance Procedure

Just as the grievance machinery was found to be one of the principal facets of management and union organization for collective bargaining, so does it constitute one of the major provisions of an agreement. As with all the mechanics of collective bargaining, the parties can mold and fashion the grievance procedure in a variety of ways to their special problems. The grievance procedure may serve many diverse purposes in a collective bargaining relationship depending upon the language of the agreement and the intention of both parties.

a) The grievance procedure may be used to locate problem situations in the relations between a union and management and to discern difficulties within both organizations. From this vantage point, the explicit grievance is not to be taken at its face value. The real problem may be a foreman or a shop steward. It may be evident that subordinates are not receiving proper instructions. The grievance is seen as a symbol of some maladjustment, and the skillful representative of the union or management will seek out the real and submerged difficulties.

So also in the complaints of single employees, there may be little overt basis for the grievance but the real difficulty may be a health condition, or a family situation, or a long standing personality problem. In a day when more than 60 per cent of the visits to the doctors' offices of the country are found to have a psychic rather than a purely physical basis, it should not be surprising that a large proportion of grievances of individual employees should also have their roots in psychic difficulties. A careful study of British experience[1] has shown that 30 per cent of factory employees suffer from some form of neurosis. The well-known fact that many grievances are filed by the same persons is a reflection of the problems of individual adjustment that are involved.

The clinical approach to a grievance must be used with care. Such an approach is likely to be inappropriate for most grievances filed by groups of employees or by the union and management as such. The problems of individual personalities

---

[1] Russell Fraser, *The Incidence of Neuroses among Factory Workers*, Great Britain Industrial Health Research Board Report 90 (London, 1947).

must not be allowed to so engross the attention of representatives of both sides that they overlook the task of accommodating the two organizations. There is no question, however, that the grievance procedure can be made to serve the function of discovering problem situations, both of individuals and of parts of the organization, when the grievance is approached as a symbol of some maladjustment.

b) The grievance procedure may be utilized by both organizations as a device by which information is channeled both ways between the top and the bottom of the hierarchy. In language that has become popular, the grievance procedure is a channel of communication. The top-management officers and the union leaders who follow carefully the status of grievances are frequently able to keep in touch with developments at the level of the individual worker. New problems are rapidly reflected in the grievance procedure.

As a channel of information, the grievance procedure is likely to be more reliable than most chains of command in a hierarchy since both the union and management (steward and foreman, or plant manager and business agent) are aware that the grievance may go a step higher or even to arbitration. Any statement they make will be subject to check by the other side before a superior officer. In this way the grievance procedure as a channel of information may be expected to be less subject to self-serving statements of fact than most chains of command within an organization.

In most grievance procedures, when a unique problem is presented, there may be considerable advance consultation with higher levels of authority before action on a case at a lower stage. This practice may be carried to the detrimental extreme in which all decisions are in fact made at the top. The practice of advance consultation, however, is indicative of the way in which the grievance procedure is used as a channel of information and policy-making within an organization.

c) The explicit purpose of the grievance procedure is to interpret the provisions of the agreement, to apply the contract to the new and changing aspects of everyday relations between a union and a management. This procedure must translate the necessarily general language of a contract into particular decisions in specific cases. It will also be used to achieve uniformity of interpretation in various units of management and divisions of the union.

The grievance procedure is related to the periodic negotiations of a new agreement in at least three ways. First, the general policies and language agreed upon in contract negotiations, as has been noted, are applied through this procedure. In this sense the grievance procedure is sometimes referred to as "collective bargaining." Second, the contract negotiations may re-examine and alter interpretations established by the grievance procedure. One side or the other may request a reconsideration of the whole problem in the light of experience. Third, the grievance procedure discovers and records many problems which one side or the other may wish to raise at the next contract negotiations period.

d) The contract language of some grievance procedures is so broad as to permit the raising of any problem or difficulty that may arise. The procedure is not limited to contract interpretation. Under these circumstances the whole relationship of the parties may be shaped through the grievance procedure. Each side is committed to discuss and settle any question that may be raised during the contract period. The grievance machinery in these circumstances serves the purpose of providing an orderly and systematic way in which problems may be studied and decided.

It is apparent that a grievance procedure may serve a variety of purposes. In a single union-management relation, the two organizations may not necessarily regard the grievance procedure in the same light or expect from it the same results. Thus, any particular grievance may have many facets and there will be a variety of types of grievances.

There are undoubtedly a great many ways of classifying the types of grievances that arise. It may be helpful to consider grievances in their relation to the contract and to the two organizations as follows: (1) Some grievances involve a conflict between two or more sections of the agreement. The union will point to one clause, and the company will refer to another. The problem may involve a reconciliation or clarification of conflicting sections of the agreement. (2) The contract may be silent on the specific problem. The issue may clearly involve a subject treated in the agreement; in this sense the grievance is within the scope of the agreement. The problem in such a grievance is to fill in the gap in the agreement. (3) The grievance may raise the question of the applicability of a general rule to a particular case. (4) Some grievances present exceptional circumstances, the type of situation no general rule or regulation can be formulated to handle. (5) At times a grievance presents no contract problems but arises as a device to "save face" for one side or the other. A union or management representative may find it expedient to pass along a grievance rather than to make an obvious settlement. These various types of grievances are represented in the cases that have been selected for this volume.

The Arbitration Step

Arbitration is the final step in the grievance procedure. Just as with other aspects of the grievance procedure, the parties may mold and shape this step to their special problems and predilections. There are a variety of ways in which the last step may be arranged. These various systems will influence the results of arbitration and the confidence which each organization will have in its operation.

The parties may select a number of different arrangements regarding the neutral person in arbitration. Some contracts provide for a single *impartial umpire*. A continuing relationship has the advantage that the neutral becomes familiar with the technical operations of the industry, with the special problems of internal organization of both parties, and with the personalities on each side. Where the parties intend to present a great many cases to a neutral, the continuing umpire eliminates the time and energy required to select an arbitrator for each case. A variant of the impartial umpire arrangement provides for a panel of three or five names from which a single name may be selected when a case reaches the final step. Other contracts provide for a succession of *ad hoc* arbitrators selected for a single case or a group of grievances. In this way the parties may select a neutral whose background qualifies him to solve the special problems of a particular case. The parties may also have in mind the fact that an arbitrator may become too familiar with a relationship; they would prefer to take a chance on a new man.

The parties may shape the arbitration process in another way by electing to associate with a neutral a representative from each side. The result is a *tripartite arbitration board*. This board may in turn be a continuing-umpire arrangement (as in the case of the steel-producing subsidiaries of the U.S. Steel Corporation in their relationship with the United Steelworkers of America, CIO) or a case-by-case appointment. The addition of a representative from each side has the advantage of giving the parties a method of directing and channeling the mind of the neutral. When problems are complex and technically peculiar to an industry, the arrangement has advantages. It permits the neutral to establish through these representatives on the board particularly close relations with both sides.

In some tripartite boards the chairman alone has a vote, while in others the parties provide that a majority vote shall decide the case. The difference between these forms of arbitration can be substantial. When the chairman alone has a vote, he may decide the case as he sees it. When a majority vote is required for a decision, he may have to compromise his position in order to secure the vote of one representative or the other. In cases in which the parties are quite far apart and the neutral finds neither position acceptable, the requirement of a majority vote may introduce a three-way bargaining process into arbitration.

The parties may further influence the arbitration process by the arrangements agreed upon for the selection of the neutral. The role of the parties is greatest when they agree in advance upon a simple umpire or upon a panel of names. Their role is less prominent when they simply agree upon an agency to appoint the neutral. The agencies most commonly designated in contracts are the Federal Mediation and Conciliation Service and the American Arbitration Association, the latter a private organization. Both of these agencies have attempted to restore to the parties some participation and responsibility for the selection of the arbitrator by furnishing a list of names from which the parties may agree upon the neutral. The role of the parties in the selection is ordinarily least when they merely designate a person, such as a governor or a judge, to name the neutral.

The precise language of the issue presented in arbitration is shaped by the parties. The definition of the issue is decisive to the results of arbitration. On many occasions when the parties may not be able to agree on a grievance, they can agree on the formulation of the issue to be arbitrated. The decisive nature of the definition of the issue in dispute is illustrated in the cases presented in this volume.

The arbitration process in the relationship between a particular union and management will be shaped by the internal policies of each toward arbitration. For instance, either side may follow a policy of carefully screening cases that go to arbitration. The objective may be to present only "good cases" so that the record before the arbitrator of cases won will be as nearly perfect as possible. This record may be intended to create the impression in negotiations with the other side over a grievance that, whenever arbitration is threatened, the other side ought to concede the case. The policy may be effective in doubtful cases and may be instrumental in reducing the number of grievances. The policy may be derived from a desire to avoid the creation of precedents that may be unfortunate. If an issue is to be tested in arbitration, a careful selection of cases may be made to secure the most favorable case on which to contest the issue.

Another possible policy in arbitration may be designated as the "percentage theory." Either side may elect to present any doubtful case to arbitration on the theory that arbitrators will tend to compromise as among cases. On this basis, the party following this policy may expect to win certain points that it might otherwise have conceded.

In a given union-management relationship the parties may adopt opposite policies; one side may elect to screen cases carefully and the other may adopt the percentage theory. It is basically for this reason that the "box score" of cases won or lost in arbitration decisions is meaningless. One side may be carefully selecting cases, and the other side may be permitting any case to go through to arbitration.

Two statements are made about the arbitration process, both of which have a measure of truth. Neither is a complete description by itself. It is said that "arbitration is an extension of collective bargaining." It is also held that "arbitration is a judicial process." The simple fact is that the arbitration process is flexible. While both elements are involved in most cases, the parties are in a position to alter the proportions of collective bargaining and judicial content within very wide limits. The careful specification of the issues in dispute, the designation of a single arbitrator, and a contract which provides only for the arbitration of questions of interpretation of the agreement—all tend to increase the judicial element. The absence of a clearly defined issue, a three-man board with a majority vote, and the possibility of arbitrating "any difficulty or problem" arising during the contract period tend to enhance the collective bargaining feature of an arbitration. If one examines the arbitration arrangements between a great many unions and managements, it will be evident that actual experience runs the full range of these extremes.

SUGGESTIONS FOR FURTHER READING

DIVISION OF LABOR STANDARDS, DEPARTMENT OF LABOR. *Settling Plant Grievances*. Bulletin 60. Washington, D.C., 1943.

GARDINER, GLENN. *When Foreman and Steward Bargain*. New York: McGraw-Hill Book Co., 1945.

ROETHLISBERGER, F. S. *Management and Morale*. Cambridge, Mass.: Harvard University Press, 1946.

SELEKMAN, BENJAMIN M. *Labor Relations and Human Relations*. New York: McGraw-Hill Book Co., 1947.

SLICHTER, SUMMER H. *Union Policies and Industrial Management*. Washington, D.C.: The Brookings Institution, 1941.

Chapter V

STANDARDS FOR WAGE DETERMINATION[1]

THE debate over wage rates in the public press and in proceedings between management and labor organizations has popularized economic analysis. A limited number of clichés or standard arguments have come into use, which are employed by the side that regards them as most effective at the time in negotiation or in arbitration proceedings. Illustrative of these phrases are "comparable wages," "productivity," "cost of living," and "ability to pay." These slogans are not the distinctive trade-mark of any one side. Either party may use one of these arguments today and repudiate it tomorrow as a factor in wage determination under a different set of circumstances.

The interest in arguments and slogans in wage negotiations has increased spectacularly in recent years with the growth of private arbitration, the participation of government in wage-setting through the machinery of the Railway Labor Act, the wartime experience under the National War Labor Board, and the postwar vogue of fact-finding boards and boards of inquiry. The employment by management and labor organizations of technicians, such as lawyers, economists, statisticians, accountants, actuaries, industrial engineers, and publicists, who produce voluminous briefs and statistical appendices, has given wide currency to such wage-determining principles or slogans.

[1] The chapter is adapted from an article by the author, "The Economics of Wage Dispute Settlement," *Law and Contemporary Problems*, Spring, 1947, pp. 281–96.

The purpose of this chapter is to appraise some of the more prominent arguments and slogans used in wage negotiations. Much of the discussion will be devoted to exploring problems that arise in giving meaning to these standards and in translating them into definitely measurable guides to decisions in particular situations. The problems will be found to be stubborn and not always tractable. This emphasis is not, however, fundamentally defeatist with respect to the contribution of economics to wage-dispute settlement. The identification of problems is the beginning of economic wisdom.

Comparable Wage Rates

No argument is employed more frequently in wage discussions than that wage rates in one bargaining unit should be equalized with, or related by a particular differential to, wage rates in other "comparable" bargaining units. While other arguments are more decisive in the "key" wage bargains affecting the general level of wage rates, the appeal to comparable rates is frequently employed in transmitting the impact of these critical decisions throughout the rest of the wage structure. Resort to this standard is also frequently the basis for the numerous changes in differentials that are made among occupations, plants, and industries each year.

The principle that wage rates in one bargaining unit should be adjusted to the level of wage rates in comparable plants has an alluring simplicity. The economist indicates that in equilibrium the same wage rate will be paid in a "market" for a specified type of labor service. The slogan "equal pay for equal work" commands wide support. However, for reasons which will now be surveyed the illusion of simplicity vanishes in the attempt to give meaning to the concept of "comparable" wage rates in any particular situation.

1. The content of job classifications designated by the same job title varies widely among different employers. The

range of duties assigned to a single worker has not been as standardized among plants as is widely assumed. The varying ages and types of equipment, the differing scales of operation between large and small plants, and the different techniques of various managers are factors making for different job contents among firms producing roughly similar goods. Various arrangements may be made, for instance, in machine operations for the cleaning, oiling, and greasing of equipment. The flow of materials to a machine and the handling of processed parts and waste products permit different plans of organization. The extent of supervision and inspection in a job may also vary widely from one plant to another.

For instance, a study of the distribution of spinning-room duties in forty-seven cotton textile firms divided the work of five customary job classifications—spinner, cleaner, oiler, sweeper, and doffer—into twenty-five separate operations.[2] No two of the mills divided these operations in the same way among the job classifications. Except for the operation of "creeling" and "piecing up," performed by the spinner in all cases, no operation was assigned to the same job classification in all mills. The total duties of the spinner varied from these two operations in one mill to as many as ten in another. The comparison of the wage rates by job classification among these various cotton textile mills under these circumstances requires a certain amount of temerity.

At the request of the Federal Mediation and Conciliation Service in particular disputes, the Bureau of Labor Statistics has made a number of surveys of occupational wage rates in comparable establishments. The most recent of these studies examines the differences between duties among the various firms studied. The ordinary occupational wage-rate survey of the Bureau of Labor Statistics starts with a single description

[2] Presented as an exhibit before the National War Labor Board in the cotton textile cases decided February 20, 1945, *War Labor Report*, Vol. XXI, p. 793.

for a "standardized" job classification.[3] As long as a common core of duties is performed, the wage-rate data are collected from a particular firm and compared with rates from other firms. The newer special studies for the Conciliation Service recognize that there are wide variations in the actual content of jobs that roughly fit the same job description. These inquiries uniformly reveal the same range of diversity in job content illustrated by the distribution of spinning-room duties.

2. Comparability in wage rates is impaired by variations in the method of wage payment. Some workers and job classifications are remunerated on an hourly-rate basis, others are on individual piece rates or incentive rates, while still others are paid on group incentive plans. The content of job classifications may be identical, but the amount of services performed and purchased will ordinarily vary with the method of wage payment. Commission methods of wage payment add the further complexity of variations in the price structures of the products being sold. Among incentive systems. there are substantial differences in the definitions of the "standard performance" and the extent of "incentive pull" for additional output. The provisions regarding minimum guarantees, including rates for machine breakdowns, poor materials, etc., and the method of calculating these guarantees—by day, by week, or other period—affect the meaning of interplant comparisons of wages.

3. The influence of regularity of employment upon wage rates must be assessed in defining comparable wages. The level of rates for maintenance occupations with steady employment is frequently, although not always, below the level of rates for the same crafts engaged in seasonal construction work. While there are some important differences in job

[3] "Wartime Wage Movements and Urban Wage-Rate Changes," *Monthly Labor Review*, Vol. LIX (October, 1944), pp. 684–704.

content, the regularity of employment is usually indicated as the principal reason for this difference. The difference between wages of mechanics in the repair shops of taxicab and truck companies and those of their fellow-craftsmen in commercial garages also reflects the factor of regularity of employment, although job content and methods of wage payment again differ. In fact, wage rates in "captive" departments of a company with relatively steady work opportunities are typically below those of the "outside" or "contract" firm with greater fluctuations in available work. Comparison of two groups of employees for wage-setting purposes will be complicated by the task of assessing the extent to which wage rates reflect differences in the regularity of employment.

4. The terms and conditions of employment typically include not only the occupational rate but also other "money" conditions, such as shift premiums, vacations and holidays with pay, sick leave, pensions, social and health insurance, paid lunch periods, Christmas bonuses, etc., to mention the more prominent terms. The total contract of employment involves many other items that are less immediately "money" terms, such as union recognition seniority, management rights and grievance machinery, and arbitration. In the bargaining process there is frequently give-and-take among the "money" terms. Substitution is likely among basic rate adjustments and shift premiums, vacations, and health insurance plans. There may even be important trades between the "money" items and other provisions of a contract. Comparison of wage rates under these circumstances may become particularly tenuous.

5. The geographical implications of "comparable wages" can be most perplexing. The concept of a "labor market" has no direct correspondence in geography. Specifying the labor market in accordance with the cost of transportation or the knowledge of job and wage opportunities does not yield

precise results. The inclusion of suburbs and satellite communities in a grouping has definite effects. The War Labor Board for the Boston Region was plagued throughout the war with the question whether to include Torrington (16 miles away) in the Waterbury, Connecticut, labor market for metal-trades occupations. The areas of uniformity of wage rates may vary widely among occupations even in the same industry. In the construction industry the rate for ironworkers typically extends over many counties or even a state, while the rate for laborers is usually confined to each locality. The areas of uniformity have been extended in recent years, although uniformity appears to be greater in periods of high employment than in loose labor markets. If the standard of comparable wages is to be employed, we cannot escape the difficult task of defining the geographical limits of the appropriate labor market.

6. The complications of "comparable" wage determination developed so far in this section relate to labor-market difficulties. They derive from comparing the exact work performed by the wage-earners in different bargaining units or from what are essentially labor-market influences on wage rates. However, another group of problems must be faced in giving meaning to "comparable wage rates." These have their roots in the product market or, more precisely, in the divergent competitive positions of the firms employing the wage-earners.

Business enterprises are ordinarily regarded as clustering into industries, segments, or smaller groups among which product competition is relatively closer than with firms outside the group. But every business, except for a few cases of perfectly competitive markets, has its specialized market and clientele. The grouping of firms according to similarity of product-market conditions is a convention always subject to further subdivision. The definition of these clusters of "comparable" firms is probably as difficult as any issue in applying the wage standard discussed in this section.

The local transit industry includes primary and feeder-line companies; hotels are divided into first-line and several other classes; bakeries may be classified as large-scale businesses and specialty shops. Are the larger or smaller units appropriate for comparison? The trucking firms in an area may be subdivided into over-the-road and local trucking enterprises. The latter may be classified in turn into product groups—oil, coal, grocery, department store, express, etc. Any one of these groups, such as oil, in turn could be further subdivided into: national distributors, local companies, home delivery, industrial uses, etc. While many of these groupings are associated with important differences in job content (type of equipment) and method of wage payment, competitive conditions among these various groups no doubt vary widely. The important question is to determine when these differences in competitive conditions are so significant as to warrant a separate wage determination regardless of labor-market influences.

The problem may be posed even more sharply by an instance in which labor-market influences are relatively more uniform than in the trucking case. An engine-lathe operator may work for companies ordinarily classified in such groups as electrical machinery, textile machinery, machine tools, and shoe machinery. In determining the "comparable" wage rates, what grouping of firms should be selected?

There can be little doubt that wage rates do in fact vary by virtue of the influence of divergent product-market conditions. Maintenance workers, for instance, have rates that vary substantially through the range of industries even where job content is quite similar. The choice of groupings among firms presents the most difficult of problems.

The foregoing discussion of six groups of problems is

adequate to divest the slogan or standard of "comparable wages" of any alluring simplicity. It is doubtful that there are any royal answers to these problems in principle or in measurement. The difficulties arising from the product market can be mitigated, however, if agreement is secured from the parties as to a list of comparable firms. This device has been frequently used by mediators.

Productivity

No argument is used with more conviction or sophistication than that wages should vary with changes in productivity. In the mid-twenties, the American Federation of Labor Convention adopted the policy that wage-earners should share in rising productivity in the form of wage-rate increases. In recent days management, editorial writers, economists, and some labor leaders have been preaching that increased productivity alone provides the basis for wage increases. These views have normally been associated with the conviction that wage rates have already outstripped productivity. As part of the mores or folklore of an industrial community, there may be little objection to the contention that productivity is a basis for increases in the general level of wage rates in the long run. As a guide or a rule of thumb in any particular negotiation, the principle has grave difficulties which may be briefly summarized.

1. The rate of change in productivity in our economic system varies widely among the component segments. Within an industry the rate is normally quite different among firms. Even within a firm or plant the rate varies among departments, machines, and operations. The wage structure of a particular plant or department, if it were geared absolutely to changes in productivity, would soon become intolerable. Employees in continuous strip mills and on tin-plate oper-

ations in the steel industry, for instance, would have had enormous wage increases in the last ten years in comparison with employees in other sectors of the industry. Under such circumstances the wage structure would bear very little relationship to skill, experience, or other factors typically taken into account in settling rate structures. Nor would the wage structure bear any relationship to wages paid for comparable operations in other industries in steel centers. The exclusive adoption of the principle of adjustment according to changes in productivity would result within a very short time in an utterly chaotic wage structure within a single plant or industry.

In the same way, the adjustment of wage levels among industries exclusively in proportion to productivity would distort the wage structure of the country. Industries in which productivity increased rapidly would experience large wage increases, while in others in which productivity did not increase or actually declined (especially in extractive industries) wage rates would remain relatively unchanged. Either as a matter of allocation of resources or as a means to the maintenance of industrial peace, the absolute adoption of such a principle for determining the structure of wages among industries would be a catastrophe.

All this is not to say that changes in productivity do not have effects upon the structure of wages within plants or among industries. It can be established, for instance, that wages in the last twenty-five years have increased more rapidly than the average in those industries in which employment and productivity have increased more rapidly than the average. Similarly, the wages have increased less rapidly than the average in those industries in which employment and productivity have either increased less rapidly than the average or actually declined. A substantial part of the in-

crease in productivity, where productivity is increasing fast-
est, is translated into price declines, increases in profits, and
improvements in quality.

2. The term "productivity" seems to have a fascination
that impels many devotees to regard it as a formula for wage
adjustments. The measurement of productivity presents, however, one of the most difficult problems of economic analysis,
econometrics, and statistical measurement. The customary
measure of productivity is "output per man-hour," a measure
secured by dividing a measure of product in physical units by
a measure of man-hour inputs.

In many industries the task of constructing an index of
physical production is formidable, if not impossible. There
may be many different products, and their proportions in total
output, or the "product-mix," may change frequently. While
changes in quality and specifications will be particularly
important in a job-order business, these factors are present
to some extent in almost every case.

3. Between any two periods, output per man-hour may
vary as a result of a great many different factors, among which
are the following: a change in the level of output, a change in
the composition of production, changes in the average effectiveness of plant and equipment (as a result of scrapping
obsolete facilities and bringing in new ones), increased effort
and application on the part of the work force, a change in the
composition of the work force, improvements in earlier stages
of production (as in the concerns which supply materials
and parts), and the substitution of other factors for labor as
a result of a wage-rate increase. These circumstances are
hardly equally valid bases for an increase in wage rates in a
particular plant or company.

In negotiations and public discussion, little effort has
been made to separate the effects of these factors influencing
"productivity," in the sense of output per man-hour. The

union may argue, on the basis of general knowledge of the industry, that productivity increases which have taken place provide a basis for wage increases. The Steel Workers Organizing Committee, as an illustration, argued in the Little Steel Case in 1942 that "workers should receive an equitable share of the proceeds of increasing productive efficiency."[4] In addition to generally available output-per-man-hour data, the union gave examples of man-hour savings through important technical changes. In a later case the United Steelworkers of America supported its case by pointing in detail to new capacity, to the abandonment of obsolete facilities, to changes in the quality and composition of the labor force, and to the effects of further integration.

Evidence of changes in productivity is not readily transformed into cents-per-hour wage adjustments. In a number of industries, such as local transit and utilities, wage costs are to some extent a fixed cost, so that changes in output substantially influence output per man-hour. A higher wage rate in some industries may induce more careful inspection or use of higher-quality materials. Such a change would be reflected in output per man-hour. As has been indicated, these various types of factors affecting output per man-hour are not equally valid grounds for a wage-rate adjustment. Not only is the measurement of productivity changes difficult, but their interpretation for relevant wage negotiations is even more ambiguous.

4. Depending upon the precise meaning given to the productivity argument, the problem of the relation of wage changes to declines in productivity may have to be faced. In the normal case, changes in productivity may be regarded as typically in one direction. There are instances, however, in which performance per average-unit-of-labor input may

---

[4] Brief submitted by the S.W.O.C. to a panel of the National War Labor Board (1942), p. 75.

decline as a result of the exhaustion of a resource, the use of a less-skilled labor force on the average, or as the result of less-intensive application. Under these circumstances is there an argument for a wage decrease?

Cost-of-Living Index

The change in the cost-of-living index[5] has been used during some periods as a standard to determine changes in wage rates. The relative emphasis placed on the cost of living by management and labor organizations depends on whether living costs are rising or falling. The attention given to this influence in wage discussions is greatest during periods of pronounced changes in living costs. In a number of collective bargaining situations, sliding scales have been established to adjust wage rates automatically to changes in the cost-of-living index. The more typical case involves using the cost-of-living argument as one factor among many in negotiations or in other forms of wage-fixing.

As an absolute principle of wage determination the cost of living has severe limitations:

1. The cost-of-living index typically contains important components, such as food and rent, whose price movements are not necessarily good barometers of the change in other wage-determining factors. For reasons peculiar to agriculture and housing, these prices may be out of line relative to the general level of prices. If this were the case, there would be serious question as to the propriety of altering the general level of wage rates, or any rate, by the application of the cost-of-living standard. There have been periods, such as the

[5] In 1945 the Bureau of Labor Statistics changed the name of its index to "Consumers' Price Index for Moderate-Income Families in Large Cities." This index "measures average changes in retail prices of selected goods, rents, and services, weighted by quantities bought by families of wage earners and moderate-income workers in large cities in 1934–36. The items priced for the index constituted about 70 per cent of the expenditures of city families whose income averaged $1,524 in 1934–36."

twenties, in which industrial prosperity has been associated with agricultural depression. To contend that this fact should be binding in industrial wage-rate determination is dubious, just as a temporary rise in the cost-of-living arising from a disappointing harvest would hardly be regarded as an appropriate basis for an upward revision in wage-rate levels.

The absolute application of the cost-of-living standard would force practically uniform wage-rate adjustments in all cases. (Admittedly, there are minor geographical variations in rates of change in the cost-of-living index.) But there may be occasion for important variations in the rates of change in wages among firms and industries.

2. Labor organizations have frequently indicated that application of the cost-of-living principle over any considerable period would result in a stationary real standard of living for wage-earners. The gains of productivity in our system have normally been translated in part into increases in wages and salaries. The rigid application of the slogan of cost-of-living would result in a stationary real wage rate.

3. Mention may be made briefly of the difficulties of measuring changes in the cost-of-living. These problems received widespread attention during the recent war period.[6] It is not always clear whether the proponents of the principle in collective bargaining are interested in measuring the price of a constant bundle of goods and services, or whether they are attempting to measure the change in average expenditures. The latter concept includes the effect of changes in income levels, the effects of administering price structures so as to make available particular price lines of commodities and "forced" substitutions of the type necessitated by wartime conditions.

[6] *Report of the President's Committee on the Coast of Living* (Washington, D.C.: Office of Economic Stabilization, 1945). The various reports by labor and management representatives and by technical experts are appended.

56808

EMORY & HENRY LIBRARY

4. The application of any cost-of-living principle to wage determination must surmount the difficult problem of an appropriate base period. If wages are to be adjusted to the changes in the cost-of-living, there must be some starting point. The unions normally would select the period of the last wage change, in cases of increasing cost-of-living, while employers would emphasize the point that some more representative period of real earnings should be selected.

5. Automatic adjustment of the general level of wage rates to the cost-of-living index is not always appropriate policy. There may be times of high employment and output in which such a policy would result in cumulative wage and price increases. High employment is always loaded with inflationary dangers, and wage-rate adjustments at such periods must be approached with care in order to avoid unstabilizing consequences.

Ability to Pay

The slogan, "ability to pay," has received particular attention in the course of postwar wage discussions in the public press and before fact-finding bodies. The argument is not new; probably it is as old as collective bargaining. In its simplest form the argument should be looked upon as a mere reflex of a wage demand. A union would not normally make a wage demand without at the same time stating that the demand could be met. There are, no doubt, some exceptions to this view, as in cases involving marginal concerns, but a union cannot make a demand with conviction unless it also implies that the company or industry can afford the wage increase. In much the same way, in the initial stages of bargaining, the employer in rejecting the demand almost has to imply as a stratagem that it cannot be afforded. There are situations in which a company rejects a demand, admitting that it can afford the requested adjustment, but these are not typical circumstances. On the most elemental plane, consequently, statements regarding ability to pay have been necessary adjuncts to the demand or to the rejection of the demand.

Any discussion of ability to pay in more serious terms in wage negotiations necessarily raises a host of conceptual and statistical problems regarding the meaning of the phrase in any particular case. Among the more prominent of these problems are the following:

1. What is the period over which one is concerned with ability to pay? A firm may be able to pay a specific increase for a short period, but not for a longer one. A large part of the difficulties in the postwar period arose from the fact that the unions demanded immediate wage adjustments, while the view of many companies in the reconversion industries was that wage adjustments should be postponed until output had been raised to more nearly normal conditions. Here was a conflict concerning in part the period of time to be considered in decisions concerning ability to pay.

2. How shall one estimate the effect of wage-rate changes on costs? This question involves the problem of labor productivity, which is dependent, not alone on the efforts of wage-earners, but also on the flow of materials and supplies and the effectiveness of management organization. In estimating the effect of wage-rate changes on costs, a decision must also be made on the allowance, if any, to be made for the indirect effects of the wage adjustment on materials, prices, purchased parts, and equipment.

3. The volume of production will no doubt materially affect ability of an enterprise to pay wages. This difficulty concerns not merely the level of production but also the way in which production may be distributed among different types of goods (broadly, the product-mix), particularly among high- and low-profit items.

4. The character of competition in the markets in which the products must be sold will substantially affect the ability to pay wage increases. These circumstances will influence the extent to which wage adjustments may be translated into price increases and the effect of such adjustments upon volume of output.

5. The rate of return on investment to which the company is regarded as entitled will create a problem in determining the ability to pay wages. The familiar complications that have arisen in the regulation of public utilities indicate that this is not a problem to be treated lightly. Differing views on rates of return and valuation will significantly influence the content of the ability-to-pay slogan.

6. The ability to pay wage increases before and after income taxes will vary substantially. Which measure is appropriate? The handling of other tax issues, such as the carry-back adjustments, may present serious problems in defining ability to pay.

Several recent attempts have been made to apply the ordinary multiple-correlation technique to the problem of determining the capacity of enterprises to pay wage increases.[7] The analysis of the General Motors Corporation, for instance, determined the level of profits by these variables: the level of output, average hourly earnings, cost of materials, prices of the finished products sold by the company, and a productivity time trend. By solving for the values of these relationships to profits on the basis of average relationships for the period 1929–41, it is possible to estimate the level of profits with specified values for output, wage levels, prices, material costs, and productivity (a function of time). The effects of wage-rate changes on profits may be estimated under desig-

[7] "Purchasing Power for Prosperity, the Case of the General Motors Workers for Maintaining Take-Home Pay," presented by International Union, UAW-CIO G.M. Department, Walter P. Reuther, Director, (1945), pp. 55–74. Also see Harold M. Wein, "Wages and Prices—A Case Study," *Review of Economic Statistics*, May, 1947.

nated conditions regarding prices, material costs, and output.

This type of analysis no doubt warrants further examination. At least it should contribute to a better understanding of the quantitative relations among production, prices, and costs. The method cannot, however, provide any automatic formula for measuring ability to pay. Its proponents have never claimed that it does. The problems summarized and enumerated above are not suddenly dissolved. The level of output for the future contract period remains dubious. There may be grounds to question whether productivity will be above or below levels predicted from any time trend.[8] The statistical technique does not eliminate these problems; it may present them in different form.

The correlation technique may present its results in the better-known form of a "break-even chart," showing the level of output or the percentage of capacity operations at which the enterprise "breaks even." This point will vary with changes in the prices of the products of the firm, the wage rates, and the productivity of the enterprise. This simple device may provide a helpful basis for discussion in collective bargaining over the economic position of the enterprise. What level of output should an enterprise regard as normal for wage-setting purposes? The analysis may help to suggest that temporarily high or low levels of output are not satisfactory standards by which to fix wage rates expected to be maintained over relatively long periods.

As an absolute principle of wage determination, the ability-to-pay principle is widely recognized as having severe limitations. The general adoption of the principle of determining wage rates absolutely in accordance with ability to pay would result in very unequal wage levels among different firms. It would be incompatible with many union programs

[8] See "General Motors Reply to UAW-CIO, Brief Submitted in Support of Wage Demand for 52 Hours Pay for 40 Hours Work" (1945), pp. 14–19.

for equalization of wage rates among firms in the same industry or locality. The principle would appropriate to wage-
earners the incentives that lead the more profitable firms to
expand production and employment.

Just as unions have stressed that employers have the ability
to pay wage increases in good times, so managements have
emphasized inability to pay on other occasions. For instance,
one of the major headings in the brief of a company resisting
a demand for a wage-rate increase stated: "The financial condition of the company with revenues of practically the lowest
point in twenty years makes it impossible to increase wages
already adequate and at the same time maintain the present
standard of transportation service, retain the present number
of employees, and continue to render unified service."[9] The
ability-to-pay argument has been employed frequently by
companies attempting to make a case for a lower wage scale
than other companies in an industry or locality. By virtue of
location, machinery, size, or temporary financial embarrass-
ment, an enterprise may seek to secure special wage treatment
on grounds of inability to pay.

There will be wide differences of judgment in any particular situation concerning the net effect of the factors defining
and measuring ability to pay wages—differences not only between parties but also within any group of relatively disinterested observers.

Fundamental Problems

The analysis of the slogans and principles of wage determination summarized in the four preceding sections indicates
that there are fundamental limitations to the application of
these principles to particular situations. These limitations
must be faced with candor.

[9] "Brief on Behalf of Pittsburgh R. Co., Arbitration between Pittsburgh R. Co.
and Div. No. 85, Amalgamated Ass'n. of Street and Electric R. Employees of America"
(hearings held from July 16 to August 18, 1934).

First, the range of possible wage rates which would follow from the various possible applications of each of the principles would generally be wider than normal variance between the parties in collective bargaining. The alternative meanings and measurements of each one of these standards are so diverse that the principle frequently can provide little help as an authoritative determination of wages. The same point may be made in alternative language: the differences between the parties are simply translated into alternative meanings and measurements of a particular wage slogan or standard. The range of disputed application of any of these principles is likely to be much wider than the normal range of disagreement between the parties.

Second, since all wage determination must be considered with reference to a prospective period, conflicting expectations as to the future are certain to result in divergent applications of any set of wage principles. The point is not merely that the future in general is uncertain but that uncertainty exists in respect to the magnitude of specific factors—such as output, price, and productivity—vital to *present* wage determination.

Third, the application of wage slogans or principles is complicated by the fact that the parties frequently have conflicting and divergent basic objectives. These are particularly contentious when the "time horizons" of the parties are markedly different. The company may be interested in remaining in business over the long run; whereas, a union may be interested, by virtue of the political problems of leadership, in its position during the next year. Or the union may be interested in maximizing the position of union members during their lifetime without regard to new and younger employees. A further illustration of this basic conflict exists in a situation in which the management of a particular company may be interested in the continuation of its own position over a period of time, while the union may be concerned with the industry more broadly. Such conflicts in basic objectives are certain to yield divergent wage levels.

Fourth, even if any one of these standards could be applied in an unambiguous way, the problem would remain of choosing among these alternative standards or weighting the results they yield. No two of the principles would result in the identical wage-rate change in a specific situation. The successive application of these four standards, however, may serve to delimit the range of controversy. In arbitration proceedings the limits indicated by the various standards help to identify the practical range of judgment of the arbitrator.

These basic difficulties may seem to suggest a pessimistic conclusion as to the contribution that economics can make to the solution of wage disputes. There is no royal road to the application of economics to wage determination. There is no simple formula that may be simply applied to particular cases. The rigor of the classroom diagram blurs in the face of the complexities of collective bargaining when the rigid assumptions of the formal economic analysis have been removed. In fact there are no "economic" problems in the real world. There may be economic aspects of problems, but the real problems which require decision must be faced as entities. The more frankly and explicitly technical economists admit this fact, the greater the assistance they may eventually give in the solution of practical problems of wage determination in particular cases.

Criteria for the General Level of Wage Rates

The slogans and clichés used in discussions of the general level of wage rates would require another major chapter. Only some of the more prominent issues can be indicated. There is fairly general agreement among economists that the average increase in productivity constitutes the appropriate norm for the long-term movement of the general level of wage rates. As average productivity increases, the level of money wage rates and salaries should rise. The price level as a whole should remain relatively stable. These norms would roughly continue the actual relationships of the past century.

In order for the price level to remain constant, however, industries with greater-than-average increases in productivity must decrease prices. In a day of extensively administered prices, these decreases may not be forthcoming. The pricing mechanism may not have the flexibility requisite to this standard of wage-setting. Moreover, the internal requirements of the labor movement may necessitate larger wage-rate increases than are possible under the productivity standard. Intense leadership rivalries may produce greater wage-rate increases, with a consequent rise in the price level.[10]

Purchasing power is a slogan that has received as much attention as any other in discussions of the general level of wage rates. While the cliché is used in particular cases, a separate section has not been devoted to it in the preceding discussion since no single wage bargain is so extensive as to permit a particular wage change to affect directly and appreciably the purchasing power expended on the products of the firms in negotiation. The standard of purchasing power must refer to the general level of wage rates.

The crudest form of the argument identifies wage-rate and purchasing-power changes. There is no need here to expand on the fact that the relation between changes in wage rates and the aggregate expenditures for consumption and investment in any period is not simple nor direct.

A more sophisticated form of the purchasing-power standard relates to the balance between wage rates and prices. The

[10] See John T. Dunlop, "American Wage Determination: The Trend and Its Significance," a paper read before the Chamber of Commerce Institute on Wage Determination, Washington, D.C., January 11, 1947.

Nathan Report was cast in these terms.[11] The level of wage rates was regarded as too low at the existing level of prices to sustain high levels of employment. Decreases in the price level were regarded as unlikely. "Businessmen show no signs of exercising such self-restraint in their natural search for profits as would bring about a decline in prices except in the face of a sharp reduction in demand."[12] The Nathan Report concluded that a substantial increase in the level of wage rates without corresponding price increases was required to sustain purchasing power and high-level employment.

The Nathan Report raised the fundamental question of the standards to be applied in appraising whether the levels of wages and prices are in balance. If a lack of balance is determined, the issue must be faced whether wages or prices should be corrected. These questions cannot be answered by rote. Judgment as to appropriate policy must be based not only on the level of profits but also on the structure of wage rates and prices. Judgment as to appropriate wage-price policy must also be influenced by the level of interest rates.

An annual appraisal of the economic outlook, such as is provided by the Council of Economic Advisors to the President, can promote a widespread understanding of the problems to be confronted in particular wage negotiations. A greater economic literacy among the rank and file of union members and business executives can improve the atmosphere in which specific wage conferences take place.

The Contribution of Economic Analysis

The restraint of the previous sections follows not so much from modesty as from candor. It must not be concluded, however, that the economist has nothing relevant to say in the

[11] Robert R. Nathan and Oscar Goss, *A National Wage Policy for 1947* (Washington, D.C., December, 1946).
[12] *Ibid.*, p. 3.

process of wage determination, whether it be collective bargaining, arbitration, or governmental wage-fixing. Economic analysis can make at least these distinctive contributions to the settlement of wage disputes:

1. The parties or other wage-fixers need to be reminded of the longer-run consequences of any decision. While no simple formula or standard may be available to fix a wage, the possible effects of any decision on the employer and the union involved need to be explored. Regardless of the standards used in setting wage rates or the objectives of the parties, economic analysis calls attention to the channels of effect of any wage decision on output, prices, and employment. It can serve as the conscience of the parties as to many of the less immediate effects of a wage-rate decision.

2. Economic analysis points to the impacts of wage rates in sectors of the economy outside the immediate decision. It is particularly concerned with the effects of wage changes on the total national income and the aggregate level of output and employment. "What is true of a firm or of a particular industry or of a set of industries need not be true of the economy as a whole. To draw attention continually to such relationships between the parts and the whole is probably the most distinctive function of the economist."[13]

The processes of wage-dispute settlement need to develop, as they are developing, specialized personnel within unions, employers' organizations, and public bodies who are skilled in the exercise of judgment in the intricate and complex business of wage determination. A person so skilled may profitably utilize the technical services provided by statisticians, lawyers, economists, actuaries, accountants, publicists, industrial engineers, and others; but the primary need is for the mature practitioner to exercise judgment.

[13] A. P. Lerner, "The Relation of Wage Policies and Price Policies," *American Economic Review Proceedings, 1939*, p. 158.

Economic analysis purports to deal with one aspect of human behavior. Wage-setting must involve the totality of behavior. Any practitioner must develop the art of applying the tools of the technicians in the light of all of the complexities, and frequently the perversities, of human behavior.

Part Two

Collective Bargaining Cases

Section A

DISCHARGE AND DISCIPLINE

PROBLEMS of discharge and discipline go to the heart of the collective bargaining relationship. Many seemingly trivial situations conceal issues fundamental to each party. Few questions are charged with more emotion and are more explosive in day-to-day relations. The volatile character of these cases is not surprising since the right of management efficiently to direct the operations and personnel of an enterprise and the desire of employees to seek protection from arbitrary and discriminatory discipline are vital to both. These basic objectives are at times in conflict.

To the individual employee, a job is his only means of a livelihood. In 90 per cent of the cases of those who work for a living today outside of agriculture, the employee is not his own boss. In the absence of a union he holds a job subject only to the decision of the enterprise and at the pleasure of a superior. A job entails a variety of rights other than wage rates, such as seniority, vacation, and health and pension benefits. The worker comes to think of having "property rights" in *his* job. The threat of discharge under these circumstances is a serious risk to livelihood in the customary manner. Moreover, a job typically implies a pattern of friends and social life in our society. The union emerges as protection against the risk of arbitrary discharge and the loss of economic and social status.

To the management of an enterprise, efficient operations are a necessary objective in a competitive world. Consequently, the development of an efficient and loyal work force is a fundamental concern to management. The removal of certain employees may be required, not alone on account of their deleterious or inferior work and conduct, but also to serve as an example to keep other employees up to the standards required by the management. The right to direct the work force carries with it the authority to discipline those who deliberately or otherwise fail to perform their work.

The importance of discharge cases in collective bargaining varies with the regularity of employment. In the typical case, where employees work steadily for the same employer, discharge assumes most importance. Where migratory employees are hired by continuing firms, as in the case of agricultural and allied operations, or where the same employees are hired by a succession of migratory firms, as in the case of construction, discharge becomes a much less serious problem since the loss of a particular job is a frequent and normal occurrence.

It has already been observed that one of the most significant aspects of decision-making is the location or level in an organization at which decisions are made. Decisions on discipline are no exception. In the management organization, should the foreman have final authority to discipline? Should the responsibility at the foreman level be limited to recommending discharge or discipline? How far up into the management hierarchy should the case be carried before discharge or for review after the decision? In the same way, the location of decision-making regarding discharge cases in the union organization is important. Under what circumstances should the individual member's case for redress against discharge be overruled by the union organization? Should the local union steward ever take this responsibility? Can he ever afford to do so politically, in view of the fact that he must normally face an election in the department? Is the international union the level at which cases should be settled by the union against the individual employee when the member seems to have no case? Or, should union policy be to take all cases, regardless of their merits, to arbitration?

In the typical collective bargaining agreement, the right to discharge appears in the enumeration of the "rights" of the company under the "management" clause. The following clause is representative: "The management of the works and the direction of the working forces, including the right to . . . . suspend or discharge for proper causes . . . . is vested exclusively in the Company, provided that this will not be used for purposes of discrimination against any member of the Union."[1]

Many contracts in recent years have developed special clauses indicating the procedures to be used in discharge cases. A significant development in some of these clauses is the provision that no employee shall be discharged peremptorily. The immediate supervisor may suspend the employee for a nominal period, such as five days, during which higher levels of management may investigate the case. If a discharge is decided upon by the management, the period permits the filing of a grievance in the event the union is to contest the case. The device of the initial suspension period removes many of the explosive qualities that accompany a flat discharge in tense circumstances. There is less danger of direct action by other employees. The disciplined employee can more readily be removed from the department or plant. Moreover, the management hierarchy has the opportunity to review a decision of the first line of supervision. Such procedures are a good illustration of creative negotiations which evolve contract terms that protect the "fundamental" rights of each side and yet result in more orderly and workable relations.

A great many issues arise in the day-to-day handling of discharge and discipline cases. Some of these problems are peculiar to management; they present difficult questions of company policy. Others are unique for the labor organization and the union officer. Still others are issues only for the

[1] Carnegie-Illinois Steel Corporation and United Steelworkers of America, CIO, March 13, 1945.

arbitrator in cases where all other steps in the normal grievance procedure have been exhausted. Among the more frequently encountered problems that arise in discharge and discipline cases are the following:

1. Is the right of discharge and discipline limited to misconduct on the premise of management? May an employee be disciplined for acquiring outside of working hours a reputation that would be regarded as inimical by the management?

2. What is the status in discharge cases of company rules that are not a part of the collective bargaining agreement? May the reasonableness and propriety of such rules be challenged in a particular case?

3. May rules that are frequently and openly violated be invoked to discipline a particular employee?

4. Is ignorance of a rule defense against a penalty?

5. Should an employee ever be discharged who has not been warned after an initial offense? What would be a sound company policy? Is every employee entitled to a second chance?

6. When a number of employees are involved in a breach of contract, as a wildcat strike, must penalties be invoked only in proportion to responsibility?

CASE 1

CONDUCT OFF THE COMPANY PREMISES

Union: United Automobile Workers of America, CIO, Local 6

Company: General Motors Corporation, Buick Motor Melrose Park Division

Two Negro employees became involved in a dispute with a white employee and a member of his family outside the plant. After the white employee had brought the situation to the attention of management, the Negro employees were discharged. The Union protested their discharge.

The Union based its protest on the grounds that, since the

entire situation occurred outside of the plant, the Company lacked authority to impose discipline. It therefore requested that the two men be reinstated with reimbursement for all time lost.

Management's position was that, although the incident occurred outside the plant, it gave rise to a latently extreme racial issue, which had already evidenced itself in several ways within the premises of the plant. Management claims that it is within its rights in discharging the complainants whose actions outside of the company's property resulted in the existence of dangerous tensions among the company's employees while they are actually working on the job.

QUESTIONS

1. Do you agree with the position of management? What limitations, if any, would you place on the principle advocated?
2. On what basis would discipline be applied to some employees and others excused? In this case, should not all employees involved in the dispute be disciplined, if any are to be subject to company action?
3. Can an employee be disciplined for getting into trouble outside the plant? Would the company have a right to discipline a worker who had served a short term in prison for an offense occurring outside the company premises?
4. Do you think it possible to establish a clear relationship between events outside the plant and a real threat of trouble within the plant? What kind of evidence would be required?
5. Do you accept the principle that anything that happens outside of working hours is of no concern to the management? If not, under what circumstances would you hold otherwise?

CASE 2

CONDUCT AFTER WORKING HOURS

UNION: United Automobile Workers of America, CIO

COMPANY: Chrysler Corporation

A. J. Kennedy became an employee of the Chrysler Corporation on September 29, 1936. He was made chief steward in his department in October, 1937. Thereafter, he continuously held various offices in DeSoto, Local 227 of the UAW. At the time of his discharge on January 26, 1943, he was President of the local.

The Company and the Union do not agree on his record as an employee. The Company maintains that Kennedy's record was not good. It cites repeated warnings and several disciplinary layoffs. The Union maintains that Kennedy's record was good, that certain charges made against him were not properly based, and that he had been largely instrumental in avoiding and preventing work stoppages at the plant.

But on the night of January 15, 1943, and the early morning of January 16, Mr. Black, the DeSoto Plant Manager, Mr. Ranney, the Operating Manager, and Mr. Carmichael, the Labor Relations Supervisor, received repeated phone calls from a person who said he was Joe Kennedy. When these first calls were made around 8:00 P.M., the caller said he wanted to discuss a grievance involving two employees who had been discharged in December, 1940, for gambling during working hours in the DeSoto plant. The speaker became less intelligible and less coherent with each subsequent call. He eventually stopped talking about the two gamblers and began criticizing the Corporation and calling Black, Ranney, and Carmichael profane names. About 4:00 A.M. on January 16, Black told the caller that he would not countenance this vile language and the annoyance of the constantly ringing phone. He told the caller that he was discharged.

The Company stated that all of the plant officials called were familiar with Kennedy's voice and recognized the voice of the caller of January 15 and 16 as Kennedy's.

In the final step of the grievance procedure, it was denied by the Union that Kennedy made the calls in question. This denial was not made in earlier days. The Company felt that the combination of his past record and this incident justified Kennedy's discharge.

The Union contended that Kennedy did not make the calls and added that, even if he did, they were not grounds for disciplinary action since they did not take place on company property or during the business hours of any of the parties directly concerned. The Union offered no proof to support its denial of Kennedy's guilt. No provocation by the persons called is claimed or shown by the Union. The testimony before the umpire brought out that had Kennedy, without provocation, used the language charged in the manner described in the presence of management's representatives at the plant, the discharge would have gone unchallenged by the Union.

QUESTIONS

1. How would you decide this case?
2. If the facts as stated by the Company are accepted, does the management have the right to discipline for conduct beyond the limits of the plant after working hours?
3. If the previous question be answered in the affirmative, how far would you extend the principle? Must the conduct for which discipline is applied concern officially the Company or its representatives?
4. How would you appraise the argument that the company's representatives had the right to call the police to prevent the nuisance but no right to discipline the employee?

CASE 3

UNAUTHORIZED WORK STOPPAGE

UNION: United Steelworkers of America, CIO

COMPANY: Jones and Laughlin Steel Corporation

Seven crews, consisting of one engineer and one brakeman per shift, operate the narrow-gauge trains that service the open hearth department at the Aliquippa works of the Jones and Laughlin Steel Corporation. These small locomotives bring raw materials to the furnace and carry away molds filled with hot steel.

On Friday, January 31, 1947, the 4-to-12 shift reported 15 minutes before the regular starting time but did not go to work immediately. Instead, they huddled together with the men of the 8-to-4 shift. After some moments of milling around, Lechman made the following statement to assistant general foreman L'Grady:

"Somebody has to tell you what this is all about, so I might as well do so, if no one else will. We've complained about the hazards here for more than three months. Yet little has been done about it. We won't work under such unsafe conditions and are giving you notice now that we will stay on the job only long enough to protect the equipment from damage."

The crews then went to work under the direction of their supervisors who ordered a general conditioning of the department preparatory for a shutdown. At a hurriedly called meeting in the mill at 8:00 P.M. on Friday, Ray Dye, management's representative, told the local union officers that, if Lechman and Cooke, two of the rebellious crew members, went out that night, he was going to fire them. At that moment Lechman and Cooke were working as were all the other crew members, and continued working until sent home by Foreman Albaugh at 9:00 P.M. Friday. On Saturday, February 1, Ray Dye told the union officials that instead of the two he had planned to discharge, it would be four, and that the other two would be Belsky and Mezmar, none of whom would be allowed to return to work.

Operations were resumed Monday at 8:00 P.M., February 3, when the Union finally succeeded in prevailing upon its membership to return to their jobs, leaving the four discharges to be resolved by arbitration or negotiation. Lechman, Cooke, Mezmar, and Belsky received their suspension notices at home by mail on February 6, 1947. The Union holds that these four employees were discriminately discharged and asks for their reinstatement with back pay.

Position of the Union

The Union, at the outset, explains that it has no intention of defending an unauthorized walkout. It views a wildcat strike, not only as a violation of a solemn assurance given to management, but also as a challenge to union responsibility and as an act destructive of democratic principles. However, the Union contends that, while it is charged with the responsibility of keeping employees at work, management has an equal responsibility, negatively at least, not to establish such conditions as will make continuous operations onerous or impossible. Work stoppages presuppose a cause. The cause must be of sufficient magnitude to persuade men to stop their own income, injure their fellow-workmen, and undermine the principles of collective bargaining.

In the present case, the Union contends that it is inaccurate to term the events of January 31, 1947, as a "work stoppage." The Union holds that, in its most extreme expression, the events constituted merely a refusal of certain employees to work under conditions that they felt to be unreasonably hazardous. It holds that the conditions of work are pertinent to an understanding of the causes of the walkout. It would be unjust to judge the relative guilt of the employees without an appraisal of the circumstances that led to the refusal to work. The Union insists that, although the employees were unwise in their choice of the walkout weapon, it was an understandable response to a series of unsuccessful frustrating efforts to remedy a dangerously unsafe condition. Had the Company been alert to its responsibilities of maintaining safe and healthy conditions of employment, the walkout would never have occurred.

The Union further maintains that the Company is especially unjust in selecting four out of a total of fifty-four offending employees and offering them as a sacrifice, presumably to "establish discipline." This is held to be contrary to Section 9 of the contract which reads: ". . . . the right to . . . . discharge for proper cause . . . . is vested exclusively in the Corporation, provided that this will not be used for purposes of discrimination against any member of the Union. . . . ." The Union insists that the discharge of the four employees is a gross example of unwarranted discrimination. They are not more guilty than any other of the fifty; yet they are discharged while no penalty whatsoever is attached to the rest. When the Company chooses to apply a penalty to some and not to others, such action is discriminatory, unjust, and consequently contrary to the plain content of the contract. The four employees should be reinstated to their former jobs and compensated for their lost time.

POSITION OF THE COMPANY

The Company considers the events that occurred on January 31, 1947 as constituting a "strike" or "work stoppage." Work stopped during the turn (shift) in question and continued at a standstill for several days. Eventually all the departments of the works were affected, thus showing no temporary or transient interruption but a serious cessation of operations. The Company argues that the aggrieved men were discharged "for their participation in that stoppage" and that it is basing its action on Section 2 of the February 18, 1946, supplemental agreement, which reads as follows:

"The Union agrees that during the term of the April 6, 1945 agreement, as amended and supplemented by this supplemental agreement neither the Union nor its agents, nor its members, will authorize, instigate, aid, condone, or engage in a work stoppage or strike. The Corporation agrees that during the same period there shall be no lockouts."

The Company also cites Sections 8 and 9 of the basic agreement, which read in part as follows:

"The Management of the Works and the direction of the working forces, including the right to hire, suspend, or discharge for proper cause, or transfer, and the right to relieve employees from duty because of lack of work, and for other legitimate reasons, is vested exclusively in the Corporation; provided that this will not be used for purposes of discrimination against any member of the Union. . . . ."

While the Company acknowledges that the "work stoppage" was not, at the time, "authorize(d), instigate(d), aid(ed), condone(d), or engage(d) in" by the Union, it insists that some, if not all, of these forbidden acts were committed by "its members." It argues that discussion of the cause of the work stoppage or of any condition precedent to the discharge is out of order. The Company holds that if the aggrieved employees had a valid complaint, if they considered their conditions of employment hazardous and unsafe, then the agreement between the Company and Union outlines in a detailed fashion the responsibility of the parties to deal with complaints brought in the specified form of a grievance. Under the terms of the agreement, either party can be held to prompt and full response on specified matters which the other party desires to have determined. The Company insists that the employees had no justifiable excuse for taking matters into their own hands, especially since they had not yet exhausted their remedies under the bargaining agreement. Complaints had been made by the employees and had received the courtesy of a response by letter from the Company. If this was not considered adequate, means were available to require further response; yet a formal grievance was never filed by these employees.

Finally, the Company argues that although fifty-four employees were involved in the work stoppage and, although all of these were in some degree guilty, its choice of four employees does not constitute a discriminatory discharge. These four employees were discharged "for proper cause," and the Company did not use its authority "for purposes of discriminating against any member of the Union." The Company contends that, so far as its own knowledge is concerned, these four employees are alone indicated to be near enough to the center of the concerned events to be surely responsible for them. It argues that if the Union desires to produce other employees who are equally guilty, the Company will deal them equal punishment. If the four discharged employees are not to suffer arbitrary penalties beyond their fellows, the only remedy would be that others be brought up to their level of pain. The Company argues that in selecting the four employees who appear most responsible, it is being lenient rather than discriminatory in its handling of the problem.

QUESTIONS

1. Does the discipline of the four workers out of a total of fifty-four constitute discrimination? Discrimination against the Union? May the Company discipline some workers as an "example" to others?
2. If the workers believed that continuing at work constituted a threat to their health, would such a cessation of work be a work stoppage? Would it violate the agreement?
3. Why did the stoppage take place? How would you assess responsibility? What steps would you advocate by the management and the Union to avoid the recurrence of similar cases?

CASE 4

ALLEGED DISCRIMINATION FOR CREED

UNION: United Packinghouse Workers of America, CIO

COMPANY: Armour and Company

Mary Jones was hired by Armour and Company in December, 1942. In April, 1945, the Company changed from a five-day to a six-day normal work week—Monday through Saturday. Mary Jones informed the foreman that it was her conviction, from her reading of the Bible, that Saturday was the Sabbath. She is a Baptist, and her own reading of the Bible convinced her that it was "wrong" to work on Saturday, although this is not the interpretation of the church with which she is affiliated. She asked to be excused from work on Saturday, offering to work on Sunday instead. But when she did not report to work on Saturday, April 28, she was discharged.

The Company offered to reinstate her as a part-time worker, but this was refused. The Union requested reinstatement with back pay on the ground that the employee was discriminated against because of her "creed" and that this was improper under Section 5 of the contract which reads: "The Company agrees that it will not discriminate against any employee or applicant because of race, sex, color, creed, nationality or because of membership in the union."

POSITION OF THE UNION

The Union states that, in the past, other employees have refused to work on the day that they consider to be the Sabbath, namely, Sunday. It has been company practice not to require people to work on Sunday, when it was against their religious beliefs. In this case, the employee considers that Saturday is the Sabbath and should be accorded the same privilege as those who consider Sunday as the Sabbath. The Union argues that to do otherwise is to discriminate against this employee. In addition, the Union stresses the right of individuals in a democratic form of society to depart from the majority practice and to exercise their liberty to make decisions for themselves.

The Union is opposed to the company's suggestion that Mary Jones be returned to work as a part-time employee since this would eliminate her vacation and seniority rights.

POSITION OF THE COMPANY

The Company acknowledges the complete sincerity of Mary Jones in her religious conviction. No implication is advanced that this was a subterfuge for getting out of Saturday work. However, the Company argues that, since the normal work week is Monday through Saturday, the Union's request that Mary Jones substitute Sunday employment for Saturday employment will mean discrimination in favor of one employee. The Company feels that it has a right to assign workers and to schedule hours. The contract specifically provides for Sunday work and the rate of pay on Sunday. No provision exists in the contract for granting special privileges to employees because of their religious beliefs. If an exception were to be made in this case, other employees might become subject to "conversion." Plant operations would be impaired. Regular employees have been discharged, under plant rules, for refusing to work on Sunday.

The Company states the sole issue is whether an employee may be discharged for refusing to follow the work schedule set by the Company. The Company further feels that, in offering part-time employment to this employee, it is going as far as it can. It states that "regular" employees, obtaining the advantages that accompany their status, should work the regular schedule.

QUESTIONS

1. Do these facts constitute discrimination under the contract on grounds of creed?
2. In deciding this case, in what sense would the arbitrator be "interpreting" the contract?
3. What limits would you place on the principle of individual freedom advocated by the Union?
4. What weight would you give to the fact that the Company lengthened the work week from five to six days? Would you be influenced by the fact that the employee took a job in the industry which at times works six days per week?

CASE 5

COMPANY DEMERIT SYSTEM

UNION: Industrial Union of Marine and Shipbuilding Workers of America, CIO

COMPANY: Cramp Shipbuilding Company

James Westfield, a truck helper, had been out on a job during the afternoon of July 17, 1945, and arrived back at the yard approximately 12 minutes prior to his quitting time of 4:00 P.M. He reported to his leadman and then proceeded to the washroom to wash up. At about 3:55 P.M., while he was at his locker with his shirt off, he was approached by a representative of supervision who asked him his number and requested that he show his badge. Westfield resented the manner in which he had been approached and replied that he had no number. Upon further questioning he stated that his number could be found at the office; he did not show his badge. At this point the whistle blew, ending the shift. On the following day Westfield was discharged for violation of company rules. The Union is protesting this discharge.

POSITION OF THE COMPANY

The Company holds that Westfield was guilty of infraction of four company rules by loafing in the men's room, leaving his job before the allowed quitting time, failing to wear his identification badge where it could be seen, and refusing to show his badge when requested to do so by a Supervisor. These offenses are considered sufficient to warrant a discharge.

Further, the Company argues that discharge is justified under its announced and established demerit system. The Company relies on its general memorandum No. 228 (Yard Routing No. 6) entitled "Demerits for Given Offenses." This memorandum provides: "Any employee who commits three offenses in any one year, each of which carry 30 or more demerits, will be subject to discharge, decision in such cases to be made by the Foreman and the Foreman's Committee." It also provides that an employee is subject to discharge when demerits total 100 or more after credits have been given for merits of 10 points for each calendar month of "good behavior." The company's demerit system allowed the point values as shown in the accompanying table for the infractions in question.

Item No.	Item	Demerits
3	Loafing in toilets.........................	40
7	Leaving job before allowed quitting time.....	40
12	Failure to wear identification badge where it could be seen........................	40
13	Refusal to show badge when requested to do so by a Supervisor......................	40

The Company did not cumulate Items 3 and 7, but rather gave 40 demerits for both offenses. However, Items 12 and 13 were judged as two separate offenses with total demerits of 80. The sum of Items 3 (and 7), 12, and 13 yield 120 demerits and makes discharge the appropriate disciplinary action. Finally, the Company argues that it has discharged other employees under its demerit system, and the Union has in the past acquiesced in these decisions.

POSITION OF THE UNION

The Union argues that Westfield's offenses did not warrant discharge either on their own merits or under the company's demerit system. It is admitted that Westfield was in the washroom before the whistle blew. However, it is felt that there was little if any productive work for Westfield to do in the few minutes of the shift which remained after he had come in with the truck. In this sense he was not really loafing, and the offense was minor as a practical matter.

Further, inasmuch as Westfield had his shirt off when the Supervisor addressed him, he could not be expected to be wearing his badge at the moment. And his failure to show his badge upon request was due to the manner in which the Supervisor had approached him by grabbing Westfield's arm and saying, "Hey, boy, where's your button?" These offenses are not considered sufficient to merit a discharge.

If analyzed purely on the basis of the company's demerit system, the Union argues that the Company still does not have grounds for discharge. The demerits against Westfield would not reach the total of 100, if correctly assessed. The Union maintains that in order to build up more than 100 demerits, the Company penalized Westfield twice for a single offense.

The Union considers the Company to have been unduly technical in charging Westfield 40 demerits for failure to wear a badge as well as refusal to show a badge. As is pointed out by the Union: "He (Westfield) could not be expected to pin it on his skin." Thus, if scored properly, 40 demerits for

Items 12 and 13 combined and 40 demerits for Items 3 and 7 combined would yield a total of 80 demerits and would not warrant discharge.

QUESTIONS

1. Does the company demerit system have any status under the agreement? Why did the Company develop such a plan? What purpose does it serve? Does the Company have to justify its discharge under the demerit point system?
2. Would the alleged conduct of the Supervisor make any difference?
3. If quitting early were a common complaint of management, would management be within its rights in singling out Westfield as an example?

CASE 6

COMPANY RULES

UNION: United Automobile Workers of America, CIO

COMPANY: General Motors Corporation

James O. Wiltone had been employed in the Buick Flint plant since December, 1935. On July 1, 1940, he was discharged for getting signatures in the plant to a petition to place the Communist party on the official ballot of the state of Michigan. The petition had been circulated in May but came to the attention of management only at the end of June when the names and addresses of signers were published in a Flint newspaper. Hence, discharge occurred weeks after the violation of a plant rule reading: "Soliciting or selling or distribution of literature for any cause, and by any person, without the permission of the Management is forbidden in the factory or on company property at any time. Employees violating this rule are subject to dismissal."

Wiltone disclaims any knowledge of such a rule, which management states had been printed, along with many others, in April, 1934, and posted on bulletin boards until sometime in 1939, when it was necessary to revise some of the rules because they had come to be in conflict with the provisions of the current agreement with the Union. Wiltone disclaims ever having seen such a set of rules posted, as does the Chairman of the Bargaining Committee. Both of these men claim that numerous petitions, political and otherwise, had all the while been circulated for signatures, with or without the permission of management, and at times these had been signed by supervisory officials.

No one had been discharged for circulating a petition. In one case, the Chairman and another employee had sought to have a worker discharged for circulating a petition offensive to the Union. Local top management disclaimed all knowledge of the matter. It declined to discharge the worker complained against but stated that he would be spoken to. The worker was placed on another shift, but it is claimed that "every time he was brought (back) on the second shift he has circulated petitions."

When Wiltone was discharged, a request was made that he be reinstated and then that notices be posted stating the penalty for any future unauthorized circulation of petitions, penalties to be equally enforced against offenders. The request was not granted. The Union claims that this was due to a feeling that, in the language of one management representative, Wiltone's case was one of "a different sort."

On appeal from an adverse decision on a claim for unemployment compensation, a referee for the Michigan Unemployment Compensation Commission rules that Wiltone had not been guilty of misconduct because the rule had not been publicized.

Management emphasizes that Wiltone admits circulating the petition. The rule had been on the bulletin board during Wiltone's period of employment. While it was frequently violated during the hectic days of 1937, and now and then violated more recently, violations were not generally overlooked when they came to the attention of management. The case cited by the Union was one in point. The worker was admonished, and the two union representatives had been personally given notice that "anyone caught passing petitions would be released." The rule, said the Company, was not a "dead letter."

The umpire's power under the agreement is different from that of an arbitrator under many agreements. Paragraph 20, reads in part: "In disciplinary lay-off and discharge cases the Umpire shall have the power only to adjudge the guilt or innocence of the employee involved."

QUESTIONS

1. Can management invoke a rule that has not been consistently enforced?
2. Does it make any difference whether Wiltone personally had knowledge of the rule?
3. The rule stated that employees violating the ban on soliciting "*are subject to dismissal*." Does this language grant management the right to use its discretion as to when to invoke the rule? From this viewpoint, management may not have chosen to use the penalty previously. What do you think of this argument?
4. Is the decision of the referee for the Unemployment Compensation Commission relevant to the problem posed to the umpire under the contract? Explain the issue confronting each.
5. What is the status of company rules under a collective bargaining contract? Has the Union agreed to this rule?

CASE 7

FAILURE TO PERFORM WORK ACCORDING TO STANDARD

UNION: United Packinghouse Workers of America, CIO

COMPANY: Armour and Company

Clem Marshall, chief steward in the park department, was discharged on Saturday, July 6, 1946, on grounds of failure to perform his work properly. This discharge was made the subject of a grievance and, upon failure to settle it through negotiation, was submitted to arbitration. The Union requested reinstatement of Marshall with retention of all rights and full back pay.

The grievance arose out of a change in work standards. During the week of the Fourth of July, the rate of speed of the hog kill was cut to an abnormally low level. A "combination job" new to the Chicago plant, but in use in certain other plants of the Company, was introduced on Wednesday, July 3. This combination job included several tasks, of which the most important was the tying of "bungs." This combination job was alternated with that of "snatch guts." The two employees performing these jobs switched from one to the other at half-hour intervals. The rate for the higher-paid job ("snatch guts") was paid to both employees.

Marshall was assigned to work on these two jobs. He was familiar with the individual tasks since he had been engaged in hog-killing work at the Chicago plant of Armour and Company for fifteen years, primarily as a "gut snatcher." On Wednesday, July 3, and Friday, July 5, Marshall worked 4 or 5 hours on the two jobs half of the time, or 2½ hours on the combination job. Protests were filed that the work load was too heavy. Marshall complained to management that he could not maintain the pace. But apparently the work progressed satisfactorily on Wednesday, despite those indications of dissatisfaction with the work requirements by the employees. On Friday, the bungs were not all tied, and this resulted in warnings by management. Marshall was present at the time of at least one of these warnings. Failure to tie bungs, according to company testimony, violated Federal Meat Inspection Regulations.

On Saturday morning, July 6, the work again was not satisfactory. One warning was given—whether to Marshall or his co-worker is not clear, although both men were present at the time. At 8 o'clock at the time of a change-over from the one job to the other, the operation was not performed on eight hogs. It is agreed that this failure occurred at a time when Marshall, rather than his co-worker, was responsible for tying the bungs. Marshall was discharged on the spot for missing the eight hogs. He left without altercation. Subsequently, a work stoppage of the hog-kill gang occurred but was called off prior to the arbitration hearing.

POSITION OF THE UNION

The Union considers discharge an "extreme penalty" in this case and a discriminatory action against a shop steward. It believes Marshall to be guilty of only a "minor infraction." It argues that other employees have in the past missed tying bungs, and have been reprimanded but never discharged. The Union feels that the Company has committed a grave injustice in discharging so hastily a man with fifteen years' continuous service, employed for a short time only on a new combination job and under conditions as to a rate of kill which had not existed for many previous years, and for an offense for which no one had previously been discharged. In this case, the Union holds that the Company has failed to give its employees the same careful consideration in personnel matters that it expects from the employees in their attention to duty.

POSITION OF THE COMPANY

The Company denies the union charge of discrimination. It considers that this case is distinguished from other cases in that the employee was warned, did not improve his work, but instead deliberately missed the largest number of bungs ever passed at one time. The Company holds that it has the right to set standards of work, to direct the working force, and to effect full output without interference. It reminds the arbitrator of the following provisions in the contract which set forth the "jurisdiction of the Contract Arbitrator on work standards":

"(*a*) The Contract-Arbitrator shall have no jurisdiction to determine the propriety of work standards set or changed by the Company. . . .

"(*b*) The Contract-Arbitrator shall have jurisdiction to determine factually whether or not a work standard has been met and to determine the propriety of discipline, if any, arising out of a failure to meet work standards."

Further, the Company protests the union action of calling a work stoppage. It argues that the Union has a duty to encourage its members to perform their work, and to abide by the provisions against work stoppages. In Section 15 of the contract the parties agreed, for the duration of the contract, to depend upon arbitration to recognize their rights when either party failed voluntarily to do so. Section 4 reads in part as follows:

"Should differences arise between the Company and the Union. . . . there shall be no strike, stoppage, slow-down or suspension of work on the part of the Union or its members, or lockout on the part of the Company, on account of such disputes, until after an earnest effort has been made to settle all such matters immediately in the following manner. . . . ."

QUESTIONS

1. Should Marshall be reinstated or permanently discharged?
2. What tests would you apply to establish whether Marshall had met the work standards established by the Company? How much variation, if any, from such standards would you allow?
3. How would you assess the argument that a period of adjustment should be allowed in the light of the new combination job?
4. Does the work stoppage have any relevance to the present case? Would you allow the stoppage to influence the decision either way?
5. Would it be possible to establish that the unsatisfactory work was a form of direct action to support the protest over work standards? How should protests against standards be handled?

CASE 8

TIME LOST IN INVESTIGATION OF ALLEGED MISCONDUCT

UNION: United Packinghouse Workers of America, CIO

COMPANY: Armour and Company

A watchman discovered some bacon concealed in the peanut butter cooler of the Armour plant. He considered this

concealment as the initial step of an attempted theft. Hoping
to apprehend the culprit, he concealed himself in the cooler—
a dark room—and waited to see who might come through to
pick up the bacon. Two men employed in the sausage manufacturing department came into the cooler. The watchman
accosted them and accused them of attempting to steal the
meat. They denied the charge. These employees were not
allowed to go to work the next morning (a Saturday) between
the hours of 7:00 A.M. and 10:00 A.M., while the charges were
being investigated. Upon investigation the next morning, "no
proof was found of their taking any product." The men were
allowed to return to work, having lost three hours, for which
they would have been paid time and one-half had they
worked. Now these employees ask three hours' lost time, on
the ground that this disciplinary action was discriminatory,
and thus improper, under Section 4 of the contract, which
reads in part, as follows:

> "The management of the plants and the direction of
> the working forces, including right to hire, suspend, or
> discharge for proper cause, or transfer, and the right to
> relieve employees from duty because of lack of work, or
> for other legitimate reasons, is vested exclusively in the
> Company, provided this will not be used for the purpose
> of discrimination against any employee, or to avoid any
> of the provisions of this Agreement."

POSITION OF THE UNION

The Union states that the accused men were taking a
"short cut" in leaving the plant and, while in the cooler,
had not taken the bacon. It considers the watchman to have
been "overzealous" and points to the joint statement of the
parties, quoted above, which says "no proof was found of
their taking any product."

Acknowledging the company's need for vigilance against
theft, the union representatives maintain: "At no time have

we ever tried to protect any employee that would steal any of the products from the Company, and at no time in the future will we protect such an individual." However, in the present case, the Union holds that the company's case is built on suspicion of intent and circumstantial evidence, and not proof of intent or the act itself. The watchman destroyed his opportunity for obtaining conclusive evidence when he "jumped the gun" and accused the men before waiting for proof. Consequently, the Union argues that, since no crime was committed, no punishment is in order.

POSITION OF THE COMPANY

The Company argues that the loss of three hours' pay was a minimum disciplinary penalty. While the men took no product, the Company considered the intent to have been wholly evident and that actual theft was prevented only by the intervention of the watchman. It is pointed out that the men needed to follow a circuitous route to reach the cooler, that the bacon was concealed there, that the men were caught standing in the cooler next to the place of concealment unbuttoning their clothes preparatory to hiding the bacon in their garments. The Company feels that it must exercise constant vigilance in prevention of theft. Theft of meat violates plant rules as well as the law of the land. The Company must take disciplinary action against those guilty of theft or of attempted theft.

QUESTIONS

1. Does the principle of "innocent until proven guilty" apply in the area of management discipline?
2. May a partial penalty be invoked on the grounds of suspicion and circumstantial evidence?
3. Should the problem involved in this case be covered explicitly by an agreement?

CASE 9

A MEDICAL REPORT AS A BASIS FOR DISCHARGE

UNION: International Association of Machinists

COMPANY: Boeing Aircraft

Wallace was employed at Renton as a tool repairman B at $1.20 per hour. He was assigned to the repairing of electric motors. On July 1, 1944, a medical restriction was placed on Wallace prohibiting him from employment at work involving the danger of electrical shock. Sometime prior to July 1, 1944, Wallace had filed a grievance with the Company in which he charged misassignment and requested the rate of $1.29½ with retroactive pay. Upon the issuance of a medical restriction, Wallace was asked to transfer to another department at a lower rate of pay. He refused to transfer and was subsequently terminated on July 28, 1944. The Union holds this termination to have been unjust and requests reinstatement with back pay.

POSITION OF THE UNION

The Union contends that Wallace had been employed as a tool repairman for almost a year prior to his termination. During this period the Company had ample time to judge his work and determine whether or not he was physically able to be assigned to his particular job. However, shortly after Wallace had filed a grievance, the Company ordered him to stand a medical examination. The medical department issued a medical recommendation (not a restriction) advising: "Our examination shows that this employee should not be exposed to the possibility of electrical shock." This recommendation was allegedly based upon the condition of Wallace's heart. Upon receiving this report, the Company took the view that Wallace should not continue his work in repairing motors; it placed a medical restriction on him.

The Union explains that it chose to verify the company's

medical report and had Wallace submit to a medical examination by an outside doctor. The second examination revealed that Wallace was in "perfect health." The Union insists that an employee has a right to consult a disinterested doctor regarding a medical restriction. Such a procedure would prevent the Company from using the medical department to punish or reprimand workers.

In the present case, the Union is concerned with the reasons which prompted the Company to place a medical restriction on Wallace. The Union holds that Wallace was discharged because he had asked for upgrading on the basis of a misassignment. The timing of the restriction is held to be significant since it came only after Wallace had filed a grievance for upgrading and retroactive pay. The Union further states that it refused to permit Wallace to transfer to another department at a lower rate of pay because it felt that the company's request arose from the fact that Wallace had filed a grievance.

POSITION OF THE COMPANY

The Company denies that there is any connection between Wallace's filing a grievance and the subsequent medical restriction. The timing is said to be purely coincidental, and the restriction is in no sense a retaliation for Wallace's actions. According to the Company, the Safety Supervisor, in a routine tour, suggested to the Foreman in shop No. 603 that it was poor policy to have a man of Wallace's age—71 years—doing repair work which involved the danger of electrical shocks. The Foreman thereupon sent Wallace to the medical department for examination. The medical report recommended that the "employee should not be exposed to the possibility of electrical shocks." The Company feels that the actual degree of risk of shock in the classification of tool repairmen is sufficiently great to preclude Wallace's continuing on the job. Consequently, a medical restriction was issued. The Company expresses its faith in the ability of its own doctors and argues that the introduction of an outside physician is unwarranted.

It is the company's view that, since the Union refused to permit Wallace to transfer to a lower-paid job, and, since the Company could no longer employ him as a tool repairman B, its only alternative was to issue an order of termination. The Company states that it stands ready to re-employ Wallace at any job for which he may be eligible.

QUESTIONS

1. Who should be the judge of the physical qualities of a worker to continue in a particular job classification? Is the testimony of an outside physician relevant? How should such a physician be selected? Who should pay his fees?
2. May the Company establish standards of risk for employees not subject to review or grievance? In this connection may the Company appeal to potential accidents and its rates for workmen's compensation?
3. How should this grievance be settled in your opinion?

CASE 10

REFUSAL TO ACCEPT WORK ASSIGNMENT

UNION: American Federation of Hosiery Workers

COMPANY: Full-Fashioned Hosiery Industry

Mrs. B was a worker in the parachute department of Company X's plant. She usually performed her operation as one member of a two-worker team, but on the evening of June 7 her partner was absent from work. The Company desired to put a learner on the job with Mrs. B and offered to guarantee Mrs. B her average earnings. The usual method of wage payment was piecework. Mrs. B requested that she be permitted to work alone, claiming that she could make higher earnings that way. The Company insisted, however, that she instruct the new girl. Mrs. B refused, whereupon she was discharged.

The Union contends that the Company had no justification for the drastic action it took and asks that Mrs. B be reinstated with retroactive pay for the time she lost as a result of the discharge.

POSITION OF THE UNION

The Union argues that Mrs. B is a very efficient worker and has co-operated fully with union and company officials in their attempt to increase production in her department. At the time of her discharge, she was not an instructor and therefore had a just complaint when the Company asked her to take on a new girl as a partner. The Union maintains that the Company had an instructor in the department on the night in question and that this instructor, not Mrs. B, should have been asked to do the teaching. Moreover, since Mrs. B was the committeewoman in her department, it is felt that the Company had no right to place her in a capacity which interfered with her union activity.

As to the company's offer to pay Mrs. B her average earnings, the Union contends that the Company was actually offering her considerably less than she could have earned by herself on the night in question. It appears that Mrs. B's regular partner was a very slow worker and pulled down the total production. The relatively slow pace of Mrs. B's partner is evidenced by the fact that the Company later removed her from this operation. Working alone, Mrs. B was able to earn considerably more than any "average earnings" figure. Thus, the performance of the instruction job requested by management would have involved a substantial monetary loss for which the Company offered no adequate compensation.

POSITION OF THE COMPANY

The Company argues that it was completely justified in discharging Mrs. B for her refusal to perform an assigned job. The regular instructor was busy on other tasks on the night in question. The Company feels that it did not make an unreasonable request of Mrs. B when it asked that she take on the learner for one night only, especially since the Company offered to pay her, her average earnings and thus avoid any loss of earnings that might have accured. In so doing, the Company contends, it acted equitably and in good faith.

But when Mrs. B refused to do the task assigned to her, management argues that it had no other choice but to discharge her. It could not permit one girl to decide what she would or would not do in the plant. The Company holds that, if one girl were permitted to make such decisions, then it would only be fair to give other girls the same privilege, and the result would be a complete lack of discipline.

QUESTIONS

1. If the Company has the right to assign work, are there any limitations on this right?
2. Is the Company under any obligation in this case to allow Mrs. B to make the maximum earnings she could by working alone?
3. Is the refusal of a work assignment grounds for discharge in this case?
4. Does this case represent a problem that should be clarified in a contract?

Section B

THE STATUS OF UNION AND MANAGEMENT REPRESENTATIVES

FEW issues are more fundamental to collective bargaining than the status of the representatives of each side. Union stewards and local union officers are typically full-time employees of a company. They are both representatives of the union and employees of the company. In an analogous way many foremen are members of a union. They have a dual role to fulfill. They are always both employees and representatives of management. Even when foremen are not members, the union may be concerned in defining and restricting the activities of foremen as representatives of management. These interests of each side in the status of representatives of the other side present many basic problems.

It is not always easy to distinguish when the union representative who is also an employee acts as an employee and when he acts as a union officer. This distinction is most difficult to draw in discipline cases when the union may contend that management is seeking to discipline for the exercise of union functions and management may insist that it is treating the union officer simply as an employee. It may be contended that the union steward should be held to higher standards of discipline by virtue of the responsibilities of union office. On the other hand, it may be held that the union officer should be permitted more freedom of action. Consider a steward who talks back to a foreman in language that might otherwise warrant discipline. Is such conduct to be immune by virtue of the union office? Are the standards that are applicable to all employees to be used? Is a higher standard to be imposed? Is an attempt to be made to distinguish between discussions of union business and problems of the steward as an individual employee?

The attempt to bifurcate the union representative is certain to meet practical obstacles. The steward is the personalized symbol of the union; almost invariably members will treat discipline of the steward as an attack by management upon the union. It is most difficult for management to convey to the rank and file that discipline is directed to the steward as an employee rather than as a union officer. Their total experience will have been to regard him as their leader and champion.

A different range of problems may arise with regard to union officers who are full-time employees of the union rather than of a company. May they have access to the plant during working hours? Under what circumstances? May they participate in the discussion of grievances with stewards and management representatives at lower steps in the grievance procedure? The answers to these questions will be influential in shaping the relationship between the parties.

Management will likewise seek to protect and fortify the status of its representatives in the collective bargaining process. The Taft-Hartley Law withdrew from foremen the protection and procedures for organization afforded to other employees. Managements have typically resisted the attempt of unions to divide a foreman between his functions as a management representative and as an employee. Managements have regarded it inappropriate for a union to propose discipline for a foreman.

Despite the concern of both unions and managements to prevent interference from the other in its own internal organization, each has a reciprocal interest in the competence and responsibility of officers in the other organization. Managements have a real interest in the quality of union leadership, just as unions have in the character of supervision. Many contracts provide for top seniority for union officers, and managements may designate a few key employees for top seniority. These provisions are intended to protect the organizations on both sides. Where collective bargaining relations are advanced, there may even be frank discussions of the problem spots in the personnel of each organization's hierarchy.

The cases in this section illustrate some of the problems that arise by virtue of one party's interest in, and concern for, the organization and operation of the other.

CASE 11

EMPLOYEE WORKING PART TIME AS FOREMAN

UNION: United Steelworkers of America

COMPANY: Mann Steel Company

The following grievance, having been duly processed through the grievance procedure of the contract between the United Steelworkers of America and the Company, was submitted to the arbitrator for final decision: "That we request that when Class A Millwrights fill in on turns [shifts] as turn foreman that they be paid the new rate of the turn foreman and that this rate be retroactive to date new rate was put in effect."

The employee involved in this grievance spends part of his time in a supervisory position known as "turn foreman." The rest of his time is spent as a millwright. The Company feels that he is not a member of the collective bargaining unit represented by the Union, while the Union on the other hand considers him to be within the bargaining unit even when he may temporarily work in a supervisory position.

POSITION OF THE UNION

The Union contends that the employee involved in this particular dispute is entitled to whatever differential exists between his rate and that of the turn foreman whose job he takes over temporarily. The Union also states that it is up to the umpire to decide whether the Company, under the terms of the contract, has to answer a grievance or accept a grievance for this particular man or any man who is working part time in the collective bargaining unit as an hourly and production worker and part of his time as a supervisor. The Union feels that this is a very vital issue because it involves not only this employee but other men who are filling the same kind of job. The Union also contends that the worker has been a member of the collective bargaining unit since an election conducted by the National Labor Relations Board and that his union dues have been checked off by the Company. The Union contends that by checking off his dues, the Company has recognized that the worker is within the collective bargaining unit.

POSITION OF THE COMPANY

The Company, at the time the grievance came up, took a position that the employee was not a member of the bargaining unit. The Company argues that this employee was excluded from the list of employees who were eligible to vote at the NLRB election. The Company also argues that the Union is attempting to bring through the grievance machinery a case involving an issue in which the Union has no interest and over which the arbitrator has no jurisdiction. The case involves compensation for work as foreman. Foremen, however, are not members of the collective bargaining unit which the Union is authorized to represent and for which the Company deals with the Union. In this case the worker's name should not have been listed by the Union on the check-off list.

ARBITRATOR'S FINDING OF FACTS

It is apparent from the testimony that the employee worked more than half his time as turn foreman. Section 1 of

Article III of the agreement states: "Subject to the provisions of the National Labor Relations Act, the Company recognized the Union as the exclusive representative of all the employees for the purpose of Collective Bargaining in respect to rates of pay, wages, hours of employment, or other conditions of employment."

"Employee" is defined in Article I: "The term 'Employee' means an employee of the company who is included in a unit, and the term 'Employees' means two or three or all of such employees."

"Unit" is defined in Section 2 of Article II:

"The Unit at each of such Plant and Works shall include all production and maintenance employees of the Company there, except all executives, office and salaried employees, foremen, assistant foremen, supervisors who do not work with tools, draftsmen, timekeepers, watchmen and guards, and full-time first aid and safety employees, and except also die sinkers in the Die Sinking Division at the Mann Plant and pattern makers at the Sarrows Paint Plant."

QUESTIONS

1. If the Company intends to classify a part-time supervisor as a foreman, should it continue to check off his dues to the Union? By checking off the worker's dues, does the Company recognize that the worker is still in the collective bargaining unit?
2. Does the checkoff list determine who is in the bargaining unit?
3. Could the worker in this case be represented by the Union in a matter involving his status as a millwright?
4. Was the worker eligible under these above circumstances to belong to the Union?
5. Would the decision in the case be different if the "employee" worked less than half the time as a turn foreman? If he worked a negligible proportion of his time as a turn foreman?
6. Is there any barrier to this employee being a *member* of the Union?

CASE 12 ✓

DISCHARGE OF UNION REPRESENTATIVE

UNION: American Federation of Hosiery Workers

COMPANY: Lehigh Silk Hosiery Company

The present case involves the discharge of a knitter, Charles Weiss, from the employ of the Lehigh Silk Hoisery Company. The discharge clause of the 1931 agreement reads, in part, as follows:

"The member [Company] shall have the free exercise of the right to employ or discharge any worker in accordance with the necessity of his or its business, provided in the case of a discharge from employment such discharge is in good faith, and provided that in exercising that right the Member shall do so without discrimination against union workers."

Charles Weiss was working on an order for 75 dozen hosiery with particular sizes specified, including the requisition to knit 10 dozen of size 8½. Apparently by mistake, this knitter made 15 dozen of size 8½ and then deliberately made 4 dozen of this same size in addition. Weiss admitted that this disregard of orders was deliberately undertaken in order that he and the toppers on his machine would not have to return to work the following day. There is no dispute over the fact that Weiss's flagrant disregard of orders was an irresponsible act and warrants some disciplinary action.

However, the Union introduces further evidence which it considers pertinent to an understanding of this case. Weiss is a representative of the union shop committee in the Lehigh plant and, as such, has functions beyond that of the ordinary knitter. It appears that Weiss had been previously warned by the Company that he would be discharged at the first opportunity because of his union activities within the mill. The Union asks that Weiss be reinstated on the ground that his act of inefficiency did not warrant a penalty as severe as discharge—rather that the discharge was related to Weiss's activities as a shop committeeman.

POSITION OF UNION

The Union acknowledges that Weiss is guilty of an act of inefficiency but argues that discharge is an excessively severe punishment. Weiss's record as a knitter is that of at least an average workman, and his first major misdeed normally would have been followed by a warning and by discipline other than discharge.

In this particular case, the Union argues that the company's warning to Weiss, namely, that he would be discharged at the first opportunity because of his union activities, provides grounds for questioning the basis of the subsequent discharge. No evidence was submitted to show that Weiss used his position as a shop committeeman in an overt manner. The Union admits to the fact that there are limits to the privileges that are to be accorded to the shop committeemen. But the Union holds that the shop committeeman's effectiveness cannot be hindered by a threat of discharge, for the representatives of the Union within each shop constitute an integral part of the industrial relations plan that has been developed under the National Labor Agreement in the hoisery industry.

In the opinion of the Union, Weiss's discharge was not related to his act of inefficiency but rather represented the carrying out of the previous warning that Weiss would be discharged at the first opportunity. Discharge was meted out as punishment for an act which, under more normal circumstances, would have been met with a mere warning. The Union asks that Weiss be reinstated and a more moderate form of discipline be imposed.

POSITION OF THE COMPANY

The Company contends that this is a simple and straight forward case of gross inefficiency and flagrant disregard of orders. No amount of excuse can justify such an irresponsible act. Weiss's actions are particularly censurable in view of the fact that he is a representative of the union shop committee in the plant, and in such a position should be most anxious to insure efficient workmanship and prevent waste. The Company holds that discharge is the only suitable form of discipline in this case.

QUESTIONS

1. In your judgment what standard of conduct should be applied to Weiss—the same standard that is applied to other employees or a higher standard?
2. Did the Company have any right to warn Weiss with respect to his conduct as a union officer?
3. May a Company discipline an employee who is a representative of the Union when his union activity interferes with his most efficient work as an employee?
4. What arrangements would you suggest to minimize the conflicts between a union representative acting for the Union and as an employee?

CASE 13

TRANSFER OF A UNION OFFICER

UNION: United Automobile Workers of America, CIO

COMPANY: Link-Belt Company

Neville Waldrep was first employed by the Company on March 24, 1942, as an inspector on the night shift in the south steel shop. Subsequently, he was transferred to the day shift in the north steel shop and was elected a shop steward. During a period in 1944, Waldrep was transferred from his job as inspector, class C, out of this department, and shifted between a number of jobs which included fitter's helper, blacksmith's helper, bucker, rivet heater, and general laborer. A grievance was filed protesting his separation from the group of employees he represented as a union steward. The grievance was carried to arbitration, and on November

14, 1944, an award was entered to the effect that Waldrep, as a steward, should not have been transferred out of his department. He was replaced on the job as class C inspector and in the early part of 1945 was elected President of the Local Union. Waldrep retained the assignment of class C inspector (in the meantime continuing in office as the Union President and Chairman of the Bargaining Committee) until June 24, 1946, when he was transferred at the company's request, to Layout B Job 1106-B. Subsequently, Waldrep filed a grievance protesting his transfer as discriminatory and in violation of the company-union agreement.

The pertinent sections of the agreement relating to grievance procedures and seniority read, in part, as follows:

"ARTICLE IV
"*Grievance Procedure*

"*Section 4.* Any shop committeeman shall have the right to visit departments other than his own after receiving permission from his foreman and notification to the foreman of the department he wishes to visit. Grievances may be presented at any time, but preferably outside of working hours. The investigation and settlement of grievances shall be done outside of working hours unless the Company and the shop committee agree that it is necessary for the Chief Steward or the shop committeeman to investigate or settle the particular grievance during working hours.

"ARTICLE V
"*Seniority*

"*Section 7.* Whenever new jobs are created or permanent vacancies occur, such jobs shall be filled with employees on the basis of their plant-wide seniority when their respective abilities to do the work available are relatively equal in accordance with the procedure set forth below.

"Employees shall state in the order of their preference not more than six (6) jobs for which they desire to be considered in the event of an opening. Preference forms will be furnished by the Company. Such forms may be filed with the personnel department and amended at any time by the employee involved. In the event of an opening only those employees who have stated a preference for the job shall be considered unless none with the ability to do the work has stated a preference, in which event the Company shall make the selection among other employees. An employee who has received a promotion in this fashion shall be ineligible to file another job preference form for six (6) months from the date of his last promotion.

"*Section 8.* There will be no discrimination against any employee who does not wish to transfer to a new job or permanent vacancy. Any employee who wishes to return to his old job may do so within sixty (60) days after having accepted such a transfer. In the event he transferred from another division he shall return to such division with his seniority in such division intact plus the time he spent on the new job. Any employee so transferred shall continue to hold his original seniority in his original division until he has accumulated sixty days seniority in the new division, at which time he shall receive his combined seniority.

"*Section 9.* Seniority and the employment relationship shall be broken and terminated when:

. . . .

"(*c*) An employee is absent for three (3) consecutive working days without notifying the Company, unless he is physically unable to do so in which case he must notify within three (3) days after he is physically able.

. . . .

"*Section 12.* Not more than two (2) employees selected or appointed to serve the International or Local Union on a full time basis shall be granted a leave of absence without pay, with accumulated seniority.

"ARTICLE IX
"*Management*

"The Company shall manage the plant and direct the working forces. The management of the plant includes the right to assign work to employees, to plan, direct and control plant operations, to hire, promote, suspend or discharge for proper cause or to transfer employees from one occupation to another, or from one division to another, and the right to lay off and relieve employees from duty because of lack of work or for any other legitimate reason, and to make and enforce shop rules in order to carry out the management of the plant and the direction of the working forces, and the right to introduce new or improved production methods or facilities or to change existing production methods or facilities. The choice, control and direction of the supervisory staff is vested exclusively in the Company. Such authority shall not be used for the purpose of discriminating against any employee, nor shall it be applied in any manner inconsistent with any of the other provisions of this agreement."

POSITION OF THE COMPANY

The Company notes that as a class C Inspector Waldrep worked in the inspection bay of the south steel shop with one or two other inspectors on the day shift. All of the steel work in this shop is channeled through the inspection department, and this department influences the speed with which the work passes through the shop. Thus, if the inspection process is slowed down, the steel shop production is impeded. The Company introduced evidence as follows: (1) During the first half of 1946, Waldrep was absent from work 31 days out of 124 scheduled workdays. (2) During this period he was scheduled for 1,080 hours of work and actually worked only

787.4 hours and, therefore, was absent 27 per cent of his scheduled work hours; he constantly left his work station and his department to engage in Union business. (3) The hours shown to represent Waldrep's attendance at work did not take into account Waldrep's frequent tardiness or partial absences from work. (4) During the 8-month period prior to Waldrep's transfer, shipments were delayed because of the amount of work that was bottled up in the inspection department, and an excessive quantity of field back-charges were received (production errors not disclosed during inspection). (5) As an inspector he did not handle a fair share of the more complex jobs but left this work to the other inspector on the job. (6) On several occasions, Waldrep was reprimanded for his absenteeism, his unsatisfactory work, and the amount of time he devoted to duties outside his work as an inspector. (7) Waldrep's conduct would not have been tolerated if he were not the union President.

It is the company's contention that numerous warnings failed to improve Waldrep's unsatisfactory performance as inspector C. It was imperative to remove him from his inspection job and secure the proper flow of materials through the department. While the Company asserts that Waldrep's conduct warranted discharge, in the interest of maintaining harmonious industrial relations, it chose to transfer Waldrep instead. This right to transfer employees from one occupation to another is said to lie within its managerial authority and to be affirmed by the agreement. (See Article IX, above.)

The Company argues that transferring Waldrep to the layout job was not required by increased production. On the contrary, the job was made specifically for Waldrep to avoid his discharge. The Company insists that it is not a new job available to other employees, that therefore Article V, Sections 7 and 8, do not apply, and that it is ridiculous to contend that the job-preference procedure should be applied. Moreover, the union's claim of discrimination is without foundation since there is no significant change in working conditions. Also, the new job has the same basic hourly rate as the inspection job and, in addition, has an incentive rate which makes the earning opportunity greater.

Finally, the Company asserts that it refrained from taking disciplinary action against Waldrep only because he was a top union officer. If the Company is prevented from making possible the reasonable alternative to disciplinary treatment, it argues that the Union must be prepared to accept Waldrep's immediate discharge.

POSITION OF THE UNION

The union's interpretation of Waldrep's activities prior to his transfer is quite different from that of the Company. The Union maintains that 90 per cent of Waldrep's full-time absences were attributable to arthritis and chronic appendicitis which finally resulted in an emergency appendectomy. As the top local union officer, employees frequently consulted Waldrep to determine whether they had justifiable grievances. This is regarded as in accord with the mutual policy of the Company and Union to adjust grievances as quickly as possible. Waldrep's official position required him to take care of innumerable duties, and restrictions of his activities would make it impossible for him to operate effectively.

The Union argues that it was agreed that Waldrep would secure permission to leave the department if his foreman was readily available, otherwise he would leave without being checked out. Further, according to the agreement, Article V, Section 12, permits the withdrawal at any time of a maximum of two members to engage in union business for such periods as is deemed appropriate at the discretion of the Union; and Article V, Section 9, specifies that absences of less than three days' duration do not need to be reported. Finally, the Union disputes the company's evaluation of Waldrep's working efficiency and insists that his work as an inspector was equal in quality to that of the other inspectors with whom he worked.

The Union contends that the transfer of Waldrep against his will constituted an act of discrimination against this employee and was an infringement of and in violation of the employee rights guaranteed by the agreement. The Union holds that the agreement prohibits the exercise of the company's rights to transfer for the purpose of discriminating against any employee, safeguards the privilege of refusing a transfer to a new job as a permanent vacancy, and preserves the license to return to the old job within sixty days after having accepted a transfer (Article V, Sections 7 and 8). Thus, the company's violation of the agreement cannot be justified by consideration of convenience or by alleged violations on Waldrep's part. The Union admits that, if the alleged charges against Waldrep had been sustained, they might have supported a disciplinary layoff or discharge, but they cannot be used to justify a contract violation. Finally, the Union contends that, if the company's assertions that Article V, Section 7, is not involved on grounds that the job was created especially for Waldrep (and was not a new job or permanent vacancy as spelled out in Section 7), then the same excuse could be used to avoid the application of this clause whenever the Company desired to place a particular individual of its own choosing on a given job.

QUESTIONS

1. State carefully the grievance involved in this case.
2. Has the Company the right under the agreement to create a job for Waldrep?
3. What is the bearing of the arbitration decision upon the present case?
4. May the Company transfer a union officer if union duties require frequent absences? Is the Company obliged to provide a substitute employee for such absences?
5. How should such a problem be handled?

CASE 14

MANAGEMENT'S INTEREST IN UNION DISCIPLINE

UNION: International Federation of Hosiery Workers

COMPANY: LaSalle Hosiery Company

When the 1931 National Labor Agreement in the hosiery industry expired on August 31, 1932, the Union called strikes in the shops of those firms which had been parties to the 1931 agreement but which had not renewed the agreement. Strikes were called on September 1, 1932, at a number of companies, including the LaSalle Hosiery Company, whose employees were collectively and individually notified of the strike.

While negotiations were being carried on to have LaSalle sign the 1932 agreement, that Company began limited operations under union conditions. Three union workers who had previously worked at LaSalle acted as strike-breakers for about one day, after which the plant ceased operations again. This act of the union members was considered at a meeting of the local executive board of the Union, where it was deemed necessary to discipline these members. The discipline was to the effect that the three members were not to be permitted to accept employment at the LaSalle Hosiery Company, although they could be employed by any other union mill.

The Company protested this ruling of the executive board on the ground that it constituted oppressive dealing and was in violation of Article B, Section 3, of the national agreement, which reads in part as follows: "The members (companies) shall also have the right to re-employ any worker who shall have disobeyed the orders of the Union, although it is understood and agreed that such worker may otherwise be disciplined by the Union. . . . ." It asks that the three employees be reinstated to their former positions in the company employ.

POSITION OF THE UNION

The Union argues that a strike was definitely under way at the LaSalle Hosiery Company at the time when the three union members resumed employment with the Company. A strike for the purpose of securing the company's signature to the agreement represented, in September, 1932, an important issue. Moreover, regardless of its intentions, the LaSalle Company had not actually signed an agreement with the Union at the time of the strike. The Union holds that it might be seriously handicapped in conducting certain strikes, if its members could act as strike-breakers without being subject to discipline. It insists upon its right to discipline those of its members who act as strike-breakers.

In the present case, the Union maintains that the Company is trying to limit the union's right of discipline by invoking a particular clause of the agreement. But at the time of the act complained of, that agreement was obviously not effective; and it cannot be considered as providing any rule for the case at issue.

POSITION OF THE COMPANY

The Company holds that the Union has been excessively severe in dealing with the three workers concerned in this case. The Company claims that the acts of its employees complained of by the Union could not be construed as strike-breaking. It maintains that its known intentions were to operate a union shop or not to operate at all, and it points out that shortly after the incident complained of it did sign the 1932 agreement. Furthermore, the Company states that, when it operated to a limited degree before signing the agreement, it paid union rates and operated under union conditions.

Finally, it is pointed out by the Company that the disciplined workers were skilled in operating the Company's particular type of equipment and on working upon its style of work. To replace them would entail a training expense which the management desires to eliminate.

QUESTIONS

1. What interest has the Company in the discipline of union members by the Union in accordance with its constitution and by-laws?
2. Can the Company invoke a contract provision when there was no contract in effect at the time of the strike? Does the fact make any difference that the contract was in effect at the time of the discipline of the three members?
3. Does the arbitrator have power to review the internal operations of the Union?

4. What would be the status of this case under the provisions of the Taft-Hartley Law which holds that it is an unfair labor practice for an employer to discharge, and presumably to refuse to hire, an employee at the request of the Union for other reasons than nonpayment of union dues?

CASE 15

UNION INTEREST IN DISCIPLINE OF FOREMAN

UNION: United Automobile Workers of America, CIO

COMPANY: General Motors Corporation

At the Pontiac plant of General Motors, discipline was imposed by management upon a foreman for alleged improper remarks of a personal nature about a committeeman. The Union insisted that the foreman be discharged. In any event, the Union claims it should be informed by management of the discipline that was imposed upon the foreman since such information would be necessary for a proper answer to the grievance filed by the Union.

The Supervisor referred to by the Union had been a foreman over two departments for five years. His record was good, and he worked well with the employees. Union representatives charged this foreman with having made derogatory remarks of a personal nature about a committeeman. The Union insisted on his discharge.

POSITION OF THE PARTIES

Management states that it thoroughly investigated the case. The foreman vigorously denied making the statement attributed to him. Management thought him guilty, however, and reported that "proper action has been taken." The foreman was not discharged but was disciplined in some other way, according to management.

The Union then requested a written answer to its grievance, which answer would detail the discipline that was imposed upon the foreman. The case should not be closed, con-

tends the Union, merely by a general report from management
that "proper action has been taken." It is held by the Union
that a proper answer to its grievance under the terms of the
agreement,[1] requires information concerning the exact nature
of the discipline imposed upon the foreman.

Management refused to comply with this demand, on the
ground that "foremen are a part of Management" and that
any discipline invoked upon them is a matter not covered by
the national agreement and one that is the sole function and
responsibility of management.

Management claims that the request of the Union in this
case is really that the discipline imposed by management upon
its foremen, at least in certain kinds of cases, should be considered by collective bargaining procedure. This, it says,
would mean a reversal of the traditional rules of the two
parties.

The issue, says management, comes down to this: Does
the Union have a right to be informed of the discipline imposed by management on the foreman in this case? It should
not be overlooked, says the management, that the provision
of such information would most likely lead to an appraisal
by the Union of the adequacy or inadequacy of the penalty
and possibly to an effort to discuss its findings in collective
bargaining procedure.

After a discussion of the matter, the Union recognized that
the disciplining of foremen was the sole responsibility of management and that the terms of any such disciplinary action
were not subject to collective bargaining. The Union insisted,
however, that "as an equal" under the agreement it is entitled
to information concerning the discipline that was imposed on
the foreman. Management resists giving such information in
the belief that, once given, the Union might then proceed to
pass judgment on the decision and to strive to encompass such
penalties within collective bargaining.

Nothing in the agreement gives the Union the specific

---

[1] Part of the terms under the grievance procedure read: "Written answers will be
given by the Management to all written grievances presented by the Shop Committee."

right to receive information on discipline meted out to foremen in such cases. It should be noted, however, that, in the Statement of Unadjusted Grievance, management noted: "On personal grievances between a foreman and an employee, that the Union should be told of whatever action was taken."

Management's argument closes with the statement:

"When a foreman violates the Agreement, he subjects the Corporation to possible penalty. Management has the sole responsibility for taking steps to prevent a further violation of the Agreement by the foreman and must be accorded latitude of action in this direction so as to enable it to balance the necessities of efficient operation of its business with the need for avoiding exposure to penalties for Agreement violations by the foreman."

QUESTIONS

1. What is the issue before the umpire? State it precisely.
2. What intent has the Union in requesting the information? What purpose would the information serve the Union?
3. What is the meaning of "equal partners to the contract"? Would the Company have a right under the contract to demand information concerning the discipline of union members by the Union?
4. If you accept the position of the Union, how far up the hierarchy of the Company would you carry the principle?
5. If the Union is informed of any action taken in a personal dispute between a foreman and employee, why should not the Union also be informed of disciplinary action to foremen?
6. What does this case indicate concerning the relationship of the parties?

CASE 16

UNION CLAIM TO BE PRESENT AT TIME STUDY

UNION: United Automobile Workers of America, CIO

COMPANY: General Motors Corporation

The committeeman in zone 1 of the Hyatt Bearings Division several times requested that additional time studies of particular operations be made following failure to adjust certain disputes. He further requested that he be permitted to be present at such studies on the grounds that Paragraph 79 of the agreement should permit him this privilege. Paragraph 79 states:

"When a dispute arises regarding standards established or changed by the management, the complaint should be taken up with the foreman. If the dispute is not settled by the foreman, the committeeman for that district may, upon reporting to the foreman of the department involved, examine the job and the foreman or the time study man will furnish him with all the facts of the case. If there is still a dispute after the committeeman has completed his examination, the foreman or the time study man will then reexamine the operations in detail with the committeeman on the job. If the matter is not adjusted at this stage, it may be further appealed as provided in the Grievance Procedure."

POSITION OF THE UNION

While the Union did not cite a specific instance of failure of management to abide by Paragraph 79, it was indicated that the grievance had been filed following a disagreement on an actual case. The Union claims that management has often refused to make additional time studies on disputed operations and has not permitted the committeeman to be present in instances when studies have been made as part of a re-examination of a job following a dispute. The Union states that it has appealed this case to the umpire in order to "get the correct interpretation of Paragraph 79."

POSITION OF THE COMPANY

Management takes the position that Paragraph 79 of the agreement permits the committeeman to "examine the job" or to be present with the foreman or the time-study man when there is occasion to "reexamine the operations." Management maintains that nothing in Paragraph 79 can be construed as giving the committeeman the right to be present when actual time studies are being made.

QUESTIONS

1. Does Paragraph 79 require that the Company make additional time studies when a standard is in dispute?
2. Does Paragraph 79 prescribe how time studies shall be made?
3. What part of Paragraph 79 would the Company violate (*a*) by refusing to make additional time studies or (*b*) by refusing to make time studies in the presence of a union representative?
4. Would the Company be wise to ask the Union to have a representative present when time studies are being made?

CASE 17

WHAT IS A "CONDITION OF EMPLOYMENT"?

UNION: American Communications Association, CIO

COMPANY: Postal Telegraph Company

The Union complained that the Company violated the 1940 agreement by requiring all operators to keep hourly averages of their outgoing wires.

Keeping hourly averages requires the operator to mark upon a slip each hour the total number of messages sent by him in the course of that hour, the channels worked by him during that hour, and the number of messages sent over each channel. Operators check in by a time clock, and their time slips indicate the number of hours worked. Furthermore, number sheets are kept for each wire. On these sheets the operator is required to indicate the time he starts sending over a particular wire, the time he stops, and the number of messages sent by him over the entire period.

The Company introduced the system of keeping hourly averages in 1908. Operators were then being paid on a bonus system, earning extra compensation for sending messages in excess of certain determined standards. The keeping of hourly averages, however, bore little relationship to the bonus system, for the averages were introduced after the bonus system had been initiated, and they remained in effect after the bonus system was abandoned in 1919 and 1920. In 1938 the employees in a number of offices objected to the keeping of these hourly averages. The local unions, despite the fact that the 1937 agreement was operative at the time, determined to abandon the system. They took matters into their own hands, not by refusing to fill out the slips, but by entering thereon the arbitrary number of twenty messages, regardless of the number actually sent. Protestations by the Company were met by "job action" or threat to strike, which sometimes actually were carried out. The Company retreated in the face of these threats, and, from 1938 to September, 1940, the practice of keeping hourly averages was abandoned in these offices. Other offices, however, notably New York, continued to keep them as theretofore.

The problem was not covered explicitly by either the 1939 or the 1940 agreements and seems never to have been discussed by the parties in the negotiations which preceded the latter agreement. The Company, however, believed that the 1940 agreement empowered it to reinstitute the practice of keeping hourly averages, and it did so throughout the entire system. The Union then complained that this action constituted a violation of the agreement, and the matter was referred to a board of arbitration on April 22, 1941.

POSITION OF THE UNION

The Company's action in ordering reinstatement of compulsory keeping of the hourly averages of wires sent violates Section 1(a) of the 1940 agreement. This section is headed "Recognition." Part 1(a) of the section reads:

"(a) The Company recognizes the Union as the exclusive representative for collective bargaining in all matters pertaining to rates of pay, wages, hours of employment, and other conditions of employment, for all employees of the Company including wire chiefs and traffic chiefs who were eligible to vote in the election held pursuant to the Direction of Election dated November 22, 1938, as amended, issued by the National Labor Relations Board, except employees, who, because of their positions, shall be deemed ineligible for membership by the Union.''

In support of the argument it is submitted that, although not related to an incentive system, the mandatory recording of hourly averages represents a change in the ''conditions of employment'' referred to in the section quoted above. In the first place, the number of messages which any operator may send over any particular wire during any particular period of time depends upon several factors besides the speed of the operator. It depends upon the condition of the wire, the supply of messages to be sent, and the length and type of the messages—they may be news messages at reduced rates, on the one hand, or standardized messages, such as greetings, which require only the transmission of code numbers, on the other. Interruptions occur frequently on longer wires, holding up the sending of messages for periods of minutes or even of hours.

Employment of the system of recording hourly averages has as its objective a speed-up of the work force. Furthermore, it will furnish invalid data on which to base such a speed-up, for, since these averages reflect important conditions removed from the control of the operator, records of different individuals are not comparable. Finally, the mere knowledge on the part of the operators that management collects this data and considers its accumulation important speeds up work by instilling in the employees a sense of the necessity of unremitting attention to duty and a competitive spirit in increasing the hourly average.

For the reasons cited above, then, the reinstatement of this practice constitutes a change in the ''conditions of employment'' within the meaning of Section 1(a). And since this section specifies that the Union is recognized as the exclusive bargaining agent for the employees in all matters pertaining to conditions of employment, the Company's action in promulgating a change in such conditions without prior notification to, and negotiation with, the Union constitutes a violation of the collective agreement. Matters for which the Union is designated as bargaining agent must be subject to collective bargaining and are removed from the sphere of permissible unilateral action on the part of the Company.

Position of the Company

Recording of hourly averages is intended only to furnish the chief operator with data which will be helpful to him in making proper force assignments. The extra-personal factors stressed by the Union are admitted, but the keeping of hourly averages is definitely not related to any type of speed-up. The Company's action in requiring such records does not involve any change in "conditions of employment" within the meaning of Section 1(a), but is a matter of managerial action which is reserved to the company's sole determination under Section 1(b), which reads as follows:

"(b) The Union recognizes that the management of the Company's business and the assignment and direction of the working forces, including the right to hire, suspend or discharge for proper cause, or to release employees because of lack of work or for other legitimate reasons, is vested exclusively in the Company: provided that this right shall not be used for purposes of discrimination against any member of the Union, nor in any manner contrary to the provisions of this agreement."

However, if it be assumed for the sake of argument that Section 1(a) is controlling, it does not follow that the union's interpretation of that section is correct—i.e., that Section 1(a) operates to exclude unilateral action by the Company in instituting changes in conditions of employment. In other words, it is the company's contention that working conditions can be changed either as a result of negotiations between union and management or by action on the part of management alone. The obligation to bargain collectively, which is implied in this section, reserves to the Company the right to act unilaterally whenever the Union does not request bargaining to take place. The Union is obliged to take the initiative in demanding that a given matter be bargained collectively. Thus Section 1(*a*) carries no obligation on the part of the Company to bring about a change in working conditions *only* by negotiation with the Union.

This position was brought out in the following testimony:

"*The Chairman:* It seems to me, we are threshing over old ground here. My understanding of the company's position in reference to a matter like this and a matter like averages, is that this is one of those things which comes within the power given to the Company under Section 1(*b*) of the contract, namely, a thing that it is entitled to do without any reference to the union.

"*Mr. Peck:* That's right.

"*The Chairman:* Whereas, the union's position is that this is a thing that comes within Section 1(*a*) of the contract, and because it comes within Section 1(*a*) of the contract, the company is not entitled to initiate a policy of this nature unless it has bargained with the union.

"*Mr. Peck:* You have quite correctly stated our position, sir, but we would go one step further and that is that even if these came within 1(*a*), and is the proper subject of bargaining, nevertheless all that means is that the union has the privilege to take these matters up with us and that we are then obligated to bargain with them about it. It doesn't mean that before we do anything such as this order of October 7 that we have to initiate negotiations with the union.

"*The Chairman:* That is something new. That is a new thought.[1] Mr. Chinlund, you would like to mention a point in that connection.

"*Mr. Chinlund:* I thought that mention was made, but perhaps not. So there are two points under 1(*b*). This is something which is our absolute duty and discretion and decision about it, and not a matter of a working condition, which is a proper subject for bargaining under 1(*a*) at all. But going a step further, if it were regarded as a working condition, which was the proper subject for bargaining under 1(*a*), nevertheless that means only it is the privilege of the union to bargain when they want to bargain and it is not an obligation on the part of the company to initiate negotiations."

The Company buttresses its position in this respect with reference to two matters:

1. During the extended negotiations preceding the execution of the 1940 contract, the Union made two proposals concerning the company's right to make changes by unilateral action in personnel or in methods of operation due to mechanical and technological changes. These proposals were rejected, but it is claimed that the Union would not have made them if the construction which the Company puts upon Section 1(*a*)—that it does not preclude unilateral action by the Company—had not been accepted by the Union at that time.

2. In interpreting this contract, consideration should also be given to a contract made between the American Communications Association and the Radio Corporation of America on September 20, 1940, renewing an earlier contract of April 28, 1939. The RCA contract contains language

[1] This position was not adopted by the Company in the opening days of the proceedings, as is indicated by the following testimony of the President of the Company: "*Mr. Chinland:* If I were convinced that it was a working condition as covered by Section 1(*a*), and were not precluded from being that kind of a working condition by the rights of management as outlined under Section 1(*b*), I certainly would ask that it be negotiated; but I do not consider it so."

substantially similar to that in Sections 1(*a*) and 1(*b*) of the 1940 Postal contract, but it has a separate section which specifically states that no major change in conditions of employment not covered by the agreement shall be made except after discussion with the Union. The fact that the Union found it necessary to insert such a clause in its contract with RCA is evidence that it considered a provision similar to that of Section 1(*a*) insufficient to rule out unilateral changes in working conditions.

THE ARBITRATION AWARD

1. The union's contention that reinstitution of hourly averages is a change in "condition of employment" and is therefore governed by Section 1(*a*) and not by 1(*b*) is upheld. In the first place, the physical and psychological effect which the keeping of averages exerts upon the employees in their daily routines causes them to change "significantly their attitude toward the responsibilities that attended their jobs." In the second place, a matter "which has historically been an issue between the management and its employees comes within the category of a matter pertaining to a condition of employment."[2]

2. With respect to the company's citation of certain union proposals which were rejected in the 1940 negotiations:

> "But more than this, the Company's contention proves too much. If mere rejection of the proposal to limit the Company's right to make changes in personnel were sufficient to establish that right, Section 1(*a*) being no barrier to unilateral action in this connection by the

---

[2] "The very fact that these words in Section 1(*a*) are borrowed from the National Labor Relations Act would indicate that any matter pertains to a condition of employment if it is a matter which customarily is the subject of bargaining between an employer and a union. The institution of so-called efficiency methods designed to produce speed-ups would be such a matter. Strikes have resulted from such action and collective bargaining has concerned itself with placing limitations upon management's action in this respect. Similarly a matter such as this which has historically been an issue between the management and its employees comes within the category of a matter pertaining to a condition of employment."

Company, nothing would be required to be inserted in the 1940 contract affirmatively to establish that right. Yet that right is affirmatively set forth in Section 1(*b*), a provision seemingly unnecessary if no restriction were otherwise present in Section 1(*a*)."

3. With respect to the company's citation of the ACA–RCA contract: The contract is not admissible as evidence, because, although the ACA was a party to both contracts, the negotiating committees responsible for these contracts had different memberships, the problems covered by the two contracts were different, and the backgrounds from which those problems originated were not identical.

4. Section 1(*b*) did give the Company the right to act unilaterally in the fields which it covered, but it reversed prior practice "only with reference to those matters that it covered, leaving untouched what formerly by dint of custom and practice was subject to the negotiation process."

QUESTIONS

1. What is "a condition of employment"? Would it be a change in conditions of employment if the Company required all typists to make two carbon copies of letters instead of one? To use dictaphone machines in place of person-to-person dictation?
2. Does the recognition clause constitute an undertaking by the Company to make no changes in conditions of employment without first bargaining with the Union if the Union so desires?
3. What is the purpose of the recognition clause?
4. When a company agrees to recognize a union as an exclusive bargaining agent, does it agree to freeze all existing working conditions except as changes may be bargained with the union?
5. When a management and a union enter into a contract, is each to be presumed to reserve all freedoms not specifically given up under the terms of the contract? As a general rule, should clear and unmistakable language be required to establish the surrender of a freedom by either party to the contract? Does the recognition clause contain such language?

6. Was the board of arbitration correct in holding that the contract between the American Communications Association and the Radio Corporation of America sheds no light on the reasonable construction of the contract in this case and should be ignored by the board?

Section C

~~~~~~

UNION SECURITY

UNION security contract provisions concern the relation
between the union as an organization and individual
employees or members. While the agreement is between the
management organization and the union as an entity, these
provisions may require that individual employees be members
of the union in good standing and may authorize the deduction from wages and salaries of financial obligations to
the union. Union security provisions are directed toward the
preservation and security of the *union organization*. It may
appear strange that *management* should by contract assume
any obligation for the relations between a union and its members. That intimate area might be held to be the sole concern
and responsibility of the union.

Union security contract provisions are indeed unique to
the labor movement in the United States. They no doubt
arise from the fact that the American wage-earner has been
less class-conscious and more difficult to organize and keep
organized than the industrial work force of other countries.
American employers have historically opposed the growth of
unions more vigorously than the employers of other countries.
The union utilizes the agreement with the employer to prevent disintegration by loss of interest or financial support on
the part of members and to ward off raids from rival unions
during the contract term. These provisions also strenghten
the organization in dealing with a hostile or unpredictable
management. In a social milieu in which workmen "naturally" join and support their unions, where union rivalries are not intense, and where there is little tradition of

hostility by employers to the *existence* of unions, union security contract provisions would not be expected to be prominent. These factors account for the absence or relative unimportance of union security provisions in agreements in England, Sweden, and other European countries. They also account for the pivotal attention given to union security provisions in collective bargaining in the United States.

There are a variety of contract provisions relating to union security; the most important provisions can be grouped under the two headings: the checkoff and union membership as a condition of employment. Checkoff provisions require that union dues, and sometimes union assessments and fines, be deducted from the pay of each employee and forwarded by the management directly to the union. A checkoff may be *voluntary* in the sense that the personal authorization of an employee (member) is required before deduction. The authorization ordinarily is valid for the contract period and may even run indefinitely. A checkoff is said to be *automatic* when it applies without individual authorization to all employees under the scope of the agreement. A checkoff provision may on occasion be the only form of union security provision in a contract.

There is a rich diversity of contract provisions requiring union membership as a condition of employment. The most common shop types are: the *closed shop* under which union membership is required before employment; the *union shop* under which union membership is required after an initial period of employment, frequently thirty days; the *maintenance of membership* provision according to which any employee who is a union member or who joins the union must maintain membership as a condition of employment during the term of the agreement; and the *preferential shop* in which union members have first claim on employment opportunities. There is great variety within each of these types, and there are numerous conbinations of the several shop types with the forms of the checkoff. As with other contract provisions, the collective bargaining process typically has "tailor-made" the union security provisions to the special problems of the industry and to the traditions of the two bargaining organizations. Thus, the intermittent nature of employment in the longshore industry has produced the union hiring hall. Some unions are not interested in the checkoff; their traditions lead them to prefer to collect dues directly from members on the grounds that the process of personal collection is significant to the union member and to the union officer.

The relative importance of these various forms of union security is indicated by the percentage of all employees covered by union agreements under each type. The Bureau of Labor Statistics reported for 1946 that of the 15 million under agreements 33 per cent were covered by the closed shop, 17 per cent by the union shop, 25 per cent by maintenance of membership, an additional 3 per cent by preferential hiring arrangements, and the remaining 22 per cent simply by check-offs or by no explicit form of union security.[1] The same investigation revealed that 24 per cent of all employees under union agreements were covered by automatic checkoff provisions, 17 per cent by the voluntary checkoff, and the remaining 59 per cent by no checkoff.

It should be recalled from Chapter II that the Taft-Hartley Law sought to regulate for the first time provisions of contracts specifying union security. The closed shop was made illegal, and other forms of union security can be effective only after a majority of employees by election have authorized union membership as a condition of employment. The check-off was limited to the voluntary type.

A great many problems arise in the administration of

[1] "Extent of Collective Bargaining and Union Recognition, 1946," *Monthly Labor Review*, May, 1947, pp. 765–69.

union security provisions of agreements. Some of the more prominent issues may be grouped under these headings. (*a*) What is the range of interest of the management in the relations between the union and individual members? Can an employer refuse to enforce a union security provision on the grounds that the action of a union requesting discharge or discipline of a member is inappropriate or discriminatory? It is to be recalled that the Taft-Hartley Law made it an unfair labor practice for an employer to discharge or discriminate against an employee, under a union security provision, for other reasons than nonpayment of dues. (*b*) May an individual employee (member) use the provisions of the contract to seek redress against any action of the union? May the grievance and arbitration provisions of an agreement be used to establish the facts as to payment of dues and other requirements of membership? Or, is the statement of the union on such matters final? (*c*) What is the range of activity open to a union under an agreement in dealing with employees who are not union members and who need not become members under the form of union security? What are the limits of activity in treating employees who may have been expelled from the union but who may still remain as employees?

These problems are suggestive of the range of issues which confront union and management representatives in the administration of union security contract clauses. Some of these questions are illustrated in the cases which follow.

CASE 18

DISCHARGE UPON EXPULSION FROM THE UNION

UNION: United Automobile Workers of America, CIO

COMPANY: Ford Motor Company

Twelve to fifteen test-drivers were employed at the Ford plant in Edgewater, New Jersey, whose job was to take trucks

from the final assembly and subject them to a prescribed run
and inspection. Two of these drivers were John Elvin and
Neil Smith.

On January 16, 1944, the local Union notified local management that Smith and Elvin had been expelled from the
Union and requested that they be discharged by the Company,
pursuant to Section 2 of the parties' agreement which reads:

"It is a continuing condition of employment with the
Company that employees covered by this agreement, both
present employees and new employees, shall be and remain good standing members of the Union. Persons losing
their membership in the Union shall not be retained in
the employ of the Company."

The Company refused to discharge the two men. It claimed
that they were expelled from the Union only because they
did their work quickly without soldiering and thus "spoiled"
an easy job for the other drivers who, it was asserted, were
accustomed to doing the work more slowly and with considerable loafing. The Company charged that, in expelling
the men and asking for their discharge, the Union was abusing
and perverting the union shop provision of the agreement in
order to deprive the Company of its rights, particularly those
provided by Sections 11, 12, 13, and 62. Section 11 pronounces
management's right to hire and maintain order and efficiency;
Section 12, the right to promote, discipline, and discharge;
Section 13 is a general statement of management's functions
and prerogatives; Section 62 is the no-strike, no-slowdown,
etc., no-lockout clause which reserves the right to management of disciplining violators of this section.

The situation thus created attracted wide public attention.
The Company charged that this case was but an instance of a
general condition, that its costs had greatly increased and its
production had been impaired by concerted slowdowns which
pervaded its plants. The Union made public answers and
countercharges. Accusations concerning lack of patriotism
were hurled. There was widespread comment in the press.

After the matter was discussed by top officers of the Company and the Union, it was submitted to the impartial umpire on the union's claim that Elvin and Smith must be discharged, and on the company's defense and counterclaim that the expulsions should be set aside.

The detailed provisions of the international constitution of the UAW with respect to appeals from sentence of expulsion or other disciplinary penalties imposed by subordinate bodies show that the danger of unjust expulsion exists as well as that precautions have been taken against it. And the records of the International Executive Board and of the Convention, in reversing the sentences of subordinate bodies, indicate not only that the safeguards are operative but also that the danger of injustice is real and that subordinate bodies do occasionally take unjustifiable action.

The Company concedes readily that the protection of union members against unjust expulsion in general is not the function, privilege, or duty of the employer. His interest in the general justice of an expulsion is no different from or greater than that of any outsider. His special interest, says management, is in the maintenance of a proper level of efficiency in the business.

The Union recognizes its responsibility for guarding against injustice. It has by constitution prescribed the procedure for trial of members on charges. It has provided a number of opportunities for appeals, including appeal to the International Convention. And it submits that it has administered the machinery seriously and with vigilance against injustice, as evidenced by the instances of reversal or modification of penalties with compensation for loss to the member when deemed justified. The Union is proud of the fact that since the beginning of the union shop at Ford there have been relatively few trials on charges and not more than a half-dozen expulsions of Ford employees.

The Company concedes that the justice or injustice of an expulsion, as an issue between the member and his union, is none of its business. But it insists that management of its operations and efficient production are its business; that an expulsion for the purpose of slowing down production is an attack on it and not merely on the expelled member; that the expulsion of a member for doing his work faithfully and refusing to engage in an illegal slowdown is an infringement of its rights under the contract and a violation of the union's duties thereunder; that expulsion for such a reason is an abuse of the union shop provision not warranted by the contract; and that it cannot be bound to co-operate in an illegal attack upon itself by effectuating such an expulsion. The Company claims that the expulsions in this case were of this character.

The Union denies that the expulsions were of this character. It contends that the evidence presented by the company as proof is highly complex and controversial and that it is not essential to an understanding of the more general issues involved here. More important than the specific facts in this case is the union's contention that, in any event, neither the Company nor the umpire have any power to go behind the fact of expulsion and inquire into its causes or purposes. Its position is that

"the question of whether a worker is a good-standing member of the Union is one which is for the sole determination of the Union, arrived at through the procedure established by the constitution of the Union, the worker having all the benefits which the procedure affords for the protection of members who may be dissatisfied with the decision of any Union tribunals at any stage in the trial and appellate proceedings."

It also states that "decisions of the Union respecting the standing of its members are not and cannot under any circumstances be the concern or responsibility of the employer"; that the umpire "has no jurisdiction over such questions"; and that they "are not arbitrable under the contract."

Interpreting the contract, the umpire comments:

"There can be little doubt that the Umpire does not have the power to order the reinstatement of an expelled worker into good standing in the Union. The Umpire's office is a step in the grievance procedure. That procedure is prescribed for grievances between employer and employees. It does not apply to grievances between the Union and its members. Disciplinary penalties imposed on the Union by its members are, as such, not subject to the grievance procedure and the Umpire's jurisdiction. But this case does not come to me on complaint of the expelled workers against the Union. It comes on the Union's demand of the Company that Smith and Elvin be discharged. And the issue is whether the Company has any defense to such a demand in any circumstances. I must decide not whether the Union should reinstate the men but whether the Company should discharge them."

In answer to a direct inquiry the Union deliberately and unequivocally stated its opinion as follows: Assuming, if you can, that an employee is admittedly expelled only because he refuses to slow down production and for the purposes of impairing the company's right to a fair day's work for a fair day's pay, Section 2 of the contract would nevertheless obligate the Company to discharge him upon notice of the expulsion; and the remedy for such action would be elsewhere than in a refusal to discharge.

Commenting on the union's assumption as to the cause of the expulsion, whether or not true in the case of Elvin and Smith, the Company asserts that this assumption is one of a real possibility and not of a wholly imaginary situation. The Company says:

"It can be fairly granted that the International Executive Board and the International Union would not sanction expulsion for such a cause. The danger that some of its many locals may employ the threat of expulsion to gain adherents to an interference with production is real. . . . . To protect the interest in the proper performance of a worker's duties as employee, safeguards against the improper use of the threat of expulsion are much more important than those against improper expulsions themselves."

As further argument the Company states that the provision for a union shop at Ford is not the whole argument of the parties. The agreement sets down many other rights, obligations, and procedures. It sets down, for example, the union's "adherence to the principle 'a fair day's work for a fair day's pay,' " and its agreement to "use its best efforts in behalf of the Company both as to work and as to conduct in its performance." The contract states the agreement of the Union and of its members not to cause or to take part in any "slowdown, curtailment of work, restriction of production, interference with work" and the like; and it recognizes the right of the Company to discipline any employee "taking part in any violation of" this provision (Sections 29, 17*a*). And implicit in the right to discipline "for cause" (Section 12) is the right to discipline an employee for failure to maintain production in accordance with fair production standards properly set or for sleeping or loafing on the job.

QUESTIONS

1. How would you decide this case?
2. Do you agree that the issue is that formulated by the umpire?
3. Has the management any right under a union shop to inquire into the reasons for expulsion or suspension from membership?
4. Would management have any interest in the problem presented by this case if the Union had fined rather than expelled the two employees?
5. Does the principle proposed by management permit the Company to review every expulsion decided by the Union? What happens to the principle of the union shop under such circumstances?
6. What is the effect of the Taft-Hartley Law on this situation?

7. How would you define the relative jurisdictions of the National Labor Relations Board and the arbitrator in this type of situation? What would be the status of the decision of the arbitrator in any proceeding before the National Labor Relations Board?

CASE 19

REPLACEMENT OF EMPLOYEE SUSPENDED BY UNION

UNION: International Brotherhood of Teamsters, Chauffeurs, Warehousemen and Helpers, Local 584, Unit No. 3

COMPANY: Sheffield Farms Company, Inc.

A wholesale route-rider at the company's Richmond Hill branch was given a two weeks' suspension by the Union. The Company in compliance with the contract displaced him. It replaced him with a foreman for four days of the suspension period and with routemen working on their other days off for eight days.

Paragraph 4 of the collective agreement provides that: "In the event that any employee is expelled or suspended by the Union, the Employer agrees to discharge such employee from his employment within seven (7) days after receiving notice from the Union of such expulsion or suspension."

The instant grievance arose when the Union complained that the replacement procedure adopted by the Company was improper and that it should have filled the vacancy created by the wholesale route-rider's suspension by hiring another union member for the interval.

POSITION OF THE UNION

The company's action in putting a foreman and regularly employed routemen on the job temporarily vacated by the suspended employee deprived an unemployed union member of two weeks' pay. Therefore the impartial chairman is requested to award the Union the equivalent amount of wages for distribution to an unemployed member. He is also requested to direct the Company to follow correct procedure in future instances of similar nature. The procedure indicated for the Company consists in posting a temporary rider's job for bid. If a qualified man enters a bid, the vacancy created by the union's suspension of an employee would be filled from the union's list; if not, the temporary job would be directly filled by an unemployed man.

Position of the Company

The suspension of an employee by the Union and the resulting discharge inevitably causes the Company inconvenience and some expense. While compliance with the terms of the contract makes this unavoidable, this inconvenience and expense ought not to be permitted to exceed reasonable limits. In the first place, it is noted that the sentence of suspension falls within the exclusive sovereignty of the Union. The so-called "discharge" necessitated by a suspension is not a true discharge; being temporary in nature, it does not terminate the employment liability of the Company. In the second place, to have followed the procedure recommended by the Union would have resulted in a decidedly unfair and unreasonable inconvenience and expense entailed in breaking a new man in on the suspended employee's route. The suspended rider in this case had an unusually difficult territory. To break in a new man for his job would have required two or even three days for each route, or from twelve to eighteen days for the entire section. Thus, the Company would have derived absolutely no benefit from the trouble and expense of breaking in a new man because the period of suspension would have terminated before the very earliest time within which the training could have been completed.

QUESTIONS

1. How would you decide this case?
2. Distinguish between the following terms: expulsion, suspension, discharge, layoff, leave of absence.

3. Would the present case have arisen if the employee had been expelled rather than suspended from the Union?

CASE 20

AN INCREASE IN UNION DUES

UNION: United Electrical, Radio, and Machine Workers of America, CIO

COMPANY: Clayton Mark and Company

The issue to be determined in this case is whether the Company is obliged to honor the request of the Union that, effective February 1, 1947, the union dues are to be increased from $1.50 to $2.00 per month.

On January 28, 1947, the Union mailed the following letter to the Company:

"Mr. Clarence Mark, Jr.

"Clayton Mark and Company

"1900 W. Dempster Street

"Evanston, Ill.

"*Dear Sir:*

"This is to inform you that the following amendment to the constitution and by-laws of Local 1114, UE (CIO), was adopted by the membership of the union at a special meeting held Sunday, January 26, 1947: 'Article 13 Finances, Section 1. Dues shall be $2.00 per month per member payable in the current month.'

"This increase in the dues from $1.50 to $2.00 per month for all members of Local 1114 employed in your plant shall be effective February 1, 1947. Therefore, in making dues deductions for the month of February, please conform with the amendment adopted by the membership of Local 1114 referred to above.

"We would appreciate your cooperation in this matter and trust that you will give the necessary instructions to your payroll department for the next checkoff in accordance with the terms of our contract.

"Very truly yours,

"LOUIS TORRE

"Business Manager

"Local 1114, UERMWA"

The Company refused to increase the union dues checkoff to $2.00 per month. The parties agreed to submit the case to arbitration.

The applicable sections of the labor agreement read in part as follows:

"ARTICLE I
"*Recognition*

"The Company agrees that all such employees who fifteen (15) days after the execution of this Agreement are members of the Union in good standing, and those employees who may thereafter become members, shall during the life of this Agreement as a condition of employment remain members of the Union in good standing as to dues, initiation fees and uniform assessments (which assessments shall not exceed Six Dollars [$6.00] per year).

"The Company for said employees shall deduct on the first payday of each month, the Union dues for the current month of One Dollar and Fifty Cents ($1.50) and remit the same within ten (10) days after said payday by check made out to 'Financial Secretary—Local 1114—U.E.—C.I.O.' and mailed to 'United Electrical, Radio and Machine Workers of America, C.I.O., 166 W. Washington Street, Chicago.'

"The initiation fee of Three Dollars ($3.00) for new members upon notification to the Company shall be deducted by the Company and remitted in the same manner as dues collections.

"Uniform Union Assessments (which shall not exceed

Six Dollars [$6.00] for each employee during the term of this Agreement) shall be deducted by the Company and remitted in the same manner as dues collections.

"The Union will furnish the Company with a notarized list of members in good standing as of the fifteenth (15th) day after the execution of this Agreement and may from time to time submit notarized lists of employees who thereafter become members.

"Any dispute which may arise between the Company, the Union or an employee as to

"(1) Whether an employee has been coerced into membership in the union; or

"(2) As to the meaning and application of this Article I shall be regarded as a grievance and shall follow the procedure outlined in Article III of this Agreement. . . . ."

POSITION OF THE UNION

The Union holds that the express language of the collective bargaining contract permits a checkoff of $2.00 per month, pursuant to the union's notice to the Company. In the opinion of the Union, the arbitrator is not being called on to alter the collective bargaining contract nor to determine the amount of union dues. The amount of union dues is held to be the internal affairs of the Union, and is none of the company's business. The Company has no right to interfere in the union's internal affairs on any paternalistic pretext.

The Union argues that the company's only proper interest in the matter is in its own bookkeeping practices and reasonable convenience. The amount of union dues proper for carrying on the functions of the Union is to be determined exclusively by the union members according to its constitution and bylaws.

An increase of dues under the terms of the union constitution and bylaws is equivalent to a uniform union assessment, which is clearly permissible under the agreement. An increase in dues and a uniform assessment have the same consequences on the bookkeeping convenience of the Company.

POSITION OF THE COMPANY

The Company argues that the clear and unambiguous language of the contract limits the company's obligation with respect to union dues checkoff to $1.50 per month. The Company insists that the contract is determinative of the extent of the company's obligations and must be so regarded by the arbitrator. It is held to be beyond the arbitrator's power to alter or amend the contract between the parties.

The Company points out that under the voluntary maintenance of membership provisions of the contract, employees were led to rely on the $1.50 limitation of the dues checkoff. The Union is thereby estopped to demand an increase in the dues checkoff. In the opinion of the Company, the present issue does not concern internal union affairs but deals with the company's obligation to check off union dues under the terms of the labor agreement.

"Dues" and "assessments" have separate and distinct meaning. The Company insists that since the Union is requesting an increased dues checkoff, the provision covering dues rather than the one covering assessments is applicable. The contract provides for a distinction between dues, assessments, and initiation fees, and sets forth the specific amounts under each category which shall be deducted through the checkoff procedure. Thus "dues" is not used to indicate all things of a characteristic nature but is limited and confined to its generally accepted meaning.

QUESTIONS

1. What are the relative interests of a union and a management in including an explicit figure for dues in the agreement?
2. How do you appraise the argument that dues are equivalent to a uniform assessment?

3. Does the fact that the union members have approved the change in dues influence your decision? Has this fact any bearing on the case?

4. How do you appraise the general argument that management has no legitimate interest in the level of dues?

5. Is the "reasonableness" of the dues a factor to be considered?

6. Does the contract permit the dues to be increased?

CASE 21

A CHECKOFF FOR MEDICAL SERVICES

UNION: United Steelworkers of America, CIO

COMPANY: Bethlehem Pacific Coast Steel Corporation

A medical and hospitalization service was established about thirty years ago by a predecessor of the Company. The Company never assumed any responsibility for the service other than to check off the monthly payments. The service was provided by the South San Francisco Hospital which made individual or family contracts with employees of the Company. Any employee could take the service if he could qualify from a health standpoint, and he could withdraw at any time by discontinuing the monthly payments. The Company was never a party to the contract or the service. It simply inherited and followed the practice of checking off the monthly payments established by its predecessor until May 31, 1946, when the hospital discontinued the service altogether. At that time 287 out of 1,400 clerical and production employees of the Company were subscribers to the service.

Upon discontinuance of the service by the South San Francisco Hospital, Local 1069 took steps to make a substitute group service available. A committee was appointed and several services were canvassed. The services were considered by the committee and were discussed at union meetings by representatives of the services and by the committee. The membership finally took a vote and selected one service that required an initial sign-up of 500 members. All of the services canvassed, regardless of their quality, required a checkoff by the employer.

The Company and the Union did not bargain about a substituted service. However, the services under consideration were discussed informally with the company's Manager of Industrial Relations who pointed out a number of disadvantages in the service finally selected by the Union. The Company, in turn, proposed a service which the Union rejected.

On October 14, 1946, the following grievance was lodged:

"We, the employees, feel that we are being discriminated against in that the Company will not grant the checkoff of Hospitalization for the Hospital Plan that we have selected. Previously this has been done under our contracts signed to date. Under Past Practice this has always been the consideration from the Company. This is a vital necessity for ourselves and family."

The Company contends that the subject is not covered by the agreement and hence is not a proper grievance. The Union holds that the agreement does cover this situation. The case was finally presented to an arbitrator for his decision.

The relevant sections of the agreement read in part as follows:

Article III, Section 1

"Subject to the provisions of the NLRB, the Company recognizes the Union as the exclusive representative of all the employees for the purposes of collective bargaining in respect to rates of pay, wages, hours of employment and other conditions of employment."

Article XI, Section 1

"Should any difference arise between the Company and the Union as to the meaning and application of the provisions of this Agreement or as to any question relating to the wages, hours of work and other conditions of employment of any Employees, there shall be no suspension of work on account of such difference, but an earnest effort shall be made to settle them promptly and in accordance with the provisions of this Agreement in the manner hereinafter set forth."

Article XI, Section 2

"An umpire to whom any grievance shall be submitted in accordance with the provisions of this Section, shall in so far as shall be necessary to the determination of such grievance, have authority to interpret and apply the provisions of this Agreement, but he shall not have authority to alter in any way any of such provisions."

Article XIV

"The Company will continue to make every reasonable effort to provide safe and healthful conditions of work for Employees at the Plants and Works and to provide Employees with any necessary protective equipment in accordance with the practices prevailing at the respective Plants and Works at the date of this Agreement. In so far as reasonably practicable, considering the nature and requirements of the respective operations, suitable heating and ventilating systems shall be provided.

"The Union will co-operate with the Company in encouraging Employees to observe the safety regulations which shall be prescribed by the Company and to work in a safe manner."

POSITION OF THE UNION

The Union argues that the checkoff for medical and hospitalization service, which it requests, is one of the "other conditions of employment" about which the Company is obligated to bargain collectively with the Union, by way of recognition pursuant to Article III, Section 1, and by way of adjustment of grievances pursuant to Article XI, Section 1, of the agreement. On the basis of Article XI, Section 1, the Union maintains that an arbitrator is authorized to make an award on the subject of a medical and hospitalization service because it is one of the "other conditions of employment."

Further, the Union relies on Article XIV, the safety and health provision. The Union argues that participation in the establishment of a health and hospitalization service is a "safe and healthful condition of work" which the Company is obliged to "continue to make every reasonable effort to provide." A well man makes a better employee and hence can better serve the Company.

Finally, the Union holds that established practices not inconsistent with the agreement are, by necessary implication, as much a part of the agreement as what is written into it. The argument is founded upon the fact that the agreement is negotiated on a national basis and governs seventeen plants or works of the Company located throughout the United States; that such an agreement could not be translated into effective performance except in some relation to the habits and customs of work in each particular plant or works; and that a proven long-established practice such as this checkoff cannot therefore be unilaterally discontinued by the Company. The Union insists that the minor differences which may result from this new service plan is not the issue since the Company bears no responsibility for the service. The issue is the continuance of the checkoff system which is a practice of long standing.

POSITION OF THE COMPANY

The Company contends that while payroll deductions for Union dues are specifically required by the agreement, deductions for medical and hospitalization services are not provided. Since the agreement does not authorize this kind of a payroll deduction, the subject does not lie within the scope of the grievance procedures; and Article XI, Section 1, is inapplicable. Rather it is held that Section 2 of Article XI is applicable, and this article prohibits the arbitrator from altering any provisions of the existing agreement. As for Article

III, Section 2, the Company admits that this obligates it to bargain on "other conditions of employment," and that a medical and hospitalization plan falls under this category. However, the Company insists that the present case calls for an interpretation of the existing agreement and is in no wise related to bargaining obligations in negotiations of a new agreement.

The Company further maintains that Article XIV, the safety and health article, is also inapplicable to the issue at hand. Article XIV relates strictly to conditions within the plants and works of the Company and not elsewhere; to the structure and equipment of the plants and works, and not to the physical condition of the personnel; and to the observance of safety regulations. Nothing in Article XIV obligates the Company beyond doing something about an employee's physical surroundings in the plants and works, and about his implements of work.

As for the union's contention that the Company cannot discontinue an existing practice without union consent, the Company argues that it may act unilaterally upon any subject except upon those which are specifically covered by the agreement. The Company insists that there is no provision in the agreement which stipulates that payroll deductions will be made for any purpose except for union dues. And finally, the Company holds that it did not of itself eliminate the medical plan. The hospital eliminated the service and when it did, the checkoff died for want of a payee. Thus, the Union is actually advocating a new practice, i.e., one in which a different service is substituted. This, the Company insists, is a subject for collective bargaining and not for either a grievance procedure or an arbitrator's ruling under an existing agreement.

QUESTIONS

1. Could the Company have unilaterally discontinued the checkoff of the South San Francisco Hospital service under the provisions of the agreement? How do you appraise the argument that the

Company may act unilaterally on any matter not specifically covered by the agreement? What does this position imply as to the nature of the agreement?

2. Could the Union have made a demand for a checkoff of medical services under the agreement if no plan had previously been in effect?

3. How do you interpret the obligation of the Company to bargain under Article III, Section 1? Does this section mean that the Union has a right to raise any question for negotiation at any time regardless of the term of the agreement?

4. Can the Company discontinue any long-established custom not explicitly covered in the agreement without approval of the Union?

5. Is the type of checkoff involved in this case related to union security?

6. Is the present dispute a "grievance" within the meaning of the contract?

Section D

EMPLOYMENT RIGHTS IN JOBS

A LARGE part of the agreement defines the relative rights of individual employees (members) in particular jobs. These "property rights" in a job are specified in terms of contingencies which reoccur in the work community—an increase in the work force, temporary layoffs, transfers, promotion opportunities, a permanent reduction in the work force. When men are to be rehired following a temporary shutdown, in what order shall they be returned to work? When vacancies arise, which individual employee shall be promoted? Who shall be laid off when work is slack? These questions are not only vital to the individual employees whose personal lives are immediately affected, but they equally concern the union and management organizations as well.

Management is presumably interested in developing an efficient work force. It may be even more interested in some flexibility of discretion over the selection and assignment of the work force. Decisions on whom to hire, to promote, or to lay off will have significant consequences not only on costs but also on the morale and tone of the whole organization. The range of discretion on these problems will condition the adaptability of the enterprise in the face of unforeseen changes in demand and production methods.

The union is concerned that these questions on employment rights in particular jobs are not answered in a manner discriminatory to individual employees (members), or to the union as an organization. It will seek to have decisions on hiring, layoffs, and promotions conform to the prevailing views of union members. The mores of the work force may place a high value on length of service, or military service, or dependency, or some other factor. The union will seek to establish the relative status of different employees in terms of the standards that are widely accepted among its members.

At times the interests of a management and a union in employment rights to a job may be conflicting. The management may desire to lay off workers it regards as less efficient; the union may not recognize management's judgment of performance as a suitable basis for distinguishing between two workers for layoff purposes. The management may desire to promote an employee it regards as qualified for a vacancy; the union may reflect the aspirations of many older employees, who have been looking forward to advancement, in urging a different standard or basis for promotions.

There are other occasions when the union and management organizations may have no conflicting interests; yet difficult problems arise in establishing a hierarchy of relative rights among employees. When two departments are combined the men from each department may insist on superior job rights in the combined work area. Relative seniority rights in such a case may be of little concern to the union or management. When men are to be laid off temporarily, there may be a conflict of interest between those men who have worked a long time with the employer but only a short time on the particular job and those who have longer seniority on the particular job but a shorter service record with the company. Such conflicts arise in the process of determining the relative status or rights of individual employees in the available or potential job opportunities. The establishment of these relative rights frequently illustrates that a union is not a homogeneous whole. It is composed of different employees— young and old, men and women, long-service and new employees, skilled and unskilled, and workers from different departments. Their interests are not always the same.

The agreement typically specifies the principles or general rules which are to govern hiring, temporary layoffs, re-employment, transfer, promotion, and a permanent reduction in force. These rules as a group define relative employment rights in particular jobs. The contract provisions on these problems bargained by the parties are certain to reflect the objective conditions of employment. Layoff rules in a seasonal industry are likely to be different from those in which work is steady the year around. Transfer arrangements must reflect the ability of employees to perform other work and the length of time required to learn new operations. Lines of promotion are related to the training and experience required to perform the better job. The provisions in contracts on these problems consequently are not likely to be standardized since such objective circumstances vary widely among firms.

The cases which follow illustrate some of the more common problems of administering contract provisions which define relative employment rights in jobs. An examination of the contract provisions under scrutiny in these cases will reveal many of the considerations entering into management and union negotiations over these provisions.

CASE 22

THE HIRING OF OLDER WORKERS

UNION: International Brotherhood of Teamsters, Local 584

COMPANY: Sheffield Farms Company

The Sheffield Farms Company called on the Teamsters Union, Local 584, for two helpers for its automotive division (garage department) on January 13, 1941. Since the unemployed list for this craft had been exhausted, the Union sent unemployed members from other crafts. The applicants were rejected because they did not satisfy the company's employment requirements.

A controversy ensued. The Union refused to send other men, insisting that the original applicants were qualified and that their rejection by the Company was arbitrary and unreasonable. The Company maintained that its requirements were proper and reasonable and that, if the Union would not, or could not, send applicants who could satisfy them, the Company had the right under the contract to hire workers outside of the Union.

The Union does not deny that the Company is entitled to set standards for hiring. These standards are not, however, a part of the contract. The case was not carried to the umpire by the Union, but by the Company. The union's position seems to have been to "sit tight" in its refusal to supply men other than those originally sent.

The relevant contract clauses are as follows:

Paragraph 4:

"Throughout the term of this agreement, the employer agrees to hire only members of the Union in good standing. Men laid off through no fault of their own, shall, in the order of their company seniority of their respective crafts, for a period of two (2) years from the date of lay-off, be sent by the local or unit having jurisdiction to fill vacancies as they occur. If none are available, the local or unit having jurisdiction shall send other men to fill the vacancies. Any such other men shall be competent and shall meet the employment requirements of the Employer. If no such men are available, the Employer shall have the right to employ men not sent by the Union, provided such men are or become members of the Union in good standing. Any new men so employed shall for a period of thirty (30) days, be on trial subject to dismissal at any time within such thirty (30) days. Each man however employed shall present an O.K. card signed by the Secretary-Treasurer of the Union, and shall present the same to the Superintendent or the man in charge before being employed. The Superintendent or man in charge shall immediately notify the Shop Steward of the employment of any new man who under this agreement is required to be a member of the Union."

Paragraph 24:

"Any and all disputes and controversies arising under or in connection with the terms or provisions of this agreement, or in connection with or relating to the application or interpretation of any of the terms or provisions hereof, or in respect of anything not herein expressly provided but germane to the subject matter of this agreement, which the representatives of the Union and the Employer have been unable to adjust, shall be submitted to arbitration by Arthur S. Meyer, as the impartial chairman, whose decision shall be binding and conclusive on both parties."

The company's requirements are that the applicant pass an "aptitude test for garage helpers," and that he be not more than 25 to 27 years of age.[1] The aptitude test was examined, and the Union raised no serious objection to it provided that the Company applied it fairly. But the Union strenuously objected to the imposition of any age limit; the Company as strenuously urged its necessity.

The Union points out that because of decreasing employment opportunities it has for years not accepted new members. As a result, the average age of its members is constantly increasing—a trend that is likely to continue for an indefinite length of time. There are few among its unemployed whom the Company today looks upon as "young" men; there will be fewer in future years. Unemployment has been caused, the Union continues, partly by steps taken by the Company to effect economies, such as the consolidation of branches and the laying off of routes; partly by the trend from retail to wholesale delivery; and partly by the technological change

[1] Ordinarily the Company would not hire an inexperienced man for this job older than 25 but would accept experienced men up to the age of 27. It concedes that it might even employ a person older than 27 if he were particularly well qualified.

from horse-drawn to motor-driven vehicles. Thus, concludes the Union, there is a body of men, unemployed through no fault of their own, who, because of an arbitrary and unreasonable age requirement, are deprived of jobs in the only field of operations—the automotive division—where employment is expanding.

The Company claims that it is imperative, because of seniority rules, to place an age limit on the position of garage helper. These rules provide that the senior garage helper has the right to bid for a vacant mechanic's helper's job; the senior mechanic's helper, for a vacant mechanic's job. In the ordinary course of events it takes many years for a new garage helper to become a full-fledged mechanic. Unless the Company is permitted to restrict helpers' jobs to relatively young men, the result will be that eventually the Company will have in its employ only mechanics who are well past their prime of life and whose average efficiency will consequently be below the level the Company has a right to expect.

Since July 1, 1937, the Company has hired 28 garage helpers divided into age groups as follows:

Under 20 years	5
20 years but under 25	15
25 years but under 30	5
30 years and over	3

The approximate age of the 28 helpers at the time they were hired was 24 years; the Company, it would seem, is not attempting to step up its employment requirements, but is actually proposing standards somewhat less restrictive than those which prevailed in the years preceding this controversy, 1938, 1939, and 1940. On the other hand, during these years the exigencies of unemployment have thrown an even heavier burden on the Union.

QUESTIONS

1. Does promotion by seniority affect the need for an age limit in the hiring of new employees?
2. Is the concern of the management for the age distribution of its force a legitimate one? Under the circumstances, is an age limit

for new employees a reasonable way of achieving a better balance in the age distribution of the work force?

3. In view of the shrinking employment in the industry, does the Company have an obligation toward the unemployed members of the Union which the Company would not have if employment were expanding?

4. Distinguish carefully between the *needs* of the employer and of the Union and the *rights* of the employer and of the Union. Employment trends in the industry create certain needs for both the employer and the Union. Do these needs affect the rights conferred upon the employer and the Union by the labor agreement between them?

5. Does Paragraph 4 provide an argument for the Union?

6. Should the contract be written so as to define the word "competent" and the "employment requirements of the Employer"?

7. Should the Union be allowed to review, as part of the grievance procedure, management's estimate of the men the Union supplies?

CASE 23

ARE INDIVIDUALS REQUIRED TO BE PRESENT AT HIRING HALLS?

UNION: International Longshoremen's Association, Local 38–82

COMPANY: Marine Service Bureau of Los Angeles

BACKGROUND

The section of the award in dispute provided as follows:

"*Section 4:* The hiring of all longshoremen shall be through halls maintained and operated jointly by the International Longshoremen's Association, Pacific Coast District, and the respective employers' associations. The hiring and dispatching of all longshoremen shall be done through one central hiring hall in each of the ports of Seattle, Portland, San Francisco, and Los Angeles, with such branch halls as the Labor Relations Committee, provided for in Section 9, shall decide."

The issue which has developed as a result of conflicting interpretations of the above cited section of the award and which is submitted to the local arbitrator for consideration and decision is: "Whether, within the meaning of Section 4 of the Award gangs and individual men are required to present themselves physically at the Hiring Hall in order to be dispatched to work."

Position of the Union

It is the purpose and intent of Section 4 of the award to have eligible employees present themselves physically at the hiring hall for the purpose of being dispatched to work. Such physical appearance, it is urged, is indispensable, not only to complete compliance with the Award, but also to the smooth and efficient functioning of the dispatching system and assurance of an adequate and qualified labor supply when, as, and if, needed by the employers.

Position of the Company

Although the award establishes central hiring, it nowhere stipulates that longshoremen must present themselves physically at the hiring hall for the purpose of being hired. The physical presence of the longshoremen is not necessary in the operation of the centralized hiring system. On the contrary, a requirement of physical appearance for dispatching, not only would constitute an inconvenience and expense to both employers and employees, but would occasion serious risks for nonunion employees and is totally unnecessary in view of the practicability of dispatching by means of telephone communication, as demonstrated in other parts.

The Arbitration Award

Neither the language nor the intent of Section 4 of the award can reasonably be construed to compel or require the physical appearance of regular gangs or individual employees at the hiring hall for the purpose of being dispatched to work.

The sole purpose of Section 4 is to provide for the centralized hiring and dispatching of men under a jointly organized and administered system. In establishing such a system, the International Longshoremen's Association and the Marine Service Bureau undoubtedly have sought to avoid the difficulties which in the past have resulted in discordant relations between employers and unionized employees.

Centralization of hiring and dispatching is an imperative condition of economical, efficient, and equitable distribution of employment among the relatively large number of men depending upon the industry for a living. Physical appearance of the men at the hiring hall is not, however, an absolute essential of centralized dispatching. Centralized dispatching undoubtedly does require that all placements of longshoremen shall be cleared through the medium of the hiring hall, but it is quite probable that this could be done more economically and more efficiently by means of telephone communication.

There is nothing in the award which prohibits the voluntary physical appearance of men at the hiring hall for the purpose of obtaining work.

The arbitrator is of the opinion that the requirement of physical appearance at the hiring hall as a condition for assignment to work is objectionable for a number of reasons:

a) It is impossible to escape the conclusion that in presenting themselves at the hiring hall employees who are not members of the ILA would subject themselves to mental discomfort, if not physical injury.

b) A dispatching system that makes mandatory the physical appearance of men at the hiring hall is necessarily cumbersome, expensive, and inefficient. This would seem to be especially true in the part of Los Angeles where the longshoremen reside in such widely distributed communities and where the places of employment are spread over such a wide area.

c) If members of regular or preference gangs were required to report physically at the hiring hall the inconvenience and loss of time would be so great as to entail considerable injustice to highly valued employees, not to mention the probable waste of time for the employing companies.

d) The facilities of the hiring hall as now organized are totally inadequate to provide for the physical dispatching of two thousand or more men within the short period of time allotted to the hiring and distribution of employees, especially on the "peak" days.

QUESTIONS

1. What do you deduce past practice has been concerning the men's personal or physical appearance at the hiring hall?
2. Would the convenience of the men be served by requiring them to report in person at the hiring hall in order to obtain job assignments?
3. Would the requirement that the men report in person at the hiring hall help prevent favoritism and discrimination in making job assignments?
4. Would the appearance of the men at the hiring hall promote the smooth and efficient functioning of the dispatching system?
5. If the Union had the closed shop, would you expect it to demand that the men appear in person at the hiring hall for assignment to jobs?
6. Was the Union in this case representing the interests of the longshoremen?
7. Assume that the positions of the parties were reversed—that the Union had the closed shop, that employers were asking that the men be required to appear in person, and that the Union was opposing it. Would the language of Section 4 justify the arbitrator in requiring the men to appear in person at the hiring hall?

CASE 24

THE PRACTICABILITY OF STRICT SENIORITY IN LAYOFFS

UNION: Textile Workers Union of America, CIO

COMPANY: The Pantasote Company

The case involves the interpretation of the layoff provisions of the agreement. The contract provides that layoffs shall be in accordance with straight seniority "so far as is practicable."

In April of 1946, a lack of certain raw materials made it necessary for the Company to lay off 65 people out of a total employment of 205. If 12 so-called key people could have been retained without regard to seniority, 30 additional lay-offs could have been avoided, because these 12 men were embossing machine operators, mill men, and laboratory assistants, all of whom do preparatory work. A strict interpretation of the seniority provision would not have permitted these 12 men to continue in their jobs during this "slack" period since the men did not have sufficient seniority ratings. However, to train other employees to do the work would have required 2 or 3 weeks. It was tentatively agreed between the parties that the 12 would be retained but that 12 senior employees would immediately be trained to replace them. The 12 incumbents, however, declined to work on this basis, and they and 18 others were laid off. The Union insisted that the Company would have to train senior employees for the job. The Company held that it could rightfully retain the key men without regard to seniority. The dispute was referred to arbitration under the agreement.

POSITION OF THE UNION

The Union contends that the seniority provision is one which needs to be rigidly interpreted and enforced. Seniority would soon cease to have much meaning if it could be disregarded as lightly as the Company seemingly desires. The "practicable" expression, according to the Union, has reference to a person like a boiler engineer or a fireman without whom the plant could not operate.

The Union argues that several provisions of the agreement evidence the company's stated obligation to train employees for more than one job. In fact, the capacity to handle more than one job in this plant is expected. For example, Section 7 of the contract provides as follows:

"The parties recognize that in the operation of the plant the employees may be required to work on different jobs and are subject to transfer from one job to another as the exigencies of the business may require, subject to the provisions of the agreement and to the collective bargaining rights of the Union."

And in Section 16, it is stated: "Promotion shall be made on the basis of seniority and other necessary qualifications to perform the job."

The Union argues that, if the Company had been sincere in fulfilling its responsibilities and if it had been efficient in the conduct of its business, it would have given its qualified seniors training for these key or higher-paying jobs before the layoffs became necessary. The Company is in a position to plan promotions and transfers and should not wait for some emergency situation to arise. The present dilemma is felt to be a product of the company's poor management. The Union insists that the principle of seniority is so important for the maintenance of harmony within its own ranks that only a strict interpretation should be allowable.

POSITION OF THE COMPANY

The Company maintains that the contract provision which stipulates that layoffs shall be in accordance with straight seniority "so far as practicable" contemplates the very type of situation here under consideration. The Company interprets "so far as practicable" to mean that there are situations where strict seniority should not be followed. A long layoff is not in prospect, and the Company feels that there is no good reason for wasting time and money in the training of senior employees for highly specialized jobs. It argues that the best way to resolve the issue would be to allow the 12 men to continue their jobs for this short "slack" period. The Company maintains that it would be foolhardy to penalize 30 people. It holds that a logical interpretation of "practicable" would allow the retention of any person out of seniority when a layoff is necessary if his work is such that his senior would require at least 2 weeks of special training.

QUESTIONS

1. Why do you suppose the 12 incumbents refused to work in accordance with the tentative agreement between the Company

and the Union? What should the parties do under such circumstances? What methods are open to the union organization to secure approval of the agreement? Should union government provide that such an agreement be approved by the members directly affected?

2. What are the major possible meanings of the word "practicable"?

3. What do you suppose the Union and management meant when the term "practicable" was included in the contract? Do you approve of such language in an agreement?

4. How do you appraise the rule proposed by the Company? Do you think the Union would accept such an administrative interpretation? Why?

5. How would you phrase the administrative interpretation of "practicable" that is suggested by the Union?

6. How do you appraise the contention of the Union that management should have prepared for the contingency by training senior employees more broadly in advance of such a situation?

7. Why is the Union willing to let 30 additional men be laid off rather than allow the 12 men to be retained out of seniority? What is the interest of the Union in this case?

CASE 25

A TRANSFER OR A LAYOFF?

UNION: United Electrical, Radio and Machine Workers of America, CIO

COMPANY: Cory Glass Coffee Brewer Company

Employees in the stripping department of the Cory Glass Coffee Brewer Company are engaged in painting lines on glass bottles to be used as part of coffee-brewers. The bowls are placed on a wheel, and the employee applies platinum paint with a camel's-hair brush. Three lines are painted on each bowl. The task of applying the lines to the bowls is highly skilled work. Employees who begin work in this department receive an hourly rate and a guaranteed day wage. The rate is 57½ cents an hour for a beginner, 60 cents after 60 days, and

62½ cents after one year. When the employee's wage equals the day rate, the employee is placed on a piecework basis. The earnings of the skilled pieceworkers are substantially in excess of the employees in other departments.

For the past 8 years the practice has been followed in the plant of transferring employees in the striping department to assembly work when work falls off in the striping department. The transfers have been made on a rotation basis without regard to seniority in point of service.

In November, 1945, the Company signed an agreement with the UERMWA containing the following provisions:

Article II, Section 3:

"To facilitate shipments getting in and out of the plant, employees may be transferred from floor to floor and from department to department."

Article IV, Section 1:

"It is understood and agreed that in all cases of increase or decrease of the working force, length of service shall govern (except as outlined in Section 2 of this Article). The seniority date of all present employees shall be placed on a list and a copy furnished to the Union. The list shall be kept up to date."

Article IV, Section 2:

"The seniority of the striping and firing departments shall be by department."

Article IV, Section 3:

"When there is a decrease in the working force because of insufficient work, the following procedure will be observed:

"*a*) All probationary employees will be laid off first.
"*b*) No further layoffs will be made except such as may

be necessary to maintain a work week of 32 hours. Those employees having the least seniority will be laid off first.''

The Union filed a grievance on behalf of 5 employees of the striping department in February, 1946. It complained that, when there was a lack of work in the striping department, employees were transferred to other departments without regard to seniority. This is held to be in violation of the provisions of the agreement, as cited above.

Position of the Union

The Union argues as follows:

a) Under Section 2 of Article IV, seniority in the striping department is on a departmental basis; and, under Section 3 of Article IV, when there is a decrease in the working force, all probationary employees are to be laid off first; and thereafter employees having the least seniority will be laid off. Under these provisions, the Company is obliged to transfer employees in the striping department to assembly work in the order of their seniority of service, and the practice of transferring them on a rotation basis is in violation of these provisions.

b) Since it is specifically provided that all probationary employees will be laid off first, the practice of retaining trainees in the striping department for sixty days, while at the same time experienced employees with seniority are being transferred to the assembly department, is also a direct violation of seniority provisions of the contract.

c) Section 3 of Article II, relating to transfers, applies to departments of the plant where there is no departmental seniority, and therefore this provision does not apply to the striping department, which is specifically given departmental seniority in Section 2 of Article IV.

d) The seniority provision in Article IV applies to transfers as well as layoffs because the Company, in effect, says that, if you will not transfer, you will be laid off.

Further, the Union puts considerable weight on the fact that the Company by its policy and practice is able to maintain a pool of employees in the striping department at the expense of the older employees by transfers to the assembly department. It is argued that this means a substantial reduction in earnings to experienced stripers, and the loss incurred is one which the stripers should not be asked to absorb since the transfer is really made for the accommodation of the Company.

Finally, the Union denies that the Company has handled transfers from the striping department in any established uniform way. The Union insists that it has never accepted what the Company considers its adopted practice and that, in at least one case, an employee actually quit work in 1944 because she did not want to be transferred to assembly work out of the order of her seniority.

POSITION OF THE COMPANY

The Company argues as follows:

a) For the past 8 years, the Company has followed the practice of transferring employees from the striping to the assembly department by the rotation method. Eight years is considered a sufficiently long time in which to formulate an "established practice."

b) The Union is attempting to place a meaning on the contract which was contemplated by neither party, up to the date the grievance was filed.

c) Article IV on seniority, by its language, clearly applies to layoffs only; and, while it is true that an employee may lay off rather than accept a transfer, the layoff is optional at the employee's request and is not made by the Company.

d) The only provision of the contract which relates to transfer is Section 3 of Article II, and the language of this section permits the Company to transfer employees from floor to floor and from department to department without regard to seniority.

e) Section 3 of Article II was placed in the contract at the company's request in order to make possible the transfer of employees from department to department without regard to their seniority.

f) It is impractical to provide for transfers on the basis of seniority from the striping department to the assembly department. The contention is made that it takes some time for trainees to learn how to do striping and that probationary employees would suffer particular hardship by transfer because the transfer would take place before they had mastered the skill of striping. This would work a hardship not only on the employees, it is contended, but also on the Company.

g) The rate of absenteeism is high, and it is difficult to maintain a supply of skilled stripers. Unless the Company is enabled to keep trainees in the striping department for the 60-day period, it would not be able to build up an adequate supply of skilled labor in the striping department.

The Company presents the general proposition that the collective bargaining agreement cannot be considered .as an abstract legal document. It must be construed in the light of the practices existing at the time the agreement was made. One of the conditions of employment that existed at the time the agreement was made was the Company's practice of transferring employees from the striping department to the assembly department on a rotation basis without regard to seniority. The Company holds that the Union did not attempt to change the existing practice. The language of the agreement is in no way designed to correct or change the practice existing between the parties. The Company argues that in entering into the agreement the Union, in fact, acquiesced in the rotation plan of transfer by its failure to insist upon a change in the agreement and that the present agreement must be read as though the provision for transfers appearing in Section 3 of Article II permits transfers out of the striping department on a rotation basis in accordance with the established practice.

QUESTIONS

1. Which section of the agreement applies to this case?
2. May the Company use the transfer provision of the agreement to avoid a layoff in a particular department?

3. Why does the Company favor the established practice?
4. Why does the Union demand strict departmental seniority on layoffs? Under the union view what would happen to the junior employee in the striping department in the event of a reduction in work?
5. What would you expect to be the relative views of the striping and assembly department employees toward the established practice?
6. Do conditions and practices which antedate an agreement have status under an agreement? Does the long-established practice affect the status of the grievance under the contract?

CASE 26

A TEMPORARY OR PERMANENT LAYOFF?

UNION: International Photographers of the Motion Picture Industries, International Alliance of Theatrical and Stage Employees

COMPANY: Walt Disney Productions

During the latter part of July, 1946, Walt Disney Productions found itself in difficult financial conditions and was obliged to undertake a drastic curtailment in its production schedule. A substantial number of layoffs were involved. A meeting was held in the company cafeteria where the circumstances were explained to the business agents of all the unions whose members were employed by the Company in order that these business agents and the members of their unions would fully understand the conditions which necessitated a reduction in staff.

On July 29, 1946, a memorandum was addressed by John Reedes, Vice-President and General Manager of the Company, to the cameramen. Each cameraman was notified that he would be included in the general layoff effective at the close of work, August 1, 1946. The memorandum stated that the Company took this action with reluctance and that the layoffs were dictated entirely by economic considerations. Nine cameramen were affected.

The Company had found it impossible to operate without further financial assistance and had applied for bank loans in order to work out its problems over a period of time. It was not known at the time of the layoffs just when a decision might be forthcoming on the bank loans. Consequently, no promise or commitment was made regarding recall or any future work.

Prior to this last day of work, August 1, 1946, all of the cameramen, excluding one man who was on vacation, were advised by their immediate superiors that the outlook was very "dark" and that they should not rely on the chances of obtaining future employment with the Company. They were advised to seek other jobs. The acceptance of other work would not prejudice their future employment opportunities with the Company, or the accumulation of benefits under the contract.

After August 1 most of the cameramen involved secured work in other studios. During the month of August, the Company gradually began to rehire its former employees. On August 8, 1946, Roy Hoar was offered and accepted re-employment. On August 20, Paul Martin was re-employed. On September 15, Leonard Pickley, who had been on vacation when the layoff occurred, was offered a job and returned to work.

On September 27, 1946, Herbert Aller, the business representative of the Union, addressed a letter to Bonar Dyar, Personnel Director of the Company, stating that a reasonable length of time had expired since the layoffs and that, therefore, he was requesting severance pay for the members of his Union under the terms of the contract. Section 11 of the collective bargaining agreement between the Company and Union reads as follows:

"Upon dismissal, employees with one year or over of continuous service will receive one week's severance pay; and employees with two years continuous service or more shall receive two weeks' severance pay to be computed at the highest rate of pay received by said employee during the twelve months prior to dismissal."

Negotiations and discussions regarding the severance-pay claim continued for more than two weeks, but no agreement was reached.

On October 15, 1946, two additional jobs became available, and re-employment was offered, in turn, to each of the remaining six cameramen according to their seniority. Messrs. Sharpe, Mann, Wilkins, and Nave refused the offer of re-employment on the grounds that the work was only temporary and they had already secured other employment of a more permanent or desirable nature. Messrs. Brandenburg and Gunderson accepted re-employment on October 15 when they were reached on the seniority list.

The Union submits that the laid-off cameramen are entitled to their severance pay. The Company opposed payment of this benefit.

POSITION OF THE UNION

The Union takes the position that under the terms of the severance-pay provisions of the contract each cameraman became entitled to his severance pay immediately upon being laid off. The Union contends that there is nothing in the agreement which provides for the withholding of the severance pay pending a later determination of available re-employment or which distinguishes between a permanent and a temporary layoff. According to the Union, severance pay had been paid on numerous occasions to cameramen during the war years, and in 1941 similar payments were made during a shutdown caused by a strike, in spite of the fact that it was commonly accepted that the plant would reopen and the men would be re-employed.

In the present case the Union points out that absolutely no commitments were made or could have been made regarding re-employment at the time of the layoff on August 1. Attention is called to the fact that the layoff notice received by the cameramen makes no mention of re-employment and that the advice given to the employees to secure other jobs naturally left them with no expectations of being re-employed by the Company at any predictable time in the future. The Union introduced the testimony of several of the cameramen involved to the effect that, when re-employment was offered and refused by some of the men on October 15, such re-employment was offered on a purely temporary basis. The Union argues that the refusal of these men to accept temporary work does not prejudice their rights to severance pay since they should have received this pay before the offer of temporary re-employment was made.

The Union answers the company's argument that it has an established practice of waiting ninety days after layoffs before making severance payments, with the statement that the terms of the contract contain no reference to any such practice, and that the decision in this case must be made on the terms of the contract.

The Union also answers the company's contention regarding the accumulation of vacation rights and other benefits under the contract with the argument that these matters are separate and apart from the severance-pay provision and have nothing whatsoever to do with the application thereof.

In summary, the essence of the union's claim is that, under the terms of the severance-pay provision, an employee who is laid off, dismissed, terminated, or discharged, becomes immediately entitled to the amount of severance pay for which he qualifies by length of service. The Union argues that this holds regardless of whether the employee is to be re-employed by the Company after one week, two months, or any other period of time.

POSITION OF THE COMPANY

The company's position is that on August 1 it was forced by circumstances to put a general layoff into effect and that the circumstances surrounding this action were made very clear to all of the union business agents and the cameramen involved. It contends that there never was any question regarding the desire and intent of the Company to increase its production schedule as soon as its financial condition permitted and to re-employ as soon as possible all the men who were laid off.

The Company maintains that the cameramen involved were not discharged or dismissed but were laid off temporarily until such time as conditions permitted their re-employment. Furthermore, the Company insists that it has long had a policy of carrying employees who were laid off on the payroll for a period of ninety days during which time such employees' seniority rights, vacation, sick leave, and other benefits were accumulated so that, if an employee returned to work, he suffered no loss of such benefits as a result of the layoff.

According to the company's description of the practice, after the ninety-day period has expired, the Company either makes a final discharge or termination of the employee and pays him everything to which he is entitled under the contract up to that date, or notifies the employee that he is entitled to such things if he wants to claim them or that he can continue on a laid-off status for a longer period if there is a possibility of future employment.

The Company insists that everything it has done in connection with the reduction in force supports its contention that the layoff was, so far as the cameramen were concerned, of a temporary nature. It places a great deal of emphasis on the fact that re-employment was actually offered to each of the men involved and accepted by some of them. The Company states that under its practice, if the top men on the seniority list had accepted re-employment, leaving those on the bottom of the list unemployed after the ninety-day period, then those cameramen who were not re-employed would have become entitled to their severance pay.

Thus, the essence of the company's claim is that, when an employee is laid off with the possibility of future rehire, it is entitled to follow an allegedly established practice of waiting ninety days and then either paying severance pay to the employee or allowing him to exercise his option of taking such severance pay or waiting further for re-employment.

QUESTIONS

1. How could the question posed by this case be avoided in the future? Would you propose any contract language? Would you suggest any internal administrative rule which might be adopted by the Company?
2. Is it always possible to know at the time of a layoff whether it will be temporary or permanent? Who should bear the costs of this uncertainty?
3. If employees were told that they were laid off permanently and were offered re-employment a week later, would they be entitled to severance pay under the contract provision?
4. What is the status of the alleged practice of the Company under the agreement?

CASE 27

PLANT-WIDE SENIORITY OF EMPLOYEES DISPLACED BY TECHNOLOGICAL CHANGES

UNION: United Automobile Workers, CIO

COMPANY: General Motors Corporation

Six separate grievances bearing on the same matter were presented at the Atlanta Chevrolet plant on September 30, 1941. The language of one of them may be considered as typical. It reads: "Request that I be placed on job in line with my seniority as to Paragraph 59 in the contract, also request I be reimbursed in pay difference due to my transfer."

On September 29, changes in operating methods resulted in the elimination of three jobs in the new-car conditioning department, four jobs in the inspection department, and one job in the repair department.

The provisions of the agreement between the union applicable to these changes were Paragraphs 59 and 63. Paragraph 59 reads in part:

"When changes in methods . . . would otherwise require the permanent laying off of employees, the seniority of the displaced employees shall become plant-wide and they shall be transferred out of the group in line with their seniority to work they are capable of doing, as comparable to the work they have been doing as may be available, at the rate for the job to which they have been transferred."

Paragraph 63 reads in part:

"The transferring of employees is the sole responsibility of the Management. In the advancement of employees to higher paid jobs when ability, merit and capacity are equal, employees with the longest seniority will be given preference."

Management took the following action in the above cases:

New-Car Conditioning Department.—Three men had been inspectors in the New Car Conditioning Department at $1.08 per hour. This department is a separate seniority group. When the three inspecting jobs were eliminated on September 29, management reasoned that, in compliance with Paragraph 59, their seniority was sufficient to let them remain in the same department as "tighteners" at $1.04 per hour. The junior tighteners then replaced or "bumped" the three youngest men in the department who were transferred out of the department to the unloading dock at $0.95 per hour. Three employees on the unloading dock were "bumped" and laid off.

The claimants remained on the tightener jobs until November 3, 1941, when two of the three men were transferred to the inspection department as assembly inspectors at $1.08 per hour. The third man remained on the tightener job until November 11, 1941, when he was offered a job as a road-tester in the inspection department at $1.08 per hour; but evidently he preferred to stay on the tightener job.

Inspection Department.—Four men who had been employed as road-testers at $1.06 per hour, when their jobs were eliminated, were transferred to the unloading dock at $0.95 per hour. On September 30, one day after the transfer, employee H was transferred to an assembly job at $1.10 per hour; on October 1, T was transferred to Assembly at $1.10. F went to the Assembly on October 16 at $1.10. Management reports that "he remained on this job for seven working days and was unable to 'carry the operation' so he was transferred back to the Unloading Dock." O was on the unloading dock until October 27 when he was transferred to a tightener job in new-car conditioning at $1.04.

Repair Department.—S had been employed as a paint-touch-up man at $1.08 when his job was eliminated on September 29. He was transferred to the unloading dock at $0.95, and on October 6 to the assembly at $1.10.

THE ISSUE

What jobs are "available" to employees who become entitled to plant-wide seniority in accordance with the provisions of Paragraph 59 as a result of permanent discontinuance of their jobs?

POSITION OF THE UNION

The Union feels that "the real issue to be settled in this case is: when is a job available when an employee is entitled to plant-wide seniority"? It contends that an available job is "any comparable work that the employee is capable of doing, in line with his seniority."

The Union notes that each of the employees who filed the grievances in question "have more seniority than employees working in the following departments at a rate of $1.10 an hour on work they are capable of doing: Paint Department, etc. (five others)." It is contended by the Union that such jobs in these departments should have been assigned to the claimant employees on the ground that "any comparable job that the employee is capable of performing is available under Paragraph 59, if he has sufficient seniority to take the job."

With specific reference to the three inspectors in the new-car conditioning department, the Union claims that, since their jobs had been discontinued, the men should have been transferred out of the group in line with their new plant-wide seniority on the basis of Paragraph 59. The Union contends that they were entitled to an assignment to work comparable to that which they had been doing rather than to demotion within the departmental seniority group. The Company had stated that they had sufficient seniority to remain "in the same occupational group."

POSITION OF THE COMPANY

Management contends that the employees whose jobs were eliminated by a change in method were properly transferred in accordance with Paragraphs 59 and 63 (above) of the agreement. It is said that the three men, whose jobs were eliminated in the new-car conditioning department, had sufficient seniority to remain in the same seniority group, and Management maintains that they properly "replaced the three youngest men in the department who were transferred out of the Department to available jobs on the Unloading Dock." The four eliminated jobs in the inspection department properly resulted, says management, in the transfer of the four men to the unloading dock "which was the only place where there were jobs available." The unloading dock had always been considered, states management, as a "clearing house" for hiring, laying off, and transferring employees.

Management does not interpret "as may be available" as contained in Paragraph 59 "to mean the right to bump an employee with less seniority, who has sufficient seniority to be working, even though it may be a job comparable to the work that he had been doing." In its statement of unadjusted grievances, management specifically contended "that a job is not available when another employee is working on the job" and further maintained that the plant-wide seniority of an employee whose job has been eliminated only gave a man a right to a job and did not entitle him to a job comparable to the work he had been doing until such jobs became vacant.

Supplementing their general position upon the issue, management and the Union offered the following comments upon their stand in specific cases:

Transfers of Three Inspectors in the New-Car Conditioning Department.—Management contended that these three employees were not entitled to plant-wide seniority. In a previous decision, the Union replied, the umpire had interpreted that part of Paragraph 59 which reads: When changes in methods, products, or policies would otherwise require the permanent laying-off of employees. . . . ." It was held then by the umpire that this provision makes Paragraph 59 applicable "when job changes occur which would require the permanent laying-off of an employee unless his job classification is changed." Since these three claimants were inspectors in the new-car conditioning group, it is obvious, says the Union, that the changes in method required a change in job classification in order to prevent their permanent layoff. They were thus clearly entitled to plant-wide seniority under Paragraph 59. Management had erred, says the Union, in contending that the "bumping" had to be initially confined to the new-car conditioning department with the employees displaced from the department "bumping" others on the loading dock.

Management had contended that the three men had sufficient seniority to remain "in the same occupational group." (The Union replied by noting that the men actually were not retained in the same occupational group but in the same seniority group.) Management reasoned that the elimination of jobs in any seniority group, because of technological change, results in transfers, with its attendant bumping, within the seniority group wherever that is possible. The union's counterargument held that, under such an approach, the status of such displaced employees would be entirely dependent upon the setups of the local seniority agreement—whether ratings were determined on an occupational, department, or plant basis. There is no evidence, the Union argued, of any understanding that the local seniority agreement in this plant is to be applied to determine the transfers of employees upon the elimination of their jobs for technological reasons. The Union went on:

> "At any rate, however, Paragraph 59 applies on a national basis to all employees who are displaced by technological change and it cannot be modified by local agreements. Under Paragraph 59, displaced employees are those whose job classifications must be changed because of technological change and they are entitled to plant-wide seniority."

Transfers of Four Road Testers in the Inspection Department.— These four men, upon the elimination of their $1.08 jobs, were transferred to the unloading dock at $0.95. Management's reason was that, under Paragraph 59, these jobs were as comparable to the work they were doing as was available. It interprets this paragraph as giving a displaced employee only a right to a job on the loading dock or on some job where no more than one "bump" is required.

Transfer of Man Out of Repair Department.—This man had worked on a paint-touch-up job. He was transferred to the unloading dock where he worked for about a day and was then transferred, at his own request, to a driver's job. These may properly be considered "clearing assignments" to fill the gap while management made the necessary "bumping" adjustments. He was then transferred to a job that represented a promotion to him.

QUESTIONS

1. The Company relies in part upon Paragraph 63 of the Agreement which states: "The transferring of employees is the sole responsibility of management. In the advancement of employees . . . when ability, merit, and capacity are equal, employees with the longest seniority shall be given preference." Are the shifts resulting from the discontinuances of jobs because of technological or operating changes "transfers" within the meaning of Paragraph 63?

2. Assuming that the shifts involved in these cases are transfers within the meaning of Paragraph 63, does the phrase in Para-

graph 63 stating that "the transferring of employees is the sole responsibility of Management" mean that the discretion of management is not limited by Paragraph 59?

3. Under the terms of Paragraph 59, which employees in the inspection department should be regarded as having acquired plant-wide seniority—the three inspectors who could "bump" within the departments or the three junior men who were transferred out of the department when they were bumped by the junior employees among the tighteners?

4. May an employee be regarded as threatened with "permanent layoff" by a technological change when he has seniority rights which would enable him to take the job of a junior employee in the same department? Is the answer to this question affected by whether or not the jobs within the department from which the employee might "bump" other workers pay less than the job destroyed by the technological change?

5. Is Paragraph 59 to be interpreted as an attempt to implement the principle that no employee shall suffer a wage reduction from technological change so long as there are jobs in the plant which are held by men junior in seniority and which the employee is capable of doing?

6. Does the seniority system embodied in the agreement between the Union and the Company contemplate that adjustments to changes in methods shall occur insofar as possible within seniority groups or within departments before men acquire plant-wide seniority?

7. Is the management correct in holding that "a job is not available when another employee is working on the job" even though the employee on the job has less seniority than the employee who would like to "bump" him? Would the management's interpretation of "available" be consistent with the purpose of Paragraph 59 of the agreement?

8. The Union in asking that Paragraph 59 be interpreted to confer plant-wide seniority upon employees displaced by technological change, even when these employees have seniority which enables them to "bump" other employees in the seniority group or department, is requesting that employees have greater seniority rights in cases of displacement by technological change than in cases of displacement by ordinary falling off in business. Are there sound reasons, in your judgment, for the union's seeking to es-

tablish such a distinction? For the Company's opposing it? Bear in mind that the seniority system establishes a distribution of rights among the workers—the more rights some workers have as a result of seniority, the fewer rights other workers have. Why give greater rights to the employees displaced by a technological change than to employees displaced by a decline in business?

CASE 28

DOES "REASONABLE CONSIDERATION OF SENIORITY" REQUIRE A TRIAL ON THE JOB?

UNION: United Automobile Workers of America, CIO

COMPANY: General Motors Corporation

John Harding held top seniority ranking in occupational group 11 of department 1, consisting of 189 employees at the Southern California Division of General Motors. When a job in the inspection department became available, Sam Holt was chosen for transfer to it since management considered him the man best qualified to fill the vacancy. He held the fourth highest seniority in the same group.

The consideration required to be given to seniority by management in making transfers is stated in Clause 8 of the seniority section of the agreement between the Company and the Union as follows: "In transferring employees, seniority will be secondary to other qualifications but will be given reasonable consideration. Any claims of discrimination for union activity in connection with transfers may be taken up as grievances." The Union made it clear that no charge of union discrimination was being made in this case.

The Union objects to the transfer of Holt on the ground that he has less seniority than the claimant. Holt's seniority date was June 17, 1936, while that of Harding was June 3, 1936. Management stated that "Harding is one of our best men" but also insisted that Holt was better qualified for the inspection job because he was younger, better educated, and better adapted to inspection work, whereas "Harding likes to work with his hands." It was pointed out that both men had been "under observation" for transfer and that both were assigned to better jobs for which they were qualified.

On April 8, 1941, two months after he had filed the grievance, Harding was assigned to the emergency operators' occupational group and to a job which carried a rate of pay equivalent to the inspection job which is involved in this case. This assignment of Harding to a new job occurred two days before the consideration of his grievance at the third step of the grievance procedure.

It was recognized by both parties at the umpire hearing that the issue concerned only the basis of selection for transfer that had been used by the management in this case and specifically whether it gave reasonable consideration to seniority.

POSITION OF THE UNION

The union's position is that "the man having the most seniority should be given a fair trial on the job involved, and the filling of a vacancy should not be left up to the judgment of the Foreman." Such a procedure is necessary, contends the Union, in order to provide the "reasonable consideration" to seniority that is required by Clause 8 of the seniority section. It is also claimed by the Union that the transfer in question should have been provided to Harding because a representative of management had promised him an inspection or a better job "if he would cooperate by not requesting a transfer into the service building."

POSITION OF THE COMPANY

The Company claims that John Harding merely was informed that he was under observation for a transfer. It is pointed out that he was transferred to a better job in April. The Union feels, however, that, since neither Holt nor Harding had worked on the inspection operation in question, Harding should have been assigned to it because he worked next to it for a long period of time and "by having more seniority would be better qualified to hold the job."

Management contends it chose the best man for the job. Reasonable consideration was given to seniority, it is contended, as is amply shown by selection for the job of the fourth man in order of seniority in the group of 189 men. Management states that it feels "reasonable consideration" was given to seniority since the selection for the job was made from the first ten of the group of 189. The selection was entirely proper, it is held, under the contract which states: "In transferring employees, seniority will be secondary to other qualifications, but will be given reasonable consideration."

In making this selection, management was governed, it states, by a realization that "inspection is intimately and inseparably associated with the quality phase of the production, and Supervision must select for the inspection jobs those employees they feel are qualified to do the work." By choosing the best-qualified employee holding fourth greatest seniority, management contends it conformed fully with the agreement.

QUESTIONS

1. How would you test whether management gave "reasonable consideration" to seniority in making transfers? Do you agree that the selection of any one of the ten men with greatest seniority out of 189 indicates that "reasonable" consideration was being given to seniority?
2. How would giving a man a trial on the job help the management give reasonable consideration to seniority?

CASE 29

DEMOTION FOR INEFFICIENCY

UNION: Textile Workers Union of America, CIO, Local 77

COMPANY: Fish Net and Twine Company

On November 19, 1945, Mrs. Mary Mellett was demoted from net machine operator, with a guaranteed minimum basic rate of 65 cents per hour, to bobbin-winder at 55 cents. On November 30, the Union requested the Company to reinstate

Mrs. Mellett on the net machine. The Company refused to reinstate her, and the Union took the matter to arbitration, claiming that the company's action constituted a violation of the agreement.

Mrs. Mellett entered the employment of the Company as a bobbin-winder on April 5, 1943. After a few months she became a net machine operator, in which capacity she remained until about August 22, 1945, when wartime contracts were canceled which necessitated the layoff of many employees and the reorganization of those who were retained. For twenty-eight weeks prior to V-J day Mrs. Mellett made an average of 58.54 cents per hour, or 6.46 cents below the guaranteed basic minimum rate. In no one of these weeks did she make the basic rate. (The classification is on piece rates, and employees are guaranteed a minimum rate. Actual earnings depend on production.) The record of other operators on the same machine under the same conditions during this period shows such rates as 80.8, 70.77, and 70.25 cents per hour. Furthermore, on or about October 22, Mrs. Mellett was again put on the net machine. Her production record showed no improvement, however, and she was once more demoted to bobbin-winder on November 19, 1945.

POSITION OF THE UNION

The Union claimed that this demotion violated the following sections of the agreement:

"*Section 5* (in part). If during slack periods work should fall below twenty-four (24) hours in any one week for the workers in any one department, the Employer may lay off workers in that department according to their departmental lack of seniority. Whenever possible during the slack periods in one department, workers with less seniority in that department shall be temporarily transferred to another department which has available work, if they are capable of doing the work therein. New employees or learners hired after the signing of this agreement may be given less, but no more work hours than employees with greater seniority in the particular department."

"*Section 9*. In the event that new help is hired or laid off it shall be done on a seniority basis; i.e., the last one to be laid off shall be the first one to be taken back. This rule shall apply to anyone who has been employed for three (3) months or more."

"*Section 20(a)*. In the event an employee at the request of the Employer is temporarily transferred to another job, then the employee's average earnings or the higher rate of pay shall be paid to such employee while working on that job."

It is the union's contention that the contract envisages only layoffs due to lack of work and that such layoffs shall be governed by seniority when they do occur. It is further argued that the rules governing layoffs should apply with equal force to demotions, provided that the individual concerned exerts his best effort at his job. Therefore, whether or not the operator maintains a production resulting in the guaranteed minimum pay for the classification, so long as said operator exerts his best efforts, the Company has no right to demote him. Mrs. Mellett, having been placed on a net machine and allowed to work on it for a considerable period of time, the Company is henceforth powerless to demote or discharge her, provided that she has performed her work consistently in a conscientious manner and provided that enough work is available to keep her machine in operation.

POSITION OF THE COMPANY

The Company claimed that, if an employee on a certain job consistently fails to produce a quota which would entitle him to at least a basic minimum rate of pay for the job, the Company has the right to demote such an employee to some other job. The demotion in this case was properly made under the following section of the contract: "Senior workers shall be given first consideration for promotion, and if promoted, such senior workers shall be given an ample trial period to prove that they can perform the duties required."

Mrs. Mellett's employment record shows that she was given more than one "ample trial period" in accordance with the terms of the contract. It is equally evident that she was not able to prove her ability to "perform the duties required." The fact that Mrs. Mellett was retained as net machine operator over so long a period of time, despite her failure to produce the quota, is explained by the wartime man-power shortage. Whereas, it had been the exception for an employee to fail to produce an output yielding the minimum basic hourly rate before the war, the company's records show that productivity fell off progressively during the war, so that from January 1, 1945 to August 18, 1945 (the date of cancellation of war contracts) only 40 per cent of the operators consistently made production for minimum basic rate, or better.

After the cancellation of war contracts, the Company cautioned all of its operators that, unless basic guaranteed minima, or better, were maintained, operators failing to meet quotas would either be transferred to lower-paid jobs or dismissed. Beginning with the week in which the warning was given, the regular operators, virtually without fail, produced better than guaranteed minimum rates. Mrs. Mellett was warned by her foreman that she would have to do better work if she desired to remain on her machine. During the four weeks of her testing period, however, her earnings were only 53.34, 63.12, 56.82, and 60.05 cents per hour—or an average of more than 10 per cent below the basic minimum rate. Another girl who operated the same machine during the identical period under the same conditions made 80.8 cents, or 24 per cent above the basic rate; and still another made 70.77 cents, or 9 per cent above the basic rate.

QUESTIONS

1. Are there any provisions in Sections 5, 9, or 20(a), cited by the Union, which prohibit the employer from demoting workers who fail to produce the "normal" amount?

2. Is the employer's right to demote contingent upon the length of time during which the employee served in the position from which he was demoted? Does the fact that the employer retained Mrs. Mellett on the net machine for about two years limit the right of the management to demote her for substandard work, assuming that her output just prior to the demotion was no worse than it had been for some time previous?

3. Would it be in the long-run interest of the Union to win this case? What would the Union gain by preventing the employer from demoting inefficient workers?

4. Does the fact that the employee was retained in the net machine operator's classification during a period of wartime labor market conditions affect the decision? Should the decision be different if the employee had been retained in the classification during normal times?

CASE 30

RIGHT OF MANAGEMENT TO TRANSFER EMPLOYEES AGAINST THEIR WILL

UNION: United Automobile Workers, CIO

COMPANY: General Motors Corporation

In February, 1941, at the Fisher Body Plant No. 1 of the General Motors Corporation at Flint, it became necessary to transfer several employees to the "low-quarters" group in the trim department and to select for transfer employees who would meet certain physical requirements of the jobs and who were otherwise qualified to perform trim operations. The three claimants in this case held jobs in the final assembly department paying them $1.00 an hour. Their long service with the Company gave them a favorable position on the seniority roster in the final assembly department. As a result, their employment was steady and regular. Although the seniority dates of the men gave the men a relatively high position in the final assembly department, these dates gave the men a relatively low position in the trim department. Consequently, the men protested the transfer to the trim department because they claimed they would be better off to remain on the $1.00 job where their seniority would make it more likely that they would secure relatively full-time employment.

After discussion with the shop committee, management stated that the men would be returned to assembly because it was not considered desirable "to have the men work in the Trim Department against their will." Management emphasized, however, that it held the right to make such transfers, and that the return of the men to the assembly department would have to be "at the convenience of the Company." The shop committee expressed concern over this approach to the matter and urged that the claimants be promptly placed back on final assembly because "if the men were not placed back in their own department before sixty days were up, they would lose their seniority standing in the department." The Union then protested the management's position in the case, and brought it up as a grievance to the impartial umpire.

Seniority in this plant was, at the time of the grievance, governed by a national agreement and, secondarily, by a local seniority agreement which supplemented but did not conflict with the national agreement. The national agreement lays down the rules for acquiring and maintaining seniority. Clause 4 of the seniority section of the national agreement reads in part: "Seniority shall be by non-interchangeable occupational groups,[1] within departments, or groups of departments, or plant-wide, as may be negotiated locally at each plant, and reduced to writing."

The part of the local seniority agreement at this plant relevant to the case established a departmental seniority grouping of four major departments (four major occupational groupings). The four departments, under the national agree-

---

[1] The term "non-interchangeable groups" means that all movement in layoff and rehiring, etc., shall be by occupation, and that there shall not be "bumping," for example, of machinists by electricians. An occupational group may include one or more job classifications. These are similar enough in nature so that any worker in the group can do any other worker's job.

ment, constituted non-interchangeable occupational groups—final assembly and trim were two of these departments.

THE ISSUE

The claimants considered their transfer a demotion because of the greater likelihood of layoff in the trim department.

The Union challenges, indirectly, the right of the management to transfer men against their will so long as there is work to be done at the jobs from which they are being transferred. The Union asks for a ruling on the issue despite the fact that the men have been returned to their original jobs. The right of an employee to refuse a transfer is not specifically given to him in the agreement. The Union bases its argument on the contract (sections quoted below) which, it says, precludes transfers or promotions between occupational groups.

The union claim also raises the important question as to whether low or high seniority employees should be first transferred from $1.00 to $1.10 jobs in cases where there are other relative disadvantages connected with the higher-paying jobs.

POSITION OF THE UNION

In supporting the claims of these three men, the Union contends that their transfer was made in disregard of their wishes and was, moreover, contrary to the seniority agreement at this plant (explained above) and Clauses 3 and 4 of the seniority section of the national agreement.

Clause 3 reads:

"When an employee acquires seniority, his name shall be placed on the seniority list for his occupational group in the order of the date of hiring except as provided in the preceding paragraph. Men and women shall be divided into separate non-interchangeable occupational groups."

Clause 4 reads:

"Seniority shall be by non-interchangeable occupational groups, within departments or groups of departments, or plant-wide, as may be negotiated locally at each plant, and reduced to writing. When changes in methods, products or policies would otherwise require the permanent laying off of employees, the seniority of the displaced persons shall become plant-wide and they shall be transferred out of the group in line with their seniority, to work they are capable of doing, as comparable to the work they have been doing as may be available, at the rate for the job to which they have been transferred."

The Union maintains that it was not proper to move these three men from assembly to trim because these major departments have been negotiated in the seniority agreement as non-interchangeable occupational groups. The Union interprets the contract to mean that Clauses 3 and 4 preclude transfers or promotions between occupational groups.

The Union insisted that, once an employee has established his seniority in an occupational seniority group, he then has a right to stay in that group, and management has no right to move him against his will to another non-interchangeable group.

In addition, it was claimed that management erred in transferring the three men because management did so without giving proper consideration to their seniority standing in the assembly group. Here the Union cites Clause 8 of the seniority section of the national agreement which reads: "In transferring employees, seniority will be secondary to other qualifications, but will be given reasonable consideration. Any claims of discrimination for Union activity in connection with transfers may be taken up as grievances."

No claim was made that Union discrimination was involved.

The claims of the Union add up to a request that "these men be placed back into Final Assembly Department with full department seniority."

POSITION OF THE COMPANY

The Company argues that the transfers of the claimants are promotions because the vacancies pay 10 cents an hour more than the jobs which the men left. Clause 3(c) of the recognition section is construed by the management as giving it the sole right to select employees for promotion. The clause reads in part: "The right to hire; promote; discharge or discipline for cause; and to maintain discipline and efficiency of employees is the sole responsibility of the Corporation except that union members shall not be discriminated against as such."

The management contends that nothing in the national agreement, or in the local seniority agreement, limits or restricts its right to transfer employees from one non-interchangeable occupational group to another provided seniority is given "reasonable consideration" in the making of such transfers (as required by Clause 8 of the seniority section of the national agreement, quoted above).

The management points out that the vacancies in question in this case paid $1.10 an hour, and management determined to promote employees with seniority to these jobs rather than to hire new employees for these higher-rated jobs.

The Company disputes the union's view that Clauses 3 and 4 of the seniority section of the national agreement preclude transfers or promotions between occupational groups. Those clauses essentially concern the manner in which seniority lists are made up and the manner in which the seniority rights of employees are placed on such lists; they do not preclude transfers or promotions between occupational groups. Recognition that such transfers may be made is clearly evidenced by Clause 7 of the seniority section of the national agreement which provides that: "When an employee is transferred from one occupational group to another for any reason, there shall be no loss of seniority. . . . ." This can only mean that there will be cases where transfers will be made between occupational groups. Clause 8, the Company points out, further supports this conclusion since it provides that: "In transferring employees, seniority will be secondary to other qualifications but will be given reasonable consideration. . . . ."

In reply to the union contention that reasonable consideration, as required by Clause 8, was not given to seniority in making the transfer, management replies that it gave a very important consideration to the relatively long seniority record of these men in "promoting" them and also sought to act upon their earlier expressed desire for promotion. Management considers the transfer as a promotion because it was a change from $1.00 to $1.10 jobs. The employees seem to have regarded their transfer as a demotion because of the greater likelihood of layoff in the trim department.

QUESTIONS

1. Should the umpire dismiss the case on the ground that it is moot?

2. Were the transfers in this case promotions or demotions? Whose judgment would determine whether a transfer was a promotion or a demotion?

3. The Union argues that it was not proper to move the claimants from assembly to trim because the two departments were placed by the local seniority agreement in non-interchangeable occupational groups. Does the agreement prohibit *all* transfers by non-interchangeable occupational groups? If not, where does the line fall between permitted and prohibited transfers?

4. The Company argues that there is nothing in either the national agreement or the local seniority agreements limiting or restricting the right of management to transfer employees between non-interchangeable occupational groups provided seniority is given "reasonable consideration." Assuming that the Company is correct, does it follow that the Company may transfer men from their existing jobs against the will of these men? Must a man accept what the Company, not the man, regards as a "promotion" in order to hold a job with the Company? Would an affirmative answer to these questions be contrary to the intent and spirit of the seniority arrangements provided in the agreement?

5. Assume that the men selected for transfer from the final assembly to the trim department had been at the bottom of the seniority list in the final assembly department. Assume, however, that if they were transferred, their jobs would have had to be filled. Would these facts affect the right of the Company to make the transfer against the will of these men?

6. Assuming that neither the national nor the local agreements specifically limit the right of management to make transfers, does it follow that the management would be free to transfer men against their will from expanding departments to declining departments?

7. Assume that the management offered long-service employees an opportunity to move from a department in which the work might be expected to decrease over the long run to a department in which the work might be expected to increase over the long run. The men refuse the opportunity, and junior men are transferred. Later when work falls off in the declining department, the men who declined transfer are laid off. Under Section 4 of the agreement, does the plant-wide seniority which they acquire on being permanently laid off permit them, if necessary, to take the jobs of the junior employees who accepted the transfer which the senior men previously had refused?

CASE 31

DEMOTION FROM PREMIUM MEN TO MECHANICS

UNION: Industrial Union of Marine & Shipbuilding Workers of America, CIO

COMPANY: Cramp Shipbuilding Company

On or about September 3, 1945, approximately two weeks after a major layoff in the department, two premium ship-fitters (James Nangle and Harry Guthapfel) were called into the foreman's office and advised that the work which had justified their premium rate was being discontinued and that they were being reduced to mechanics at $1.20 per hour. Both of these men were what is known in the shipbuilding industry as "premium men." Premium men, as distinguished from premium trades in this industry, are individual employees who receive a rate of pay in excess of the rate for the classification at which they work. The higher rate is paid for exceptional skill and ability.

The Union protested the company's action and filed a grievance which read in part as follows: "The Union contends that these men should be rerated back to the premium rate they enjoyed prior to the layoffs since it is common knowledge that premium rates are established for individuals and not for individual jobs."

POSITION OF THE UNION

The Union's general position is that premium men can never be reduced to mechanics since their premium rates are paid for ability and skill and not for any particular job. So long as an individual is retained in the company's employ, he loses none of the unique qualifications which allegedly justified the original rate. Theoretically, he could be demoted to a Class A mechanic, but only if it could be shown that the employee was suffering a loss of skill and ability due to old age or some similar disabling process.

The Union argues that in the shipbuilding industry a premium man does much the same type of work as other mechanics but receives a premium-man rate almost solely because he does some of the more difficult jobs and does them so much better than the average Class A mechanic that he is entitled to a premium rate. The Union insists that, so long as he is employed and retains his health and vigor, he will both possess and use his exceptional capabilities. Consequently there is no just basis for his demotion from a premium man to a mechanic.

POSITION OF THE COMPANY

The Company made the following statement explaining its stand on the issue of the demotion of premium men to mechanics:

"It is *not* the Company's position that a premium rate is paid for the job. It is agreed that a premium rate is paid to a man who possesses exceptional skills or special qualifications, and the premium rate is paid *only* for these skills or qualifications and *not* for any particular job. *However*, the Company is obliged to pay such premium rate *only* so long as these skills or qualifications are used by the individual (for whatever reason). The Company does not appoint any individual to a premium rate unless the individual possesses exceptional skills or special qualifications and that he actually employs such skills or special qualifications. Therefore, if an individual is no longer required or able to use these skills or qualifications, the Company is no longer justified in maintaining him at a premium rate.

"In the case of the two aggrieved individuals, the premium was paid principally for the skills which they possessed *and used* in connection with the layout and processing of furnace plates. Since the cut-back in our program, furnacing of plates is not required at this time, therefore, the subject employees are no longer in a position to use such special skills as they possess, and they are now doing only such work as any 1st Class Shipfitter can do and is expected to do."

Further, the Company holds that premium rates are used in many instances to provide extra compensation for a combination of exceptional individual ability *and* type of work. This was done to avoid a multiplicity of classification rates of pay and to provide for a sensible flexibility in the wage structure. In addition, the Company points out that there are premium men whose skill is so specialized that the elimination of one or a number of specific tasks leaves them with skills which they never use, and at the regular mechanic's work they are no better than good Class A mechanics. Thus if a machinist received his premium rate only because he had a specialized skill as a planer and that machine is shut down for a long period of time on a semipermanent basis, that man would work on other machines and might be no better than an average Class A machinist on the other work. The Company argues that this is the situation in the case of the two aggrieved employees, and that the Union is unrealistic in relating premium rates to individual ability alone, without in turn relating this ability to some particular job which the employee performs.

QUESTIONS

1. Were Nangle and Guthapfel paid a higher or "premium" rate on the shipfitter job, or were they paid a rate for a specialized job classification, a subdivision of the shipfitter job?

2. How would the Company and the Union answer the above question?

3. Does the case involve the transfer between two job classifications?

4. What wage rates are paid typically during a temporary or a permanent transfer?

5. Should the case be treated as a problem of a change in job content? (See cases on wage structure, Section G.)

CASE 32

WAGE RATE OF "BUMPING" EMPLOYEE

UNION: American Communications Association, CIO

COMPANY: Marconi Telegraph Company

In June, 1941, the telegraph office of the *Monitor*, a Pittsburgh newspaper, was closed down. The manager of a press office, who had been receiving a salary of $103 a month, was displaced. In accordance with the collective agreement, he exercised his right to "bump" into an equal or lower classification and in so doing "bumped" a Morse operator. The latter's salary had been $110 a month, and the highest pay in that classification was $112 a month. The Company continued to pay the manager $103 after he had "bumped" the operator.

The Union protested that, according to the contract, the manager should have received $112.

POSITION OF THE UNION

The Union based its claim on the following sentence in the collective agreement:

"When an employee is furloughed from his normal classification, his office seniority may be exercised to bump employees with less office seniority in other equal or lower classifications for which the furloughed employee is qualified at the wage rate not less than the maximum wage rate in effect in that classification or District."

Since the classification into which the manager "bumped" was equal to or lower than his own had been, and since the maximum wage rate of that classification was $112, the Union claims that the Company violated the contract in continuing to pay him his old salary. The fact that the maximum wage rate in effect in the operator's classification was higher than that in effect in the "bumping" employee's original classification is irrelevant to the question at hand.

POSITION OF THE COMPANY

The Company claimed that the whole intent of the section covering involuntary furloughs is to assure senior employees who are about to be furloughed an opportunity of retaining employment with the Company by exercising their seniority in order to "bump" employees with less seniority. It is certainly not the purpose of this section to grant senior employees advances in compensation. The object of "bumping," in other words, is to preserve employment and not to increase pay.

The Company also presented evidence purporting to demonstrate that its interpretation of this section of the contract was in fact the established one, and that, although this provision was included in the 1939 agreement, the Union did not challenge the company's interpretation until the present case.

THE ARBITRATION AWARD

The company's interpretation is correct for the reasons presented in its argument.

The board of arbitration unanimously held that furloughed employees who "bump" into lower classifications shall receive the maximum wage rate only when the maximum is less than the rate received by the employee in the position from which he was furloughed. In case the maximum rate in the lower classification exceeds the employee's wage rate, he shall continue to receive the wage rate on the job from which he was furloughed.

QUESTIONS

1. Was the decision of the arbitration board in plain violation of the terms of the contract?

2. Is there any defense for the decision of the board of arbitration in this case? Do you attach significance to the fact that the Union representative on the board joined in the decision?

3. What, in your judgment, was the purpose of the section in the agreement relied upon by the Union in this case? Was the section well worded to achieve its purpose?

CASE 33

WHAT IS A PROMOTION?

UNION: United Packinghouse Workers of America, CIO

COMPANY: Armour and Company

The contract between Armour and Company and the United Packinghouse Workers of America provides, in part, as follows:

> "Seniority will operate on a departmental basis. Promotions, layoffs and re-employment will be based on length of continuous service, provided that the individual can perform the job to the satisfaction of the management, and provided further that this will not be used for the purpose of discrimination against any employee."

The present case raises the question of what a "promotion" is. The Company has been applying the above clause on the assumption that "promotions take place through advantageous movement at the same or to a higher rate of pay." This has led to the canvassing of men at the same or lower rate of pay when a job opens up. The Union challenges the company's interpretation of "promotion" and its administration of the seniority clause. It claims that all men, regardless of rate of pay, should be canvassed when a job opens up.

The present grievance is raised specifically in the motive power department and reads as follows:

> "On the 3:00 P.M. to 11:00 P.M. oiling job that is open at 87½ cents per hour, the management is not going to the

head of the seniority list and contacting from the oldest man down. Only those men are contacted who are making this rate or less. We contend that all men in the department should be contacted so they can accept or reject this job, so they might exercise shift preference."

POSITION OF THE UNION

The Union considers that management is interpreting the word "promotion" too narrowly. Promotion means improvement. Improvement can take place in other ways than in monetary income alone. A job on a more agreeable shift, an easier job, a cleaner job, a job with more chances of advancement, may all be a "promotion." A broad point of view should be applied, not one limited to dollars and cents. No single concept of a promotion should be applied.

The Union argues that its own interpretation of what constitutes a promotion need not necessarily be identical with management's view. The Union further holds that one employee might look at a promotion differently than another employee. Consequently, it is considered important that each man should have a chance to decide what he individually views as a promotion. In the union's opinion, this should mean that *all* persons on the seniority list should be canvassed when a job opens up. Seniority gives a man the right to bid for the job he wants most, even though at a lower rate.

Finally, the Union contends that the Company did practice complete canvassing for some period between 1943 and 1946 and that the policy imposed no burden upon the Company. The Union requests that this practice become a permanent policy.

POSITION OF THE COMPANY

The Company maintains that the contract does not require complete canvassing. A promotion is viewed as the reassignment of a worker to a higher-rate job. The Company argues that this has been its practice for seventy-five years, and the contract does not, nor did it intend, to change it. Complete canvassing would create an impossible situation. The Company points out that it would have to canvass the entire seniority list every time it wanted to hire a common laborer. This procedure is felt to be so cumbersome, fruitless, and time-consuming as to be unworkable.

The Company admits that for a short time in 1943 it did canvass the gang but this went beyond the contract, was improper, and was stopped. It was never taken advantage of by any single higher-paid man and never applied to all jobs in the gang but only to the ones involving some skill.

QUESTIONS

1. What group of employees should be canvassed under an agreement when considering a promotion?
2. What group should management consider in the case that there is no bargaining representative?
3. What elements do workers consider in determining whether or not a particular job classification would constitute a promotion?
4. What administrative rules would you suggest to minimize problems of "canvassing"? How do you appraise the device of posting job vacancies?

CASE 34

WHEN DOES AN EMPLOYEE BEGIN TO ACCUMULATE SENIORITY?

UNION: International Association of Machinists

COMPANY: Boeing Aircraft Company

Clarke Hadfield was promoted to the job of Riveter C when he had worked with the Company for a period of less than 90 days. The 4 assistant riveters who had established seniority apparently were not available or otherwise not prepared to take the promotion. The Company had to go outside of the workers who had at least 3 months of employment. In choosing one of these persons for promotion, the

Company selected Mr. Hadfield without strict regard to his seniority.

Position of the Union

The Union contends that when someone is to be upgraded, the Company should take the person highest in order of seniority regardless of the time that he has served. It is the union's view that if a person has been working 3 days he has a seniority over one who has worked a lesser period, and further that this seniority should be made effective at once. The Union argues that Article 7, Section B, of the agreement covers the situation fully. It provides, in part, as follows: "All employees coming under this agreement will be entitled to exercise their rights as established under the Arbitration procedure, regardless of length of service."

The Union further states that Article 8, Section B of the present contract was included during negotiations for the purpose of minimizing the paper work involved in calculating the seniority of employees subject to a considerable turnover. According to the Union, its purpose and intention was not to limit seniority.

Position of the Company

The Company bases its position on Article 8, Section B, of the Labor Relations Agreement which reads in part as follows:

"Paragraph 1.—The first three months of employment shall be considered temporary and without seniority.

"Paragraph 2.—Following three months of continuous service, seniority is established retroactive to the date of employment."

According to the Company, these provisions provide that there is no seniority until after 90 days. The effect of the contract clause is to give the employee a *potential* seniority during the first 3 months which becomes an *effective* absolute seniority, the first moment of the day following the 3 months' initial period. Therefore, the Company argues that in promoting persons who have not worked 90 days, it may select those best qualified to do the work, without reference to seniority.

The Company insists that the express intent and purpose of the contract is to make the date of hiring the date of seniority after a period of 3 months. It denies that the intent of the seniority contract provisions was to economize on time in keeping records on workers employed for only short periods.

QUESTIONS

1. State carefully the issue in dispute.
2. What is the purpose of Paragraph 1 of Article 8, Section B, of the agreement?
3. How do you reconcile Article 7, Section B, and Article 8, Section B?

CASE 35

REFUSAL OF A POSITION AS A BAR TO FUTURE PROMOTION

UNION: United Packinghouse Workers of America, CIO

COMPANY: Swift and Company, Omaha Plant

When the job of tank cook became vacant in October, 1943, the foreman offered it to Paul Mellitzer because of his superior seniority rights. Mellitzer at that time refused this job, although it was more advantageous in some respect, including rate, than the one which he then held. On March 28, 1944, this tank-cook job again was open. Although Mellitzer still held top seniority, the foreman did not again ask him if he wanted the job but instead gave it to another employee with less seniority. Then, about the middle of May, Mellitzer complained to his steward that he had not been offered the job and that he wanted it. On June 7, the steward filed a claim with the foreman for the job, on Mellitzer's behalf. Mellitzer got the job on June 29, 1944.

The instant grievance arose out of the union's claim that Mellitzer should have been offered the job as soon as it was open again on March 28, 1944. It contended that the company's failure to do so constituted a breach of the seniority provisions of the contract. The relevant section thereof reads as follows:

> (45) "Seniority will operate on a combination of departmental and plant basis. Layoffs and re-employment will be based on length of accumulated plant service. Promotions and demotions within the foregoing units will be based on length of accumulated departmental service, provided the employee can perform the operation or can learn the operation within a reasonable time."

The Union therefore demanded back pay for Mellitzer in the amount represented by the difference which it would have made in his earnings had he been offered the job in March and had duly accepted it.

The Company claimed that it was entitled to assume that Mellitzer, having once refused an offer of the job, still did not want it. It claimed that Mellitzer knew at the time that the job again fell open, that it was available for him, and that he could have had it merely by saying that he wanted it. The fact that he did not request it, argues the Company, is presumptive evidence that he did not want it at the time and justifies the company's assumption to that effect.

QUESTIONS

1. Is the refusal of a job by an employee to be regarded as permanent? Or is he entitled to be notified that the job is open to him on the basis of his seniority every time it becomes vacant?
2. If you hold that Mellitzer should have been offered the job, is he entitled to back pay and if so, from what date?
3. If Mellitzer knew that the job of tank cook had become vacant,

was he under any obligation to notify the management of his desire to be promoted to the job?

CASE 36

THE "HEAD-AND-SHOULDERS" PRINCIPLE IN PROMOTION

UNION: United Automobile Workers of America, CIO

COMPANY: General Motors Corporation

On August 4, 1941, a reliefman vacancy occurred on the first shift of Occupational Group No. 20, at Plant No. 3 of the Chevrolet gear and axle division of General Motors. This occupational group includes the Spring Housing job and the King Pin Support job.

Employee T was selected to fill the vacancy. A grievance submitted by employee M claimed that, in accordance with Paragraph 63 of the national agreement, his seniority and previous experience entitled him to the reliefman's job.

Paragraph 63 of the Agreement provides:

"The transferring of employees is the sole responsibility of the Management. In the advancement of employees to higher paid jobs when ability, merit and capacity are equal, employees with the longest seniority will be given preference. Any claims of personal prejudice or any claims of discrimination for union activity in connection with transfers may be taken up as grievances."

Management noted that the Spring Housing and the King Pin Support jobs had not been in regular production since 1938 and were operated at this time to supply service parts. Employees are used interchangeably between the two operations and the reliefman is also required to be able to work on both types of work. The relief job in question was not in operation at the time of the discussion of the case in the earlier steps of the grievance procedure, but the Union "requested that M be placed in line for the job so that when work is resumed he will be made the reliefman."

The previous experience of T on this work included service as a reliefman on the King Pin Support job when it was in production as a separate job. He had had other service as a reliefman in this occupational group, but no significant experience as a reliefman on the Spring Housing job. Altogether T had had about twenty months' experience as a reliefman and had a seniority date of November 21, 1930.

The claimant in this case, employee M, had served as a reliefman on the Spring Housing job when it was in regular production, but apparently had had no experience as a reliefman on the King Pin Support job. His experience as a reliefman totaled approximately eleven months, and he had a seniority date of March 12, 1924.

Neither T nor M had ever been classified as a reliefman, but had held jobs which gave them a chance to work intermittently as reliefmen.

THE ISSUE

The relative weight to be given to ability, merit, capacity, and seniority under a clause requiring that employees with the longest seniority shall be given preference when ability, merit, and capacity are equal.

POSITION OF THE UNION

The Union recognized that the relief job in question required a considerable versatility to do various operations. The Union also recognized that only a few men have such all-around experience because the jobs were for past-model service rather than for current-model production. The Union contended, however, that M was, not only better qualified for the job, but had greater seniority than T. In its brief, the Union expressed its belief that, under Paragraph 63,

"when a promotion is to be made, the Agreement implies that the employee with the longest seniority shall be the first considered and in the event he can do the job adequately, he is to be given the promotion without the personality comparisons usually made in promoting men.''

POSITION OF THE COMPANY

Management held that T had better qualifications than M to fill the reliefman vacancy. Of the sixteen machines included in the King Pin Support job, T was said to have set up fourteen and to have operated all sixteen. Of the seventeen operations on the Spring Housing job, T had set up fifteen and had operated sixteen of them. Management had weighted T's experience, which was said to provide him with better qualifications than M, who, it was claimed, had not set up any of the sixteen machines in the King Pin Support job and had operated only eight of them. Of the Spring Housing machines, management reported that M had set up experience on ten and operating experience on thirteen of them.

The selection of an employee for transfer to this vacancy had to take into account, states management, the necessity for interchanging employees between the two types of work. Therefore, it continued, the best-qualified candidate for the reliefman's job would be the one who was most familiar with the various jobs. T's longer and wider experience as a reliefman on both the King Pin Support job and later in Group No. 20 was considered to have given him superior claim to the job. The selection of T, management maintained, was a proper exercise of management's responsibility as outlined in Paragraph 63 of the national agreement.

DECISION OF THE IMPARTIAL UMPIRE

The umpire's ruling introduced the ''head-and-shoulders'' principle for interpreting Paragraph 63.

Paragraph 63 of the June 3, 1941 agreement provides, in part: ''The transferring of employes is the sole responsibility of the management. In the advancement of employes to higher paid jobs when ability, merit and capacity are equal, employes with the longest seniority will be given preference.''

There have been marked difficulties in the effort satisfactorily to apply this clause. It is difficult to define, let alone evaluate, such intangible factors as "merit and capacity." The Union certainly errs in its present arguments, however, that the clause specifies preference to the employee with the most seniority and gives him a right to promotion "in the event he can do the job adequately." Since such an interpretation would give importance to seniority irrespective of relative "ability and capacity," the approach of the local Union is obviously not in accordance with Paragraph 63 as written.

Under Paragraph 63 seniority becomes the determining factor in a selection for promotion only as between employees whose "ability, merit and capacity are equal." In order to attribute a reasonable meaning to the clause, it must be recognized that (1) the relative ability, merit, and capacity of individual employees cannot be precisely evaluated; (2) these factors in one employee's work will be differently rated by different supervisors because their appraisal involves personal judgment; (3) seniority is, however, a definite factor that can readily be measured; (4) in making a selection for certain promotions, under this clause, management may properly proceed by designating several men whose ability, merit, and capacity are considered by management to be equal. The seniority factor can then be applied in making the choice of the individual who is to be promoted.

In considering employees for promotion under Paragraph 63, it may be that an employee's record is so outstanding that he is "head and shoulders" above any other possible candidate. In such cases, he is entitled to promotion irrespective of seniority, and, if necessary, management should have no difficulty in pointing out his superior qualifications. Unless such an individual is available for promotion, Paragraph 63 can properly be effectuated by management's selection of several employees who are competent to fill the job and whose "ability, merit and capacity" are considered by management to be approximately equal. From the several candidates adjudged by management to be approximately equal in "ability, merit and capacity," it would then become possible to effectuate Paragraph 63 by selecting for promotion that individual in the group who has the greatest seniority.

Such a procedure follows Paragraph 63 in recognizing that qualifications of several employees are often approximately equal and in recognizing the compelling importance of seniority in such cases. The umpire must assume that the parties sought to give compelling importance to seniority as respects certain promotions or Paragraph 63 would have been written in different terms. It is emphasized that, under such a procedure, management retains the sole responsibility for designating the employees who are to be promoted.

How would such a procedure be applied to the facts of the present case? Management has made its choice as between T and M principally on the basis of the relative number of machines on the relief job, that had been previously operated by each of these men. To be sure, this is a factor that is important because of the nature of the job. The relative ability of these men in operating such jobs is, however, a considerably different fact, and the mentioned experience has little to do with merit and capacity. It is the opinion of the umpire that the evidence does not show that T had the outstanding "ability, merit and capacity" for the job in question.

It is to be noted that the relief job is not now being operated. This provides an opportunity to apply the above-outlined procedure when it resumes operation. At that time the job should again be considered as a vacancy. If a review of the qualifications of the candidates for the job shows that one is "head and shoulders" above all others not only in experience but in ability, merit, and capacity, it is in conformance with Paragraph 63 for management to assign him to the job. If such an individual is not available, management may designate two or three employees who are competent to take the assignment and who are considered by management as being approximately equal in ability, merit, and capacity. The individual assigned to the vacancy should be the one in the group who holds the greatest seniority.

QUESTIONS

1. Does Paragraph 63 indicate whose judgment of "ability, merit and capacity" shall govern?

2. Suppose the Union and the management disagree as to the relative abilities of two rival candidates for promotion. Is this the kind of dispute on which the judgment of an outside neutral would be useful?

3. Is it part of the skill and special competence of management to appraise the capacities of workers and to decide which workers are best fitted for which places? Is this one of the duties for which managers are hired? Is it the purpose of Paragraph 63 to transfer this responsibility from management to the umpire?

4. The umpire's decision says: "The Umpire must assume that the parties sought to give compelling importance to seniority as respects certain promotions or Paragraph 63 would have been written in different terms." Reread Paragraph 63, and comment upon the above statement of the umpire. Is it reasonable to interpret Paragraph 63 as intended to give "compelling importance to seniority" when the paragraph states that employees with longest seniority will be given preference "when ability, merit and capacity are equal"? Is it more reasonable to interpret Paragraph 63 as intended to give "compelling importance" to ability, merit, and capacity?

5. Did the umpire interpret Paragraph 63, or did he re-write the paragraph and change the meaning of the agreement? Did he exceed his authority as an arbitrator?

6. If it is held that Paragraph 63 was intended to substitute the judgment of the umpire for the judgment of the management in cases where the "ability, merit and capacity" of candidates for promotion are in dispute, is the burden of proof upon the Union to show that its view of "ability, merit and capacity" is correct and that of the management wrong? Does the "head-and-shoulders" principle enunciated by the umpire change the locus of the burden of proof? Does it relieve the complainant from the neces-

sity of making out a prima facie case? Does the opinion of the umpire indicate any view on this matter?

7. Is the principle enunciated by the umpire that the management may disregard seniority only when "an employee's record is so outstanding that he is 'head and shoulders' above any other possible candidate" consistent with the wording of Paragraph 63 stipulating that seniority will be given preference "when ability, merit and capacity are equal"?

8. The umpire implies at the opening of his decision that his interpretation of Paragraph 63 is necessary in order "to attribute a reasonable meaning to the clause." Do you agree?

9. If the Company believes that the umpire has abused his discretion in this case by altering the agreement instead of interpreting it, has it any remedy? How might a remedy be given the Union and the Company against abuse of discretion by the umpire?

CASE 37

SENIORITY RIGHTS AFTER A TRANSFER BETWEEN BARGAINING UNITS

UNION: United Automobile Workers of America, CIO

COMPANY: General Motors Corporation

On August 18, 1942, the Delco Brake Division and the Moraine Products Division of the General Motors Corporation were consolidated under one management. The new organization became known as the "Moraine Products Division." The plant buildings of the two former subdivisions are on the same property and immediately adjacent to each other. Two unions represent the employees in the new Moraine Products Division. The production and maintenance employees of the old Delco Brake Division have been represented exclusively by the United Automobile Workers of America, CIO, under an agreement dated October 19, 1942. This is a national agreement covering many plants of General Motors. Production and maintenance employees of the old Moraine Products Division had been, and at the time of this case, were represented exclusively by the United Electrical, Radio and Machine Workers of America, CIO, under an agreement dated November 2, 1942. Collective bargaining with the respective representatives under the two agreements was carried on by one set of management officials with like policies being applied to both collective bargaining units.

Since the consolidation of the two former divisions, approximately 300 employees have been transferred across bargaining unit lines to meet production requirements.

Employee B was employed in the Delco Brake Division under the UAW bargaining unit. On December 7, 1943 he was transferred to the section of the Moraine Products Division represented by the UE. There was no protest of this transfer. On January 5, 1944, he was discharged for disciplinary reasons, and two days later he presented a grievance through Local 696 of the UAW requesting that he be returned to work in line with his seniority rights under the provisions of the agreement of October 19, 1942, with the UAW. The Union asks that B be returned to work in that part of the plant represented by the UAW and that he be granted back pay for all time lost since the date of his grievance.

The Union contends that employee B holds seniority in that part of the plant represented by the UAW bargaining unit in accordance with Paragraphs 59, 64(e), 64(f), 70, and 105 of the October 19, 1942 agreement. It holds that Management's failure to return B to work under the UAW bargaining unit represented a violation of the seniority rights accorded to B by the noted provisions of the national agreement.

Paragraph 59 of the UAW contract reads as follows: "Seniority shall be by non-interchangeable occupational groups within departments, groups of departments or plant-wide, as may be negotiated locally in each plant and reduced to writing." (The remainder of the paragraph provides for plant-wide seniority when changes in methods, products or policies would otherwise require the permanent laying off of employees.)

Paragraph 64(e) and (f) of the UAW agreement reads:

"Seniority shall be broken for the following reasons:
"*e*) If he is laid off for twenty-four consecutive months. . . . .

"*f*) Employees with seniority who are laid off and who are not recalled to work on war production during the period of the war by the plant in which they now have seniority, shall not break their seniority with that plant until they are laid off for a continuous period following the date of termination of the war equal to that which would otherwise break their seniority under Paragraph 64(*e*)."

Paragraph 70 reads: "Temporary employees will not be called back until all employees with seniority capable of doing the work have been called back."

Paragraph 105 reads:

"For six months after production begins in a new plant, the Corporation will give preference to the applications of laid off employees having seniority in other plants over applications of individuals who have not previously worked for the Corporation, provided their previous experience in the Corporation shows that they can qualify for the job. When employed, such employees will have the status of temporary employees in the new plant. Such employees will retain their seniority in the plant where originally acquired until broken in accordance with the seniority rules herein."

The Union claims that transfers between the two bargaining units have been protested verbally by the Union on the grounds that the seniority rights of the individuals concerned have not been protected. It admits that it has not made the transfer of seniority rights the subject of a completely processed grievance. It holds, however, that in the particular case of employee B, management's action has taken him beyond the jurisdiction of the UAW and has resulted in his discharge without the union's being able to test the cause of the discharge. On the other hand, even if the opportunity to test the discharge had been afforded the UAW, the Union holds that management's action with regard to B while he was employed in another bargaining unit in no way affected his status in the UAW bargaining unit. It asks that he be returned to work in a job covered by the UAW bargaining unit, and that he be granted back pay for all time lost.

Management observes that the transfer of B's seniority between the two bargaining units has been handled in the same manner as other transfers between the two plants since they were first grouped into one organization. It points out that all employees transferred from one bargaining unit to the other "have carried their full seniority with the Division to the new unit after sixty days." When employees have been transferred between the two units, management states, their names have been placed on the seniority lists (in order of their original hiring date with the division) of the new bargaining unit after sixty days in the new unit.

Management holds that, if the union's position in this case was supported, it "would create a situation in which employees temporarily working in another part of the plant designated as another separate bargaining unit would be immune to disciplinary control regardless of the employee's action or conduct. . . ." and that "Management's only recourse would be to transfer the employee back to the unit in which he holds his seniority." Management interprets the results of such a procedure as creating "a double standard of conduct—one for those working exclusively in one bargaining unit and another for those whose work takes them into another bargaining unit." Management concludes, therefore, that it was "within its rights to discharge B for cause and break his seniority with the Moraine Products Division."

The Union counters by repeating that after B had been transferred out of the UAW bargaining unit into the UE bargaining unit, he still retained his seniority rights in the UAW bargaining unit. Those rights existed under the October 19, 1942 agreement. What happened to B, says the Union, as an employee when he was covered by the UE bargaining unit could be of no concern to the local UAW bargaining unit because its jurisdiction did not extend in any manner into the jobs covered by the UE bargaining unit. Whether B's discharge was for cause, then, could not be tested by the UAW bargaining unit, and B's seniority rights under the terms of the October 19, 1942 national agreement could not be affected by that discharge.

DECISION OF THE IMPARTIAL UMPIRE

The reorganization of the Delco Brake Division and the Moraine Products Division into one single organization was designed by management to effect certain efficiencies entirely within its own right of determination.

On the other hand, such a reorganization could not affect the seniority rights of the employees who gained such rights under the seniority provisions of the October 19, 1942 agreement. Those rights continued to exist in full form and effect regardless of any reorganization which management may have established.

The fact that the local union did not protest the method of transfer of employee B, and has not formally protested the transfer of other employees between the two bargaining units, affects the final disposition of the present grievance, but it cannot dissolve the seniority rights of the individual employees who are afforded such rights by the October 19, 1942 agreement. It should be observed that even if the local union and local management had entered into a local agreement permitting transfers of seniority between bargaining units, such an arrangement would have been nullified by the terms of Paragraph 168 of the October 19, 1942 agreement, which prohibits the local agreement from changing or eliminating any provision of the national contract.

When employee B was transferred out of the UAW bargaining unit, it is highly probable that a violation occurred with respect to the seniority rights he possessed under the terms of the national agreement and the local seniority agreement.

After B had been transferred out of the UAW bargaining unit into the UE, he still retained his seniority rights within the UAW. What happened to B while he was covered by the UE bargaining unit could be of no concern to the local UAW bargaining unit because its jurisdiction did not extend in any manner into the jobs covered by the UE bargaining unit. Whether B's discharge was for cause, then, could not be tested by the UAW bargaining unit, and B's seniority rights under the terms of the October 19, 1942 agreement could not be affected by that discharge.

Since seniority rights granted by the October 19, 1942 agreement do not extend beyond the UAW bargaining unit, it must be held that B still retained his seniority standing in the section of the Moraine Products Division covered by that agreement at the time of his discharge from a job covered by the UE bargaining unit. Inasmuch as he still held these UAW seniority rights, he had a right to be returned to a job in that section of the plant covered by the national agreement of October 19, 1942. It is ruled therefore that B shall be returned to work in accordance with his seniority rights in that section of the Moraine Products Division covered by the October 19, 1942 contract between the corporation and the UAW.

QUESTIONS

1. What issues are raised by this case?
2. Did employee B still have seniority in the Delco Division at the time that he was discharged from the old Moraine Division?
3. Does a discharge for cause ordinarily break a man's seniority record?
4. If the UAW had been the bargaining agent for the part of the plant in which employee B was working at the time of his discharge, how would you have decided this case?
5. Does the fact that the UAW was unable to contest employee B's discharge affect his seniority rights?
6. Could employee B have contested his discharge through the UE? Would the Union be under any obligation to represent a non-member? Is any employee in the Delco Division who is transferred

into the part of the plant corresponding to the Moraine Products Division deprived of protection against arbitrary action by the management?

CASE 38

THE USE OF AN EXCEPTIONAL LIST

UNION: United Automobile Workers of America, CIO

COMPANY: General Motors Corporation

Early in June, 1941, the management, a General Motors Fisher Body plant, decided in the face of potential extended reductions in its work force to review the "exceptional employee list" in relation to the anticipated needs of the plant. As a result a revised "exceptional list" was completed on June 17, which management holds was in keeping with Paragraph 73 of the national agreement.

The paragraph reads as follows:

"The employment of the following persons shall not be governed by seniority rules: indentured apprentices, exceptional employees as defined below. . . . . Exceptional employees are employees who have a skill needed in facilitating the start of a new model or at times working forces are reduced. A separate list of such employees will be posted in the Employment Department and be available to the Committeemen. Any employee whose name is removed from this list will be subject to the rules regarding seniority. Any complaint by the Union in regard to the listing of any employee on the list shall be handled according to the Grievance Procedure."

During the latter part of June a layoff occurred, somewhat in advance of the usual seasonal reductions at this plant, because of the curtailment in automobile production occasioned by a limitation of materials. When the layoff occurred, management used the newly revised exceptional list in selecting those who were kept on the payroll. This procedure was noted by the Union to have been unusual because for many years, when the plant curtailed operations, salaried personnel performed the necessary work and any required additions were made on the basis of seniority.

The Union objected to the use and extent of the exceptional list. It asserted that an exceptional list was not needed in this plant, and it requested the umpire to abolish the list and require management to give seniority the consideration provided under the agreement.

In March and June, 1941, just prior to extensive layoffs, extensive revisions had been made in the exceptional list. Comparisons of the list for August 8, 1940, March 10, 1941, and June 17, 1941, were made. These showed considerable turnover of those included and the inclusion of five rather than the original two departments.

Position of the Union

The Union makes six principal points:

1. It asserts that an exceptional list is not needed in the engineering plant because most of the men are skilled artisans and craftsmen of the highest rank in their respective fields. The Union notes that the work done at this plant is of an engineering nature and claims that it is recognized that craftsmen involved in such work increase in skill and ability in proportion to experience. For this reason the Union claims an engineering plant should not be included with other plants where exceptional lists are needed to provide the skilled men necessary to retooling or starting a new model. The Union contends, therefore, that in this plant the same purpose which is served by the exceptional lists in other plants could be achieved by adherence to the regular seniority provisions of the agreement. This claim, according to the Union, is supported by the fact that the exceptional list had never before been used at this plant.

2. The Union claims that the qualifications which go to make up an exceptional employee, such as "ingenuity to create new methods and short cuts" and "a superior sense of

touch and sense of symmetry" are factors which defy measurement.

3. The Union complains that management disregarded seniority in composing the list and points out that an exceptional list is a ripe field for favoritism by foremen. Seniority is of great importance, the Union concludes, and it "must be given serious consideration before being set aside for any reason." The Union declares that management has grossly misused the exceptional list and claims that the character and application of the list has led to an almost entire disregard of those parts of the agreement "which guarantee to the employees the protection and impartiality inherent in a seniority system."

4. The Union argues that the exceptional list was too large. Approximately one-sixth of the men at work before the layoff were included in the list. The Union asserts that the proportion is greater than in any other plant in this Company. In selecting men for the list, the Union asserts, management included men only because they were above the average, whereas the list should include only important "cogs." The exceptional list was so large as to nullify the local seniority agreement.

5. The Union notes many objections to the inclusion of specific men on the list and claims that many other men with greater seniority could readily equal or surpass these men in skill and attainment. Many men were included, according to the Union, whose "exceptional status" was in serious doubt. In some skilled crafts, men of very little experience and seniority were listed. There were great variations between occupations in the proportion of men put on the exceptional list.

6. The Union objects that the exceptional list was not posted as required by Paragraph 73 of the agreement.

POSITION OF THE COMPANY

The Corporation maintains that the exceptional list was included in the agreement "so that Management may retain in periods of reduced operation those employees who have a skill needed for the proper and efficient operation of the job being done," and "to operate the department properly and efficiently when and if full-time operations are resumed."

Management notes that prior to 1941, because of the demands for new models each year, this plant was not subject to periods of prolonged layoff, and consequently it did not make use of the exceptional list. It states, however, that such a list has been in existence since 1937 and would have been available had the committeemen requested to see it. However, conditions forced a severe curtailment of working forces, and it became necessary to make use of the exceptional list for the first time.

Management claims that employees were selected "who were most proficient in a variety of functions in their occupation." The right of the Union to challenge the listing of any employee on the list is recognized by management, but it reasons that such challenge should "be predicated on the ability of the employees selected, rather than the application of seniority status." The challenge has been made merely on the basis of seniority, the Company argues.

Finally, the management calls the umpire's attention to Paragraph 46 of the agreement which reads: "The umpire shall have no power to add to or subtract from or modify any of the terms of this Agreement."

DECISION OF THE IMPARTIAL UMPIRE

1. The claim by the Union that Paragraph 73 of the national agreement was not intended to apply to body engineering is wholly improper and is denied.

2. The request by the Union that the umpire abolish the use of the exceptional list at this plant and require adherence to straight seniority is denied. Such a finding would represent a change by the umpire of the terms of the agreement, a step that is specifically prohibited by Paragraph 46 of the agreement.

3. Management is held to have constructed and applied an exceptional list improperly; in making extensive revisions

in such a list and failing to post it, management violated Paragraph 73 of the Agreement. Management is in error to the extent that it has interpreted the exceptional list to mean a preferred group of men whom it determines, through subjective appraisal, to be the best workers in each occupation and who, because of their ability to do their particular jobs slightly better than others in their occupation, are thereby to be used in periods of reduced operations.

4. The umpire is of the opinion that the "exceptional status" of many of the workers on the list is extremely doubtful.

5. The question is returned to the parties, with suggestions for improvement, for immediate collective bargaining. Disputes over the inclusion of any particular employees may be resubmitted to the umpire for final decision.

QUESTIONS

1. Do you agree with the umpire that he had no authority to abolish the exceptional list? Can you imagine any circumstances under which the umpire might order the list abolished?

2. How much discretion does the management have in selecting men to be included on the exceptional list? In the event the Union does not regard a man as exceptional as defined by Paragraph 73 of the agreement and the management does, may the management be governed by its judgment? Note that the essential question is one of which men the management would like to use in maintaining operations at times when versatility is especially needed.

3. Is the Union correct in asserting that the qualifications which go to make up an exceptional employee, such as "ingenuity to create new methods and short cuts," are qualities which defy measurement? Does the agreement require that management, in determining which employees should be classified as exceptional, refrain from using qualities which are difficult to measure?

4. May the umpire order a reduction in the size of the exceptional list? What yardstick should be employed in determining the maximum proportion of employees which may be included on the exceptional list?

5. Was the umpire correct in instructing the parties to bargain over the issues involved in this case?

6. Under what sort of conditions do you regard an exceptional list as appropriate? And when is it an unwarranted change in the seniority principle? What procedures would you suggest for placing employees on such a list?

Section E

WORK SCHEDULES AND
PREMIUM PAY

FUNDAMENTAL interests of managements and unions are involved in the determination of work schedules. The hours of operations and the extent of work at premium rates are decisive for the costs of a management. The amount of leisure time and its distribution through the day and week are equally vital to workingmen.

The managements of many enterprises desire a schedule of operations different from the regular work week prevailing in the community, such as the current eight hours per day, Monday through Friday. In some instances technological and cost considerations are responsible for around-the-clock operations as in oil refineries, blast furnaces, and flat glass plants. The daily starting and stopping of these processes would be impracticable. Maintenance, heating, and protective services in most plants for these reasons require special schedules. In other cases the nature of the demand for the product creates the atypical schedule. Thus, utilities and railroads provide continuous service; the morning and evening rush hours in transit operations create unique scheduling problems; the hours of drugstores are a result of the peculiar role that institution plays in the American folkways. Managements will be interested in working schedules which permit flexibility of operations in response to changes in demand.

These illustrations indicate that a distinction must be drawn between the hours of operations of a plant or a place of business and the schedule of hours worked by an individual employee. The employee may work a fixed schedule each week, a rotating schedule among different shifts, or a staggered schedule which will constitute a cycle over a period of weeks. A simple staggered schedule which repeats itself every fourteen days is four days on and two days off followed by six days on and two days off.

It will be helpful to distinguish the following aspects of work schedules: (*a*) the schedule of operation of the plant, (*b*) the regular work schedule of the individual employee, and (*c*) the hours of work of the individual outside of his schedule. The agreement will typically contain provisions relating to all these problems.

The schedule of operations of the plant is usually listed as one of the matters on which the management may exercise sole discretion. Agreements normally specify that work performed by an individual employee in addition to his regularly scheduled work week shall be compensated for at premium rates. Unions further seek in many cases to provide by agreement that even scheduled hours of work at less desirable work periods, such as Sunday, be paid at premium rates. Managements have resisted the extension of such limitations on operations, in the form of higher costs, on the grounds that the less desirable hours of scheduled work were inherent in the industry and evident to any employee accepting a job in the industry. Unions have in effect sought to transfer to the consumer the costs of the inconvenience of undesirable schedules of work.

While managements have been concerned to secure work schedules for plants and the work force which are most satisfactory in terms of the technological, cost, and demand features of the business, a union will have other considerations in mind. Most employees probably prefer to have consecutive days off, to be away from work on Saturday and on Sunday, and to work consecutive hours daily rather than to have the day broken into several working periods (e.g., four hours on, three hours off, and four hours on again—all for eight hours' pay), as in the transit and restaurant fields. The union will seek typically to secure working schedules for individual workers which conform as closely as possible to these tastes of workingmen. Where less desirable schedules are essential, the union will typically seek not only to secure a premium rate but also to have the preferred jobs allocated among workers on a principle approved by the union, such as seniority.

The administration of a given work schedule and premium-pay provisions of the agreement will significantly influence costs. The same provisions may be made effective in a variety of ways. The cases which follow illustrate some of the problems in the negotiation and administration of these contract provisions.

CASE 39

DOES THE SPECIFICATION OF THE REGULAR WORKING DAY PRECLUDE OTHER REGULAR HOURS FOR WORK?

Union: International Longshoremen's Association, Locals 38–82

Company: Marine Service Bureau of Los Angeles

Some employers affiliated with the Marine Service Bureau have been operating with 4-hour and 5-hour shifts. This has been done by changing shifts at noon. The morning shift works 4 hours and the afternoon shift, 5 hours.

Hours of work in the industry are governed by Section 2 of a previous arbitrator's award. It reads as follows:

"Six hours shall constitute a day's work. Thirty hours shall constitute a week's work, averaged over a period of four weeks. The first six hours worked between the hours of 8 A.M. and 5 P.M. shall be designated as straight time. All work in excess of six hours between the hours of 8 A.M. and 5 P.M., and all work during meal time and between 5 p.m. and 8 a.m. on week days and from 5 p.m. on Saturdays to 8 a.m. on Monday, and all work on legal holidays, shall be designated as overtime. Meal time shall be any one hour between 11 a.m. and 1 p.m. When men are required to work more than five consecutive hours, without an opportunity to eat, they shall be paid time and one-half of the straight or overtime rate, as the case may be, for all time worked in excess of five hours without a meal hour."

Position of the Union

The substance of the union's contention is that there is a general attempt on the part of the members of the Marine Service Bureau of Los Angeles to evade the provisions of Section 2 of the arbitrator's award as set forth above, especially that part of said section which establishes a 6-hour day. The Union further contends that the 6-hour-day clause of Section 2 means that every workman dispatched to a job has a right to expect a full 6 hours of employment, provided the work is available.

Position of the Company

The employers deny that there is a concerted movement on the part of the members of the Marine Service Bureau of Los Angeles to evade the provisions of Section 2 of the arbitrator's award by the introduction of an alleged "4-hour day" and calls attention to the distinction between a 4-hour day and a 4-hour shift. The employers admit that in some cases the employers have found a shift at 3:00 p.m. vexatious and inconvenient and have adopted the practice of changing shifts at noon, thus providing 4 hours of work for one shift in the morning and 5 hours for another in the afternoon in those instances when work was continuous through the day. Such procedure, the Company claims, is quite within the right of the employers to operate their business in the manner that seems to them to be the most economical and efficient.

The employers further contend that—

1. The contention of the ILA is not subject to arbitration under the award because the question is one specifically covered thereby, which cannot be reconsidered without consent of all parties.

2. The demand now made by the ILA was not presented to the arbitration board, was not an issue before it, and the ILA cannot now obtain the arbitration of demands relating to wages, hours, and working conditions not presented to the board.

3. The spread of employment or earnings was the sole object of the award, and any method used for that purpose can be applied to a noon shift as well as to any other.

4. ILA has submitted no evidence that any other method of changing shifts would tend to spread employment.

5. If the suggestion of the ILA were adopted, it would increase costs and embarrassments of the employers by decreasing efficiency and increasing overtime.

6. The award had been construed in other parts in conformity with the views of the Marine Service Bureau.

The employers contend, finally, that adherence to a strict interpretation of the 6-hour clause would disregard certain other provisions of Section 2 which specify that: "Thirty hours shall constitute a week's work, averaged over a period of four weeks."

ARBITRATOR'S AWARD

1. That evidence submitted is not sufficient to substantiate the claim that the employers are engaged in concerted activities to nullify the 6-hour-day clause of Section 2.

On the other hand, both evidence and testimony reveal a tendency on the part of certain employers to introduce a 4-hour shift in the morning and a 5-hour shift in the afternoon, thus avoiding the establishment of the 6-hour day, even when sufficient work exists for a 6-hour day.

2. It is the judgment of this arbitrator that the first part of Section 2 means precisely what it states, namely, that "six hours shall constitute a day's work." Any worker dispatched

to a job has a right to expect 6 hours of employment, provided sufficient work is available to warrant 6 hours of employment.

Any other construction of this clause would seem to be in conflict with the Board's intention of establishing a workday of six hours and of providing a definite workday of a fixed number of hours which each employee may expect to work.

In establishing the 6-hour day the National Longshoremen's Board [award quoted above] undoubtedly sought to spread employment as widely as possible among employees depending upon the industry for a living and to discourage the tendency of establishing long shifts without the penalty of overtime.

3. Section 11(*d*) of the Board's award reserved the employer the right "to introduce labor-saving devices and to institute such methods of discharging and loading cargo as he considers best suited to the conduct of the business." This cannot be construed as giving the employer the right to nullify the 6-hour-day clause of Section 2 by the introduction of a 9-hour day consisting of a 4- and a 5-hour shift.

QUESTIONS

1. When the length of the working day is stipulated in a labor agreement, does the period designated ordinarily mean: (1) The minimum amount of work which the employer agrees to supply? (2) The standard period which the men may be required to work without being paid at penalty overtime rates? (3) Both one and two?

2. Would the workers have a grievance under Section 2 if the employer on any day on which the men were called to work failed to supply 6 hours of employment? Is Section 2 to be interpreted as a guarantee of 6 hours' employment to all men called to work?

3. Even if Section 2 does not guarantee 6 hours' work, does it prohibit employers from regularly operating less than 6-hour shifts? In other words, does an agreement which stipulates the length of the working day and provides when penalty overtime shall begin prohibit employers from unilaterally setting up worksharing arrangements?

4. If an employer regularly operated a first shift of 6 hours, would it be permissible for him under Section 2 to operate a second shift of less than 6 hours—say 4 hours? Should a 4 hour shift starting at 3:00 P.M. be regarded as hurting the opportunity of the men to earn penalty overtime?

CASE 40

PREMIUM PAY FOR SEVENTH DAY WORKED

UNION: International Union of Mine, Mill and Smelter Workers, Local 470

COMPANY: Huxley Corporation, Antic, Arizona

The company's bull gang had been scheduled to work on each of 7 calendar days beginning on Sunday, October 29 and ending on Saturday, November 4, 1944. It should be noted that Sunday, October 29, was the normally scheduled day off for these employees. This schedule was complied with; all but two members of the gang worked the full 7 days and drew premium pay at double time for the work they performed on the seventh day. The other two members presented themselves at the plant on Saturday, November 4, but were denied the opportunity of working and were sent home. They were paid for 4 hours at straight time. The Union claimed that they should have been reimbursed for the full 8 hours at double time.

POSITION OF THE COMPANY

The Company admits that it erred in sending the two men home after they had been scheduled to work and had presented themselves at the plant. It claims, however, that it has rectified this error by awarding them 4 hours' straight-time pay pursuant to the following section of the collective bargaining agreement: "When an employee who reports for scheduled work is released without performing the work, unless the reason for such release is beyond the Company's control, he shall be paid for actual time held, with a minimum of four hours at his applicable rate."

Position of the Union

The Union denies that the circumstances of this case are controlled by the section of the agreement cited by the Company. Instead, the following section is cited as controlling: "An employee who is required to work on his scheduled day off shall not be required to lay off an offsetting day during the same work week."

The facts establish that the work week had been scheduled to begin on Sunday, October 29, and to end on Saturday, November 4. Since Sunday, October 29, was a regular day off for these men, they were in fact required to work on their scheduled day off. Therefore, under the provision of the agreement cited above, they were guaranteed work during the remainder of the work week terminating on Saturday, November 4. The company's action in sending them home constitutes a violation of that agreement, because it is tantamount to requiring them "to lay off an offsetting day during the same work week in which they had been required to work on their day off." Payment of 4 hours' straight time does not relieve the Company of its obligation to pay premium time for the seventh day of a scheduled work week which included the normal day off.

QUESTIONS

1. Would the decision be any different if the Company had notified the two employees on November 3 that they would not be required to work the next day?
2. What is the intent of the type of clause in the contract cited by the Union?
3. Which of the two clauses, one cited by the Company, and the other by the Union, should be controlling in this case?

CASE 41

WHICH PREMIUM RATE SHALL APPLY?

UNION: United Automobile Workers of America, CIO

COMPANY: Ohio Steel Foundry Company

On March 17, Clarence Potter worked from 7:00 A.M. to 3:00 P.M. and on March 18 from 11:00 P.M. to 7:00 A.M. He was paid time and one-half for the second 8 hours. The Union requests that Potter be paid double time for the hours after 11 hours, that is, for the last 5 hours of work on the second shift. The Company considers this request contrary to the provisions of the contract.

The contract provision pertinent to this issue is Article XI, Section F, which reads in part as follows:

"F. Time and one-half will be paid to all employees for all hours worked in excess of 8 hours in any one day. Double time will be paid to all employees for all hours worked in excess of 11 hours in any one day. A day shall consist of 24 consecutive hours from the time any employee begins the shift in which the work is performed. . . . ."

POSITION OF THE UNION

The Union contends that, since the contract specifies that a day shall consist of 24 consecutive hours from the time the shift begins, then all of the 16 hours of work fell within a day. The Union holds that for the hours after the first 11, Potter should have received double time. The Union points out that the Company paid time and one-half for all of the second 8-hours, thus recognizing that the second shift was hours over 8 in one day. The Union contends that double time should be paid for the hours over 11 in one day, particularly since the Company apparently relied upon this section of the contract in paying the time and one-half.

POSITION OF THE COMPANY

The Company holds that the Union is misinterpreting the contract. It is argued that the intent of the parties in negotiating the contract was to protect employees from being worked more than 11 hours in a single stretch. The Company points out that Potter was swinging from one shift to another and that he had a full 8 hours of rest between the shift ending at 3:00 P.M. and the one starting at 11:00 P.M. In such a situation, the Company insists that the double-time provision is not applicable.

QUESTIONS

1. What is the purpose of the figure of 11 hours in Article XI, section F of the agreement?
2. What is meant by "swinging from one shift to another"? Under what circumstances does this scheduling problem arise? Illustrate by example.
3. What change in the contract would you suggest to validate explicitly the position of the company? Draft such a revision in the agreement.
4. Was the clause cited by the Union intended to apply to this case?
5. When an arbitrator decides this case, what relation is he fulfilling to the collective bargaining process?

CASE 42

A CHANGE IN WEEK-END SCHEDULES

UNION: Amalgamated Association of Street, Electric Railway & Motor Coach Employees

COMPANY: Hudson County Bus Owners' Association

The Hudson County Bus Owners' Association comprises fifty-five bus owners. It acts as the employment agency for the owners. It trains the drivers, negotiates contracts, and performs other similar functions. In 1946 the Association entered into a collective bargaining agreement with the Amalgamated Association of Street, Electric Railway & Motor Coach Employees, which represents the drivers of the buses operated by the Association.

The drivers have been given a staggered day off each week so that every sixth week they have had a Saturday or a Sunday off. In the summer of 1946 the Association was able to charter their buses on week ends. They assigned as drivers of these buses the men whose day off fell on Saturday and Sunday. These men were then given another day off during the week.

The Union contends that, since the drivers were requested to work on their day off, they are entitled to overtime pay at the rate of double time for the Saturdays and Sundays they were required to work. The Company denies this claim and asserts that, since the drivers were given another day off, they are entitled to straight-time pay only.

POSITION OF THE COMPANY

The Association bases its case on Section 2, Article XVII of the agreement which reads, in part, as follows: "Each employee shall be entitled to one day off in the work week." According to the Association, this provision merely obligates it to give each employee one day off in the work week; it does not obligate it to give a Saturday or Sunday off. Therefore, the Association argues that so long as a man does not work seven days in a week he is not entitled to overtime for working any of the six days.

The Association insists on its right to assign work schedules to its employees. This is held to be of particular importance in the transportation industry where the nature of the business is such as to require a maximum of flexibility in assigning men.

On the question of the rate at which overtime is paid, the Association points out that even if overtime were to be paid for Saturday and Sunday, the Union's demand for double time has no logical basis. Section 3, Article II of the agreement provides that "overtime shall be paid for at the rate of time and one half."

Position of the Union

The Union concedes the association's right to assign work schedules to its employees. However, the Union argues that the issue in this case is not whether the Association has the right to make work schedules but whether, after having made the work assignments and following them for a substantial period of time, it can arbitrarily change the schedule of certain employees for the sole purpose of avoiding overtime payments.

The Union claims that the drivers have been working on a definite schedule which was made up by the Company. This schedule provided for a staggered day off each week so that every sixth week the men would get a Saturday or Sunday off. The Union maintains that both the Association and the drivers understood that certain days could be considered as days off and the men could plan week-end trips. In the Union's opinion, it is not equitable for the Association to make out work schedules following certain principles and then assign the men another day off just to avoid the payment of overtime. It is inequitable to require a man to work on his week end off, particularly when it comes only once every six weeks, and then not pay him overtime for it. The Union holds that the inconvenience is so great as to warrant the payment of double time.

QUESTIONS

1. What is "charter work"? Would you expect such business to be profitable from the company's point of view?
2. Is a previous work schedule a bar to a change in work schedule? What is the position of the Union on this question?
3. Is the Company obligated to assign work according to a definite schedule? Could it change its schedule of assignments daily? Why

do you suppose the Company has followed a specific schedule practice?

4. Could the Company schedule "charter work" as a part of the regular schedule? Why do you suppose it has not done this?

5. Does the Union have a contract right for a day off on Sunday?

6. What contract provision would you suggest to prevent the reoccurrence of this dispute? Draft an appropriate clause.

CASE 43

SCHEDULING OF WORK IN REPAIR SHOPS

UNION: Amalgamated Association of Street, Electric Railway & Motor Coach Employees of America, AFL

COMPANY: Twin City Rapid Transit Company

The Twin City Rapid Transit Company is engaged in the local transit industry operating streetcars and buses. It bargains with the Amalgamated Association of Street, Electric Railway and Motor Coach Employees of America and, at the time of this case, was engaged in the process of negotiating a new collective bargaining agreement. This case concerns only one of many issues relative to the new agreement—the scheduling of working hours for repairmen (day crew) in the car houses.

A street railway transportation system must supply transportation facilities on a 24-hours-a-day, 7-days-a-week basis. The demand for transportation, however, varies with the hours of the day and the days of the week. These differences result in variations in the number of cars and buses which must be repaired on any one day.

The previous agreement provided as follows in respect to the issue in dispute.

"1. *Paragraph 129*.

". . . the work schedule in each car house shall be arranged so that the Company will be able to maintain a seven day work schedule. The regular work day shall be eight hours. The work week may be made up of such number of consecutive days in each week as the Company may require to permit operation upon a seven day work schedule."

"2. *Article IV, Section 1.*

". . . the Amalgamated recognizes that all matters pertaining to the conduct and operation of the business are vested in the Company and agrees that the following matters specifically mentioned are a function of the management of the business, including, without intent to exclude things of a similar nature not specified by, the type and amount of equipment, machinery and other facilities used; the number of employees required on any work in any department; the routes and schedules of its cars and buses; the standard of ability, performance, and physical fitness of its employees and the rules and regulations requisite to safety."

Under the existing working schedule repairmen on the day crew in the car houses work an average of 44 hours per week. (Time and a half is paid after 40 hours' work per week). There are 14 men employed as repairmen. This schedule is so arranged that they receive 3 days off every 2 weeks. This may vary for the individual employee from 2 days off one week and 1 the following week, to 3 days off one week and none the next. In most cases, the schedule of 11 workdays and 3 days off is so arranged that the 3 days off are together; but sometimes there is a day off separated by a workday and then 2 days off together. The men get alternately every other week a Sunday off, and 2 other days off during the week within the course of a 2-week period. On Sunday, the Company maintains a half crew of 7, on Monday, a full crew of 14, on Tuesday 13, Wednesday 12, Thursday 11, Friday 13, Saturday 7, Sunday 7, and Monday 14 again. Then 12 on Tuesday, Wednesday, and Thursday; 13 on Friday, and then 7 the next Saturday. This schedule revolves round and round.

TWIN CITY RAPID TRANSIT COMPANY
WORKING SCHEDULES

As Scheduled—Under Present Agreement
Day Crew: Repairmen

Employee No.	Sun.	Mon.	Tues.	Wed.	Thurs.	Fri.	Sat.	Sun.	Mon.	Tues.	Wed.	Thurs.	Fri.	Sat.
1	w	w	0	w	w	w	0	0	w	w	w	w	w	w
2	w	w	w	0	w	w	0	0	w	w	w	w	w	w
3	w	w	w	w	0	w	0	0	w	w	w	w	w	w
4	w	w	w	w	w	0	0	0	w	w	w	w	w	w
5	w	w	w	0	w	w	0	0	w	w	w	w	w	w
6	w	w	w	w	0	w	0	0	w	w	w	w	w	w
7	w	w	w	w	0	w	0	0	w	w	w	w	w	w
8	0	w	w	w	w	w	w	w	w	0	w	w	w	0
9	0	w	w	w	w	w	w	w	w	w	0	w	w	0
10	0	w	w	w	w	w	w	w	w	w	w	0	w	0
11	0	w	w	w	w	w	w	w	w	w	w	w	0	0
12	0	w	w	w	w	w	w	w	w	0	w	w	w	0
13	0	w	w	w	w	w	w	w	w	w	0	w	w	0
14	0	w	w	w	w	w	w	w	w	w	w	0	w	0
Total	7	14	13	12	11	13	7	7	14	12	12	12	13	7

Schedules Required—By Union Request
Day Crew: Repairmen

Employee No.	Sun.	Mon.	Tues.	Wed.	Thurs.	Fri.	Sat.	Sun.	Mon.	Tues.	Wed.	Thurs.	Fri.	Sat.
1	0	0	w	w	w	0	0	w	w	w	w	w	w	w
2	w	w	w	w	w	w	w	0	0	w	w	w	0	0
3	0	0	w	w	w	0	0	w	w	w	w	w	w	w
4	w	w	w	w	w	w	w	0	0	w	w	w	0	0
5	0	0	w	w	w	0	0	w	w	w	w	w	w	w
6	w	w	w	w	w	w	w	0	0	w	w	w	0	0
7	0	0	w	w	w	0	0	w	w	w	w	w	w	w
8	w	w	w	w	w	w	w	0	0	w	w	w	0	0
9	0	0	w	w	w	0	0	w	w	w	w	w	w	w
10	w	w	w	w	w	w	w	0	0	w	w	w	0	0
11	0	0	w	w	w	0	0	w	w	w	w	w	w	w
12	w	w	w	w	w	w	w	0	0	w	w	w	0	0
13	0	0	w	w	w	0	0	w	w	w	w	w	w	w
14	w	w	w	w	w	w	w	0	0	w	w	w	0	0
Total	7	7	14	14	14	7	7	7	7	14	14	14	7	7

Note: w, Indicates scheduled work day; 0, indicates scheduled off day.

The Union objects to the present work schedule and asks for a change from an average work week of 44 hours to one of 40 hours plus a change in the method of scheduling workdays. The Company wishes to maintain the present work schedule and objects to the proposed change.

The foregoing exhibit contrasts the work schedules as presently in force with those proposed by the Union.

Position of the Union

The Union asks for a change in the present work week of an average of 44 hours to a work week of an average of 40 hours. In a changeover from a 44- to a 40-hour average work week, the Union maintains that the Company's present method of scheduling hours would mean that certain employees would have to be assigned to work every Sunday. The Union is desirous of a work schedule which allows the maximum amount of consecutive days off at week ends. It also desires a schedule which shortens the number of consecutive working days provided under the company's working schedules. At the present time, there are some employees who work as many as 11 consecutive days. (See, employee No. 11 in the schedule.)

Under the union's proposed schedule employees would work 7 consecutive days in one week and 3 consecutive days in the next week, with time off in between the two working periods. Thus, no employee would work more than 7 consecutive days in a 2-week period. Half-crews of 7 men would operate on Sundays, Mondays, Fridays, and Saturdays; full crews of 14 on all other days. The Union argues that operations on Saturdays and Sundays are light, and therefore there is no need for full crews. It contends that a half-crew could handle any emergency or run-in repairs that occurred on Mondays and Fridays, and that the full crews provided for Tuesdays, Wednesdays, and Thursdays could take care of the heavier repairs.

The Union maintains that its proposed work schedule allows the Company to maintain a 7-day-week schedule and is thus in accord with Paragraph 129 of the agreement. Further, the Union argues that it in no way interferes with the prerogative of management outlined in Article IV, Section 1, since its proposed changes relate only to the schedule which a particular employee may work and to the distribution of employees—not to the total number of men to be employed. The Union contends that its proposed work schedule will allow the Company to operate on a 7-day basis and more efficiently than under the present scheme.

POSITION OF THE COMPANY

The Company holds that the Union's proposal is an invasion of management's prerogatives as outlined in Article IV, Section 1, and further that the proposed schedule is completely unworkable. As the Company interprets Article IV, Section 1, exclusive responsibility for the assignment of the number of men to work on a particular day and the number of men required for operation of the property on each day is vested in the Company. It is argued that the Union is impinging on this company's right to determine "the number of employees required on any work in any department" when it sets up a work schedule which tries to alter the number of men working on specified days. The Company contends that the union's proposed schedule would have the effect of making it impossible for the Company to operate on a 7-day basis.

The Company currently treats Monday as the day with the heaviest repair-work load since it follows two lighter days, on which only half-crews have been maintained. Therefore, there is a carry-over of work which has to be picked up on Monday. Similarly, Friday is considered a heavy day since repairs and preparations are made for the week end. The Company explains further that, since only a small crew is maintained on Saturdays and Sundays, there is no general inspection made of the street cars on these two days. Under the present practice, if there is a wreck or some damage to doors or windows over the week end, that work is now held over until Monday. The Company insists that there is no way of redistributing the work, and that it does not have the facilities to concentrate all of its repairs on Tuesdays, Wednesdays, and Thursdays. The work schedule proposed by the

Union is unworkable and detrimental to public safety and service.

QUESTIONS

1. What schedule would you purpose for the 14 men working as repairmen on the day crew? What is the maximum consecutive period of work your schedule requires?

2. Is Article IV, Section 1, cited by the Company, relevant to this dispute over the terms of a new agreement? What bearing does this provision have on the issue in dispute?

3. Do you consider as valid the distinction drawn by the Union between the total number of men required in this department and the number required on any one day?

4. What further facts would you request to determine the work load required in this department on Friday through Monday?

5. In what detail in your judgment should a contract specify the schedule of operations? What principles would you develop to answer this question?

6. If there are to be regular full-time jobs in this department and the Company has concluded that 14 men are required, what determines the limits to the working schedules that can be formulated for any week or two-week period?

7. Work out a schedule on a 40-hour-work-week basis for these 14 men, giving full weight to the arguments used by the Company on the pattern of scheduling during the week.

Section F

VACATION PROVISIONS

VACATION provisions became widespread in collective bargaining agreements during the late thirties and the war period. By 1944 the Bureau of Labor Statistics could report that at least 85 per cent of all employees covered by agreements received vacation benefits.[1] Collective bargaining extended to union members a form of compensation that had prevailed for a longer period among executives and office personnel. The National War Labor Board and the wartime conditions materially accelerated the extension of the vacation with pay practice.

An examination of vacation provisions of agreements will particularly underline two points made in the introductory chapters in Part I. First, while vacations with pay are a relatively simple idea, the parties have great latitude to shape and mold a vacation plan to their special needs. Some of the more prominent features of vacation plans, outlined below, indicate the luxuriant possibilities for collective bargaining. Second, vacation provisions again underscore the fact that the administration of a contract provision may be decisive for costs or benefits. Similar provisions may be made operative in a variety of ways.

The following constitute some of the more important features of vacation plans usually specified in agreements.

a) Eligibility to vacation pay may be defined and restricted in a variety of ways. Length of service is the most frequent limitation on eligibility. Employees with various service

---

[1] *Monthly Labor Review*, September, 1947, pp. 331–34. The figure is currently, no doubt, well over 90 per cent.

records, such as one, five, and fifteen years are eligible for various rates of vacation pay. Eligibility may be limited by the test of continuous service. A variety of events—discharge, sickness, voluntary quit, military service, layoff or strike— may be variously treated as interrupting continuous service and affecting vacation rights. There are many ways of applying the test of length of service. Thus, to be eligible for a vacation with pay employees may be required to serve a full year before the start of the vacation season, or before the end of the vacation season.

b) Vacation pay may be computed in a variety of ways. It may be based upon a percentage of annual earnings. It is also calculated by multiplying hours of vacation pay by a rate of pay. The hours may be the actual hours of work during a period prior to the start of the vacation season, the scheduled hours of work of the plant, or some arbitrarily bargained figure. The rate of vacation pay may be the average hourly earnings over some base period, including the effects of overtime, or straight-time hourly earnings or even the base rate on piece-rate occupations.

c) Vacation plans typically make provision for a variety of lesser matters. The time of the year during which employees may be entitled to take their vacation may be specified. The order in which various employees may be granted preference in their choice of vacation dates must be determined for any vacation allowance during which the plant is not shut down. The status of holidays with pay that occur during a vacation period must be clarified. Are employees to receive both benefits?

Each relationship must face most of the problems outlined above in contract negotiations or in the administration of the vacation plan. There are certain to be many other questions which are peculiar to the particular relationship. The cases which follow are intended to sample a few of the issues confronting the parties on vacation provisions. These cases are suggestive of the larger universe of vacation issues.

CASE 44

IS VACATION PAY A REWARD FOR PAST SERVICE OR PREPARATION FOR FUTURE SERVICE?

UNION: United Packinghouse Workers of America, CIO

COMPANY: Armour and Company

Two employees, Dominick Panek and Gus Skoglund, would have received two weeks' vacation with pay, each, in 1945, had they not died. Panek had taken one weeks' vacation with pay before his death. The Union is presenting a grievance requesting that the latter's wife be paid for the second week's vacation. Skoglund, on the other hand, had taken no vacation, and the grievance requests that a check for two weeks' vacation pay be given his wife.

The grievances read as follows:

"Dominick Panek began working for Armour and Company in 1936. On May 1, 1945, Dominick Panek took one week of vacation. On May 7, he returned to work and worked one week, and then became sick and went home. On June 8, 1945, Dominick Panek died. Some time later his wife applied for the one week's vacation pay that he still had coming, but the Company refused to give her the vacation check. It is our contention that Dominick Panek had one week's vacation still coming and therefore this money should be given his wife."

"The committee requests that the two weeks' vacation pay due Gus Skoglund, formerly of the Sausage Department, be given his wife. It is our contention that Gus Skoglund had qualified for his vacation under the vacation clause and therefore this check should be made available for his wife."

POSITION OF THE UNION

The Union contends that the two employees in this case had fulfilled their service requirements. One man had already taken part of his vacation, and the other one had requested his vacation but had no chance to take it since he dropped dead on the job. The checks for the men were already made out but had not yet been picked up. The Union argues that in the past the Company has paid "fringe issues" to the estates of deceased employees and in at least one case paid vacation benefits to the wife of a deceased employee. This is considered as establishing a precedent in favor of the payment of vacation pay to the heirs of the deceased.

The Union holds that the men had earned their vacation pay and thus accumulated a right which should not be taken from them. Death should not fortuitously enrich the Company and deprive the survivors of the deceased of their just compensation. The Union calls particular attention to Clause 35 of the contract, which provides for two weeks' vacation with pay for male employees with over five years of service, and to Clause 44, which reads as follows: "Employees who have earned vacations under this vacation plan, but who may become sick, laid off by management, or injured prior to the date selected for their vacation, may, upon request to the management, receive their vacation pay." It is the contention of the Union that deceased employees fall in the above category of employees who are specially protected in their vacation rights since death, like sickness, injury, and stay off, is involuntary in nature.

POSITION OF THE COMPANY

The Company argues that it has never had a practice of paying vacation money to the heirs of deceased employees and that the Union has no right to present these grievances. The Union represents live people, not dead people. Dead persons are not employees, thus are not in the bargaining unit, and thus are not subject to representation by the Union. Vacations are not earned; rather they are granted. They look forward, not backward. They are not a reward for past service; they are a preparation through rest, for future service. Dead men cannot take vacations.

The Company cites Section 47 of the contract which lays down the general principle that "Employees entitled to vacation will not be allowed to take money in lieu thereof." While this is qualified by Section 44 (quoted above) which permits vacation pay, in lieu of vacations, to certain groups of people, the Company insists that dead people are not included. Further, the Company points out that employees who quit are not entitled to vacation pay, and these men quit —albeit involuntarily.

QUESTIONS

1. The Company contends that a vacation is a preparation for future service, while the Union holds a vacation is a reward for past service. How do you appraise these contending positions?

2. Is there any basis in the sections of the contracts quoted on which to choose between the two positions?

3. Should such problems be treated in the contract? Should such problems be handled in company rules?

4. Is vacation pay to be regarded as part of the wage? Is it a deferred wage payment? If the employees had died without receiving their pay checks for their last week's work, would the Company be obligated to make them payable to the deceased's heirs?

5. Apply the theory you develop in this case regarding vacations (question 1 above) to the situation in which an employee is laid off for lack of work after the first three months of service in a year and not re-employed during the year. Should vacation pay be prorated? Why or why not?

CASE 45

EFFECT OF A LAYOFF ON ELIGIBILITY

UNION: Industrial Union of Marine and Shipbuilding Workers of America, CIO

COMPANY: Wilmington Welding and Boiler Works

Article VII of the working agreement between the Wilmington Welding and Boiler Works and the Industrial Union of Marine and Shipbuilding Workers of America reads, in part, as follows:

> "Every employee of the Company who has been in the continuous employment of the Company for one year commencing August 17, 1944, or for one year commencing with the date of his employment if he has been employed since August 17, 1944, shall receive one week's vacation with pay as hereinafter set forth.
> "Every employee of the Company who may have been in the continuous employment of the Company for five years commencing August 17, 1944, or for five years commencing with the date of his employment if he has been employed since August 17, 1944, shall receive two weeks' vacation with pay as hereinafter set forth."

The present case concerns a shipfitter, Frank J. Foley. The personnel record indicates that he was hired on June 25, 1945, and continued to be employed without interruption until May 20, 1946, when he received a "clearout" due to a "reduction in force." Then on July 18, 1946, he was rehired.

The Company has refused to grant Foley a week's vacation on the ground that he has not been in "continuous employment" with the Company for a sufficiently long period, that is, for one year. The Union protests this position.

POSITION OF THE UNION

The Union contends that Foley had been in "continuous employment" with the Company for a long enough period to qualify him for one week's vacation with pay under Article VII of the contract. It argues that the contract between the parties provides for continued seniority in case of layoff up to one year after the date of layoff. Therefore, when a worker is given a "clearout" due to a reduction in force, he is still an employee of the Company since he continues to accumulate seniority. Provided this employee can otherwise qualify under the terms of the working agreement, he is entitled to vacation benefits as one in continuous employment.

The Union reasons further that if "continuous employment" means that an employee must be on the payroll all the time, i.e., that he must become ineligible whenever he is laid off because of lack of work, then a ruthless employer could so plan his layoff periods so as to make most employees ineligible for vacations with pay. In the case of Foley, except for the brief layoff period over which he had no control, his seniority rights and privileges continued throughout the period. The Union holds that Foley should be considered as having remained in continuous employment in meeting the spirit of the contract provision. To rule otherwise would mean that an employee could be required to work all but a few days each year without becoming eligible for a paid vacation.

POSITION OF THE COMPANY

The Company argues that Foley was severed from the payroll, and thus his continuous employment with the Company was broken. When the employee was rehired, he came in as a new employee. At other times when a worker is only temporarily laid off, he is so told and is instructed to return to work at a definite time. In such instances his personnel records are not closed as they are when he is given a "clearout" due to a reduction in force.

The Company states that in denying Foley a vacation with pay it is not seeking to deny vacations which workers have actually earned under the terms of the working agreement. Rather it believes that "continuous employment" means employment continuously and without break except for properly granted leaves of absence or strictly temporary layoffs where the workers are told to report again for work at a definite time. The Company insists that continuous employment, in this sense, does not prevail in the case of Foley.

Finally, the Company contends that continuous employment and seniority are two separate and unrelated subjects and that it is not proper to relate one to the other. The Company concludes that, since Foley's record shows a complete severance of the employment relationship between himself and the Company, employment was not continuous as provided by Article VII, and Foley is not entitled to vacation consideration.

QUESTIONS

1. What are the possible meanings to the phrase "continuous employment"? Consider the following examples: (*a*) working every day, (*b*) working sometime during each payroll period, (*c*) name listed continuously on the payroll, whether working or not, (*d*) continuously available for work, and (*e*) name on the seniority roster.

2. Is the status of "continuous employment" to be determined finally by the Company on the grounds that it involves complex details of payroll administration?

3. What actions or events would you regard as breaking continuous service for the purposes of Article VII—sickness, layoff, quit, discharge for cause?

4. For the purposes of Article VII is it appropriate to distinguish between layoffs with a fixed date of recall and layoffs with an indefinite date of recall?

5. How do you appraise the contention that continuous employment for purposes of vacations and for temporary layoff (seniority) should have the same meaning under the agreement? Is there any necessary relationship? Seniority rights for rehire may run typically for a year or two beyond the last date of layoff. Would you place vacation rights in essentially the same category? As a matter of union or management policy should they extend as long as seniority rights after layoff?

CASE 46

EFFECT OF A STRIKE ON ELIGIBILITY

UNION: United Packinghouse Workers of America, CIO

COMPANY: Armour and Company

The contract between Armour and Company and the United Packinghouse Workers provides that employees absent for specific reasons, including illness, for over 60 working days lose certain vacation rights. Two men, Mayfield and Lloyd, were absent 62 and 64 days respectively if the 10 days of strike in January and February, 1946, are counted as working days, and thus they lose their rights; they were absent only 52 and 54 days if the 10 days of strike are not considered working days, and thus they retain their rights. The Company insists that the first interpretation is correct. The Union holds that the second is the correct interpretation.

POSITION OF THE COMPANY

The Company argues that, while very few people reported for work during the 10-day strike period, the plant was open and the Company stood ready to put anyone to work. Thus, these 10 days were working days and should be counted as such. The Company considers only the following as nonworking days, namely, Sundays, holidays, and "dark days." "Dark days" are defined as days when the Company says no work is available. The Company does not consider strike days as "dark days" since the Company stands ready to offer work on these days; so far as the Company was concerned there was no shutdown.

POSITION OF THE UNION

The Union holds that the strike was legal and authorized on a nation-wide scale. It points out that such strikes, which embody mass organization and result in complete or virtually complete withdrawal of the labor force, are an accepted phase of our national life and part of the recognized tactics of national unions. The whole industry was on strike, and thus the men could not work. Consequently, the Union argues that days on strike are not working days but rather are legal "dark days." Any other interpretation would have the effect of using strikes as a means of impairing the rights of employment.

QUESTIONS

1. What are the possible definitions of "working days" that could be applied to this case?
2. What is the basis for the distinction between "dark days" and a strike? What did the Company mean when it stated that so far as it was concerned there was no shutdown?
3. Would it make any difference in your decision whether the two employees were sick during the 10-day-strike period?
4. How should this type of problem be handled in a collective bargaining relationship? Can it be anticipated?

CASE 47

VACATION PAY FOR PART-TIME WORKERS

UNION: United Steelworkers of America, CIO

COMPANY: Carnegie-Illinois Steel Corporation

Kaercher, Junkel, and Coles were 3 high-school students who worked as part-time laborers, after school hours, in the stockhouse of the McDonald Mills of the Carnegie-Illinois Steel Corporation. Kaercher began his service with the Company on February 22, 1944; Junkel on March 14, 1944; Coles on April 4, 1944. The Company declares that they worked on the average about 16 hours per week. In June and July, 1945, these 3 employees were granted a week's vacation pay equivalent to the average hours worked by each in the 3 calculated pay periods immediately preceding their respective vacations.

The Union protests the company's interpretation of va-

cation payment for these part-time workers and holds that
the employees are entitled to a minimum of 48 hours of vacation with pay in accordance with Subsection D of Section 7
of the labor agreement which reads in part as follows:

> "Hours of vacation pay for each vacation's week shall
> be the average hours per week worked by the employees
> in the first two of the last three closed and calculated
> periods worked by the employee preceding the first week
> of the actual vacation period, but not less than (*a*) 40
> hours per week, or (*b*) the scheduled workweek of the
> plant, whichever, is larger, nor more than (*c*) 48 hours
> per week, or (*d*) the scheduled workweek of the plant,
> whichever is larger. . . . ."

POSITION OF THE COMPANY

The Company argues that the Union is incorrect in its
position—that Subsection D (quoted above), upon which the
Union bases its case, was never intended to apply to part-time
employees. The Company maintains that it was compelled to
utilize every available source of labor because of a serious
man-power shortage. In the interest of meeting production
requirements, the Company had occasion to use male minors
during time which was available over and above their school
hours. But the Company insists that the problem of vacation
privileges for such part-time employees was not considered
by the parties in their negotiations of a labor agreement.

The Company holds that the minimum and maximum
amount of vacation pay stipulated in Subsection D of the
agreement was provided as a protection against a loss of earnings for those employees who (1) were available for work but,
for reasons beyond their control, did not work the normal
schedule of 40 hours per payroll week, or (2) worked in excess
of the 40-hour schedule. It was not intended for employees
who were only available for work on a part-time basis and
who were able to work neither the 40-hour schedule nor a

regular schedule involving a greater number of hours. The Company maintains that if the same basis of calculating vacation pay were accorded to part-time employees as to full-time employees, the effect of this would be to create an inequity between those employees who were available and would work the regularly scheduled work week and those employees who were not available and did not work the regular schedule.

Further, the Company argues that in applying the seniority provisions of the labor agreement, the Union has shown its tacit understanding of the fact that part-time employees were not to be considered in the same light as full-time employees. The Union did not challenge the action of management in promoting full-time employees over part-time employees with longer continuous service. Consequently, the Company concludes that the Union recognized that part-time employees were not covered by the seniority provisions of the labor agreement to the same extent as full-time employees. The Company holds that the same conditions which make impractical and unreasonable the application of the seniority and hours-of-work section of the agreement to part-time employees apply equally well to the vacation section.

POSITION OF THE UNION

The Union argues that part-time employees who meet the eligibility requirements specified in the agreement are entitled to the full vacation benefits which the agreement provides. The 3 employees involved in the present case fulfilled the length of service requirements as well as the 60 per cent working requirement of the vacation clause in the 1945 labor agreement. As employees of the Company, they are entitled to vacation pay based on the scheduled plant work week, namely, 48 hours. The Union holds that part-time employees are in the bargaining unit and are "employees" within the meaning of the labor agreement. They have a valid claim to the same full protection of the agreement as any other employee in the bargaining unit.

QUESTIONS

1. Are the high-school students "employees" under the agreement? Are they entitled to all the benefits of the agreement? The wage clauses? The protection against discrimination? The seniority clauses?

2. May such employees be entitled to some benefits under the agreement and not to all benefits? Is there any basis to make a separation?

3. Would the problem posed by this case have arisen if vacation pay had been based in the contract upon a percentage of earnings?

4. What answer would the Union give to the argument that granting these employees the vacation benefits demanded would create inequities among employees?

5. What is the function of the arbitrator in such a case? What is he called upon to do? What does "interpreting" the agreement mean in such a case?

CASE 48

THE INCLUSION OF A NIGHT-SHIFT PREMIUM IN THE RATE OF VACATION PAY

UNION: United Packinghouse Workers of America, CIO

COMPANY: Baker and Company, Denver Plant

This case concerns the computation of vacation pay for employees who receive the night-shift differential of 5 cents per hour. The relevant sections of the collective agreement follow:

"(39) Vacation pay shall be figured on the basis of forty (40) hours base rate per week except in the case of those employees who are not subject to the forty-hour limitation. These are to be paid on the basis of their normal work week."

"(25) 5 cents per hour additional compensation will be paid for work performed between the hours of 6 P.M.

and 6 A.M., except in those plants where the regular starting time is after 7 A.M., in which case the additional compensation will be paid for the hours worked between 7
P.M. and 7 A.M. This will be retroactive to November 1,
1942."

The company's practice was to compute vacation pay on
the basis of the base rate, exclusive of any additional compensation to which an employee might be entitled. Its defense
of this practice rests in the wording of Section 39, quoted
above, which stipulates that "vacation pay shall be figured
on the basis of forty (40) hours *base rate* per week. . . . ."
(Italics added.)

The Union, on the other hand, contends that the Company should have paid its employees 40 times the *actual* rate
received as vacation pay. This would involve including the
5-cent extra night-shift compensation in the computation of
vacation pay. The Union claims that the words "base rate"
mean "what a man regularly receives per hour." Furthermore,
it claims that the Company actually paid as vacation allowance the actual rate received in instances in which such
rate included additional money for unusual danger or inconvenience like cold or wetness.

QUESTIONS

1. Should the additional compensation for night work be included
   in vacation pay under the terms of Section 39 of the contract?
2. Does Section 39, in your judgment, provide a satisfactory rule
   for determining vacation pay? Should this question be taken into
   account by the umpire in making his decision?

Section G

WAGE STRUCTURE

IT IS convenient to divide the subject of wages under collective bargaining into two headings: wage structure and general wage changes. Wage-structure problems, considered in this section, concern the methods of wage payment, the relative ranking of rates for particular job classifications, and the administration of incentive and piecework systems of payment. General wage changes, the subject of Section H, is confined to problems relating to an "across-the board" change in the rates for all job classifications covered by the bargaining relationship.

The choice of the method of wage payment—hourly rates, piece rates, or incentive rates—is one of the most important questions in a collective bargaining relationship. The choice among these methods will depend partly upon technological and economic factors, such as the standardization of product and operations, the stability of working conditions and materials, the importance of labor costs, and the extent to which individual or group effort can in fact influence output or quality. The choice will be influenced also by the traditions of the bargaining organization and their experience with different methods of wage payment. Thus, some unions are bitterly opposed to incentive systems, such as the United Automobile Workers, CIO, in assembly plants, largely as a result of periods of abuse of these systems of payment. In other cases, such as in the clothing industry, there is a long tradition of satisfactory operation of incentive plans.[1]

[1] For an extended discussion of the choice of methods of wage payment in collective bargaining, see Sumner H. Slichter, *Union Policies and Industrial Management* (Washington, D.C.: Brookings Institution, 1941), chaps. x and xi.

The choice of the method of wage payment will in turn have significant consequences for the collective bargaining relationship. Under piecework systems the union tends to concern itself with the amount and quality of output since these factors directly affect the income of wage-earners. The union may be led quite far into an interest in production problems. Managerial organization, particularly the quality of supervision, will be influenced by the method of wage payment.

Collective bargaining has tended to develop explicit wage scales irrespective of the method of wage payment. Recent years have seen the rapid extension of the practice of reducing to writing the rate paid for each job classification. The specification of the wage scale in the form of an exhibit or appendix is normally regarded as a part of the collective bargaining agreement. Under piece-rate operations, enumeration of all of the piece rates for all the various operations may run into volumes. In most cases, these explicit wage scales cannot be changed during the term of the agreement, with certain exceptions to be noted. In some collective bargaining relationships, however, the parties seem to be satisfied with provisions which permit a change in rates for particular job classifications at any time. The explicit wage scale, unchanged during the contract period, has the advantage of permitting the company to estimate labor costs more reliably. It gives both sides a period of freedom from negotiations over wage rates.

When rates are fixed for a contract period, some provision must be made for the setting of rates on new job classifications and changes in rates for jobs which have been altered in their content, normally to a "substantial degree." In industries where there are frequent changes in job content, provisions of the agreement specify the procedures to be followed in the case of new or changed job classifications.

In a collective bargaining relationship which encompasses a number of job classifications, an important range of problems concerns the ordering of rates among these various jobs. A strict craft-union relationship would not be concerned with these problems. But the growth of industrial unionism has seen these problems of the ordering of the rates in the wage structure occupy great attention. In recent years the basic steel, meat-packing, and cotton textile industries have introduced, partly under the impetus of the National War Labor Board, substantial revisions in intraplant wage structures. The growth of formal job evaluation plans is a reflection of this concern over wage structures.

A variety of forces play upon the internal wage structure of any plant. In most plants some jobs are likely to be quite similar to those in other plants in the same industry and even in other industries. It is also likely that there will be some unique jobs. (*a*) The rates for a job in one plant will be influenced by the relative supply and demand for this type of work in other plants. Labor market shortages, for instance, will affect rates. (*b*) The customary differentials in the plant will be important. Frequently they reflect social judgments of status within the work community. (*c*) The internal power alignments among departments and groups which compose the union engaged in collective bargaining will affect relative rates.

Against the background of these forces it will frequently prove difficult, if not impossible, to impose a hierarchy of job rates based upon a formal and mechanistic job evaluation plan. It may prove even more difficult to keep such a wage structure year after year. A job evaluation plan may prove a useful guide to an orderly wage structure. It may facilitate the reduction in the number of job classifications and rates. It may provide guideposts and bench marks for rate-setting in collective bargaining discussions. But the internal wage structure of a plant ordinarily cannot long be fixed by slide rule or rote under collective bargaining.

A piecework system of wage payment involves a special range of problems for collective bargaining. Shall the union take any responsibility for the system of time study and rate-setting? What information shall the company be required to furnish to the union regarding the details of its time-study methods? Shall its representatives or experts be permitted to be present at time studies? Shall the union restrict its activities to the protest of rates it believes to be too low?

a) Most piece-rate or incentive systems provide for a minimum guarantee to which all workers shall be entitled regardless of actual production. At times this is the starting rate in the plant; more frequently it is the base rate for the particular job classification.

b) Piecework and incentive systems normally indicate the rates to apply in a series of contingencies such as a breakdown in the machinery, a run of inferior raw materials, and periods of setting up new styles or products in which production is experimental. The worker may be paid on the basis of average hourly earnings or base rates in such contingencies.

One of the central problems of collective bargaining concerns the way in which the benefits of technical changes are to be shared. The administration of a rate structure, under an hourly or a piece-rate system of wage payment, compels attention to this fundamental question. Technical change normally produces some change in the nature of the work performed. A piecework system of wage payment frequently permits wage-earners to capture immediately some of the benefits of technical change. The same piece rate will permit larger output and earnings. The bargaining over a change in piece rates, when job content has been changed, is to be seen as one phase of the contest for the benefits of technical change. When the method of wage payment is by the hour, the contest must take other forms in which ordinarily the union seeks a rise in the rate. The union may seek an increase on the particular job or in effect use a number of minor technical changes as the basis for a general wage-rate increase.

It should be apparent that the administration of a wage structure may raise a great many questions. The way in which such problems are handled will ordinarily be vital to both union and management. The cases which follow illustrate a few of the diverse types of issues which arise in the administration of a wage-rate structure.

CASE 49

MAY THE COMPANY UNILATERALLY ESTABLISH A NEW JOB RATE?

UNION: United Steelworkers of America, CIO
COMPANY: Carnegie-Illinois Steel Corporation

The Company transferred the manufacture of a part of a steel product from one mill to another. The Company set a new incentive rate on the operation in the new mill. Both Union and Company recognize that the operation in question, the rolling of a section, which was previously handled in one mill becomes a *different* job when transferred to a different mill. The Union contends that the setting of the new incentive rate under such conditions should be done by negotiating a mutual agreement between the parties and not by unilateral action of the Company. The sole question in this case is the right of the Company to establish rates under these circumstances without union agreement.

Section 11 of the agreement on rate establishment and adjustment reads in part as follows:

"It is recognized that changing conditions and circumstances may from time to time require adjustment of wage rates or modification of wage rate plans because of alleged inequalities, development of new manufacturing processes, changes in the content of jobs, or improvements brought about by the Company in the interest of improved methods and product. Under such circumstances the following procedure shall apply:

"1. When a bona fide new job or position is to be established:

"*a*) Management will develop an appropriate rate by the regular procedure in effect in the Company.

"*b*) Such procedure having been conformed to, the rate proposals so developed will be explained to the grievance committee with the objective of obtaining their agreement to the installation of the proposed rate, or, to the installation of the proposed rate for an agreed upon period which will serve as a trial period. Management may thereupon establish the rate and it may subsequently be subject to adjustment as provided in Paragraph *c* below.

"*c*) Grievances may be alleged by either the employees or Management concerning such rates as follows: In the event there has been no agreement as to the rate to be installed, it shall be considered as if a grievance had been filed in writing on behalf of all employees covered by such rate as of the date of the installation of the rate and the employee commencing to work.

. . . .

"If the grievance filed hereunder cannot be satisfactorily adjusted by mutual agreement, the question as to the equity of such rates in relation to the plant rate structure or such Company rate structure as may result from Paragraph 2 hereunder and the requirements of the job or position as established by sound industrial engi-

neering may be appealed to an impartial umpire. . . . ."

Position of the Union

The Union argues that nothing in the agreement allows
the Company to install a rate or classify a section when the
product to be rolled is transferred to another mill. The Union
agrees that the contract gives the Company the right to install
new rates on their products. However, there is no provision
in the agreement applying to the setting of rates on old established products that are removed to another mill for rolling. Since the Company did not have such authority under the
agreement, the setting of new incentive rates on such old and
established products should be by negotiation between the
management and the Union. The Union insists that there
should be mutual agreement reached on the new rate prior to
its being installed. This demand is held to be thoroughly in
accord with the principles of collective bargaining.

The Union holds that the company's unilateral establishment of rates had, in this instance, adversely affected the
workers in a double manner.

a) The workers in the mill on which the section was being
rolled lose work which was yielding satisfactory earnings.

b) The workers in the mill to which the rolling of the
section was transferred get a rate for the work which is
inadequate. The Company revaluates the job and sets a rate
yielding a lower average of earnings. The Union estimates
that the drop in earnings tends to average some 15 to 20 per
cent. Inasmuch as the rolling of the section in the new mill
requires great effort and sacrifice on the part of the workers in
developing the rolling into a smooth and efficient process,
it is the judgment of the Union that the Company should give
at least average pay. Since the section to be rolled is usually
transferred to a faster mill the result is that the workers
produce more tonnage but have lower earnings because the
rate is set too low.

The Union contends that in order to protect itself against such an adverse condition, it is privileged under the agreement to negotiate the new rates to be set on the section in the new mill. Particularly, a union committeeman should be present with the industrial engineer who is making the study through which the new rate is to be set. The Union insists that a rate so negotiated and established would be satisfactory to both parties. Either the rate should be set by such mutual agreement, or else the section should be continued on an average-earnings basis.

POSITION OF THE COMPANY

The Company holds that in the operation of its plant it must often make changes in the productive process, the removal of a section for rolling from one plant to another is a case in point. The new mill in which the section is to be rolled may have a different incentive system, a different capacity, a faster or slower rate of production, and a tonnage capacity per turn (shift) entirely unrelated to the capacity per turn of the mill from which the section was removed. The standard which may have been proper in the mill from which the section came may have no application to the mill to which the section is moved.

The Company argues that the rolling of the new section in the new mill under the conditions indicated constitutes a new job. Under the agreement the Company insists that it has the unquestioned right to institute an appropriate rate for this new job and the Union correspondingly has the right to test the equity of the rate by resorting to the grievance procedure. The contract is held to make no requirements that the Company negotiate a rate with the Union prior to its establishment. The Company maintains it has a right under the agreement initially to classify a section or set the rate.

It is further argued by the Company that the procedure it follows in setting the rate is in complete conformity with the requirements of the agreement. After the rate is developed by the industrial engineering department, it is discussed between the foreman and the grievance committeeman. The latter, in turn, discusses it with the workers. Opportunity is given to the Union to express its idea as to whether the rate is right or wrong. Under the agreement, management has the right to install the rate which it deems to be appropriate. The Union is privileged to protest the rate through the grievance procedure and arbitration.

The Company points out that it has for many years followed the practice of classifying or standardizing new or previously unrated products under existing plans on the mills. The Union recognized this practice in innumerable instances by resorting to the grievance procedure to protest the equity of the rates established by the Company, without questioning the right of the Company initially to establish such rates. The Union seeks to establish by indirection a principle which it was unable to establish through direct negotiation.

QUESTIONS

1. Does the transfer of operations involved in this case fall under any one of the following headings mentioned in Section 11: "development of new manufacturing processes," or "changes in the content of jobs," or "improvements . . . . in the interest of improved methods and product"? If so, which one?

2. In your view should the contract be written in sufficient detail to include the case of a transfer of work between departments? Is there any logic to distinguish the case of transfer of work from a genuinely new operation?

3. What should happen in the union's view if the parties cannot agree upon a new rate as a result of bargaining? State carefully the union's position.

4. Why should the Union be opposed to the Company setting a rate on a part of the work transferred between mills? What would be the effects on earnings if the piecework system had many loose rates and the Company could frequently transfer work?

5. Does step 1(*b*) in Section 11 require the Company to bargain with the Union before placing a rate into effect?

6. What protection does the Union enjoy under Section 11? What rights of management are guaranteed?

CASE 50

ADJUSTMENT OF PIECE RATES FOR CHANGED JOB

UNION: United Steelworkers of America, CIO

COMPANY: American Steel & Wire Company

The Company has installed new patenting furnaces with a greater capacity. A change has taken place in the material processed in these furnaces because of an increase in the size of the starting coils. Whereas these coils were predominantly in the 200- to 300-pound range in the old furnaces, they are now predominantly in the 500- to 600-pound range.

The Company established new incentive rates for employees who operate these furnaces, namely, the reelers and blockers, on the basis of a changed job. The Union protests the installation of these new piece rates, which are lower than the old rates. It asks that the old rates be reapplied and the workers be given average earnings retroactive to the date of the written agreement.

POSITION OF THE UNION

The Union argues that the Company has violated the provisions concerning wages in Section 3 of the 1942 agreement. This section provides in part that "rates now in effect . . . . shall remain in effect for the duration of the Agreement." The contract allows for changed rates only where there has been a "substantial change in job duties or requirements." In this case, the Union holds that there has been no substantial change in job duties or requirements and that the Company was not justified in installing new rates.

The Union maintains that the work operations of the reelers and blockers, who constitute the crew, are the same on the new furnaces as on the old furnaces, except that the amount of work effort that is required has increased in direct proportion to the increase of the tonnage handled. This is estimated to be about 50 per cent.

1. *Reelers.*—The duties of reelers are the same as before. Hoists are still used to raise the bundle, and the same difficulties of disengaging are experienced. However, much more effort is required to push the loading bridge hoist than the previous monorail crane. It is much easier to roll the smaller coils than to use the hoist in the large coils.

The speed of the furnace is still variable with this exception, the speed is calculated by slide rule, the motor is set at this speed, then locked. The Union holds that the increase in speed has not changed the job in a way to merit a change in the rate, since the increase in effort of the workers is in direct proportion to the increase in the speed.

2. *Blockers.*—The Union holds that the duties of the blockers have not changed with the installation of the new furnaces. However, the enlargement of the size of the blocks, making possible the holding of the entire large coils, has increased the work of the blockers. The required effort in stripping one bundle of 600 pounds is far greater than that required in removing a 300-pound bundle or 200-pound coil. At present the rod is clawed off the block and allowed to slide down a bent pipe, coming to rest on an angle iron fastened to the floor. The bundle lies loose, in some cases binds under the turning block, causing increased effort to get it pulled out. Also sometimes the rods will drop through the gap between the end of the pipe and the block causing the blocker enormous trouble. The struggle that the average blocker has with the 500- and 600-pound coil is so great as to strain to the limit his physical strength. No satisfactory means has been evoked for stripping that has not caused the blockers to expend more effort per unit of weight than before. In addition, the hazard of this work has increased significantly.

The Union further insists that in the development of standards and of rates based on time studies, the Company has committed a serious error in merely considering the time and frequency of work tasks. It has ignored the important factor of the amount of work effort required in these tasks. *The increase in work effort of the workers has been in direct proportion to the greater production in the new furnace.* Under the new production standards the workers have to produce roughly 50 per cent more tonnage and exert 50 per cent more effort in order to receive the same earnings. The time elements do not reflect the extra exertion required in the execution of the tasks.

The new rates have resulted in a substantial reduction in earnings for the same tonnage and the same amount of work. Thus, the Union points out that on the old furnace, one rate was $1.25 per 1,000 pounds for a given size and kind of wire. The new rate is $0.755, which represents a cut of $0.495 per 1,000 pounds or nearly 40 per cent. Ten thousand pounds under the old rate meant $12.50 and under the new rate yields only $7.55. To make $12.50 under the new rate would mean an output of 16,500 pounds, under conditions which increase work effort per unit weight.

The Union concedes that some of the new rates are fair rates and that some of the combinations of sizes and rates have maintained the men's earnings. Others, however, are far out of line. Some are too low to be commensurate for the energy and speed necessary to the work. Others are too low to give even a fair return.

POSITION OF THE COMPANY

The Company argues that the installation of the new patenting furnaces constituted a genuine changed job resulting in a substantial change in job duties and job requirements. The new furnaces embody many improvements in handling equipment, in methods of operation, and in working conditions. The new patenting furnaces, together with the larger-size starting coils, allow for a substantial increase in productivity in the operation of the equipment. The expansion in the capacity of the furnaces, an increase in the speed with which the lines are run through the furnaces, and the installation of devices such as hoists and new blocks, enable significantly greater production with a shift from manual effort to machine effort. The larger-size starting coils permit essentially a 50 per cent reduction in handling elements per ton of material handled, thereby saving working time.

It is the company's contention that all of these changes and improvements constitute a significant change in the job with a resulting "substantial change in the job duties" and requirements of the reelers and blockers. The reeler now lifts each bundle from the buggy by means of an electric hoist and lowers it onto the appropriate reel, instead of having to lift by hand portions of the bundle until the entire coil was on the reel. The blocker now strips the entire bundle onto the stripper arm and consequently no longer has the necessity of cutting the larger coils into smaller units before the removal of the rod from the blocks. Previously, the blocker stripped the bundle by hand and balanced it against his leg while tying the bundle. Under present conditions, the blocker now loads the bundle directly from the stripper arm to the buggy by means of an electric hoist.

The Company maintains that an analysis of the changes in the job duties or requirements of the reelers and blockers indicates that the amount of time and effort per 1,000 pounds required of these employees has been reduced substantially. The reduction in time per bundle for the reelers averages about 13.7 per cent. For the blockers this reduction in time per bundle averages about 36.9 per cent. The Company denies that workers on these jobs have had to exert an increased incentive effort anywhere approaching the 50 per cent figure claimed by the Union. The Company recognizes an increase in activity of 3.1 per cent on the part of reelers in meeting new production standards. However, the Company argues that it has taken this increased effort into account in the setting of its new rates. The increase in activity is less than the 4.8 per cent increase in anticipated earnings that had been allowed for. Similarly, the increase in activity of the blockers in meeting new production standards is 5.7 per cent, and their anticipated earnings also had been increased 4.8 per cent. The composite increase for these two job classifications is 4.4 per cent, whereas the Company has made an allowance of 4.8 per cent for increased activity.

The Company contends that the increased tonnage which is permitted by the changed equipment comes primarily from the larger-size starting bundles. In practically all instances the handling of the larger-size coil is the same as on the smaller-size coil, hence approximately double tonnage is secured from the same number of work operations. Since all of the major handling of the coils is done by mechanical equipment, the increase in the weight of the coils does not mean added effort.

Finally, the Company argues that on one of the new furnaces the increase of earnings of both the reelers and blockers is 16.1 per cent above the level of the previous year, and on another type of furnace is 9.9 per cent above the previous level. These earnings show that the reelers and blockers are able to meet and exceed anticipated earnings consistently. This is held to be a convincing argument for the appropriateness of the company's newly established rates.

QUESTIONS

1. Do the changes in this case involve a "substantial change in job duties or requirements" under the contract? What criteria would you establish to decide whether a particular change was "substantial"?

2. Why does the Union wish to have the piece rate unchanged, and why does the Company wish it lowered? Explore the different interests in the sharing of the benefits of technical change.

3. Can the Union argue that with the larger furnaces the productivity of the men has increased?

4. How do you measure "work effort"? How do you appraise the union contention that "work effort" increased directly proportional to output, that is, to the tonnage handled?

5. If technical change does reduce physical exertion, may it not

result in an increase in responsibility on account of the larger-size furnaces?

6. For what does the piece rate compensate? Physical exertion? Responsibility? Output?

CASE 51

WAGE REDUCTION ARISING FROM TECHNOLOGICAL EXPERIMENT

UNION: United Steelworkers of America, CIO

COMPANY: John A. Foster and Sons

Al Tackas was earning $1.25 per hour under an incentive system with a base rate of $0.795 while operating his machine at the John A. Foster & Sons plant, under a contract with the United Steelworkers of America, CIO. The Company carried out an experiment on the machine for two days, during which Tackas was transferred to miscellaneous floor work for which the rate is $0.78. During these two days, Tackas received his base rate of $0.795.

POSITION OF THE UNION

The Union bases its claim for average earnings of $1.25 for the two days of floor work on Paragraph 5 of Section 3 of the agreement which states:

"An employee transferred from one department or one job to another (except (a) in order to avoid a lay-off, or (b) at his own request, or (c) because of his inability to perform the work assigned to him, or (d) in a justifiable demotion) shall not have his base rate or hourly earnings reduced. If the job to which he shall be transferred pays a higher rate than his immediately previous job, the employee shall receive the higher rate."

The Union claims that none of these exceptions applies in this case. The Union also believes that the experiment could and should have been carried out over the week end, at overtime rates, so that the operator would not have been deprived of his regular work.

POSITION OF THE COMPANY

The Company points out that this case is similar to maintenance shutdowns, which occur frequently and for which transfers are made under terms and conditions identical to the action taken in this case. The Company also claims that this case is covered by another section of the agreement, which provides that an incentive employee who, for any reason clearly not within his control, fails to earn at least his hourly base rate, shall be paid his hourly base rate. The Company, therefore, claimed originally, and still claims, that Tackas was properly paid.

ARBITRATOR'S DECISION

Past practice in this Company, the agreement between the Company and the Union, and widespread practices elsewhere would seem to support the company's position in this case. Shutting down this particular machine for experimental purposes is closely similar to maintenance shutdowns which are planned in advance. Under these circumstances, the arbitrator believes that the exception named in Paragraph 5(a) applies to Mr. Tackas and that he is not entitled to guaranteed hourly earnings under the circumstances. The arbitrator would be most reluctant to follow the union's suggestion and rule that the Company should carry out experimental work over the week end at overtime rates in order not to deprive the operator of his regular work. Such a directive would not be justified by either the agreement or generally accepted practice.

The arbitrator sustains the company's claim that Tackas was properly paid.

QUESTIONS

1. How, in your judgment, does equity demand that this case be decided? Should equity determine the decision?

2. Does this case properly fall under any of the exceptions in Paragraph 5 of the contract?

3. Was Tackas transferred to avoid a layoff? Was there a lack of work to be done on his machine? Must a layoff be for lack of work to fall under the exception in Paragraph 5?

4. May the transfer of Tackas be classified as "justifiable demotion"?

5. Is the union's argument that the experiment could and should have been carried out over the week end relevant to the issue in this case?

6. If you were writing a contract clause, how would you cover this type of situation?

CASE 52

LOSS OF PIECEWORK EARNINGS DUE TO PRESENCE OF NUMEROUS INEXPERIENCED WORKERS

UNION: United Automobile Workers of America, CIO

COMPANY: General Motors Corporation

THE GRIEVANCE

"We demand to be paid at $1.10 per hour as we always made it. Because we have a group of new men we cannot maintain production. We are working and pushed all day long and getting paid less money. Until such a time as production is maintained, we demand to be paid our regular rate."

BACKGROUND

The export department of the Chevrolet plant was shut down on July 29, 1941, for what management states was a change of model. Production was resumed on August 4, 1941, but it was found necessary to increase the number of men in the department because of expanded production requirements. The additional man power required was obtained from other piecework departments that were not working at that time. The piecework price for the 1942 model remained the same as for the 1941 model, i.e., $1.10 per hour for 100 per cent efficiency. The regular men in the department were called in, but, because of the augmented force, they were unable to obtain 100 per cent efficiency and were paid at a rate lower than the full-efficiency rate.

When the increased production in the export department made evident the need for additional men, management states that, following a discussion with two shop committeemen, it agreed that the guaranteed rate customarily applicable to the starting up of the truck line would be paid to the regular workers in the export department after the first day of operation following the shutdown. In any event, a meeting was held between management and the shop committee on August 6, 1941, at which time management made clear what it felt was the agreement it had made in this matter, viz., to pay the regular guaranteed rate of $0.95 per hour to the new men in the export department "until they were able to carry the job," but to pay the $1.05-per-hour starting-up rate of the truck line to the regular men in that department, after the first day of operation.

Because of the presence of the new men, the regular earnings for the export department for the week ending August 9, 1941, fell considerably below $1.10 per hour. However, these earnings were made up to $0.95 per hour for the first day of operation, and to $1.05 per hour for the remainder of the week. On August 12, 1941, and thereafter, this department attained 100 per cent efficiency and was paid the piecework earned-rate of $1.10 per hour.

POSITION OF THE UNION

The Union claims that the loss in production was not the fault of the regular men in this department and that, in the absence of any regular model change-over, no guaranteed rate should apply. In place of the guaranteed rate that was paid to these men, the Union maintains they should have received their regular earned rate for the job.

In the absence of a change in the model, the Union

claims management had no right to apply the guaranteed rate of pay, especially since the loss of production was caused by the presence of additional men who had little or no experience in the operation of the department. The Union feels that it is unfair to have a number of new workers placed with a group of regular workers and thereby cause a loss in earnings to the regular workers in the department. The Union contends that the guaranteed rate of pay of $0.95 per hour, contained in the local wage agreement, was not intended to apply in an instance of this nature, and that management's attempt to apply it here was a violation of that agreement. The Union therefore requests that the regular export department operators be reimbursed to the extent of their full $1.10-per-hour earnings "until such time as production was maintained."

POSITION OF THE COMPANY

Management maintains that it acted well within the terms of the local wage agreement when it paid as it did for the start-up of the export department. Management points out that notice of this addition to the regular starting rate was communicated to the operators through several committeemen and later through the entire shop committee.

The extension of the guaranteed rate, says management, rather than being a violation, represents greater liberality than required by the agreement. Management holds that these employees have no regular earned rate but rather are governed by the production on a group piecework basis which is subject to a guaranteed rate, if group earnings fall below the guarantee (except for breakdown or material shortage when regular earnings are maintained).

The local wage agreement clearly provides a guaranteed rate, which, by past practice, has been paid upon the starting up of a department after a model change-over, after an inventory period, and during certain other occurrences when earnings fell below such guaranteed rate. The only exceptions noted to the application of the guaranteed rate have been when breakdown or material shortages occur—in such cases the regular 100 per cent efficiency rate has been paid.

Says the Company: "If the guaranteed rate is not applicable in this instance, it is difficult to conceive of any circumstances to which it would apply."

QUESTIONS

1. Does management appear to have violated the local wage agreement?
2. Should the local wage agreement be changed so that regular earnings are paid in a case of this kind?
3. If, as the Union implies, the inflow of new workers which brought down the group piecework earnings was caused by poor management planning, should management be made to pay for such inefficiency, or should the employees simply accept it as one of the routine occurrences of industrial life?
4. Would the problem have arisen under a piece-rate system as distinguished from a group incentive system? Should workers under a group-earnings plan have any right to say who shall be employed in the group?

CASE 53

EXTRA COMPENSATION FOR OPERATING "OLD" MACHINES

UNION: American Federation of Hosiery Workers

COMPANY: Lincoln Hosiery Company

In the hosiery industry a National Labor Agreement is negotiated jointly by companies affiliated with the Full Fashioned Hosiery Manufacturers of America, Inc., and representatives of the American Federation of Hosiery Workers. The agreement aims at establishing uniform piece rates and working conditions for all member-firms. It further provides for the appointment of an impartial chairman to settle controversies arising under the existing agreement.

The present case is concerned with the adjustment of a piece rate to compensate for operating an "old" machine. The

Brentmore mill of the Lincoln Hosiery Company operates what is termed by the Union "old" 39-guage legging machines. The Union requests the payment of 5 cents extra per dozen to operators of these machines to compensate for the added effort and risk and the decreased production that accompanies knitting on these machines. The Company maintains that production secured from the machines is not comparatively low and therefore no extra compensation is in order. Production records show that the average weekly output, over a period of 7 recent weeks, was about 53 dozen per week.

As early as October 28, 1929, the joint negotiating committee considered the principle that extras should be paid on old equipment. At that time the minutes of that committee disclosed that such an extra was discussed in connection with the principle of uniform rates. The committee recognized "that difficulties may arise (difficulties in achieving uniformity of rates) in view of possible conditions on old equipment. In such cases, no deviation from the principle shall be inaugurated without investigations and approval of the impartial chairman."

In the present case, the decision of the chairman must serve to define the conditions under which extra payments should be made to operators on old equipment.

POSITION OF THE UNION

The Union contends that operation of the company's "old" 39-gauge legging machines requires added effort and skill for which increased compensation should be awarded. The machines are said to be of an extremely low-speed type which means that production is decreased through no fault of the employees. The low production of the old machines is not due to any lack of efficiency on the part of the operators, rather to the antiquated character of the equipment. The Union argues that it is unjust that those who work on subnormal equipment should be further penalized by having, in addition to the added effort involved, a low production which no amount of skill or effort can overcome.

POSITION OF THE COMPANY

The Company opposes the union's demand for 5 cents extra and questions the standards suggested by the Union for determination of the appropriateness of an extra compensation. First, the Company argues that the age of a machine is not in itself a sufficient factor in determining whether or not an extra should be paid. If production and earnings are adequate, then payment of extras would mean a deviation from the principle of uniformity established under the national labor agreement. Or if low production and earnings can be traced to the inefficiency of the operator rather than of the machines, then no extra compensation is in order.

It is the company's position that the necessity for securing an adequate income on old machines should be stressed rather than the necessity of securing a certain dozen pairs of production. Thus, earnings rather than production is regarded as the criterion for determination of the appropriateness of extra compensation. The Company holds that this distinction is essential because of the variations that occur in specifications in the stockings. It is conceivable that an average production of a loosely knit stocking may not result in average earnings to the knitter.

In the present case, the Company cites figures to indicate that employees on the old machines do earn the average weekly income. The average full-time production of these machines is 53 dozen a week, while the average earnings for a full-time week approximate $29. This condition is said to prevail generally on all machines at this plant. Thus, inadequate earnings do not result from the nature of the "old" equipment.

QUESTIONS

1. What is the purpose of a uniform piece rate in the hosiery industry? What does this tend to equalize among firms? Earnings of wage-earners? Labor costs?
2. What would be the effect of a 5-cent "extra" on older equipment?

3. Who should bear the costs of the lower productivity of older equipment? Should men be expected to work harder? Should they receive lower earnings? Should rates be higher or lower?

4. Under a piece-rate system, does the Union have an interest in the age and condition of equipment? What action may the Union take when it believes that equipment is not being properly maintained or is obsolete?

5. Under what circumstances would you recommend a differential in piece rates for older and less-productive equipment? Should the piece rate be higher or lower than on more modern equipment? What is the case for each position?

CASE 54

WHAT CONSTITUTES AN INEQUITY IN RATES?

UNION: Textile Workers Union of America, CIO

COMPANY: Botany Worsted Mills

The present case is concerned with the establishment of an appropriate rate for the sewing of gabardine ties. The company's present rate is $0.704 per bundle. The Union requests that the rate be increased to $0.75 per bundle to equal the rate for challis ties, on the theory that the work is equally difficult.

POSITION OF THE UNION

The Union protests the company's existing rate. It contends that piece rates should be established on the basis of the time, effort, and skill required on a normal basis of working; that hourly earnings are the result not only of the piece rates but of the energy and skill used by the workers. It argues that if earnings alone were used as the criterion, then each increase in production due to the expenditure of more energy or improvement in the skill of the worker would be reflected in a reduction in piece rates.

The Union concedes that the substitution of the rounded

edge early in 1945 did decrease the difficulty of the work somewhat and accordingly revised its request for a new rate from $0.77 to $0.75. However, it submits the testimony of a number of workers as evidence of the fact that unusal efforts were made in the months of March, April, and May to get out a large production. This is supported in part by one of the company witnesses. As final evidence in its case for a higher piece rate, the Union offers a memorandum dated November 21, 1944, over the signature of Nelson J. Rohrbach, Superintendent of the production division, in which Mr. Rohrbach expresses the opinion that gabardines "are more difficult to do" and states: "It is true that recently there has been an unusual amount of difficult work going through."

Position of the Company

The Company contends that, while an adjustment in the rate for gabardine ties may be in order, the union's proposal of $0.75 is much too high. It argues that the sewing of gabardine ties is less difficult than the sewing of challis ties and that an appropriate differential must be maintained between the two jobs. This is held to be especially true since the recent introduction of the rounded edge in the manufacturing process for gabardine ties. The Company presents figures which show that in the months of March, April, and May the percentage of gabardine ties manufactured rose from 9.4 per cent in February to 11.1 per cent in March, to 30.8 per cent in April, and to 60 per cent in the first three weeks of May. Nevertheless, in March the average earnings were $1.136 per hour, which was an increase of $0.05 over the February earnings. In April there was a decrease of $0.013 per hour, and in May the earnings increased to $1.141 per hour, which is $0.005 above the March average, in which month the percentage of gabardine ties manufactured was only 11.1 per cent.

The Company offers the results of a time study made by a company representative for the week ending April 29, which indicated that the rate for challis should be $0.756 and for gabardine $0.713.

QUESTIONS

1. Do differences in piece rates necessarily indicate an inequity?
2. Does equality of earnings indicate that the piece rates are properly set relative to each other?
3. How would you define an inequity in piece rates between two job classifications?
4. What is a time study? How is it typically made?
5. Does the time study of April 29 provide a basis for a request by the Company for a reduction in the rate for challis ties?

CASE 55

WAGE-RATE DIFFERENTIALS IN A DEPARTMENT

Union: Textile Workers Union of America, CIO

Company: Forstmann Woolen Company

Approximately 25 first-class cylinder fullers now earning $0.84 per hour claim they are entitled to an increase. Comparison with the rates for certain other jobs in the wet finishing department, it is alleged, shows that this job classification is subjected to an inequity. The first-class cylinder fullers maintain that the skill and judgment required of them has not been given sufficient weight in slotting their jobs in relation to other jobs. The comparison made by the fullers is with the dryers, the teazling operators, the wet decaters, all of whom also receive $0.84 per hour, the washing operators who receive $0.79 per hour, and the examiners who receive $1.01 per hour.

The adjustment is requested under the provisions of Article III (B) of the contract between the Company and the Union, which reads in part as follows:

"Nothing in this Article shall prevent either party hereto from requesting, at any time, an adjustment of individual rates of pay which, in its opinion, should fairly be made because of intraplant inequities or inequalities. Upon such request, which shall be submitted in writing, the rates of pay in such cases shall be negotiated and the parties shall in good faith endeavor to reach an agreement. If no agreement is reached within 15 days after receipt of such request, the dispute may be submitted to arbitration by either party thereto in accordance with Article VIII of this Agreement. A wage adjustment arrived at in accordance with this clause shall not be used by either party as a basis for claiming other inequities or inequalities."

POSITION OF THE UNION

The Union argues that the fuller's rate is too low and that the company's job description does not sufficiently emphasize the elements of skill and judgment required on the job. It is held that the fullers are left more to their own judgment and experience than are any of the persons in comparable jobs, with the exception of the examiners. All the other work is tied much more closely to machine and automatic devices. It is also true that the fullers have a greater direct responsibility for the material they are handling. Mistakes on their part would lead directly to damage and rejection of goods, either by overshrinkage or undershrinkage. While their foreman works closely with them, harm can easily be done if the fullers are careless or incompetent. Finally, it is agreed that at least 4 months and probably 6 months of training are necessary for the job. On the basis of these factors, the Union argues that no inequity would be created by raising the fuller's rate. An inequity exists in maintaining the present rate.

POSITION OF THE COMPANY

The Company holds that the existing rate for first-class cylinder fulling operator is appropriate for the duties entailed in the job. The company's job description reads as follows:

"The Operator pushes a loaded truck to the machine and places the pieces in the machine by hand, making sure to equalize the length of the strings. He measures the length and width of pieces and fills out the Work Slips. He then adds soap solution as required and sets the machine for the proper Fulling operation. The Operator remeasures the pieces from time to time during the Fulling process, and occasionally resets the machine and rearranges the pieces. After the pieces have been processed, they are opened at the seam, and folded out by hand on to a receiving truck. The Operator records the final measurement on the Process Control Card and Work Slip. He cleans, oils and greases the machine whenever necessary. One man operates two machines."

In establishing a rate of $0.84 for this job, the Company holds that it has taken adequate cognizance of the skill and judgment factors involved, also of other factors important in valuing a job, namely, the amount of physical effort required, the responsibility for the work and for the safety of others, the nature of the physical working conditions, and the exposure to dangers of accident.

The Company further contends that it has achieved a delicate balance in the components of its wage structure. Any upward movement of rates in one job would cause a certain amount of dissatisfaction in related jobs. The history of the various job rates is cited as an important element indicating the long-established character of the existing wage relationships .The Company indicates that with slight qualification, the record shows that the fullers have had the same relative rate through a whole series of adjustments since January, 1931, as have the dryers, the teazling operators, and the wet decaters, ranging during this period of 14 years from a low rate of $0.45 to the present rate of $0.84. Until September, 1941, the washing operators also had either the same relative rate or a rate only $0.02 per hour below the fullers, although they are now receiving $0.05 per hour less. The examiners, on the other hand, have always earned at least $0.15 and at sometimes as much as $0.20 more than the fullers.

QUESTIONS

1. From what circumstances may this grievance have arisen? How can the Union request an increase for some workers in a department and not for all workers?

2. How much weight should be given to the historical differentials that have prevailed within the department?

3. What are the merits and disadvantages from the point of view of both parties of a contract provision such as Article III (B) which permits the raising of a grievance on a particular job rate at any time during the contract year?

4. If the rate for a particular job is to be changed, how can the dangers of creating dissatisfaction among other workers be minimized?

CASE 56

INTERDEPARTMENTAL WAGE-RATE INEQUITY

UNION: Textile Workers Union of America

COMPANY: The American Woolen Company

The Company has 24 plants located in 6 New England and Middle Atlantic states. It employs about 24,000, of whom 1,800 work in the Devon mill, located in Devon, Massachusetts, in which this case took place.

The Company maintains collective bargaining relations with two national unions: the Textile Workers Union of America, CIO, and the United Textile Workers of America, AFL. The former represents 21,000 of the company's 24,000 employees and has been certified as exclusive bargaining agent in 20 of the 24 plants. The other 4 plants, employing about 3,000 workers in the aggregate, are represented by the ALF union. Of the 1,800 employees in the Devon mill, about 1,700 are members of one of the locals of the TWUA. Collective bargaining relations between the Company and this local began in 1938. It was one of the company's first two mills to be organized by the CIO union and certified to it in an NLRB representation election. No strikes have occurred since the establishment of collective bargaining in 1938, although some unauthorized small-scale walkouts have taken place.

The Issue

The present case involves 4 cloth-carriers and 2 floormen in the weaveroom of the plant who desire an adjustment in their rate of pay from 65 cents per hour to the rate which the floormen received in the mending and burling department in the same mill, which is 82 cents per hour. The Union contends that the duties of the cloth-carriers and the floormen in the mending department and the duties of the floormen in the weaveroom are "somewhat alike" and that the difference in rates constitutes an intraplant inequality. The Company denies the alleged similarity in job content, and the case was referred to a neutral arbitrator. Hearings took place on March 28, 1945.

Description of Operations Involved

The cloth-carriers in the weaverroom work as a 2-man team, each team handling a truck per trip. Cloth is picked up at the loom and delivered to the weaveroom perch for inspection. Empty rolls are taken from the weaveroom perch and trucked to looms wherever necessary.

After the weaving has been completed, the cloth may be subjected to an operation known as "burling" in which foreign matter is removed from the material. Then the cloth is passed on to the burling examiner or percher, who marks in yellow chalk defects in the weave which may have resulted from the burler's work. The marked material goes to the sewer for mending and then to the "blue-line" percher, or mending examiner, who may find defects which have escaped the attention of the "yellow-line" percher. If he does, the material is returned to the original mending department for further repair.

The floormen in the mending and burling departments also work in teams of two. Each stage of the journey made by the cloth is handled by a different team of floormen, e.g., from burler to yellow-line percher, from percher to mender, from mender to blue-line percher and back.

Background

The mending department was originally entirely on day-work, and the floormen in it received a slightly lower rate than was received at that time by the floormen in the weaveroom. Later, the entire mending department, including the floormen, was placed on piecework. A bonus, based on the number of pieces handled by the entire department during an 8-hour day, was divided equally among all the floormen in the mending department. Since, however, some of the cloth skips the burling and/or mending processes—and therefore is not handled at all by the floormen servicing those processes—the other floormen protested that an equal division of the bonus among all the floormen in the department meant in effect that some of them were getting paid for the work of others. The dissatisfaction thus aroused resulted in the floormen being taken off piecework in 1942. They were put on their present day rate of 82 cents per hour, which rate approximated their former piecework earnings.

Position of the Company

The Company bases its denial of alleged similarity between the duties of the cloth carriers and floormen in the weaveroom and the duties of the floormen in the mending department on the following grounds:

1. Different grades and styles of cloth are handled in the mill, and not all grades need be subjected to all the processes described above. Some of the grades may go directly to sewers, skipping the burlers; some may go directly to the examiners, skipping both the burlers and sewers. To each piece of cloth is attached a ticket which bears a style designation. It is the task of the floormen in the mending department to distribute the material correctly. This is called "booking." The weaveroom cloth carriers, on the other hand, are not concerned with

any work of segregation and distribution; they merely truck the material from loom to perch.

2. Furthermore, some of the styles are more difficult to burl, mend, or examine than others; and they consequently require more work on the part of the people performing these operations. Consequently, it is necessary for the floormen in the mending room to see that the cloth is properly distributed in order to equalize the work of the burlers, sewers, and examiners—all of whom are paid by the piece. Therefore, the Company defends the difference in the rates between the floormen and cloth carriers in the weaveroom and the floormen in the mending and burling department on the ground that more judgment and intelligence are required by the work in the mending department than the work in the weaveroom. The floormen must know where the work is to go, and they must see that it is distributed fairly among the pieceworkers so that each gets a share of easy and of hard work.

3. The existing differential of 15 cents per hour between the two jobs originated as a result of the mending department floormen's experience under piecework. Originally they, like the other floormen, were on daywork. Their day rates were then comparable to the others. At that time, however, they were not responsible for equalizing work as described above. This function was performed by a head clothman. The head clothman, however, could not handle all of the booking himself, with the result that the floormen performed that part of the work which the head clothman was unable to do. Since the floormen thus demonstrated their ability to do part of the booking, the position of head clothman was later eliminated, and equalizing work was formally added to the duties of the mending department floormen. This assumption of added responsibility became effective at the same time that the mending department floormen were placed on piecework; as a result, their earnings outstripped those of the floormen and cloth carriers in other departments. Thus, the differential in pay arose at the same time that the functions described in paragraphs 1 and 2 above were added to the duties

of the floormen in the mending department. The continuance of this differential after the latter were shifted back to day-work is therefore justified by the continuance of the additions to the content of their jobs.

4. There are a number of other classes of dayworkers in the plant, including some floormen (e.g., in the dye house and the finishing room), who receive 65 cents an hour or less and whose responsibilities are as great as those of the floormen in the weaveroom.

POSITION OF THE UNION

1. In support of its argument that the jobs of the floormen in the two rooms are substantially the same, the Union cites the fact that floormen are frequently transferred between the two rooms when an absence or other condition makes such transfer needed. Indeed, it was the fact that the same floormen who receive 65 cents an hour for a regular job in the weave-room make 15 cents an hour more when occasionally substituting in the mending department that caused the discontent which resulted in the union's demand being presented.

2. The Union concedes that, at least in the original distribution of work, the floormen in the mending room have to exercise more judgment and discretion than is required of the floormen in the weaveroom. The Union argues, however, that once the work is picked up by the floormen in the mending room, there is no essential difference in the responsibilities of the two groups of floormen.

COMPANY REBUTTAL

The Company admits that some of the floormen in the weaveroom are capable of doing the work in the mending room but contends, nevertheless, that the job requirements are different. The Company also adds that even a less-qualified man from the weaveroom could do the work satisfactorily because the floormen work in pairs. If one of the men knows how the work should be distributed, the other member of the pair can work effectively with him.

POST-ARBITRATION DEVELOPMENTS

The arbitrator denied any increase in the wage rate of the floormen and cloth carriers in the weaveroom.

Following publication of the arbitration award, the weaveroom carriers and floormen quit work. Both union and management then attempted to get other classes of employees to carry cloth, with management offering to pay them their normal rates of compensation. Thus, management offered weavers $1.15 per hour to carry cloth from the weaveroom to the mending department.

But no one in the plant volunteered for this work. Unofficial union spokesmen said that, if management could afford to pay other workers their normal compensation, which was in most cases substantially in excess of 80 cents per hour, they could afford to grant to the weaveroom floormen the increase of 15 cents. As a result, the entire plant of 1,800 employees was forced to shut down.

Management then advised the national union's director of the American Woolen Company locals of the situation. The Union, through the director, readily assented to the company's hiring new employees as weaveroom floormen. (The collective agreement guarantees union security in the form of a maintenance-of-membership clause providing that all employees who are or become members of the Union shall, as a condition of employment, remain members of the Union in good standing for the duration of the contract.) But the Company found it impossible for two reasons to hire new floormen: (1) It was difficult to induce men to work at the rate of 65 cents per hour; and (2) The population of the town of Devon, like the work force in the mill, is predominantly Finnish, and these people refuse to take anyone else's job.

The original floormen and cloth carriers in the weaveroom returned to work 5 days after the shutdown began, after the union director addressed a meeting of the entire union membership of the mill's work force and reminded them of their obligation to accept the award of the arbitrator to which they had bound themselves in advance.

QUESTIONS

1. How was the alleged wage-rate inequity created? If you were the management of the Company what would you have done at the time the floormen in the mending and burling department were placed back on day rates at 82 cents per hour?

2. Is the fact that workers may interchangeably perform two jobs an indication of their relative worth? Should wage scales be determined for the "job" or for the "men" performing the job?

3. From the point of view of the Company and the Union, what steps would you have advocated to avoid the "wildcat" stoppage?

4. Did the Company create an intradepartmental wage-rate inequity between the floormen and other employees of the mending and burling department when it placed the floormen on a time rate of 82 cents, approximating their former piecework earnings?

5. Was the argument valid for taking the floormen off of the piece-rate method of payment? Under what circumstances may the piecework method be inappropriate?

6. Do you agree with the decision of the arbitrator?

CASE 57

RATE DIFFERENTIAL ARISING FROM SUBCONTRACTING WORK

UNION: United Packinghouse Workers of America, CIO

COMPANY: Swift and Company, Denver Plant

At this plant the Company has a gang for maintenance and mechanical work which it carries on its payroll as its own employees. These employees are members of the United Packinghouse Workers, CIO. The Company obtains additional mechanical workers by contract through outside independent contractors. Such workers are not the company's employees but are employed and paid by the outside independent contractor, to whom the Company pays some agreed contract price. They are not members of the Packinghouse Workers, but of various craft unions. These employees of the outside contractor are apparently regularly employed at the company's plant and are paid in accordance with the wage schedules recognized as appropriate by the various craft unions to which they belong. Their wages are about $.50 per hour higher than those of the Company's employees who do maintenance and mechanical work at the plant.

POSITION OF THE UNION

The Union claims that this situation represents an intraplant inequality, or series of such inequalities, within the meaning of the following section of the collective agreement:

"(22) In accordance with the Directive Order of the National War Labor Board dated February 9, 1943, the parties will negotiate commencing immediately with a view towards eliminating intraplant inequalities between wage rates for individuals and between job classifications in conformance with the Board policies in this regard. All such intraplant inequalities will be handled at each plant under the grievance procedure set forth in Paragraphs 58 to 60 inclusive of this contract."

Intraplant inequalities exist because both contract and company mechanical employees work at the same plant. These inequalities should be eliminated by inaugurating throughout the mechanical gang rates conforming to those paid by the contractors to their employees who work on the company's premises.

POSITION OF THE COMPANY

The Company denies the existence of an intraplant inequality. The workers who are receiving higher wage rates for the same type of work performed by the company's maintenance and mechanical gang are not employed by the

Company but by an outside firm. Therefore, no intraplant inequalities can be demonstrated. Furthermore, there is no provision in the contract which prevents the Company from procuring work through independent contractors.

THE AWARD

There is no sanction in the contract against contracting for mechanical work. Employees of contractors are not employees of the Company and their wage rates are not set by the Company. Therefore, no intraplant inequality exists within the terms of the contract. This situation must be dealt with by collective bargaining in the future.

QUESTIONS

1. Do the employees of the outside contractors have the same prospects of employment, the same vacation and pension rights, and the same sick benefits as the employees of Swift and Company? Do you regard the answer to this question as relevant to the issue raised by the Union?

2. The Union takes the position (1) that there should be equal pay for men doing the same work in the plant even though the men work for different employers and (2) that the equality should be brought about by adjusting the wages of the Swift and Company employees to the wages paid by outside contractors. If one accepts the first point of the Union, why should equality not be established by adjusting the wages paid by the outside contractors to the wages paid by Swift and Company? In view of the fact that employees of the outside contractors are only a small fraction of the total force employed in the plant, would it not be more appropriate to adjust the wages of the employees of the outside contractors to the wages of the Swift and Company employees rather than vice versa?

3. If the wage scale for the various occupational groups in the force of Swift and Company were in proper adjustment, would adjusting the wages of the maintenance and mechanical gang to the wages paid by the outside contractor create an intraplant inequality among the various occupational groups of Swift and Company employees? In considering whether a given wage

change would remove some inequalities, is it proper to consider whether it would create other inequalities?

4. If the Company were required to adjust the wages of some occupational groups to the wages paid by every outside contractor (for example, trucking contractor, window-washing contractor, or cafeteria operator), would it be possible for the Company to maintain a properly balanced wage structure?

5. Assume that the principle were accepted that Swift and Company must pay its maintenance and mechanical gang the same wages paid for the same work by the outside contractors. Assume also that there were a change in contractors and that the new contractor paid a higher wage than the previous one. Would the Union have a case for demanding a second wage adjustment for the men in the maintenance and mechanical gang? Assume that the second contractor paid *less* than the first one. Would the Company have a case for asking a reduction for the men in the maintenance and mechanical gang?

6. Assume that the outside contractor paid less than Swift and Company. Should the wages of the maintenance and mechanical gang of Swift and Company be reduced to the rates paid by the outside contractor? If the outside contractor paid less than Swift and Company, would his employees have a case for demanding an increase on the ground of an intraplant inequality?

7. What is the practical problem which confronts the inside union in a case of this sort?

CASE 58

A DAILY OR A WEEKLY MINIMUM GUARANTEE

UNION: United Electrical, Radio & Machine Workers, CIO

COMPANY: The Morse Twist Drill Company

BACKGROUND

The company's only plant currently employs 1,240 workers, 1,125 of whom are production employees. Of these latter, between 400 and 500 are pieceworkers. The Company is a machine tool manufacturer.

Although no stoppages of work have occurred since the certification of the electrical workers' local in December, 1941 (there was, however, a half-day walkout in October, 1945, to support demands for a wage increase), the general tenor of the relations between the Union and the Company has not been entirely harmonious. The first contract was signed in 1942 only after an order of the War Labor Board. The second and third contracts, after long periods of fruitless negotiation were arbitrated, as were three other disputes pertaining to discharges (which the Union claimed had been made without just cause), an alleged refusal to give separation pay to servicemen, and a reduction in wages caused by an adjustment in piecework which involved the elimination of a rough grinding process.

Management maintains its conviction that unionism is detrimental to the efficiency of its employees because it substitutes wage-rate consciousness for a proper preoccupation with craftsmanship. It remains convinced that the great majority of issues over which the local union seeks to bargain collectively should not be removed from the sole discretion of management. The union officials, on their part, do not believe that the Company has ever bargained with the Union in good faith or that it has ever really reconciled itself to the fact that the Union would prove to be less transitory than other unpleasant innovations which the war had ushered in. During the period 1942–45, the Union estimates that the wage increases which it won amount to an average of about 28 cents an hour. It admits, however, that its dues-paying membership has declined from 1,200 in 1942 to about 350 at present.

The issue at hand arose in connection with the renewal of the collective agreement which expired on April 26, 1945, the Company having refused to negotiate with the Union on its new demands until the War Labor Board had made a final determination of several matters which it then held under consideration. The case was certified to the Board on April 25, 1945. After the Board announced its decision to cover all the matters in dispute between the Company and the Union (these involved the arbitrability of four grievances and two discharges and compliance with an arbitration award establishing labor-grade rate ranges), the Company agreed to extend the old agreement until a new one should be executed and to negotiate the union's demands. The two parties subsequently resolved all of the contract issues in dispute with the exception of the following three: (1) two 10-minute paid cleaning-up periods, (2) the checkoff, and (3) daily computation of piece-rate earnings. The Company refused to consider these three demands, and the issues were certified to the Regional War Labor Board for recommendation on October 11, 1945.

Under piecework or incentive wage systems, the earnings of workers vary with the amount of production for a great many reasons, for example: (a) variations in quality of materials; (b) state of repair of machinery; (c) flow of materials and parts; (d) breakdowns, delays, and accidents; and (e) application of the workers. Most incentive or piecework systems provide for minimum earnings to the workers. The calculation of this minimum may involve averaging earnings over a day or a week as illustrated in the table below. The issue presented by this case involves a choice between these methods of calculating a minimum.

The Union requested that the computation of piecework be changed from a weekly to a daily basis because such a change would result in increased weekly "make-up" pay being received by pieceworkers whose earnings on certain days might fall below the guaranteed day rate. The agreement provides that "the day rate shall be guaranteed employee if employee is unable to make said rate on piece-work or is waiting for piece-work at the request of the Company." It has been the present practice to compute the pieceworkers' earnings on a weekly basis and to divide the weekly earnings by the number of days worked during the week. Since this procedure involves averaging "good" days in with "bad" days, it is apparent that make-up will be greater if a daily computation of piecework earnings is substituted for the weekly computation. This is illustrated by the arbitrary numerical example given in the following table which assumes a minimum day-rate guarantee of $5.00 a day:

	Earnings	Daily Make-up
Monday	$ 5.00	None
Tuesday	10.00	None
Wednesday	4.00	$1.00
Thursday	2.00	3.00
Friday	6.00	None
Totals	$27.00	$4.00

Average daily earning:	$5.40	
Make-up computed on weekly basis:	None	
Make-up computed on a daily basis:	$4.00	

Position of the Union

If the contract (as quoted above) calls for a guarantee of the day rate, that rate should be guaranteed on a daily, and not on a weekly, basis. It is unfair to apply a pieceworker's bonus earnings—which are paid to him for his superior production—to periods of substandard output which are often beyond his control. In this connection, the Union submitted the following statement:

"As at present, operating under the terms of the current agreement, piece-rate earnings are computed weekly, with a day-rate guarantee when employee fails to reach his day rate on piece work. By this arrangement, piece workers on numerous occasions, after working diligently and making a good average for three or four days of the week have, by operating conditions, faulty material, etc., been slowed down, reducing their earnings for the remainder of the week so that the worker's take-home pay becomes average day rate and not piece-rate earnings. In some cases, the worker's day rate has to be made up, but in many cases the worker loses the compensation for his efforts for the remainder of the week, as his previous earnings, in addition to what he has been able to make under adverse conditions, often supersede his day rate which in most cases is low."

Furthermore, a system which applies earnings from superior output in one day to substandard results in another is bound to result in a deterioration of the worker's incentive and thus to defeat the very objectives of a piecework system. For "if at the beginning of the week you get hit by a bum job that don't earn anything for you, there is no incentive for you to go out and knock yourself out for the rest of the week to earn piece work, because you will end up with no better than your piece rate."

It has already been asserted that the unfairness in the practice of weekly computation lies in the individual employee's inability to govern many of the vital conditions which determine his daily output. Any one or combination of the following situations might well result in a "bum job":

1. The man might be given poor material to work up. This invariably results in his operation consuming more time than it does when performed on material of a good quality.

2. The previous operation might have been poorly executed. Thus, if a drill has been hardened inefficiently, the subsequent operation of straightening is rendered more difficult.

3. The type and nature of the job given to a worker are controlled by his foreman, and "it has been known to happen that foremen, in controlling the wages of the workers in their departments have purposely slowed down the earnings of the workers by methods of distribution and assignment of work."

4. The job might in its nature be a "tight" one. Some jobs are tighter than others. The tighter the job, the more difficult it is to make the base rate.

5. The job may be a new and unfamiliar one. Breaking in at a new type of job makes for slower work in the initial learning period.

Since the above factors are removed from the individual's

discretion, all workers, efficient as well as inefficient, are affected by the problem of make-up.

"We say that all workers, pretty nearly all workers, or the vast majority of workers, at sometime during the course of the month receive make-up pay, and that it is an exceedingly large number, which we are not able to compute, either in numbers or dollars and cents, who suffer through the loss of make-up in their base pay."

Make-up can amount to an appreciable proportion of the weekly pay of a good worker. While no precise estimates have been made, it is believed that the difference involved in a switch-over to a system of daily computation could easily come to $7.00 or $8.00 in "tough" weeks. The Union presented five cost-department slips pertaining to a particular worker whose base rate is $0.74 an hour. The amount earned which appears on the first slip is $11.89; on the second, $1.68; on the third, $3.60; on the fourth, $8.30; and on the fifth, $8.06. Since an 8-hour day's base-rate earning is $5.92, the man's earnings fell below the base figure on the second and third days by $4.24 and $2.32 respectively. Computed on a daily basis, the make-up for the five-day period would be $6.50, which is almost 20 per cent of his total earnings of $33.53.

But while the difference in make-up is financially important to the individual worker, it would be negligible to the Company which can well afford to pay it. Evidence of this is the fact that present paid make-up comprises only 3 per cent of the Company's annual payroll. Therefore, the *increase* involved in a daily computation would amount to a very small percentage of the total payroll.

Nor does the Union believe that extensive alteration or expansion of administrative or inspection procedure would be required in the switch-over, or that additional costs connected therewith would be burdensome. In the first place, there already exists, in the present system of reporting work, the machinery for computing piecework on a daily basis. At the end of the day, every pieceworker submits a slip on which is indicated the number of pieces completed on a particular job. In the event that a man has not finished a job by the end of the day, he makes out a piece slip which he submits showing the amount of work he has finished.

In the second place, the nature of the products manufactured by the Company lends itself to daily computation of output. The cycle of the jobs is such that a majority of the operations can be performed within a single working day. Long jobs form a relatively small proportion of the entire production of the shop.

POSITION OF THE COMPANY

The Company claims, first, that substandard production may be attributed primarily to the worker's own inefficiency and, second, that the administrative problems involved in changing over to a daily computation of piecework would be almost insurmountable.

The Company is currently paying make-up in the amount of $340 a week, or about $15,000 per year. Between 40 and 50 persons receive make-up weekly. While it is true that this does represent 10 per cent of the piecework force, the company's records reveal that make-up is paid for the same people, week in and week out. Furthermore, the percentage is declining, which is evidenced by the fact that the majority of workers to whom make-up is paid are "submarginal" people hired during the war to replace old employees who had entered the armed services and to handle the great increase in business during wartime. The postwar period, moreover, has resulted in a scaling down of operations which has reflected itself in a decrease in work force from a peak of approximately 2,100 to the present level of 1,200. This has enabled the Company to get rid of many of these poorer workers and also to increase efficiency per worker through more intensive supervision. These facts indicate, first, that the make-up problem is progressively becoming of less importance and, second, that the paying of make-up to an individual can be considered as a criterion of his efficiency. Complete production records of individuals are kept, and, if a man's record shows a persistent trend toward substandard output and earnings, he will be warned and finally may be discharged for inefficiency. The Union has stressed the importance of conditions for which the individual worker is not responsible and which operate to reduce his output. In so doing, however, it has presented a distorted picture.

Breakdowns do occur, but they occur rarely, and every effort is made to effect necessary repairs and maintenance after the operators have left their jobs and during week-end periods. Furthermore, the agreement provides:

> "When piece workers are unable to work on piece rates due to machinery breakdown through no fault of their own, or when they are assigned to work on unrated jobs, or to do repair work, they shall be paid an hourly rate not less than 75 per cent of their average hourly straight-time earnings for the previous week, but in no event shall such workers receive in excess of 75 cents per hour or their day rate, whichever is higher."

Furthermore, it is inevitable that waiting periods should occur repeatedly because "we are a big job shop, and . . . . we are making 22,000 different types of article and . . . . there cannot be a big continuity of these articles." However, a pieceworker is not penalized when work is not available for him. In the event that he is detained from work over 15 minutes, he is automatically shifted from piecework to a day-work basis.

It should be noted that the piece rates are fair, and it is reasonable to expect that a qualified worker can at least meet his base rates. The Company was founded in 1864, and the piece rates have been evolved out of long experience. Furthermore, the collective agreement provides that the Company will make available all rates and job descriptions for the purpose of facilitating wage negotiations and that no operative piece rates shall be changed except by consent of both the Company and the Union.

In reply to the union's assertion that the present computation of piecework results in a dampening of the worker's incentive, it is argued that a system of daily computation, on the contrary, will aggravate the practice of "banking" by which the worker will concentrate production on certain days and slack off on others in order to obtain both bonus earnings for the production days and make-up for those characterized by substandard output. Where it is possible to do so, he will report work actually produced in one day as being turned out in another.

In addition to the fact that the problem of make-up is unimportant to the efficient pieceworkers who comprise a great and, indeed, a growing percentage of the total number employed, the proposed change from a weekly to a daily computation of piecework earnings and make-up, is technically unfeasible in the light of certain peculiarities inherent in the nature of the plant's production process and in its administrative routine. After an examination of the nature of production an attempt can be made to evaluate the effects which the union's demand would impose upon it.

First, it is important to note that the Company produces in the neighborhood of 20,000 separate items. Most production is standard (according to the specifications described in the company's catalogue), although a considerable volume of business is "jobbing." The production of a given type of tool requires many different operations; thus, the production of drills involves a minimum of 22 distinct operations, each performed by a different worker. (Not all of these operations are performed by pieceworkers.) For any one product the various operations will require different lengths of time. For example, in the production of a lot of very small No. 70 drills, of which there are 1,000 to a lot, the cut-off operation will normally be completed in a few hours, whereas milling the lot will require almost a week. And, on the other hand, the completion time of any given operation will vary according to the nature of the "job" or product.

It is conceded that the majority of "job" *cycles* are less than a day in duration, but it is emphasized that items are produced in *lots*. The pieceworker's job is considered complete only after it has been passed on by the inspection department; and inspection is made by lots. The number of units in a lot varies widely with the nature of the articles turned out. For example, there are 1,000 No. 70 drills in a lot of No. 70 drills, but there is only one, 1-inch taper-shank drill to a lot of taper-shank drills. The size of the lot is determined by three factors: (1) size and weight of the article in question—originally, the determination was made with respect to the number of tools that one man could conveniently lift and carry; (2) the rate of sales of the item—large lots of slow-moving tools would result in oversized inventories; and (3) the force of custom.

Broadly speaking, the Company gears fast operations to slow ones (and vice versa) by three methods: (1) by proportioning the numbers of the various types of machines; (2) by multiple-machine operation—the worker may operate as many as six different machines simultaneously and work on several job lots at the same time; and (3) by switching jobs— a worker on a fast operation need not wait for work until a slower previous operation has been completed on the entire order for a certain type of tool; he can work on other jobs in-between. With respect to this last practice, however, it must be noted that the worker on any given process must "set up" his machine virtually every time he handles a different job. Thus, other factors remaining the same, the number of setups required for a given job will be determined by the size of the job lot. It must be noted that, while workers are reimbursed for setup time, this time is nonproductive from the company's viewpoint.

In view of the characteristics of the company's production process as above described, it must be concluded that the union's demand for completion of make-up on a daily basis would prove unfeasible and of prohibitive cost if adoption were attempted.

First, if the present system of inspection and reporting of production by lots is maintained, daily computation of piece-work would result in superseding the factors which at present determine the size of the lot by the sole criterion of any given worker's daily output. Breaking up a lot at the end of the day would thereby result in job lots of indeterminate size with resulting confusion in production control.

Second, breaking up the job lot would greatly increase in-spection work and would necessitate the hiring of an esti-mated additional 100 to 150 inspectors.

Third, the smaller the size of the job lot, the more frequent the number of setups necessitated and, therefore, the greater the proportion of nonproductive to productive time.

Fourth, if, on the other hand, it were decided not to alter the lengths of the various job lots as they now stand, there would result a very great administrative burden in the han-dling of work cards and completion slips by the cost depart-ment. In this connection, it is necessary to point out that the Union is in error when it claims that production is reported to the cost department at the end of a day for part lots. Actually, completion slips, which are the records used by the cost department, are turned in only for completed lots; memo-randum cards are indeed submitted for partial work com-pleted, but they are made available only to the production department.

QUESTIONS

1. Explain carefully what is meant by a system of weekly or daily computation of a guaranteed minima under a piece-rate system.
2. How would the character of production influence the appropriate-ness of the daily computation of the guarantee? How would the fruit-picking, hosiery, and the shipbuilding industries be suited to the daily computation of the guarantee?
3. What do you understand by the term "job cycle"? What relevance

does the length of the job cycle have to the period over which the guarantee is computed?

4. What do you understand by the practice of "banking"? How does the length of the period of computing the guarantee affect "banking"?

5. What additional administrative procedures are necessary if the guarantee is to be computed on a daily rather than a weekly basis?

6. Why is the nature of the relations between the parties particularly important in this type of situation?

CASE 59

WHEN ARE "CONDITIONS" BEYOND THE CONTROL OF THE COMPANY?

UNION: United Automobile, Aircraft and Agricultural Implement Workers of America, CIO, Local 509

COMPANY: American Foundry Company of Los Angeles, California

The reconditioning of molding sand used in the company's foundry is farmed out to an independent contractor. Molding sand must be reconditioned after each day's casting. The independent contractor accomplishes this by adding moisture to the sand in the proper amounts and running it through an aerating machine which piles the reconditioned sand in heaps near the molder's bench. It is the practice in all foundries for this task to be performed at night after the molders have completed their shift. The contract of the Company with the independent contractor provides only that the reconditioning be completed in time for the molders to go to work at 7:00 A.M.

On the night of Friday–Saturday, December 8–9, 1944, the contractor failed to recondition the sand because one of its employees failed to report for work. The American Foundry Company was not notified by the contractor of his failure to recondition the sand during the night in question. It was not

until Saturday morning at 7:00 A.M., when the foundry foreman reported for work, that the Company first discovered that
the sand had not been reconditioned. Thus, there was no sand
available for the molding operation, and the Company sent
the molders and their helpers home, requesting that they report for work the following morning.

The Union demanded that the molders and helpers affected
by the incident be paid four hours' pay under the following
section of the agreement:

> "*Section 10*. CALL IN PAY. Employes coming to work
> at the regular starting time, when they have not been
> notified that work is not available, shall be assigned to
> jobs or sent home and given four (4) hours' pay at their
> straight-time hourly rate, unless work is not available
> for reasons beyond the control of the Company."

The Company rejected the union's demand, and the issue
was referred to the impartial arbiter for decision.

POSITION OF THE UNION

The Union claimed that the Company has violated the
section of the contract quoted above. Since the Company
failed to notify the molders and helpers that no work was
available prior to their reporting for work, it is obligated to
pay the four-hour guarantee.

The Union also made the observation that failure on the
part of the contractor to recondition the sand could not constitute justification for the company's position. The Company
cannot escape its responsibilities under the collective agreement by letting out work to contractors and then claiming
that it can exert no control over their performance or non-
performance. Its ability to do so would enable it to contract
itself out of such collective responsibilities as it wished to
escape from and would nullify the intent of the collective
agreement.

Position of the Company

The Company pointed out that its obligation either to assign work or give four hours' pay to employees who have not been notified of unavailability of work prior to their reporting is a *conditional*, and not an absolute, obligation. Section 10 contains the modifying clause "unless work is not available for reasons beyond the control of the Company."

The facts in this case clearly indicate that the company's failure to notify the molders sufficiently in advance of their reporting time that no work was available for them was due to "reasons beyond the control of the Company." The party obligated to recondition the sand was an *independent contractor* rather than an *agent* or *servant* of the American Foundry Company. The Company could exercise no control or direction over the time selected or the methods employed by the independent contractor. "The failure of the independent contractor to perform this task was just as much beyond the control of the Company as a failure of the electric power company or the gas company to furnish electrical energy or fuel would be."

The question now arises as to the propriety of the company's decision to let this reconditioning work out to an independent contractor instead of performing it itself. The Union has by implication challenged the company's discretion in this connection. An exact analogy has been drawn between the failure of the contractor to provide the Company with reconditioned sand and the failure of a utility company—another contractor—to furnish it with electricity or fuel. If the latter failure can be held to constitute "reasons beyond the control of the company," so must the former. Any attempt to distinguish between the two cases boils down to a denial to management of discretionary control over business policy. "Obviously the Company could maintain electrical generators for manufacturing its own electricity, or gas generators for creating its own fuel, but in the exercise of a sound business policy it chooses to purchase these services and commodities from independent contractors.''

QUESTIONS

1. Do you regard the clause negotiated by the parties as an administrable contract provision?
2. What types of situations would you regard as clearly "beyond the control of the company"? What types of situations would you regard as clearly within the control of the company?
3. How would you guard against the repetition of the circumstances of this case?
4. Do you regard the fact of the company purchasing a good or a service from others a good test of the extent of the "control" of the company? Would you suggest other criteria?

Section H

<del>~~~~~~</del>

GENERAL WAGE CHANGES

THE discussion of standards or criteria for general wage-rate changes in Chapter V is to be regarded as an introduction to the cases in this section. Case 60, which follows, involves the comparison of a number of wage-reopening clauses in collective bargaining agreements. The demand for a general wage-rate change may be made in many situations during the life of an agreement subject to the limitations expressed in a wage-reopening clause. The precise language of such a clause is decisive in indicating under what circumstances a wage change may be demanded, the form of the demand that can be entertained, and even the extent of any wage change.

Cases 61 and 62 provide an opportunity to apply the customary standards for wage determination. These cases have been presented in considerable detail; they constitute a full account of the evidence and the arguments presented by both sides. These cases depict the economic and industrial relations environment in which the controversy over the general wage level arose.

A final problem in this section (Case 63) involves a brief survey of the facts of wage and price determination in the bituminous coal industry. The case provides the facts of a complex situation as a target for the tools of economic theory and industrial relations analysis. Attention is directed toward pervasive and longer-run aspects of a situation in which public attention has been concentrated upon the immediate and spectacular to the virtual exclusion of fundamental tendencies. The case provides a critical illustration of the interaction between economic forces and collective bargaining institutions.

CASE 60

WAGE-REOPENING CLAUSES

A number of different wage-reopening clauses have been summarized in this case. The following questions may facilitate an understanding of the differences among these various clauses as they may operate in practice.

1. What is meant by "wages" in the reopening clause? May a demand be made for "fringe benefits," such as vacations and holidays, in addition to a general wage-rate change? Does the term permit the making of demands for the rates of particular job classifications?

2. What happens in the event that the parties are unable to agree upon new "wage" provisions in bargaining growing out of demands made under a reopening clause? Is the contract still in effect? Are the parties free to strike or engage in a lockout?

3. What provisions are made, if any, for the settlement of a dispute following an impasse in bargaining when a reopening clause has been invoked? Must the parties arbitrate their differences? Do the old provisions remain in effect?

4. Who may request a reopening of "wages"? Does the clause only permit demands by the union for increases, or does it also allow the management to request decreases?

5. How often may a reopening provision be utilized in the course of a contract? Is there any limitation on the number of times or the dates on which "wages" may be subject to negotiations?

6. Are there any conditions which must be met before "wages" may be reopened? The cost of living may have had to be increased by a certain amount; there may have had to be changes in the rates paid by other firms in the industry; or "competitive conditions" in the industry must have altered. The reopening clause may be made conditional.

The foregoing questions illustrate the variety of ways in which the parties may shape a reopening clause of a contract to their special problems and relationships. The reader is urged to compare and contrast the implications of the clauses which follow in terms of the questions which have just been posed.

1. *Textile Workers Union of America, CIO, and Botany Worsted Mills, 1946*

"Wages may be revised twice a year upon the request of either party by the giving of sixty days' written notice. Wage revisions shall be effective only on the 1st Monday of August or the 1st Monday of February following such notice.

"If the parties are unable to agree within fifteen days . . . . either party may require arbitration thereof. . . . ."

2. *The Oil Workers International Union, CIO, and The Texas Company, 1946*

"It is agreed that, upon presentation of a request in writing for a general change in wage rates by one party to the other, negotiation in relation thereto will be initiated within 30 days from date of such request, unless such time is changed by mutual agreement."

3. *International Longshoremen's and Warehousemen's Union, Wholesale and Warehousemen's Union, and A. S. Beck Shoe Corporation, 1945*

"This agreement shall continue in full force and effect up to and including the 31st day of January, 1948, subject to the right of the Union or the Employer to request a modification of the previous fixing—

"*a*) The minimum weekly wages to be paid to such employees covered hereby, and

"*b*) The weekly wages of such employees, for the period of the contract commencing on the 1st day of February, 1947, and ending on the expiration day, to wit, January 31, 1948; the party desiring a modification of the provisions referred to in the said items '(*a*)' and '(*b*)' of this paragraph shall give written notice thereof to the other party . . . . , if, within five days after the sending of such notice the parties will be unable to agree with respect to such modification, then the question . . . . shall be submitted to arbitration for final settlement and adjustment. . . . ."

4. *United Electrical, Radio & Machine Workers of America, CIO, and Champion Aero Metal Products*

"At the option of the Union, this Agreement shall be reopened on December 1st, 1946, for the purpose of negotiating an upward revision of the wages provided therein. In the event the parties are unable to agree as to the amount of the wage increase, the matter shall be arbitrated in the manner provided under the arbitration provisions of this Agreement. . . . ."

5. *United Rubber, Cork, Linoleum & Plastic Workers of America, CIO, and Cords, Limited, Inc.*

"This agreement is the final settlement of all wage issues between the parties for the period hereof, provided, however, that if at the end of nine months from the date hereof there has been a general wage adjustment among the Company's competitors in the Company's industry, which adjustment brings the basic wage rates of the employees of said competitors to the level of or in excess of those agreed upon herein, the Company agrees to reconsider the wage structure provided for herein, within thirty days after a request therefor by the Union."

6. *International Longshoremen's & Warehousemen's Union, CIO, and Waterfront Employers Association*

"Semi-annually during the life of this contract, as of March 31 or September 30, the rates of pay and overtime rates shall, at the request of either party, be reviewed and if the parties cannot agree, shall, at the request of either party, be determined by the Impartial Chairman. The party desiring wage review shall give notice of such desire not less than thirty days prior to the semi-annual date on which wage review is requested."

7. *United Steelworkers of America, CIO, and Carnegie-Illinois Steel Corporation*

"The terms and conditions of this Agreement shall continue in effect until Midnight April 30, 1949, provided, however, that either party may, on April 1, 1948, give written notice to the other party of its desire to negotiate a general and uniform change in rates of pay. Within 5 days after the giving of such notice, the parties shall meet for the purpose of negotiating such issue. Failing agreement on such issue on or before April 30, 1948, this Agreement shall remain in effect until Midnight April 30, 1949."

CASE 61

HOURLY EARNINGS VERSUS PIECE RATES

UNION: International Ladies' Garment Workers' Union

COMPANY: Three Associations

REOPENING OF THE WAGE QUESTION

On November 13, 1945, the joint board of the Dress and Waistmakers' Union of Greater New York of the International Ladies' Garment Workers' Union demanded a "20% increase in wages to all workers in all crafts covered by (their) collective agreement (s)." These agreements had been entered into on February 14, 1941, and were to remain in effect until January 31, 1944. On January 25, 1944, the expiration date was extended to February 29 of the same year; on February 28 it was further extended to March 6; and on March 22, as of March 6, 1944, the agreement was extended for the third time until January 31, 1947. The Union invoked the wage-reopening clause in the agreement, which reads:

"The parties hereto are aware of the policies and measures which the federal government had adopted relating to wage stabilization. Whenever, during the term of this agreement, the wage stabilization policies of the federal government are changed or amended by any law, order, regulation, formula or decision, etc., which will permit further increases in wages, the Union shall have the right to demand that each member of the Association shall increase the wages of all of the workers covered by this agreement who are employed in his inside shop, if he maintains one, and in the shops of his contractors. The Union's demand shall be made upon the Association in writing, and immediately thereafter, the Union and the Association shall confer for the purpose of considering the same. Any agreement reached between them shall be jointly submitted for approval to the National War Labor Board or to any other government agency which may replace it, if such approval be required by law.

"In the event the Union and the Association fail to meet, or having met, are unable to reach an agreement within seven (7) days from the date of the Union's demand, the matter shall be decided not later than ten (10) days thereafter by the Impartial Chairman. . . . . His decision shall be submitted for approval to the National War Labor Board, or to any other governmental agency which may replace it if such approval be required by law."

Action was taken by the joint board of the Dress and Waistmakers' Union after the joint board of the Cloak and Suitmakers Union had reopened the wage clause in their contract. The general manager of the Dress and Waistmakers board wanted the Cloak and Suitmakers case decided first; he was agreeable, therefore, to several delays, requested by the employers, which resulted in a three-month interval between the union's presentation of its demands and the commencement of arbitration proceedings on February 18, 1946.

The Union claimed that the 20 per cent increase was required to adjust a discrepancy arising between an alleged 35 per cent rise in the cost of living between January, 1941, and September, 1945, and two wage increases in the same period allegedly totaling only 15 per cent.

The employers, represented by three associations—the Affiliated Dress Manufacturers' Association, the National Dress Manufacturers' Association, and the Popular Priced Dress Manufacturers' Group—rejected the demand, and the matter was referred to the impartial chairman for arbitration.

BACKGROUND OF THE INDUSTRY

The issues in this case are to be understood only in terms of the history of collective bargaining in the metropolitan dress industry and the extent of the union's participation in that industry's structure and functioning. The joint board of the Dress and Waistmakers' Union of the International Ladies' Garment Workers' Union, has jurisdiction over the area embracing eight states: New York, New Jersey, Pennsylvania, Massachusetts, Connecticut, Rhode Island, Maryland, and Delaware. The dress industry in this area employs 72,965 workers. The employers are affiliated with five associations, the membership of which is broken down as shown in Table 1.

TABLE 1

Association	Jobbers	Manu-facturers	Contractors	Total Firms
Affiliated.............	86	194	...	280
National.............	151	200	...	351
Popular..............	145	118	...	263
United better.........	...	...	804	804
United popular.......	...	...	644	644
Total............	...	...	...	2,342

Thus 72,965 workers are employed in 2,342 establishments; the average number of employees per establishment is 31.

The extremely small size of the industrial unit reflects the dominance of the element of style in determining the industry's structure. Where style is all-important, the potentialities of standardization are slight; mechanization is thereby limited, and with it the size of the shop. It costs little to enter an industry in which the size of the establishment is small and in which there is a low degree of mechanization. As a result, "cutthroat" competition prevails, and turnover of firms is high. In 1937, the mortality rate of jobbers and manufacturers was 17 per cent; in 1938, 23 per cent in 1939, 22 per cent. Of the 1,687 firms reported doing business in Manhattan in 1925, 1,411, or 83.6 per cent, had gone out of business by 1933.[1] "In Manhattan alone, from 1927 to 1935, the percentage of firms which retired each year was never less than 22.2% of the total. . . . ."[2] And turnover among contractors is higher than among manufacturers. In some years as many as one-third of the New York contractors went out of business.[3] An investigation of 927 contracting establishments over the period 1926–33, revealed that in 3 years 68.2 per cent and in 7 years 81.7 per cent were discontinued.[4]

Another effect of the paramount influence of style upon the organization of the industry stems from the fact that designing and skill in marketing are more important than skill in manufacturing. This has been in great part responsible for the emergence of the dress jobber who performs the key roles of designer and distributor. "Dressmaking is only partly an industry—the rest is art. . . . . He is caught halfway between the business world and the unstandardized sphere of artistic invention."[5] Manufacturing is not of primary concern to the jobber; he "farms out" most or all of the fabrication of his dresses to contractors whom he supplies with the necessary materials. The contractor manufactures the dresses and charges the jobber for labor cost and overhead. Thus "the contractor has relieved the jobber of concern with the processes of dress production and has enabled him to

[1] Teper, Lazare, *The Women's Garment Industry*, pp. 17–18.

[2] Hamilton, Walton, and Associates, *Price and Price Policies* (New York: McGraw-Hill Book Co., 1938), p. 324.

[3] Teper, *op. cit.*, p. 18.

[4] Hamilton, *op. cit.*, p. 343.

[5] *Ibid.*, p. 331.

concentrate on the problems of style and sale. The selling of dresses is an exigent, intricate, and time-consuming affair in which specialization is requisite for success. It has been greatly to the advantage of the jobber to free himself from the technical aspects of dressmaking and from the detailed shop adjustments known as labor problems."[6]

Furthermore, it is the essence of styles that they change frequently, thereby causing great irregularity in production with resultant loss on overhead during slack seasons. These conditions contributed to the emergence of the contracting system which has enabled the jobber-manufacturer to reduce the underutilization of his own productive resources by restricting the size of his "inside shop" and farming out extra work to contractors. These latter, competing for work and operating on a very narrow profit margin, sought to minimize their costs of operation. Labor being the chief element in their cost structure, wages were thereby depressed and hours lengthened.

The union members themselves contributed to this process. Since piece rates were settled by collective bargaining in each individual contractor's shop, workers in different establishments competed against each other in order to win the jobber's work for the particular contractors by whom they were employed. Furthermore, when work was short, a contractor's employees would often secretly agree to work under conditions below those stipulated in the union agreement.[7]

The importance of the contractor system is evidenced by the fact that approximately 61 per cent of the establishments in the metropolitan dress industry are contracting shops and that these shops turn out 62 per cent of the total output by volume.

The union found, therefore, that in order to achieve and maintain higher wages, shorter hours, and better working

[6] *Ibid.*, p. 345.

[7] Seidman, Joel, *The Needle Trades* (New York: Farrar & Rinehart, Inc., 1942), pp. 253, 265.

conditions, it had to effect a modification of the jobber-contractor relationship and to institute a uniform system of "settling" piece rates in the individual shops. In the collective agreements of 1936, the Union was able to insert provisions which limited the number of contractors to whom a jobber would give work to that "actually required by him to manufacture his garments," which stipulated that contractors work only for jobbers designating them, and which required that the jobber settle piece rates "for all of the piece workers of his inside shop, if he maintains one, *and of all of his contractors' shops at the same time*" (italics added) and that he pay his contractors an amount covering overhead[8] and profit in addition to the wages and earnings to be paid to the workers. Thus, not only was a brake set upon the intense competition among contractors and their incentive to depress labor standards removed, but responsibility for setting wage scales was shifted from them to the jobbers. The Union in effect now treated the contracting shops as departments of the jobber's enterprise. It therefore altered the latter's economic role of designer-seller by making him participate more directly in manufacturing than hitherto had been his practice. In this connection, it is significant to note that, in the present case, the representatives of the two contractors' associations did not argue against an increase in wages but merely sought assurance that the jobbers would reimburse their members for any increase which might be made.

The 1936 agreements also provided that the practice of determining piece rates by bargaining in each individual shop —often resulting in the establishment of different rates for the same garment—be superseded by bargaining on the jobber's premises and by the determining of rates in accordance with a "unit system" or "schedule" drawn up by an administrative board composed of representatives of the Unions and the Associations. When a new style is "settled," the garment is analyzed into its component operations, for each of which a piece rate (customarily called a "price") appears

[8] *Ibid.*, pp. 8–12.

on the schedule. The "price" of the garment is then determined by adding the monetary values of the several components. It should be noted that the schedule "price" for an individual operation is itself determined with reference to (*a*) the number of "units" of time required to complete the operation, (*b*) the minimum hourly earnings set forth in the collective agreements, and (*c*) the price line of the garment—the higher the price of the garment, the higher the money value of the component unit. If the price of the garment is raised, its schedule "prices" (piece rates) also rise—even if no change in style, quality, or workmanship is involved.

Piece rates are determined by a price committee in the employer's shop consisting of representatives of the employers and the workers in the establishment. In the event that they are unable to agree on the proper application of the system described above, either side can refer the matter to the price adjustment bureau of the industry's administrative board.

STIPULATED FACTS

The following facts, which bear upon the controversy, were generally recognized by both sides and referred to by representatives of both the employers and the unions during the hearings before the impartial chairman:

1. During the war years, the dress industry enjoyed a great expansion of production. Sales volume increased from $344,504,569 in 1940 to $680,000,000 in 1945—an increase of 97.4 per cent. Production of units increased from 77,000,000 in 1940 to 99,000,000 in 1945.

2. During the same period of time, however, the number of workers employed by the industry declined by 14.6 per cent. Employment stood at 85,439 in 1940; by 1945 it had fallen to 72,965. Thus, annual production per worker increased approximately 50 per cent in terms of physical output.

3. Part of this increase in annual productivity may be ascribed to a rise in *hourly* output per worker, which in turn can be accounted for by the following facts:

a) Increased managerial efficiency.

b) Increased effort on the part of the workers, who were stimulated by the large volume of work available as well as by the pressure exerted upon them by a rising wartime cost of living.

c) Sharp reduction in the number of styles settled by the industry—from 124,000 in 1939 to 34,586 in 1945. Styles, furthermore, were *simplified* during this period.

d) Quality of workmanship generally suffered some deterioration during the war years.

4. Annual output per worker was also greatly increased by a rise in the number of hours worked per day and weeks worked per year.

5. Within the framework of the sharp increase in over-all production by value and by unit, noted in paragraph 1 above, the percentage increase in the output of higher-priced lines

TABLE 2

Net Sales by Price Ranges

Price Range	1940	1944
$4.75–$ 5.50............	$74,205,263	$92,500,000
$9.75–$10.75............	38,499,703	95,000,000

was much greater than the relative increase registered by the lower-priced lines, as shown in Table 2. Thus, the average price per dress rose. The increase from $4.46 in 1939 to $6.86 in 1944 is in excess of 50 per cent.

6. Annual take-home pay per employee in the metropolitan dress industry has increased during the war period (taken either as 1940–45 or 1941–45). Referring to data presented by the Union revealing that an increase in sales volume of 97.4 per cent over the period 1940–45 had been turned out by 14.6 per cent less workers, and assuming that the cost of labor bore the same proportion to the volume of sales as price lines shifted upward, the employers contended that wages increased in the same proportion as volume, namely, 131 per cent.

The Union, in a supplemental memorandum, affirmed:

"The Union recognized that the take-home pay of the workers in the industry was higher in 1945 than it was in 1940 and 1941. For that matter, the Union showed that the dollar volume of business of the dress industry increased 97.4% since 1940. As Mr. Hochman put it, the workers made more dresses, and, therefore, they received more pay. The Union demonstrated that in view of the reduction in the number of workers in the industry between 1940 and 1945, an average worker turned out during 1945, 50.2% more units than in 1940. This factor alone would have been responsible for the rise in annual earnings in that amount. Mr. Kolchin claimed that, as a result of the upward shift of price lines, the piece rates for operators would have shown a difference of 38½% (without any advance in rates over those prevalent in 1940). The combined effect of increased output per worker and of different piece rates caused by the change in the nature of work equals 88.7%. When the two wage adjustments of 10% under the collective agreement and 6% awarded by the National War Labor Board are also taken into account, it may be said that the average annual earnings of the workers would show a rise of around 105%."[9]

7. Between January, 1941, and September, 1945, the cost of living rose in the neighborhood of 33 per cent. This estimate, established by the Economic Stabilization Director for the country as a whole, was finally accepted by the employers, although they had originally contended that the increase should be taken at 31.8 per cent, an amount indicated by the Board of Labor Statistics index. The Union claimed that allowance should be made for the higher cost of living in the New York area and for the fact that the cost of living rose further after the month of September, 1945. Therefore, it claimed that a rise of 35 per cent was more accurate than the 33 per cent figure.

[9] Supplemental memorandum submitted on behalf of joint board of Dress and Waistmakers' Union of Greater New York, pp. 25–26.

The Union based its claim for a 20 per cent increase on the difference between a 35 per cent rise in the cost of living between January, 1941, and September, 1945, and the wage-rate increases allegedly totaling 15 per cent which it had received in that period.

POSITION OF THE UNION

The great expansion in production and sales volume experienced by the industry during the war years in the face of a 15 per cent reduction in its work force was made possible in great part by the stable nature of the industry, in the achievement of which the Union had played the major role through its introduction in 1936 of the system of limiting contractors and also by the longer hours which it authorized its members to work.

It is readily acknowledged, therefore, that the annual take-home pay of the union members increased, but it should be borne in mind that such increase was occasioned by greater output per worker. Annual, weekly, and hourly earnings in 1945 are presented in Table 3.

No attempt has been made to compare annual, weekly, or hourly earnings between 1941 and 1945 because no adequate data are available. In this respect, it is noted that "employers' books examined by the union and employers' payrolls submitted to the union do not show hours worked. Nor do they show the amount of time spent in the course of a year, week, or even an hour by the workers in the actual process of work as distinguished from the total time spent in the shop." (The worker spends the entire day in the shop regardless of the amount of work available for him to do. When things are slack, he works slowly and converses with his fellows; his output per hour is low. In rush periods, on the other hand, the social aspect of the shop organization is subordinated to the economic one; he works more intensively, and his output per hour increases.) It is true that comparisons are submitted by the employers, but their data are drawn from samples which are too small for reliability and which are not representative of true conditions prevailing in the industry.

Even if a comparison of annual earnings for the period were possible, however, it would be valueless as a yardstick against which to measure an increase in the cost of living. A worker's annual earnings vary with the amount of work available for him to do in the course of a year. This, of course, varies from year to year. Right now, the industry is enjoying good times. But the future is uncertain. Furthermore, it may

TABLE 3

ANNUAL WEEKLY AND HOURLY EARNINGS, 1945, BY CRAFTS*

CRAFT	WORKERS		ON 52-WEEK BASIS		ACTUAL EARNINGS†	
	No.	Per-centage	Annual	Weekly	Weekly	Hourly
All crafts............	72,965	100.0	$2,317.89	$44.57	$54.03	$1.35
Week workers........	14,228	19.5	1,858.63	35.78	41.58	0.97
Cutters............	2,846	3.9	3,768.96	72.48	78.52	1.83
Sample makers.......	1,824	2.5	1,684.90	32.40	48.14	1.18
Floor..............	9,558	13.1	1,446.00	27.81	31.78	0.73
Pieceworkers.........	58,737	80.5	2,250.71	43.28	57.27	1.46
Pressers............	6,566	9.0	3,800.51	73.09	88.59	2.11
Operators..........	44,218	60.6	2,384.82	45.86	55.72	1.46
Finishers..........	7,953	10.9	1,767.51	33.99	40.82	0.98

* Memorandum submitted on behalf of joint board of Dress and Waistmakers' Union by Julius Hochman, General Manager, before impartial chairman on demand of Union for wage increase, February 18, 1946.
† Includes overtime (2,253 shops).

be expected that a large number of union members who left the industry during the war will return. Assuming no increase in output, an increase in labor force will result in a reduction in the individual's yearly take-home pay.

Thus, an increase in yearly earnings is only *temporary*. The Union demands a *permanent* increase in wage *rates* which will be unaffected by the factors mentioned above. Annual take-home pay can be acceptable as a yardstick only if the Union and its members are assured of a guaranteed annual wage. Since no guaranteed annual wage prevails in the industry, the only acceptable criterion is wage rates—and specifically, since 80 per cent of the workers are pieceworkers, this means piece rates.

Piece rates in this industry must be defined as flat rates in the case of pressers and as schedule rates (i.e. the monetary value of the units) in the case of operators and finishers. The unit system, or schedule, is the basis for determining the labor cost of the garment; in the case of contractor-made garments, it directly determines the entire cost.

The schedule system of settling garment "prices" prevails throughout the industry. The 40 firms which do not use the operating schedule account for only 3.3 per cent of the 1945 dollar volume of sales of the entire industry; and only 9 per cent of the firms, accounting for only 11 per cent of the business volume in the New York market, have no pressing schedule.

Furthermore, the system of settling rates by collective bargaining is rigidly adhered to. The Union produces evidence to show that when manufacturers (largely because of the OPA's maximum average price regulations) introduced lower-priced lines, the settlements were made on the basis of lower unit rates consistent with those price lines, even though no changes in the style or quality were involved.

Whenever a pieceworker is employed on a higher-priced line, it is true that his piece rate will rise, but the Union points out that it is possible that his hourly and weekly earnings will decline because more workmanship and detail go into the fabrication of a higher-priced garment and the worker is able to turn out less garments per hour or per week.

Whenever a manufacturer *simplifies* styles by eliminating an item of a garment, the settlement price is reduced by an amount equal to the product of the "price" of the item appearing on the schedule and the number of such items eliminated.

It is a fact that production of dresses in the higher-priced lines accounts for a much greater proportion of total output than it did before the war, but this must not be construed as an *increase* in the basic *wage rate*. It is merely a *change* in the *job.* "It merely means that the workers became employed by a higher price line firm."

Julius Hochman, general manager of the joint board, summarized the position of the Union as follows:

> "On what system do the pressers work? They work on piece work. How do they settle their prices? They settle their prices by collective bargaining. . . . Now when you agree with me to pay a flat rate, it makes no difference what the style; that is my price for your labor. This is not a question of hours; this is not a question of yearly earnings, but this is the point to discuss. In other words, it is not a question of how many thousands of dollars he makes a year, or how much he makes a week. The question is, what increase have you given to the pressers on these flat rates for which you have collectively signed with him and for which he has contracted to work with you, and for which he does work for you.
>
> . . . .
>
> "Therefore I say to you, gentlemen, what you have contracted to pay a finisher for sewing on so many snappers, basting a bottom, or making a loop, is the basis on which you must readjust your wages in accordance with the inflation that took place during the last few years."

Taking the average settled price, then, as the yardstick against which to measure a 35 per cent increase in the cost of living over the period January, 1941, to September, 1945, the Union finds that the only increases in average settled price consisted in one of 10 per cent in 1941 and one of 5 per cent (plus an additional 1 per cent in lieu of retroactivity), both of which were approved by the War Labor Board. A study of the average settled prices of all (52) firms which have maintained the same price lines since 1941 or 1942 reveals no additional increases over and above a 10 per cent "tolerance" or leeway allowed by custom in the process of settlement as a permissible difference—either positive or negative—between the settled price of the garment and the amount obtained by application of the schedule.

Therefore, the Union is demanding a 20 per cent increase required "to equalize the dollar value of the wage rates paid today with the dollar value which they had in January 1941."

POSITION OF THE COMPANY

A comparison of annual, weekly, and hourly earnings between the year 1940 or 1941 and 1945 will reveal far greater increases than the increase in the cost of living which the Union alleges to be 35 per cent but which should be taken at 33 per cent, the estimate of the stabilization director. The data on annual increases submitted by the affiliated and national groups is summarized in the accompanying table. The

PERCENTAGE OF INCREASE IN ANNUAL EARNINGS, 1940–45

Price Lines	All Workers	Pieceworkers	Week Workers
Below $6.75...........	121%	125.0%	89.0%
$6.75 and above........	128	145.8	74.4

Popular Price group estimated that the annual earnings of their employees rose 105 per cent between January, 1941, and September, 1945. And, since it can be reasonably assumed that the proportion of the cost of labor to total volume of sales did not decline as price lines shifted upward, it can be concluded that the percentage increase in per worker productivity by volume will also measure increase in annual earnings. From the union's own estimates of a 97.4 per cent increase in volume accounted for by a work force which decreased by 14.6 per cent, this can be taken at 131 per cent for the period 1940–45.

Weekly earnings, according to the New York State Department of Labor's *Industrial Bulletin and Employment Review*, rose from $25.87 in January, 1941, to $56.62 in September, 1945, an increase of 119 per cent. (It should be noted that, since adjustment was made for the lesser number of weeks worked in January, 1941, this figure can also be used to measure the increase in annual earnings.)

According to the Popular Price group's calculations, *straight-time* weekly earnings rose 88 per cent since January, 1941.

Comparisons of *straight-time hourly earnings* by the Affiliated and National Associations reveal increases above the cost of living in two out of three groups as shown in the accompanying table. The Popular Price group's estimate, based on its 88 per cent figure for straight-time weekly earnings, is 61.2 per cent if we assume that the average straight-time work week in 1941 was five hours shorter than in 1945, or 50.4 per cent if a seven-hour difference is assumed. It should also be noted that the report of the Bureau of Labor Statistics on

PERCENTAGE OF INCREASE IN STRAIGHT-TIME HOURLY
EARNINGS, 1940–45

Price Lines	Pieceworkers	Week Workers
Below $6.75..........	Not submitted	44.4%
$6.75 and above.......	95.8%	32.1

"Adjusted Average Straight-Time Hourly Earnings by Industries" set the increase for the women's clothing industry at 86.8 per cent for the period January, 1941, to October, 1944, as compared with 36.7 per cent for all manufacturing employees. Although this estimate covers the industry as a whole, "there is every reason to believe that wages in the dress industry paralleled the others."

Thus it is evident that earnings—annual, weekly, and hourly—have by far outstripped the cost of living. The Union objects to using annual earnings as a yardstick, but, since the Union is basing its demands for a 20 per cent wage increase upon a cost-of-living argument, it is a worker's take-home pay that is relevant to the issue, and not his *rate* of pay. Quoting Chester Bowles: "There are all kinds of figures tossed around about basic wage rates, straight-time hourly earnings, and average hourly earnings. But let's remember that it is take-home pay that buys groceries." Mr. Hochman can be quoted against himself on this point, and in 1940 he told us that the rates were high enough—it was more work that was needed.

The Union argues that an increase in annual earnings may only be temporary because it varies with the amount of work available for the pieceworker to perform from year to year. The Union admits that annual earnings have risen, but it bases its claim for an increase in wage rates on the possibility that the volume of business may decline in some future period. Of course it may, but that is irrelevant to the *current* situation. Adjustments to future changes in annual earnings should be bargained over *when such changes occur*, not in anticipation of them. Quoting Mr. Nizor:

> "Mr. Hochman says, 'Well, it may get worse.' When it gets worse, he should have come in. He should have had a case before he arose on his feet. He shouldn't stand here now and say, 'I predict that there will be trouble. Therefore, I want an increase to take care of it.'"

Even if it is assumed for the sake of argument, however, that piece rates should be adopted as the criterion, it can be demonstrated that piece rates, too, increased more than the cost of living. This increase was caused by certain benefits which the workers enjoyed during the war period:

1. The upward shift in price ranges resulting in a 50 per cent rise in the average price of a dress between 1939 and 1944. Schedule rates are higher for operations performed on higher-priced garments than on lower-priced ones.

2. The upward shift in price range does not reflect a corresponding shift in style ranges as it would have before the war. Women have been paying more money for the same quality dress. It will be noted that this point refutes the union's claim that a higher schedule rate for a higher-priced garment may be offset by a decrease in the worker's hourly output occasioned by the superior workmanship required. Moreover, when higher schedule rates are paid as the result of a shift to a higher-priced garment which requires no more skill or workmanship than did a lower-priced one, this rep-

resents an increase in piece rate and not a bona fide job transfer, as the Union maintains. When the two increases of 10 per cent in 1941 and 7 per cent in 1943 are considered, this upward shift in price lines amounts to a 12 per cent increase in piece rates.

3. Reduction in the number of styles from 124,000 in 1939 to 34,586 in 1945.

4. Simplification of styles with respect to details. Reduction in the number of styles and simplification have resulted in increased "lays" of dresses, increased hourly output.

> "If we will agree that garments have become simpler, I say that constitutes an increase in the wage schedule, because you can increase a wage rate in one of two ways:
>
> "You can either give an operator more money for the same quantity of work that he is doing, or you can give him the same amount of money for less work than he did before. And by simplifying the garment you are giving him less work for the same amount of money, thereby increasing the rate."

5. Deterioration in quality of garment. With less rigid inspection standards to meet, the worker's output increases because (a) he devotes less time to the production of each garment and (b) less time is "wasted" in rectifying mistakes.

6. Improved conditions of production, such as reduction of the waiting time of pieceworkers by improved messenger service, which has resulted in a greater portion of the working hour being devoted to "productive time." Since pieceworkers are paid by the piece and not by the hour, this increase in efficiency serves to increase their hourly earnings.

7. "Tolerance" in the schedule rate. This has been acknowledged by the Union as being 5 or 10 per cent and is the difference between the actual settled price of the garment and the price which would have obtained under a rigid arithmetic application of the schedule. These disparities arise because, in over 90 per cent of the cases, garments are settled by bargaining in the shop between the shop price committee and the

employer; only when the parties fail to agree are rate-fixing problems referred to the price adjustment bureau. Under wartime conditions of labor scarcity and greatly increased consumer demand, employers were not likely to resist their employees' settlement estimates. As one employer representative put it:

"We know that when, under the bargaining pressures of this prosperity, the workers came in to settle the price, that they had a bargaining weapon which they exercised. . . . .

"We know that the employers, because of the same pressures, were not even inclined to argue too much at certain times. They wanted to do anything to get the product out, but they went up. . . . .

"It went up because this unit system, this schedule device, merely puts ropes around the ring. But we know very well that in that ring you can do lots of things. You have lots of room to run around and expand, and that room was fully taken advantage of by the workers."

In conclusion, it must be recognized that it is impossible to divorce the schedule rate from hourly earnings. The collective agreements provide for minimum hourly earnings for pieceworkers, and the schedule rates are themselves determined so as to assure the worker a living wage. Two elements enter into the determination of "units" and "schedules":

"(1) the time that it takes a person to sew those snaps into the dress; and (2) how reasonably can we expect or calculate the number of weeks that the worker will have to do that operation in, in order to get a conclusion of a wage which we can say we have a right to expect a person to receive and on which he can live."

Thus it is impossible to divorce the piece *rate* from the hourly *earning*.

QUESTIONS

1. Distinguish carefully among wage rates, straight-time hourly earnings, gross hourly earnings, weekly earnings, and annual

earnings. Make a list of the factors which influence the variation of each from period to period. Decompose the extent of increase in annual earnings in this case into its separate components.

2. How would you expect companies and unions to argue for the relative influence of *rates* and *earnings* during the course of good and bad times?

3. What weight would you attach in this arbitration proceeding to the extent of wage changes made in other industries? Does this argument constitute a distinctive basis for a change in wage rates?

4. In applying the standards of cost of living, productivity, or comparable wages to the facts of a particular case involving the issue of a change in the general level of wage rates, should comparisons be made with *wage rates* or *hourly* or *weekly* earnings?

5. Write an opinion supporting your decision in this case.

CASE 62

THE APPEAL TO DIVERSE WAGE STANDARDS

UNION: Amalgamated Association of Street, Electric Railway and Motor Coach Employees of America

COMPANY: Indianapolis Railways, Inc.

The arbitration proceedings arise over a demand of Division 1070, Amalgamated Association of Street, Electric Railway and Motor Coach Employees of America, AFL, for a general wage rate increase of $0.30 an hour to be effective May 1, 1947. The request of the Union was made under the following reopening provision of the current contract, entered into as of December 1, 1946, and to continue until April 30, 1948:

"It is further agreed by the Company and the Association that either party shall have the right to request changes in the wages at any time from and after May 1, 1947, upon giving the other party sixty (60) days' notice in writing, delivered by registered mail, and that such requested changes shall be subject to arbitration in the same manner as provided in Section 7 of this agreement."

THE PARTIES

Indianapolis Railways, Inc., was established as a reorganization of the Indianapolis Street Railway Company and took over the transportation system from a receiver on June 1, 1932. Transit operations in Indianapolis date from 1864.

The Company provides mass transportation by streetcar, trackless trolley, and bus, servicing a city with a population over 400,000. It operated 63.3 miles of track, 62 miles of trackless trolley, and 143.5 miles of motor coach routes as of December 31, 1946. On the same date, the Company operated 446 streetcars and motor coaches and employed 1,606 employees. At the end of 1946, a total of 1,432 employees were in job classifications covered by the agreement with the Union, of whom 894 were operators. At the time of the hearings, total employment amounted to 1,775, with 1,575 represented by the Union.

Indianapolis Railways, Inc., operates under a 99-year lease the property of the Traction Terminal Corporation which consists of an office building, bus terminal, and parking lot.

Division 1070, Amalgamated Association of Street, Electric Railway and Motor Coach Employees of America, is the collective bargaining agency for operators and maintenance employees of the Company. The Union also represents in the same unit the employees engaged in operating the office building of the Traction Terminal Corporation. The current contract contains a list of all job classifications covered by the agreement. Division 1070 was organized in 1936.

POSITION OF THE UNION

The following major points are advanced by the Union in support of its request for a general wage-rate increase of $0.30 per hour.

1. The Union makes a number of comparisons with the rates for (one-man) operators in Indianapolis with those in effect on transit systems in other cities. The use of the rate for operators in intercity and intercompany comparisons is in

accord with the long-established practices of collective bargaining in the transit industry. Such comparisons were also utilized in the wage stabilization program developed for this industry.[1]

a) The present rate of $1.20 per hour for operators in Indianapolis is compared with the rates in effect on all other properties in the country serving populations of 400,000 or more and under contract with this international union. There were 19 such companies with a weighted average rate in August, 1947, of $1.34 for those companies that had established 1947 rates. The Union contends there is a movement in these cities toward the rate of $1.50 per hour requested in this case.

b) The Union submits a list of transit companies in which the rate for operators in August, 1947 was $1.30 per hour or more by agreement with the international union. The list included 28 companies.

c) The Union also indicated the extent of wage-rate increases for the operator's rate from V-J Day to August, 1947 in these companies with rates in August, 1947, of $1.30 per hour or more under contract with the international union. The average increase (unweighted) calculated from the data presented by the Union yields $0.361 per hour increase from V-J Day to August, 1947.

d) The Union compares the pattern of wage-rate changes for operators in the period since 1939 in Indianapolis Railways, Inc., with those in the Connecticut Company and the Connecticut Railway and Lighting Company. The Union selected these companies on the grounds that the population served, number of vehicles operated, number of employees, total revenue, revenue per mile, hours, and vacation provisions of the contracts are all comparable to the Indianapolis operations. In the case of Indianapolis Railways, Inc., the operator's rate rose from $0.70 on May 1, 1939, to a current rate of $1.20. During the same period, the rate in the Connecticut Company rose from $0.69 to $1.35.

[1] *Policy Directive Regarding Wage Adjustments for Transit Company Employees*, issued by Economic Stabilization Director, April 14, 1944.

2. The Union makes a number of comparisons with rates paid outside the transit industry in the Indianapolis area and with national averages for other industries.

a) The Union compares rates for a number of job classifications in the shops division (electrician, machinist, painter, etc.,) and the Terminal Building (janitor) with rates for job classifications it regards as comparable in industrial plants in the Indianapolis area. The Union cites rates in the General Motors Corporation, Marmon-Herrington Company, Inc., Chevrolet Commercial Body and United States Rubber Company to show that maintenance and custodial rates are $0.20 to $0.30 lower in Indianapolis Railways, Inc.

b) The Union also refers to the average hourly earnings reported by the Bureau of Labor Statistics for a number of industries—automobiles, iron and steel, machinery, printing, petroleum and coal, rubber products, and transportation equipment. The Union points out that the national averages for these industries range between $1.33 and $1.49 per hour compared to a weighted average of $1.179 for operators on Indianapolis Railways, Inc. (The average is less than $1.20, the top rate, because of lower rates for operators with less than two years' experience.) The Union emphasizes that the averages for these manufacturing industries include unskilled and semiskilled workers, while operators constitute a group of skilled workers. The Union stresses the skilled character of the work of the operator as a factor warranting comparison with highly skilled jobs in other industries rather than merely with average earnings for all employees in other industries.

3. The Union contends that these employees are entitled to share in the benefits of increasing productivity that normally takes place in the country as a whole. "I think it is an accepted axiom of American ideals, as well as the necessities of the American economy, that there be a gradual improvement in the real purchasing power of the American employee generally."

The Union points out that the real wage rate of operators

for June 15, 1947, was only 7.1 per cent over that of May 15, 1939. (The hourly rate increased 71.4 per cent, but the cost of living rose 60.1 per cent in the same period.) The Union compares this 7.1 per cent rise in real wage rate with an increase of 26.7 per cent which would have taken place had the real wage increased cumulatively 3 per cent per annum over the period since 1939, a rate of increase which the Union regards as "normal." A rate of $1.42 or an increase of $0.22 would be necessary to provide these employees with the "normal" increase in real purchasing power.

The Union presents correlate estimates for the movement of real monthly earnings. Monthly earnings for operators in this case were reported to be $242.91 for June, 1947. This constituted only a 3.2 per cent increase in real monthly earnings over those of May, 1939. Weekly earnings in real terms in manufacturing as a whole are 32 per cent over May, 1939. The Union compares the 3.2 per cent rise in real monthly earnings with a rise of 26.7 per cent which would have yielded a 3 per cent per annum increase in real earnings since 1939, a rate of increase the Union regards as "normal."

4. The Union cites the cost of purchasing the Heller quantity-and-cost budget for a family of a man, wife, and two children as a basis for its wage demands. The Union estimates that the cost in June, 1947, of purchasing this budget in Indianapolis to be $3,210.05. The annual wage of operators, even after an hourly rate increase of $0.30, would amount to $3,156.00 calculated on a 40-hour week for 50 weeks a year (including 25 minutes per day for preparatory and turn-in time). This figure would not cover the $3,210.00 estimated cost of the Heller budget in Indianapolis in June, 1947.

The Union emphasizes the point that current weekly and monthly earnings contain substantial overtime payments. The Union estimates that actual hourly earnings would be reduced $0.173 if all work over 40 hours each week were eliminated, except preparatory and turn-in time. The Union believes that the earnings of the operators should be judged on the basis of the contract work week of 40 hours.

5. The Union repeatedly urges that special weight be attached to the fact that during the 1930's the transit industry was depressed relative to other industries and as a consequence wage rates were kept below their appropriate level. The wartime prosperity of the industry could not be adequately reflected in wage rates because of the wage stabilization program. The Union contends that larger increases have recently been negotiated or arbitrated on other transit properties than in industry generally, reflecting recognition of these factors that retarded rates in this industry for many years.

6. The Union points out that a wage-rate increase is required to restore the real wage rate freely bargained between the parties at the conclusion of the wage stabilization program. On March 10, 1946, the wage rate was raised to $1.05 per hour (plus a $0.035 bonus) for operators by agreement. Between March, 1946, and June 15, 1947, the cost-of-living index for Indianapolis rose 21.5 per cent. Wage rates have risen only 10.6 per cent in the same period (when account is taken of the withdrawal of the bonus). An increase of "ten per cent or more" would be required merely to restore the real wage freely bargained between the parties at their first opportunity after the end of wage controls.

The Union points out, moreover, that in the immediate future the cost of living may be expected to rise further. The recent increases in the wholesale price index were introduced to support this conclusion.

7. The Union regards considerations of ability to pay advanced by the Company in these proceedings as irrelevant to a determination of the issue in dispute. The Union believes that an examination of the financial condition of the Company will refute the contention of the Company that it cannot afford an increase.

The Union cites the opinion of the Supreme Court in *Ames et al.* vs. *Union Pacific Railway Company*. It refers to a number of recent arbitration awards and opinions in cases in the transit industry to support the view that wages should be fixed without particular attention to ability to pay. In the words of one recent arbitration opinion cited by the Union:

> "Wage rates are fixed by objective standards, just as are the prices of materials and products. It is the duty of this Board to fix wage rates on the basis of those objective standards. Public Service Commissions and courts must determine for themselves what their duties are. . . . ."[2]

The Union contends that if consideration is given in these proceedings to the higher costs of materials and new equipment, which are partly attributable to wage increases in other industries, the Company is in effect asking transit employees to "contribute" part of the wage increase granted to other workers.

8. The Union believes that the pending fare case before the Public Service Commission and the courts should be no bar to a wage-rate increase. The Union holds that it is the task of the duly constituted public body to set fares. The arbitration board is charged with the responsibility of determining a fair and equitable wage rate. "We do not feel that the employees of Indianapolis Railways should be called upon to subsidize the cost of transportation to the public in the form of the wage rates that are now being paid."

POSITION OF THE COMPANY

The Company advances the following major points in support of its position that no general wage-rate increase should be awarded in these proceedings.

1. The employees of Indianapolis Railways, Inc., can have no case for a wage-rate increase on the basis of increased living costs. The Company voluntarily agreed to two general wage-rate increases aggregating $.27 an hour during 1946. One increase was for $.15, effective March 10, and the other increase amounted to $0.12, effective December 1. (The second

[2] In re Gary Railways, Inc. and Division 517 of the Amalgamated Association of Street, Electric Railway and Motor Coach Employees of America, award of June 23 1947.

increase in rates was $.15 per hour, while a bonus which amounted to $.03 per hour was discontinued.)

During the period March 10, 1946, to June, 1947, the cost of living for Indianapolis increased 21.5 per cent, from an index of 130 to 158 (1935–39 equals 100), while the net increase in the operator's rate of $0.27 equals an increase of 29 per cent over the rates in effect prior to March 10, 1946 ($.93 per hour including bonus).

If wage rates and the cost of living are compared for the period since January, 1941, the base date for the wage stabilization program, the employees are entitled to no increase. The operator's rate increased from $0.72 cents in January, 1941, to the current rate of $1.20, an increase of 66.7 per cent. The cost-of-living index for Indianapolis for June, 1947, was 54.9 per cent higher than in January, 1941. Moreover, except for a brief period in 1942, the real wage rate throughout the period 1941–47 was higher than in January, 1941. At the present time it is higher than at any other time.

2. The Company emphasizes the date, April 6, 1944, as appropriate for a base from which to compare the rise in wage rates and living costs. On that date the Director of Economic Stabilization approved an operator's rate of $.90 per hour on this property. The top stabilization authority found the $.90 rate to be the maximum sound and tested rate at that time. Between April, 1944, and June, 1947, the cost-of-living index for Indianapolis rose 27 per cent. In the same period the operator's rate increased 33.3 per cent. If the bonus, equal to $.04, be added to the operator's rate for April, 1944, the wage per hour increased 27.7 per cent. In either event, wage rates have risen more than the cost of living since the date of the decision of the Director of Economic Stabilization.

3. The Company points out that there is no basis for a wage-rate increase in that the weekly earnings of the operators have increased more than the cost of living. The operator's average weekly earnings in the 6-month period January 1, 1947, to June 30, 1947, was $55.96 compared to $32.85 in the 6-month period November 1, 1940, to April 30, 1941. In

this comparison weekly earnings have increased 13.5 per cent more than the cost of living in Indianapolis.

A similar comparison is made with the 6-month period September 1, 1945, to February 28, 1946, during which the 44-hour week was still effective. In that period the operator's average weekly earnings were $45.43 as compared with $55.96 for the period January 1, 1947, to June 30, 1947. In this comparison, likewise, the operator's weekly earnings have increased more than the cost of living in Indianapolis.

4. The Company contends that there are no grounds for a wage increase on the criterion of comparison of the $1.20 rate in effect for operators in Indianapolis with the rates in effect in other comparable cities. The Company points out that there are many cities with a population of 400,000 or more which do not have a rate even as high as $1.20.

The Company presents a wage comparison with the 9 cities in the north central section of the country with population of 400,000 or more which shows that between January, 1941, and August, 1947, the operator's rate in Indianapolis has increased .48, which is equal to or greater than the increase in 6 of the cities. Only Chicago, Detroit, and Cleveland, with $.54, $.56 and $.49 increases respectively over January, 1941, exceed the increase in Indianapolis.

Moreover, the Company argues that, when two additional factors are taken into account, the intercity position of the Indianapolis operator's rate appears even more favorable:

a) The cost of living in Indianapolis is relatively lower than in other cities of comparable size in the North Central States. Living costs in Indianapolis rank eighth in a group of 9 cities. The relative position of Indianapolis has remained unchanged since 1942. The cost of a budget for a 4-person manual worker's family at maintenance levels in Indianapolis is estimated for June 15, 1947, to be $2,035.19 compared to $2,268.02 in Chicago. The difference in living costs should be considered in comparing rates between cities.

b) The fare structure of Indianapolis Railways, Inc., is relatively lower than other cities of comparable size. The present fare in Indianapolis is $.10, or 3 tokens for $.25. In Detroit and Chicago, for example, there are no tokens, and the fares are $.10 and $.09 respectively. The Company argues that these fare differences are significant in intercity comparisons of wage levels. (The problem of the level of fares in Indianapolis is discussed in detail below.)

The Company emphasizes, moreover, the unique aspects of Indianapolis. The question before the arbitration board is the rate in Indianapolis. Other rates can only be of limited relevance. "We cannot extend our business out of this state or this city. . . . . When you begin to compare wage rates in different areas you must know all the facts as to what makes for a fair wage determination or a permissible wage determination."

The Company points to the fact that, at the present time, and continuously since 1938 except for two brief periods during the war, the average weekly earnings of its operators have exceeded the weekly earnings for the average of all manufacturing in the Indianapolis area, and, further, that since 1938 employment in the company's service has been regular and has shown a steady increase, while employment for all manufacturing in the Indianapolis area has been subject to severe fluctuations. It contends that such regularity and continuity of employment is an important factor to be taken into account in determining the wage rates to be paid by the Company.

The Company points out that the wage rates which it now pays in the Traction Terminal Building are greatly in excess of those paid by competitive office buildings in the city of Indianapolis and contends that the wage rates to be paid by this Company for those classifications should be determined with relation to those of its competitors.

5. The Company refers to the many special compensation provisions of its agreement with the Union. These provisions include premium time for a spread in excess of 11½ hours per day, 8 hours' pay for runs having as much as 7 hours and less than 8 hours, 16 minutes' paid preparatory time, paid turn-in

time, paid travel time, minimum pay time of 3 hours, etc.

6. The Company holds that "a dangerous imbalance already exists between that part of the Company's revenue which is required to pay its labor cost and what is left of its revenue for other requirements, and that imbalance would be aggravated by a further increase in labor costs." The Company compares the movement of operators' total payroll and gross revenue to show payrolls have increased substantially relative to revenue. It also compares the movement of operators' total payroll in dollars with car miles operated to show that, while units of transportation service have increased only 20 per cent since 1940, the dollar labor cost of said units of service has increased 180 per cent. The Company cites the fact that operating expenses have risen from 65.5 per cent of transportation gross revenue in 1936 to 70.5 per cent in 1945 and 84.7 per cent in 1946. (Revenue excludes money impounded in the fare proceedings in the courts.)

7. The Company is a public utility, and the fares it charges for transportation services are subject to public regulation. "So as a practical consideration this employer cannot even fix its prices to undertake to absorb the increased wage; it is between two millstones in that regard and is doing its best to keep from being ground to pieces itself." In the view of the Company, the fares prescribed by the Public Service Commission will not allow the Company to pay any further wage-rate increase and remain solvent. Since June 29, 1943, the Company has been in continuous dispute before the Public Service Commission and the courts concerning its fare structure.

The unions which represent the employees of the Company, including that involved in these proceedings intervened in the fare proceedings to impress the commission that they have an interest in what the rates and the revenues of this utility are.

The principal features and events of the controversy over the fare structure are outlined in the following paragraphs. These developments indicate how slow and difficult it has been for the Company to secure any increase in fares despite substantial increases in operating costs.

a) From the organization of the Company on June 1, 1932, until September 15, 1945, the same fare structure was in effect as charged by the predecessor company. That structure consisted of a $.07 cash fare on streetcars and trackless trolley cars, with a token fare of $.06¼ (4 for $.25), a charge of $.02 for transferring from through-line to through-line and a $.10 straight cash fare for motorbus lines.

b) As an outgrowth of proceedings that had been initiated in 1943, the Public Service Commission entered a temporary order, effective September 15, 1945, for a 90-day trial schedule consisting of a $.10 cash fare, a token fare of $.06⅞ (8 for $.55), and a transfer charge of $.02 on all vehicles. This schedule was in effect until January 20, 1946.

c) The Commission on January 9, 1946, reduced the token fare in the trial rate schedule from $.06⅞ to $.06¼. The Company objected to this action but agreed to a 90-day trial period on this reduced schedule. The Company states that revenue was reduced $90,000 per month from the trial schedule introduced on September 15, 1945 and $30,000 below the revenue derived from the rate schedule in effect from 1926.

d) Following the wage-rate increase of March 10, 1946, the Company petitioned the Commission for an emergency rate schedule of a $.10 cash fare, an $.08⅓ token fare, and a $.02 transfer charge. After this petition had been denied by the Commission on June 27, 1946, the Marion Circuit Court on August 12, 1946, issued a temporary injunction enjoining enforcement of the order and prohibiting the Commission from interfering with the collection of the higher emergency fare schedule until final hearing and judgment. The court ordered, however, the difference between the $08⅓ and the $.06¼ token fare impounded until final determination of the case. On April 17, 1947, the Supreme Court of Indiana affirmed the temporary injunction.[3] A sum of $1,382,172.18 was impounded while the temporary injunction was in effect. The

[3] 72 N.E. 2nd 434.

Marion Circuit Court subsequently entered a permanent injunction against the Commission enjoining it from enforcing its June 27, 1946, order and from interfering with the $.08⅓ token rate until the Commission fixes nonconfiscatory fares. The impounded funds were ordered turned over to the Company. The Commission has appealed this final injunction to the Supreme Court of Indiana.

e) Since November 30, 1945, the Company has been seeking from the Public Service Commission, under Clause No. 17782, a full investigation to determine "just and reasonable" fares. The Company has repeatedly presented to the Commission additional information as wage and other costs have changed. On July 1, 1947, the Commission entered a rate order providing for a $.10 cash fare, an $.08⅓ token fare, all transfers to be free, and required the Company to submit a schedule for a $.05 school fare. The reduction in revenue from the present schedule the Company estimates to be $450,000 a year. The July 1, 1946, order is under review in an appeal now pending in the Circuit Court of Hancock County.

8. The Company estimates that each cent-per-hour wage increase would cost the Company approximately $37,800 a year. This estimate is derived from the fact that during the first half of 1947 the Company paid for 1,889,652 hours of work (exclusive of student operators). The demand of the Union for $.30 per hour would increase operating costs by more than $1,100,000. This estimate of the cost of the demand of the Union is to be appraised in terms of the financial position of the Company.

a) Any examination of the financial position of the Company must take into consideration the fact that revenue for 1946 and 1947 will depend on whether the Company ultimately receives funds impounded by court order. Whether depreciation is figured in accordance with the books of the Company or in accordance with that approved by the Public Service Commission in its rate order of July 1, 1947, will also affect the measurement of the financial position of the Company.

At one extreme, if the impounded funds are not granted to the Company ultimately and depreciation is figured on the basis of the books of the Company, the first half of the year 1947 will show a loss of $521,222.13. At the other extreme, if the impounded funds are awarded to the Company and depreciation is calculated as ordered by the Commission, the first half of the year 1947 will show net income before taxes of $285,006.81 or $176,704.22 after taxes. If the fares as ordered by the Commission on July 1, 1947, were to have been in effect during the first half of 1947, the Company would have shown a loss of $53,655.92 using its depreciation methods or a profit of $20,052.73 after taxes if the depreciation methods approved by the Commission were used. These figures in the view of the Company indicate no room for any wage adjustment.

b) The Company points out that gross revenue has been falling as a result of reduction in traffic. Through the first 7 months of 1947 total passengers carried were 66,350,904, compared with 69,515,068 for the same period of 1946—a decrease of 3,164,164. This reduction in volume may be expected to continue.

The Company stresses the unfavorable underlying conditions and long-term trends to which the transit industry is subject. It further points out that the pre-war wage rates in the transit industry, to which the Union refers as unduly depressed, in reality reflected the economic impact of these conditions and trends. The Company contends that the industries with which the Union makes comparison, are not subject to the special factors which have influenced the transit industry. It emphasizes that at the present time these unfavorable trends are becoming increasingly manifest, particularly in the form of declining traffic, increasing competition from the private automobile, and increasing operating costs over which the Company has little control.

c) The Company emphasizes that the cost of materials and new equipment has risen substantially. These increases further limit the capacity of the Company to pay any wage increase.

d) The Company stockholders have gone a total of nearly 11 years of its 15 years of existence without dividends. No dividend has been paid since March, 1946. A further wage increase would deny the stockholders all opportunity for a dividend.

9. The Company emphasizes its record of modernization of equipment and service in its statement that:

"you are not dealing with an employer who is indifferent to its obligations to the public but one that has done and wants to do its best. You are not dealing with an employer that it indifferent to its employees, or believes in low wages . . . . but you are dealing with an employer who wants to stay alive and well."

10. The Company rejects the contention of the Union that the Heller budget is applicable to this case. The Company points out that 1,282 out of 1,741 employees claim 2 or less dependents, compared to the 3 (family of 4) assumed in the Heller budget calculations.

11. The Company concludes that "if any wage increase is awarded it should be conditioned on obtaining approval from the (Public Service) Commission of a commensurate increase in the Company's rates (fares)." The Company points out that in a recent arbitration between the Amalgamtaed and the Oklahoma City Company a wage increase provided in the award was made conditional upon the granting of an increase in fares and that in recent contracts negotiated between the Amalgamated and the Portland, Oregon, and Chattanooga, Tennessee companies wage increases were similarly conditioned.

The Company calls attention to the fact that recent arbitration awards in some 8 cases in the transit industry, particularly at Kansas City, Missouri, and St. Louis, Missouri, expressly take into account the ability or inability of the employer to pay the wage increases contended for, referring to conditions similar to those under which this Company operates as reasons for refusing wage increases which might have been justified by other standards and rejecting union contentions that the financial condition of the employer should be wholly disregarded. These awards stress the fact that the transit industry is, not only a public utility which is not at liberty to increase its charges at will and is subject to rate regulation by public authorities, but also a public utility of a very special kind which is subject to competition in various forms and to economic hazards with which other public utilities do not have to contend. They call attention to the long history of receiverships and reorganizations in the transit field with their resulting large losses to investors, the declining trends in traffic, the necessity for constant modernization of system and equipment, the necessity for attracting new capital for the purpose of carrying out such programs, and the necessity for providing in revenues for the retirement of property made obsolete thereby. And they call attention to the danger of resort to public subsidies or municipal ownership with their burdens upon the taxpayer.

ANALYSIS OF THE ARBITRATION BOARD

The question presented in these proceedings is a straight forward wage-rate issue—the extent of a general wage-rate increase, if any. The Company and the Union have each suggested different standards by which the arbitration board is invited to measure the appropriateness of the demand for a general increase. Moreover, the same standards have been applied quite differently by the two sides.

The Union pointed to higher rates in some companies and localities; the Company referred to lower rates in other situations. The Union cited the rise in living costs from the first postwar negotiations; the Company pointed to the comparative movements of wage rates and living costs from earlier dates. The Union held that the employees in question are entitled to the "normal" increase in productivity in American industry; the Company insisted it cannot afford any further wage-rate increase. As is normally the case in wage issues, the parties have appealed to conflicting standards or have applied a proposed criterion in conflicting ways.

The problem presented to the arbitration board is consequently that of appraising and balancing conflicting standards. The task is to decide how much weight to give to one standard as compared to another. The case presents no serious dispute over facts; they have been carefully and clearly presented by the parties. The decision must consequently be a judgment of the relative significance to be assigned to each of the standards proposed by the parties. The arbitration board has not attempted to develop any criteria or standards of its own; it has applied only those proposed by the parties. There can be no simple formula nor system for determining the wage rate.

The principal standards proposed by the parties are briefly summarized below, including the wage rate which each standard or each interpretation of a standard would yield. The discussion is confined to the rate for operators in accordance with the collective bargaining practice in the industry and the explicit argument of both parties in these proceedings.

1. *Cost of Living.*—Both parties compare the movement of the operator's rate and the cost-of-living index for Indianapolis. But the Company and the Union propose different base dates for this comparison. The Company proposes January, 1941, used in the Wage Stabilization Program, and April 6, 1944, the date on which a $.90 rate was approved on this property by the Director of Economic Stabilization. The Union proposes to compare the movement of the operator's rate and living costs from the date of the first postwar wage-rate increase, March 10, 1946. The Union holds that the real wage rate established in these "free" collective bargaining negotiations should at least be maintained.

The increases in the operator's rate and living costs from selected dates are summarized in Table 1.

The choice of the base period is clearly decisive for the question whether any wage-rate increase is appropriate solely on the criterion of the cost of living. The base periods proposed by the Company yield no wage-rate increase under the cost-of-living standard, while the base period urged by the Union indicates an increase of $.132. The strictest application of the cost of living standard, from the base dates proposed by the Company, would indicate a decrease in wage rates since they have risen more than living costs.

TABLE 1

	Operator s Rate*	Index of Living Costs, 1935–39 Equals 100
January,1941.................	$0.72	102.0
April, 1944..................	0.90 (0.94)	124.4
March, 1946................	1.05 (1.085)	130.0
June, 1946..................	1.20	158.0
Percentage increase:		
January, 1941—June, 1947....	66.7%	54.9%
April, 1944—June, 1947......	33.3 (27.7)	27.0
March, 1946—June, 1947.....	14.3 (10.6)	21.5

* The operator's rate and percentage changes in parentheses include the bonus in the operators' rate.

2. *Rate Levels in Other Transit Companies.*—The Company and the Union both refer to the level of wage rates for operators on transit properties in other cities. Both parties are agreed, apparently, that size of population served is a decisive factor limiting comparisons since each side presented comparisons with properties serving cities with a population of 400,000 or more. The Union stressed rates on those properties organized by the Amalgamated. The Company presented rates on all properties in this population group, including those unorganized or under contract with other unions. The unweighted average of the operator's rate in the companies cited by the Company is $1.245 or $0.045 more than the current rate in effect in Indianapolis Railways, Inc. The Company also compared the level of rates in Indianapolis with the rates in effect on August 15, 1947 on 9 properties in other cities

having a population of 400,000 or more in the north central part of the United States. The unweighted average rate was $1.256. The average of the operator's rates in the list of companies cited by the Union was $1.341, or $0.141 more than the rates currently in effect in Indianapolis. There is one further difference between these averages—aside from the question of contract with the Amalgamated. The union's average only includes properties on which a rate "has been established for 1947," while that calculated from Company data includes all company rates in the size-of-city group as of August 15, 1947.

The parties in their previous collective bargaining have not regarded the rates in any other single city or the rates in any fairly carefully defined group of cities as decisive to wage-rate determination in Indianapolis.

3. *Rate Increases in Other Transit Companies.*—The application of the standard of rate increases in other transit companies can yield divergent results, not only because different companies are included in the group used for comparative purposes, but also because different periods are selected for the wage-rate changes. The Union reports that wage-rate increases have averaged (unweighted) $0.361 per hour between V-J Day and August 15, 1947, for a group of companies in which the rate equaled or exceeded $1.30 per hour on the later date. On this standard an increase of $0.09 is appropriate since Indianapolis rates have increased $0.27 since V-J Day.

The Company refers to the $0.48 per hour increase in the operator's rate on Indianapolis Railways, Inc., since January, 1941, compared to the increases granted in the same period on 9 properties in the North Central States serving cities of comparable size. The Indianapolis increases are exceeded only by Chicago, Detroit, and Cleveland ($0.54, $0.56, and $0.49 respectively).

4. *"Normal" Increase in Productivity.*—The Union proposed that the "normal" increase in productivity in American industry, which the Union holds to be 3 per cent per year, be used as a standard in this case. The Union finds that since 1939

the real wage rate has risen 7.1 per cent while an increase of 26.7 per cent would be appropriate on this standard. An increase of $0.22 per hour the Union seeks to justify on this basis. The Company rejects this standard.

5. *Ability to Pay and Fare Limitations.*— The Company proposes as a significant standard the financial capacity of the property to stand any further wage-rate increase which in turn has been affected by the inability of the Company to secure higher fares. The Company believes that if any wage-rate increase is awarded in these preceedings it should be conditioned on securing a commensurate increase in fares.

. The Union, on the other hand, contends that the ability to pay a wage-rate increase—including the question of adequate fares—is an irrelevant standard to these proceedings.

The application of the ability-to-pay standard in this case presents more than the ordinary complications of interpreting financial statements and weighing conflicting estimates of the trend of business conditions. In the first place, certain funds derived from fares have been impounded by the courts, and while the Marion Circuit Court has ordered these funds returned to the Company the case is on appeal. In the second place, Indianapolis Railways, Inc., has made every effort for many months to secure higher fares for its services in the face of mounting operating costs. Undoubtedly these factors materially affect the ability of the Company to pay the existing wage-rate structure, not to mention any increase in wage rates. The arbitration board, however, is in no position to predict the outcome of those court and commission proceedings.

The relation of wage-setting to price or fare determination can logically be conceived in three possible forms: (*a*) wages could be fixed first and fare- or price-setting could assume these costs; (*b*) prices and fares could be fixed first and assumed as given for purposes of determining wages; and (*c*) both wages and prices could be set simultaneously. In public utilities, including the railroads, there appears to be a long tradition of separation of wage- and rate-setting. This does not mean that rates and prices are irrelevant to wage-setting, but rather that wage rates have tended to be fixed with some general reference to financial capacity and then these costs in turn have been taken into account by the rate- or fare-making body. Such has been the actual relation between collective bargaining or emergency boards determining wage rates and the Interstate Commerce Commission setting railroad rates and fares. The transit industry has tended to follow an analogous practice.

In addition to these five standards the parties have emphasized a number of other considerations which the board has taken into account. The Union has argued the depressed condition of the industry in the 1930's and the stabilization program entitle these employees to special consideration. The Company has strongly urged that the board decide the case in the light of all the unique factors in Indianapolis.

QUESTIONS

1. Complete the arbitration award indicating your decision and the basis for your award.
2. Write a critical appraisal of the way each side applied the principal standards noted above—cost of living, comparable rates, productivity, and ability to pay. (See Chapter V.)
3. What do you think of the suggestion that any wage increase be made conditional upon a fare increase?

CASE 63

THE ECONOMICS OF THE BITUMINOUS COAL INDUSTRY

The following pages constitute a summary of the development of the economic position of the bituminous coal industry. These data are arranged under the following headings:

> Organization for Collective Bargaining
> Production and Utilization of Bituminous Coal
> Employment, Wages, Hours
> Prices, Profits, Realization

Cost Structure
Production and Mechanization

This summary of some of the more important aspects of
the industry is intended to provide a basis for reflection on
the appropriate wage and price policies of the union and the
mine operators in the industry. This material will also be
relevant to the question of outlining public policy in this area
of the economy. Some of the more prominent questions of
policy are posed in the final section of the statement.

ORGANIZATION FOR COLLECTIVE BARGAINING

The bituminous coal industry offers an illustration of the
operations of national collective bargaining. Both workers
and employers are well organized—the workers into the
United Mine Workers, and the commercial operators into
employer associations based on competitive market areas or
geographic location. Employer and union representatives conduct their bargaining at a joint conference where the many
diverse competitive interests in the industry are represented.
The product of this conference—assuming that negotiations
do not break down—is the National Bituminous Coal Agreement which sets the pattern for the industry on the general
conditions of employment, hours, and wages.

This national agreement serves as a model for the negotiations of district agreements. The district agreements are more
detailed than the basic agreement, even specifying such items
as house rent and charges for light bulbs. There are 25 such
agreements corresponding to the territorial districts which
comprise the UMW organizational structure. These UMW districts are not to be confused with districts set up by the Bituminous Coal Act for pricing purposes. For example, UMW
District 5 covers the Pittsburgh area, while the Coal Act Production District 5 covers the state of Michigan.

PRODUCTION AND UTILIZATION OF BITUMINOUS COAL

Until the close of World War I, the demand for bituminous
coal rose rapidly. Between 1880 and 1918, the year of maxi-

mum production prior to World War II, annual output rose from 42.8 million tons to 579 million tons. This twelvefold growth in demand during this 38-year period may be attributed to the increase in population, the expansion of the West, the rise of cities, the development of railroad networks, and the growth of manufacture, particularly the iron and steel industries.

Even in this stage of increasing demand, the coal industry faced the problem of alternate periods of high and low operation. The widely scattered abundant supply of bituminous coal deposits and the ease with which these surface deposits could be extracted meant that producing fields were developed with great rapidity. In an economy characterized by serious cyclical variations, excess capacity became typical of the coal industry.

TABLE 1

PRODUCTION OF BITUMINOUS COAL, 1880–1945*

(In Millions of Tons)

Year	Production	Year	Production	Year	Production
1880	42.8	1931	382	1939	395
1890	111	1932	310	1940	461
1900	212	1933	334	1941	514
1910	417	1934	359	1942	583
1918	579	1935	372	1943	590
1923	565	1936	439	1944	620
1929	535	1937	446	1945	576
1930	468	1938	349		

* *Minerals Yearbook 1944*, p. 844; *Monthly Labor Review*, August, 1946, p. 167.

After 1918 but especially after 1923, a period of decline in output developed. By 1929 production of bituminous coal had fallen 7.6 per cent below the 1918 peak. Because bituminous coal is largely an industrial fuel, the business depression accelerated this downward trend. By 1932 production was 45.1 per cent below the 1923 level. As recovery started in 1933 and grew in later years, the conditions of the industry improved. Production moved to much higher levels, and new mines were opened. By 1939 production was 27.4 per cent above the 1932 level. But the industry was still 30.1 per cent below its 1923 production level. Table 1 traces the movement of production from 1880 to 1945.

Several factors may account for the serious curtailment that characterized the 16-year period between 1923 and 1939, the earlier years of which were among the most prosperous of American business. Very important was the substantial encroachment of competing fuels—especially oil and gas, and to some extent water power—upon the bituminous coal market, as shown by Tables 2 and 3.

TABLE 2

INDEX NUMBER OF RELATIVE RATE OF GROWTH OF COAL, OIL, AND
WATER POWER IN THE UNITED STATES*

(1918 = 100)

Year	Anthra-cite	Bitumi-nous	Total Coal	Domestic Oil	Imported Oil	Natural Gas	Water Power	Grand Total Fuels and Water
1889....	46	17	21	10	..	35	11	20
1899....	61	33	37	16	..	31	16	34
1909....	82	66	68	51	..	67	49	65
1920....	91	98	97	124	282	111	116	103
1930....	70	81	79	252	165	270	222	109
1940....	52	80	75	380	113	369	313	125
1945....	55	99	93	481	197	473	518	162

* *Minerals Yearbook 1937*, p. 809; *Minerals Yearbook 1943*, p. 848; *Minerals Yearbook 1945*, p. 846

TABLE 3

PERCENTAGE OF TOTAL B.T.U. EQUIVALENT CONTRIBUTED BY THE SEVERAL MINERAL
FUELS AND WATER POWER IN THE UNITED STATES, 1889–1945*

(Water Power Counted at Constant Fuel Equivalent of Approximately
4 Pounds per Kilowatt Hour)

Year	Anthra-cite	Bitumi-nous	Domestic Oil	Imported Oil	Natural Gas	Total Mineral Fuel	Water Power	Grand Total, Fuels and Water
1889....	28.7	58.1	4.9	...	6.2	97.9	2.1	100.0
1899....	22.1	68.2	4.6	...	3.3	98.2	1.8	100.0
1909....	15.5	70.2	7.7	...	3.7	97.1	2.9	100.0
1920....	10.9	66.3	11.8	2.9	3.8	95.7	4.3	100.0
1930....	7.9	51.4	22.5	1.6	8.8	92.2	7.8	100.0
1940....	5.1	44.2	29.7	0.9	10.5	90.4	9.6	100.0
1945....	4.2	42.8	29.0	1.3	10.4	87.7	12.3	100.0

* *Minerals Yearbook 1937*, p. 810; *Mineral Yearbook 1945*, p. 847.

There was increased efficiency in the use of fuel encouraged by the high prices during the war years. Other factors include:

the development of the southern fields which could produce better quality coal at lower costs because of higher seams, lower wage levels, and modern equipment; the shift in manufacturing from crude heavy products to lighter products required less fuel; and the great increase in the volume of secondary metals returned by industry as scrap retarded the use of virgin pig iron requiring greater quantities of coal.

The defense program of 1939 and World War II stimulated the demand for bituminous coal. Coal played a vital role in railroad transportation, in power production, and in manufacturing. Production rose to a new all-time high in 1944 with 620 million tons, 7.1 per cent above the earlier 1918 high.

In the present postwar period, the outlook for the bituminous coal industry revolves around the general level of industrial activity and the extent of competition offered by other fuels. The consumption of soft coal follows closely the trend of industry, and the present accumulated demand is likely to stimulate industry for several years; but inroads on coal by competitive fuels will be resumed. Coal is in a vulnerable position as the consumption of natural gas expands and as plans for hydroelectric development materialize. In the long run, atomic energy may be expected to be a competitor of coal.

EMPLOYMENT, WAGES, HOURS

How have the workers in the bituminous coal industry fared over the historical period? Table 4 summarizes available statistics for employment, hours, and average earnings for the period 1909–45. The level of employment has fluctuated somewhat, but the trend has been consistently downward since 1923. Between 1923 and 1940 employment decreased by 35.5 per cent, between 1940 and 1947, by 21.0 per cent. This trend may be attributed to (1) overdevelopment of the mines as reflected in part-time operation and (2) increased productivity, especially in the period following 1940.

The overdevelopment of the industry is further characterized by the statistics on the average number of days worked per year and the average number of hours worked per week.

The industry seldom afforded its workers as many as 200 days per year. Also, before World War II, the average weekly hours exceeded 35 hours in only 2 years, 1928 and 1929—and this despite the fact that the standard 35-hour week was not introduced until 1934.

TABLE 4

Statistics of Employment, Wages, Hours, 1909–47*

Year	Employment (In Thousands)	Average No. of Days Worked per Year	Average No. of Hours Worked per Week	Average Weekly Earnings	Average Hourly Earnings (Cents)
1909	512	...	37.7	$11.50	32.3
1919	546	...	35.5	25.65	75.9
1923	643	179	31.3	25.60	84.5
1929	459	219	38.4	25.71	68.1
1930	441	187	33.5	22.21	68.5
1931	408	160	28.2	17.68	64.7
1932	350	146	27.2	13.91	52.0
1933	366	167	29.5	14.47	50.1
1934	423	178	27.0	18.10	67.3
1935	436	179	26.4	19.58	74.5
1936	450	199	28.8	22.71	79.4
1937	461	193	27.9	23.84	85.6
1938	406	162	23.5	20.80	87.8
1939	371	178	27.1	23.88	88.6
1940	415	202	28.1	24.71	88.3
1941	407	216	31.1	30.86	99.3
1942	435	246	32.9	35.02	105.9
1943	386	264	36.6	41.62	113.8
1944	354	278	43.4	51.27	118.7
1945	322	...	42.3	52.29	123.5
1946	307	...	40.3	58.03	140.1
1947	328	...	37.2	60.55	157.5

* *Minerals Yearbook 1944*, p. 829; *Minerals Yearbook 1945*, p. 854; National War Labor Board Report, Appendix A–10, p. 38; Bureau of Labor Statistics statistics on employment and earnings *Report on Wages and Related Problems in the Bituminous Coal Industry*, April, 1943.

As for wages, both average hourly and average weekly earnings have fluctuated considerably. Since 1933 the trend has been steadily upward. Average weekly earnings increased more than average hourly earnings, 318.5 per cent as against 214.3 per cent between 1933 and 1947. If we compare 1947 with 1923, average weekly earnings have increased 136.5 per cent, average hourly earnings 86.3 per cent. Between 1940 and 1947 average weekly earnings increased 145.07 per cent, average hourly earnings 78.4 per cent.

A comparison of average hourly earnings in bituminous mining with average hourly earnings in manufacturing and railroads indicates that the *absolute* level of wages in bituminous mines usually has been higher than in the other industrial sectors. This differential would seem to reflect the serious risks and hazards associated with the mining industry. A comparison of percentage changes over time shows that, although wages for bituminous mining have increased considerably, the increase has been less than that of other industries. Between 1923 and 1947, average hourly earnings increased by 86.3 per cent in bituminous mining, by 104.5 per cent in railroads, and by 132.8 per cent in manufacturing. This trend continued in the period between 1940 and 1947 with the mines increasing their wages by 78.4 per cent as against 79.7 per cent for railroads, and 83.7 per cent for manufacturing. Table 5 compares the average hourly earning in the three industries.

The figures on average hourly and weekly earnings need to be supplemented with data on the structure of wages in the coal industry—on the differences in wages as between jobs, on the differences in wages as between plants or geographic areas, on the methods of wage payment, on the provisions for overtime, on the practice of premium payments, etc. The wage structure of the industry is highly complex and is affected by the provisions of the National Bituminous Coal Wage Agreement. This agreement provides for different hours and computation of pay for inside dayworkers, for inside pieceworkers, for outside workers on continuous operations, and for outside workers on noncontinuous operations. This point is best illustrated by the wage and hour provision in the National Bituminous Coal Wage Agreement of July 1947 which reads as follows:

"1. (*a*) For all inside employees a work day of eight hours from portal to portal is established, including a staggered thirty minutes for lunch, and without any intermission or suspension of operation throughout the day. For inside workers these eight hours shall be paid for at straight time rate. Overtime beyond eight hours per day and forty hours per week shall be paid for at time and one-half with no pyramiding of overtime. Straight time rates for inside day workers shall be the total daily normal shift earnings for eight hours divided by eight (8) hours.

TABLE 5

AVERAGE HOURLY EARNINGS IN BITUMINOUS COAL MINING, RAILROADS, AND MANUFACTURING*

(In Cents)

Year	Bituminous	Railroads	Manufacturing
1909	32.3	21.9	19.3
1919	75.9	53.7	47.7
1923	84.5	58.1	52.2
1929	68.1	63.0	56.6
1930	68.5	55.2	55.2
1931	64.7	51.5	51.5
1932	52.0	44.6	44.6
1933	50.1	44.2	44.2
1934	67.3	53.2	53.2
1935	74.5	55.0	55.0
1936	79.4	55.6	55.6
1937	85.6	62.4	62.4
1938	87.8	62.7	62.7
1939	88.6	63.3	63.3
1940	88.3	66.1	66.1
1941	99.3	72.9	72.9
1942	105.9	85.3	85.3
1943	113.8	96.1	96.1
1944	118.7	101.9	101.9
1945	123.5	102.3	102.3
1946	140.1	111.1	108.4
1947	157.5	118.8	121.5

* Bureau of Labor Statistics

"(b) For all outside employees: except those covered in paragraph (c) hereof (including all strip mine and coke oven employees), a work day of seven hours and fifteen minutes is established including a staggered thirty minutes for lunch, and without any intermission or suspension of operations throughout the day. These seven hours and fifteen minutes shall be paid for at straight time rate.

Overtime beyond seven hours and fifteen minutes per day and thirty-six and one-quarter hours per week shall be paid for at time and one-half with no pyramiding of overtime. Straight time earnings for outside day workers covered by this paragraph shall be the total daily normal shift earnings for seven hours and fifteen minutes divided by seven and one-quarter (7.25) hours.

"(c) For all outside continuous employees who are engaged at power houses, sub-stations and pumps operating continuously for twenty-four (24) hours daily, and hoisting engineers, a work day of eight hours is established, including a staggered thirty minutes for lunch and without any intermission or suspension of operations throughout the day. These eight hours shall be paid for at straight time rate. Overtime beyond eight hours per day and forty hours per week shall be paid for at time and one-half with no pyramiding of overtime. Straight time earnings for day workers covered by this paragraph shall be the total daily normal shift earnings for eight hours divided by eight (8) hours.

"(d) All mine workers, whether employed by the month, day, or tonnage, yardage, deadwork or footage rate, shall receive $3.05 per day in addition to that provided for in the contract which expired March 31, 1946.

"(e) Work performed on the sixth consecutive day is optional, but when performed shall be paid for at time and one-half or rate and one-half.

"(f) Holidays, when worked, shall be paid for at time and one-half or rate and one-half. Holidays shall be computed in arriving at the sixth and seventh day in the week.

"(g) Employees paid by the day or by the ton who start to work, that day shall be counted as a day's work in computing the sixth and seventh day in the week provided they do not leave their employment when work is available for them.

"(*b*) Rockdusting shall be done at the expense of the coal operator."

Approximately 90 per cent of all the production workers in underground mines work at inside jobs, 10 per cent at outside jobs. All of the outside workers are paid on a time (hourly) basis. Twenty-two per cent of the underground miners are paid on an incentive basis, all of these being inside workers; 78 per cent are paid on a time basis.

The Bureau of Labor Statistics made a study of the wage structure of bituminous coal mines for the fall of 1945, selecting key jobs to indicate the earnings throughout the industry at various skill levels. Table 6 summarizes some of this material. In the underground bituminous mines, slate pickers—paid on a time basis—received the lowest average straight-time hourly earnings for the country as a whole, an average of $0.95. Short firers—paid on an incentive basis—received the highest average straight-time hourly earnings, an average of $1.42. Six occupations accounted for the great majority of the estimated number of workers in all of the selected occupations, with hand loaders the most important numerical group, and with cutting machine operators and helpers, motormen, trackmen, brakemen, and timbermen also of comparative numerical importance. Table 6 (pp. 398–99) shows how earnings for these occupations varied according to the method of wage payment and as between geographic areas.

In the strip mines, straight-time averages ranged from $0.97 for groundmen and slate pickers to $1.64 for power shovel operators. The workers were largely concentrated into two occupations—truck and tractor operators and power shovel operators.

It should be noted that "fringe issues," covering working conditions and other provisions that affect real income without raising hourly rates of pay, became increasingly important during the war years with the wartime stabilization of wage rates. Both in underground and strip mines, $.04 and $.06

per hour additions represented the differential paid for work on the second and third shift respectively. A paid lunch period of 15 minutes was the most usual provision in bituminous coal mines, with the lunch period considered part of working time in figuring average hours per start and average straight-time earnings. The present contract provides for a staggered 30-minute lunch period. Nonproduction bonuses (profit sharing, safety, attendance, Christmas) were introduced in a few mines. Formal provisions for paid vacations to workers in the mines was the common practice. The present agreement provides for $100 vacation compensation after 1 year's employment.

Another important wartime development was the principle of portal-to-portal pay. It had been a long-established practice in the industry to pay the tonnage men on a piece basis (i.e., per ton, goot, or yard, depending on the nature of the work performed) and inside day workers for time at work which was computed after they reported at their working places in the mine proper. Since the working places may be some distance from the mine entrance, the workers spent a certain amount of time (varying from 10 to 15 minutes to 2 hours per day) going to and from their work places in the mine for which they were not paid. The 1945 agreement allowed for an estimated average of 1 hour for travel time, to be included as part of the regularly scheduled workday and compensated at the regular hourly rate.

In 1946 the broad outlines of a health and welfare program were written into the agreement. The program consisted of (a) a welfare and retirement fund, and (b) a medical and hospital fund. In 1947 the two funds were co-ordinated and the United Mine Workers of America Welfare and Retirement Fund was established. The details for administration and operation of the fund became the subject of serious controversy between the United Mine Workers and the mine operators, but by 1948 the fund became a working reality. According to the 1948 agreement mine operating managers pay into the

TABLE 6

Average Earnings for Selected Occupations in Underground Bituminous Coal Mines*

Occupation	United States				Eastern Pennsylvania				
	No. of Workers	Average Straight-Time Earnings per Hour	Average Straight-Time Earnings per Start	Average Gross Weekly Earnings	No. of Workers	UMW Negotiated Rate	Average Straight-Time Earnings per Hour	Average Straight-Time Earnings per Start	Average Gross Weekly Earnings
Brakemen, underground	12,267	0.99	8.93	50.46	952	1.00	1.00	8.96	57.02
Cutting machine operators:									
Inside, time	4,125	1.19	10.72	67.68	584	1.286	1.21	11.12	73.46
Inside, incentive	1,125	1.27	11.33	75.49	388	....	1.25	11.25	73.30
Helpers, inside, time	2,494	1.11	10.02	58.89	300	1.286	1.20	10.93	68.95
Helpers, inside, incentive	669	1.19	10.62	69.85	268	....	1.20	10.77	69.20
Loaders, hand, inside, time	12,107	1.07	9.57	49.17	236	....	1.08	9.68	61.51
Loaders, hand, inside, incentive	65,080	1.06	9.39	50.92	12,000	0.87	1.04	9.33	53.91
Mechanics, maintenance, inside	3,208	1.22	11.44	80.48	512	....	1.23	11.64	79.89
Motormen, inside	18,409	1.02	9.25	57.05	1,564	1.023	1.02	9.22	60.18
Shot firers, inside, time	4,288	1.09	9.79	58.59	356	1.143	1.10	9.93	62.44
Shot firers, inside, incentive	343	1.42	12.54	72.34	88	....	....	....	....
Slate pickers, outside	5,405	0.95	7.91	47.51	380	0.857	0.96	8.01	49.67
Timbermen, inside	10,856	1.00	8.98	53.81	1,060	1.00	1.00	9.03	60.32
Trackmen, inside	14,653	1.00	8.94	53.78	1,332	1.00	1.00	9.01	59.18
Trimmers, inside	115	0.83	7.50	40.63	....	....	....	....	....
Trimmers, outside	1,606	0.98	8.21	49.89	60	0.891	1.01	8.32	51.52
AVERAGE EARNINGS FOR SELECTED OCCUPATIONS IN STRIP BITUMINOUS COAL MINES									
Groundmen	1,122	0.97	8.39	52.00	80	....	0.86	7.30	43.03
Power shovel operators	2,189	1.64	14.33	98.22	168	....	1.48	13.03	91.69
Slate pickers	1,335	0.97	8.04	43.54	136	....	0.78	6.41	34.53
Truck and tractor operators	2,418	1.03	8.90	50.49	108	....	0.95	8.06	48.87

TABLE 6 (Continued)

AVERAGE EARNINGS FOR SELECTED OCCUPATIONS IN UNDERGROUND BITUMINOUS COAL MINES

Occupation	Western Pennsylvania					West Kentucky				
	No. of Workers	UMW Negotiated Rate	Average Straight-Time Earnings per Hour	Average Straight-Time Earnings per Start	Average Gross Weekly Earnings	No. of Workers	UMW Negotiated Rate	Average Straight-Time Earnings per Hour	Average Straight-Time Earnings per Start	Average Gross Weekly Earnings
Brakemen, underground	1,581	1.00	1.00	9.09	56.74	80	0.857	0.88	7.68	42.41
Cutting machine operators:										
Inside, time	1,383	1.286	1.24	11.23	72.42	215	1.043	1.04	9.13	54.10
Inside, incentive	564	....	1.27	11.42	78.77	30	0.050	1.07	9.62	51.28
Helpers, inside, time	837	1.286	1.25	11.21	70.60	195	0.971	0.98	8.63	50.90
Helpers, inside, incentive	298	....	1.20	10.73	75.49	....	....	....	....	....
Loaders, hand, inside, time	11,954	0.83	1.04	9.23	54.13	1,210	....	0.84	7.14	42.42
Loaders, hand, inside, incentive	806	....	1.24	11.56	83.92	80	....	1.04	9.90	79.27
Mechanics, maintenance, inside	....	....	....	....	....	5	....	....	....	....
Motormen, inside	4,030	1.023	1.02	9.32	60.63	180	....	0.96	8.48	52.17
Shot firers, inside, time	1,178	1.143	1.10	9.97	63.06	25	....	0.83	5.82	40.56
Shot firers, inside, incentive	....	....	....	....	....	335	....	0.83	7.00	41.32
Slate pickers, outside	589	0.857	.98	8.08	50.36	200	....	0.88	7.64	48.14
Timbermen, inside	2,561	1.00	1.00	9.10	57.02	205	0.857	0.87	7.50	44.81
Trackmen, inside	2,821	1.00	1.00	9.03	58.07	....	0.857	....	....	....
Trimmers, inside	....	....	....	....	....	55	0.714	0.82	6.93	44.68
Trimmers, outside	136	0.891	1.01	8.58	55.85	....	....	....	....	....

AVERAGE EARNINGS FOR SELECTED OCCUPATIONS IN STRIP BITUMINOUS COAL MINES

Occupation	Western Pennsylvania					West Kentucky				
	No. of Workers	UMW Negotiated Rate	Hour	Start	Gross	No. of Workers	UMW Negotiated Rate	Hour	Start	Gross
Groundmen	74	0.891–0.912	0.96	8.23	60.21	56	0.714	0.90	7.63	43.35
Power shovel operators	291	1.715	1.82	15.14	103.69	158	....	1.51	13.13	89.55
Slate pickers	223	0.857	0.97	8.03	43.87	94	....	0.88	7.89	47.27
Truck and tractor operators	267	0.891–0.983	1.05	8.53	53.61	160	....	0.99	8.76	58.81

* Bureau of Labor Statistics, *Wage Structure of Bituminous Coal Mines*, Fall, 1945, Tables 4 and 5.

fund $.20 on each ton of coal produced for use or for sale. The fund is managed by three trustees, one appointed as a representative of the employers, one appointed as a representative of the UMW, and one selected by the other two as a neutral party.

The purpose of the fund is to make payments of

"(1) benefits to employees . . . . their families and dependents for medical and hospital care, pensions on retirement or death of employees, compensation for injuries or illness resulting from occupational activity or insurance to provide any of the foregoing, or life insurance, disability and sickness insurance or accident insurance; (2) benefits with respect to wage loss not otherwise compensated for at all or adequately by tax supported agencies created by federal or state law; (3) benefits on account of sickness, temporary disability, permanent disability, death or retirement; (4) benefits for any and all other purposes which may be specified, provided for as permitted in Section 302 (c) of the 'Labor Management Relations Act, 1947,' as agreed upon from time to time by the Trustees . . . . ; and (5) benefits for all other related welfare purposes as may be determined by the trustees within the scope of the provisions of the aforesaid 'Labor Management Relations Act, 1947.' "

Subject to the stated purposes of the Fund, the trustees have full authority with respect to questions of coverage and eligibility, priorities among classes of benefits, amounts of benefit, methods of providing or arranging for provisions of benefits, and related matters. A portion of the payments into the Health and Welfare Fund is separated and designated as a special fund to be used for providing pensions and annuities. In 1948 a pension plan was instituted by the trustees providing for a $100-a-month pension to miners at 62 with 20 years of service who retired on or after May 29, 1946.

PRICES, PROFITS, REALIZATION

In Table 7 are summarized statistics which relate to the value of production, prices, and profits of the bituminous coal industry.

TABLE 7

VALUE, PRICE, PROFIT, 1909–45*

Year	Value (Realization) per Ton	Total Value (Realization (in 1,000,000) Net Tons	Average Retail Price	Net Income or Deficit (in 1,000's)
1909........	$1.07	405	....	.....
1919........	2.49	$1,161	....	$+62,260
1923........	2.68	1,515	$10.33	.....
1929........	1.78	953	8.85	−11,822
1930........	1.70	795	8.83	−42,071
1931........	1.54	580	8.33	−47,745
1932........	1.31	407	7.71	−51,167
1933........	1.34	446	7.65	−47,549
1934........	1.75	628	8.26	− 7,584
1935........	1.77	658	8.29	−15,576
1936........	1.76	771	8.42	− 3,310
1937........	1.94	864	8.58	− 777
1938........	1.95	679	8.61	−26,667
1939........	1.84	728	8.52	− 6,168
1940........	1.91	879	8.60	+14,481
1941........	2.19	1,125	9.10	.....
1942........	2.36	1,374	9.51	.....
1943........	2.69	1,585	9.94	.....
1944........	2.92	1,810	10.27	.....
1945........	3.08	1,774	10.48	.....

* *National War Labor Board Report*, p. 8; *Minerals Yearbook, 1944*, p. 844; Bureau of Labor Statistics; *Minerals Yearbook, 1945*, p. 838.

A comparison of 1923 with 1940 shows that total value decreased by 42 per cent, average value by 28.7 per cent, retail prices by 16.7 per cent, and throughout most of the twenties and continuing until 1940, the industry showed a deficit. From 1940 on, the industry improved its position, total value increasing 101.8 per cent by 1945, average value 61.3 per cent, and the price of coal 21.9 per cent.

The Office of Price Administration furnished data for 22 companies which illustrate the significant advances made by the industry during the war period, as shown in Table 8.

TABLE 8

PROFITS*

YEAR	PROFITS BEFORE TAXES (Thousands of Dollars)	PROFITS AFTER TAXES (Thousands of Dollars)	PERCENTAGE OF NET WORTH	
			Before Taxes	After Taxes
1938........	− 2,993	− 3,587	0.9†	0.6†
1939........	3,586	2,458	1.1	0.7
1940........	12,002	9,675	3.6	2.9
1941........	21,248	14,942	6.3	4.5
1942........	33,283	20,441	9.6	5.9
1943........	39,805	23,136	11.0	6.4
1944........	38,788	23,637	10.2	6.2

* Figures adjusted to exclude excess depreciation.
† 1936–39 average.

COST STRUCTURE

The OPA collected statistics of operating data for the period 1939–45, as shown in Table 9. An analysis of the figures indicates that between 1940 and 1945, labor costs per ton increased by 58.8 per cent, total costs by 52.6 per cent, realization by 61.1 per cent and margin by 133.1 per cent.

TABLE 9

OPERATING DATA

(Per Ton)

Year	Labor Costs	Total Costs	Realization	Margin
1939........	$1.1291	$1.9321	$1.8450	$−0.0871
1940........	1.1034	1.8953	1.9080	+0.0127
1941......	1.2350	2.1110	2.1890	+0.0780
1942........	1.3270	2.2472	2.3711	+0.1239
1943*.......	1.4895	2.4987	2.7062	+0.2075
1944*.......	1.6666	2.7126	2.9364	+0.3238
1945*.......	1.7517	2.8916	3.0733	+0.1818

* Cost data for 1943, 1944, and 1945 have been adjusted to exclude excess depreciation. The retroactive portal pay included in 1944 costs has been shifted back to 1943 when the liability was incurred.

In view of the large increase in labor costs, it is interesting to note that over the 7-year period an average of 59 per cent of total costs was attributable to labor costs.

PRODUCTION AND MECHANIZATION

As was earlier pointed out, the production of coal between the two world wars, although quite variable, tended to decline—but to a smaller extent than employment. (See Tables 1 and 4.) The largest amount of coal produced in any one year before 1944 was 579 million tons in 1918. This volume of production was almost equaled in 1926, with an output of 573 million tons. In 1944 production reached a peak of 620 million tons.

Yet the average number of wage-earners employed in that year was only 354,000, in contrast to 542,000 in 1926. Thus,

TABLE 10

INDEX OF AVERAGE OUTPUT*

(1939 = 100)

Year	Output per Wage-Earner	Output per Man-Hour
1935	80.3	82.4
1936	91.7	86.3
1937	90.7	88.1
1938	80.6	92.9
1939	100.0	100.0
1940	104.1	103.9
1941	118.7	105.8
1942	125.6	107.1
1943	143.5	106.8
1944	164.3	116.0
1945	167.9	119.6

* Bureau of Labor Statistics, *Productivity and Unit Labor Costs in Selected Mining Industries, 1935–1945*, p. 2.

production in 1944 was 8 per cent larger than in 1926, and average employment was 35 per cent smaller. Between 1940 and 1944 production increased by 34.5 per cent, but this increase was accompanied by an actual reduction of about 14.7 per cent in average employment. These trends may be explained in part by the lengthened work week and in part by a rise in productivity or output per man-hour.

The Bureau of Labor Statistics productivity series (see Table 10) for the bituminous coal industry shows that between 1935 and 1945, output per man-hour increased by 45.1 per cent, output per wage-earner by 109.1 per cent. Between 1940 and 1945, output per man-hour increased 15.1 per cent, output per wage-earner 61.3 per cent.

This increased productivity is largely explained by the extensive mechanization of bituminous coal mines. Mechanization of the mines continued during the war period, despite the war's demands for materials used in manufacturing necessary equipment. This would seem to indicate that more rapid mechanization can be predicted in the present postwar period. Table 11 shows the influence of increased mechanization on production.

TABLE 11

Mechanization, 1936–44

Year	Percentage of Underground Production		Percentage of Total Production Mechanically Cleaned
	Cut by Machine	Mechanically Loaded	
1936.........	84.8	16.3	13.9
1937.........	...	20.2	14.6
1938.........	87.5	26.7	18.2
1939.........	87.9	31.0	20.1
1940.........	88.4	·35.4	22.2
1941.........	89.0	40.7	22.9
1942.........	89.7	45.2	24.4
1943.........	90.3	48.9	24.7
1944.........	90.5	52.9	25.6

Source: *Minerals Yearbook, 1944*, pp. 842–43, *Minerals Yearbook 1945*, p. 852.

QUESTIONS

1. What policies should the bituminous coal industry develop toward competitive fuels? What part should the union play in any program?

2. What action would you expect this industry and Union to take toward the expansion of hydroelectric power?

3. What procedures would you advocate to determine the "public interest" in this area of competitive fuels? How would you implement any policy?

4. In the light of the long-run position of the industry, what policies would you advocate for the Union with regard to mechanization, the level of wage rates, and the entrance of new miners?

5. How would you analyze the effects of a further wage increase in this industry?

6. How are tonnage rates set among various mines? With mines of various widths of seams and ease of mining operations the Union is presented with a dilemma. Equal tonnage rates would result in very unequal earnings among miners in different mines although labor costs per ton would be equal. If earnings are equalized, then tonnage rates and labor costs are higher in the less favorably situated mines.

SUGGESTIONS FOR FURTHER READING

BUREAU OF LABOR STATISTICS. "The Changing Status of Bituminous Coal Miners, 1937–46," *Monthly Labor Review*, August, 1946, pp. 164–73.

BUREAU OF LABOR STATISTICS. *Productivity and Unit Labor Cost in Selected Mining Industries*. Washington, D.C., June, 1946.

BUREAU OF LABOR STATISTICS. *Wage Structure of Bituminous Coal Mines*. Washington, D.C., Fall, 1945.

FISHER WALDO E. "Bituminous Coal," *How Collective Bargaining Works*, pp. 229–79. New York: Twentieth Century Fund, 1942.

National Bituminous Wage Agreement, April, 1945.

NATIONAL LABOR RELATIONS BOARD. *Written Trade Agreements in Collective Bargaining*, pp. 93–114. Bulletin No. 4 (November, 1939).

NATIONAL WAR LABOR BOARD. *Report of the Panel in the Bituminous Coal Dispute, May 21, 1943*.

NATIONAL WAR LABOR BOARD. *Report on Wages and Related Problems in the Bituminous Coal Industry, April 28, 1943*.

U.S. DEPARTMENT OF THE INTERIOR. *Minerals Yearbook, 1944*, pp. 823–908. Washington, D.C.: 1946.

Section I

MISCELLANEOUS CASES

CASES 64–66
THE USE OF COMPANY BULLETIN BOARDS

CASE 64

Early in July, 1944, the officers of the Textile Workers Union, Local 140, submitted to the manager of one of the mills of a large woolen company the following notice:

Textile Workers Union
on   T.W.U.A.
The Air   C.I.O.
                      on the
                      air!

Emil Rieve
President TWUA

on Program "Labor Speaks"

Help Bring This Important Message to Our Members and the General Public

1. Copy this leaflet and distribute
2. Post on bulletin boards
3. Take an ad in your local newspaper

This notice was submitted in accordance with Article X of the agreement between the Company and the Textile Workers Union, dated February 22, 1943. This article reads as follows:

ARTICLE X
Bulletin Boards

"The employer will provide an adequate number of bulletin boards for the convenience of the union in posting official union notices, which shall be submitted to the mill manager before posting."

The manager declined to permit the posting of the notice on the ground that it was not an "official" union notice within the meaning of Article X.

Both sides agreed that a notice to be "official" within the meaning of the contract must come from the proper officers of the Union. It was agreed here that the notice had fulfilled this condition.

The Company held, however, that in order for a notice to be an "official" notice under the contract it must be one that pertains to matters that would be of concern to the Union in its relationship with the Company, and in particular, with the relationship between the parties under the agreement as expressed in the preamble.

The Union claimed that the sole test of whether or not a notice is "official" within the meaning of Article X is whether or not it comes from the proper officials of the Union. The content of the notice has nothing to do with determining its "official" character, the Union claimed. The purpose of Article X, according to this view, is to prevent unauthorized individuals from posting notices in the name of the Union.

CASE 65

Local 390 of the Textile Workers Union of America complained that the Branch River Wool Combing Company denied it the use of the bulletin board for union announcements which included a notice suggesting that the members tune in to radio broadcasts pertaining to the CIO program. The Company also forbade the posting of notices from the Textile Workers Union international office.

The Union based its claim on Article XVIII of the contract providing that: "The union shall have the use of department Bulletin Board in the mill for the purpose of posting union notices."

Accordingly, any notice, the Union stated, that it desires to post is a union notice and the Company should not deprive the Union of this right granted under the contract.

The Company contended that this clause was intended only to be used for union notices in the strict sense, notices limited to union meetings or other announcements confined to Local 390. It was not intended, the Company claimed, for use in posting notices involving controversial matters such as partisan politics, religious questions, or general questions not directly connected with production and personnel problems of the mill.

Testimony revealed that Union and Company had not discussed their respective intentions concerning the use of the bulletin board, and that there was no specific agreement as to the meaning of the term "union notices."

The Union urged that union activities at present included active participation in political matters as well as strictly economic matters affecting the local membership.

It is emphasized that in a great many contracts the posting of notices is accompanied by limitation wherein the Company reserves the right to approve notices before they can be posted. In this contract, however, no such condition was stipulated.

The term "union" was held to include the international union and the CIO, since the TWUA, CIO, was a party to the contract.

CASE 66

During July, 1946, the Retail, Wholesale and Department Store Employees of America, Local 13, was conducting a strike at the Atlas Dry Goods Company in Columbus, Ohio. In an effort to bolster the strength of the small unit at this store, the Union sent out a call for aid on the picket line to other units of the Local. One of these requests was received by the unit at the Schwab-Karnow Company in Columbus. The local bargaining committee then posted a notice on the bulletin board provided by the Company, calling for volunteers to serve on the Atlas Company picket line. The notice which originated at the local union office read: "Atlas Co. Employees Need Your Help. The Picket Line at Atlas needs support from other units. 10 Schwab-Karnow members are asked to volunteer for picket duty. Report to your local committee. Check in at the union office tomorrow morning at 9 o'clock."

The notice was read by most of the employees, and subsquently ten employees were absent from work the next day while they participated in the picketing of the competitor company. The Schwab-Karnow Company protested to the Union on the same day and itself removed the notice in question.

The Union claimed that it had the right under the contract to post such a notice and demanded that the Company restore the notice to the bulletin board. The Company, after reiterating an old complaint about absenteeism and asserting that every available employee was needed on the job at this time, refused to replace the notice. The Union brought the matter to a grievance.

The Union argued that the contract permitted it to post this notice. It referred to Article XI, Section 1 of the agreement which reads: "The Union shall have the right to post Union notices on the bulletin board which carry the imprint of Local 13 of the U.R.W.D.S.E.A. and are official union notices."

The Union claimed that all requirements of the contract with respect to this notice had been met.

The Company argued its case on the basis of two points in the contract. First, it cited Article X, "Management," which reads:

"The Management of the Company, including but not limited to the establishment of rules not in conflict with this agreement, *the direction of the working forces* (emphasis by the Company), the right to hire, promote, suspend or discharge for cause, the right to relieve employees from duty because of lack of work or for other just reasons, and to transfer employees from one department to another, is vested exclusively in the Company. This authority will not be used for purposes of discrimination against any employee."

The Company called special attention to its exclusive right to direct the working forces. In addition, the Company claimed that Section 3 of Article XI expressly forbade this action by the Union. The section reads:

"The Union agrees that during the term of this agreement there shall be no strikes, slow-ups, stoppage of work, or *any other form of Union interference with the business or employees of the Company* (emphasis by the Company) and the Company agrees that there shall be no lock-outs, nor shall there be any discrimination because of Union membership."

The Company maintained that the posting of this notice constituted a "form of union interference" in violation of the contract. The Union countered with the statement that Section 3 had not been intended to cover legitimate strike activity at the plant of another company, and asserted that at times they were forced to place the exigencies of union strategy before concern for the company's welfare.

QUESTIONS

1. What distinguishes "official" notices from other notices?
2. Is any notice an "official" notice which is issued by the officers of the Union in their capacity as officers?
3. Must an "official" notice pertain to matters which concern the Union in its relations with the Company? Must it pertain to union business of some kind?

4. Is there a difference between an "official" notice and a "union notice"?

5. What is meant by the phrase: "The union shall have the use of the Department Bulletin Board . . . ."? Does this give use of the bulletin board to any member of the Union?

6. In the case of the Schwab-Karnow Company was the notice posted a "union notice"? Did the agreement between the Company and the Union give the Union the right to post *any* notice pertaining to the affairs or business of the Union regardless of the content of the notice? Might the Union post a notice asking all employees to strike in violation of the agreement?

7. Did the contents of the union notice in the Schwab-Karnow Company case violate the union's obligations under its agreement with the Company? Was the notice an "interference" with the business or the employees of the Company? If the Union might ask for ten pickets, might it ask for fifty? Might it ask *all* employees of the Company to absent themselves for picket duty? Would the Union be within its rights if it asked only a "reasonable" number of employees to be absent for picket duty?

8. Assume that the contents of the notice posted by the Union in the Schwab-Karnow case were a violation of the union's obligation under the agreement. What would be the proper procedure for the Company to pursue? Was the Company within its rights in removing the notice?

CASE 67

ELIGIBILITY FOR HOLIDAY PAY

UNION: United Furniture Workers of America, CIO

COMPANY: Steinway & Sons

The present case concerns a Union claim that 18 employees were denied holiday pay for Washington's Birthday, February 22, 1947, in violation of the contract between the parties. The pertinent section of the contract (Article XV) provides in part as follows:

"The following shall be holidays during the term for which employees shall be paid, without working, at the employee's then regular hourly rate for 8 hours; Thanksgiving Day, 1945 and 1946; Christmas Day, 1945 and 1946; New Year's Day, 1946 and 1947; Washington's Birthday, 1946 and 1947; Independence Day, 1946 and 1947; Election Day 1946; provided that the employee works his regular shift on the regular work days immediately preceding and following the holiday, unless prevented from working because within 2 months immediately preceding the holiday date, he was either bona fide ill or laid off."

On Friday, February 21, 1947, the regular workday immediately preceding the holiday in question, a snow storm of blizzard proportions struck the New York metropolitan area, in which the company's plant and the residences of the employees involved are situated. Normal means of transportation to the plant were disrupted, and many employees were unable to get to work on that day. The Union is of the position that this failure to appear at work on the day prior to the holiday should not make the employees ineligible for holiday benefits. The Company holds that the agreement clearly spells out the conditions of eligibility for holiday payment. The 18 employees involved in this case cannot meet these requirements and hence are ineligible.

POSITION OF THE UNION

The Union contends that the failure of the 18 employees involved to report for work on February 21, 1947, was due to conditions beyond their control. The extremely bad weather conditions adversely affected the health of many of them; yet all of these employees made reasonable efforts to get to work but were unsuccessful. Since the failure of these employees to work was not intentional or willful, the Union argues that they should not be penalized by a denial of holiday benefits due them under the contract. The Union further claims that it was not intended by the parties that the conditions precedent in the contract, entitling employees to holiday benefits, were to be applicable to a situation or to circumstances present in this case.

POSITION OF THE COMPANY

The Company concedes that the failure of the 18 employees to report for work on the day preceding the holiday was not willful nor intentional and was attributable to the adverse weather conditions prevailing that day. The Company, however, contends that the contract between the parties specifically sets forth the conditions under which employees shall receive the holiday benefits, and that unless these conditions are met, irrespective of the reason, or unless the employees fall within the stated exceptions, they are not entitled to the holiday benefits. The Company further claims that even though the circumstances present in this case are unusual, it was the intention of the parties to avoid the acceptance of excuses that led them to put in the restrictions in the holiday provision. The Company frankly concedes that if any of the employees involved were genuinely ill on the preceding day, they fall within one of the stated exceptions and would be entitled to the holiday pay. However, the Company insists that to extend the contract provision to include a further exception of "special circumstances" as is requested by the Union would be contrary to the intentions of the parties and is beyond the authority of the arbitrator.

QUESTIONS

1. What standards can be applied to this type of a case?
2. What is the function of the arbitration process in these circumstances?
3. What is the purpose of the limitations on holiday pay included in Article XV of the contract?
4. How would you decide this case?

CASE 68

UNION REQUEST FOR A COPY OF A GROUP INSURANCE POLICY

UNION: Textile Workers Union of America, CIO

COMPANY: New Bedford Cotton Manufacturers' Association

Under Article III of the agreement between the parties, the member mills agree to procure and maintain in force an insurance policy providing certain benefits for their employees. Following a general outline of the benefits to be provided, these statements appear:

"It is understood that the member mills will not operate this insurance benefit plan themselves, but will obtain a policy from a reputable and established insurance company, which will administer the benefits described above. These benefits will be subject to such conditions and limitations as standard practice in the insurance business prescribes. New employees shall become eligible for these benefits after such period of time following their employment as prescribed in ordinary group policies of this type."

The Union contends that it has been refused a copy of the policy issued to the mills and requests that the Association be required to furnish a copy. The Association holds that nothing in the agreement requires it to furnish a copy of the policy. The issue has been submitted to an arbitrator for this decision.

POSITION OF THE UNION

The Union argues that as bargaining agent for employees of the Association it has a right to know the details of any policy which affects its members. It holds that it would be at a disadvantage in negotiation or discussion of questions arising under Article III if it were kept in ignorance of matters affecting the benefits available to employees. In the opinion of the Union, a reasonable interpretation of Article III, as a part of a collective bargaining agreement, would seem to indicate that the Union should be fully informed on such matters, particularly in view of the references to "standard" and "ordinary" practices.

Further, the Union holds that in the absence of a copy of the policy, disagreements will arise as to coverage. In fact, the mere refusal by the Company to furnish a copy of the policy is said to create an atmosphere of suspicion among the employees "that there is something wrong." The Union insists that the certificate and bulletins furnished to employees give only limited information. It is held that additional conditions with respect to the receipt of benefits are included in the master policy, and the Union and the employees are less than fully informed when they are not made aware of these additional conditions.

Position of the Company

The Association agrees that there is nothing in the wording of Article III which requires that a copy of the master agreement between the mills and the insurance companies be furnished to the Union. It holds that each employee is provided with a booklet and with certificates in which the details of the plan are fully set forth. The terms of the master policy relating to such conditions would serve merely to confirm this fact. However, the Association maintains that such data in the master policy as relate to costs and rates, to the financial arrangements between the mills and the insurance companies, are confidential matters. The Association argues that disclosure of such information might prove detrimental to the interests of its members, and further, that nothing in the agreement can be interpreted so as to require such data to be submitted to the Union.

QUESTIONS

1. For what purpose does the Union desire a copy of the policy issued to the mills?

2. What use could the Union make of the information contained in such a policy?

3. When the Association says that disclosure might prove detrimental to the interests of its members, what specifically do you suppose it means?

4. What principles should govern questions which are not covered in the agreement? Does the absence of an affirmative right to the policy in the contract create a presumption against the union's demand?

5. How do you appraise the position of the Association? Does it have a right to withhold the information? Is it wise in so doing?

CASE 69

IS THE DEMAND FOR A HEALTH AND WELFARE FUND A DEMAND FOR WAGES?

UNION: Hotel and Restaurant Employees' International Alliance and Bartenders' International League of America, AFL

COMPANY: United Restaurant and Liquor Dealers of Manhattan, Inc.

On December 21, 1945, the Association and the Union entered into a five-year collective bargaining agreement. Paragraph 20 of said agreement provides in part as follows:

Reopening Provision

"20. This contract shall continue in existence for 5 years from date of formal agreement, but wages and working conditions set forth in paragraphs 6, 7, 8 and 9 may be the subject of negotiations each year upon 30 days' notice by either party prior to the annual termination date."

Paragraph 6 of the agreement establishes the number of hours to be included in the workday and the regular work week. Paragraph 7 of the agreement establishes a minimum weekly salary, provides for overtime at the rate of time and a half, and fixes the minimum rate to be paid to extra bartenders. It also provides that wages shall be paid in cash at the end of each week's employment. Paragraph 8 of the agreement establishes a vacation schedule. Paragraph 9 refers to holiday pay.

Pursuant to the provisions of Paragraph 20, and within the period therein allowed, the Union reopened the agreement. Included in the demands made by the Union was a request for the creation of a health and welfare fund for the benefit of its members to be financed by contribution by members of the Association equal to 5 per cent of their respective payrolls. Agreement was reached by the parties on all of the demands raised by the Union with the exception of the demand for a health and welfare fund. The parties agree to submit this demand to an arbitrator for his decision.

Position of the Union

The Union argues that the language of Paragraph 20 is ambiguous and that it was the intent of the parties, in framing the clause, to include in the annual discussions all "bread-and-butter" matters. It states that in executing a five-year agreement, the parties intended only to fix, for that period, the union shop and the unlimited right of the employer to discharge any bartender. Therefore, it contends that any matters relating to compensation, including its demand for a health and welfare fund, may properly be raised by the Union, as a matter of right, in the annual negotiations.

The union counsel, who participated in the negotiations leading to the agreement of December 21, 1945, stated that the original contract presented by the Association to the Union did not contain the reference to Paragraphs 6, 7, 8, and 9 in the reopening clause but only stated that wages and working conditions might be reopened each year. This clause was accepted by the Union in the course of the negotiations. When oral agreement had been reached on all of the issues, counsel for the Association drafted the final agreement and inserted the reference to paragraphs 6, 7, 8, and 9 in Paragraph 20 and submitted the same to counsel for the Union. The union counsel made some minor changes in this draft and redrew the agreement but made no change in Paragraph 20, which now included the reference to Paragraphs 6, 7, 8, and 9. The agreement as thus drawn was signed by the parties. The Union insists that no discussion was had during the negotiations of any limitation on its right to reopen annually all so-called "bread-and-butter" clauses. It argues that the insertion of the reference to Paragraphs 6, 7, 8, and 9 was not intended to alter the basic agreement between the parties that wages and working conditions might be renegotiated each year.

Lastly, the Union points out that counsel for both sides in the negotiations were members of the New York Regional War Labor Board, and the term "wages," as used in the agreement, was used in the sense in which it was interpreted during the war by the NWLB and the Director of Economic Stabilization, to include payments by an employer to a health and welfare fund.

Position of the Company

The Association contends that the reopening clause is not ambiguous but is specific and precise; that it does not permit the raising in the annual negotiations, as a matter of right, of the issue of a health and welfare fund; that such a demand does not come within the scope of any of the subjects dealt with in Paragraphs 6, 7, 8, and 9 of the principal agreement, which are the only subjects expressly specified for annual renegotiation. It also argues that contributions to a welfare fund are not wages since they are not paid to the workers, and that they are not considered wages under the provisions of the Internal Revenue Code, the Fair Labor Standards Act, or the regulations of the Director of Economic Stabilization in effect during the war.

The Association is of the opinion that the addition of the words of limitation in Paragraph 20 at the conclusion of the negotiations between the parties indicated their intent to limit the subjects of renegotiation. It holds that the interpretation of counsel for the Union finds no support in the language of the agreement or the history of the negotiations. It further points out that Paragraphs 6, 7, 8, and 9 do not include all of the "bread-and-butter" clauses in the agreement. Thus, Paragraph 13 requires the employer to supply all bartenders one warm meal a day; and Paragraph 14 requires the employer to furnish and launder uniforms, coats, and aprons at its expense. Finally, the Association points to the language of the supplemental agreement of January 23, 1947, wherein the parties referred to the fact that only Paragraphs 6, 7, 8, and 9 might be reopened. It concludes by stating that the stability of the relationship between the parties requires that the union's request be denied and that any other determination would destroy the integrity of the collective bargaining agreement.

QUESTIONS

1. To what extent is the history of negotiations to be used as a basis for deciding a case in the face of explicit contract language? Does it make any difference whether the specific point was dismissed in the negotiations?
2. What is the issue in arbitration? Is it the demand for a pension on its merits or the arbitrability of the demand for a health and welfare plan?
3. Would a strike for a health and welfare fund under the circumstances of this case constitute a contract violation?
4. As a matter of union policy, is there any way in which the Union could reinstate its demand if the arbitrator decided against the Union?

CASE 70

THE POSITION OF A SINGLE LOCAL UNION UNDER INDUSTRY-WIDE BARGAINING

UNION: Pacific Coast Pulp & Papermill Employees' Association

COMPANY: Pacific Coast Association of Pulp and Paper Manufacturers

PROBLEM

This is a case of union administration and self-government and is concerned with the operations of a labor agreement applicable to a number of plants and local unions. It poses the question of whether all local unions must be bound by a contract signed by a majority of the locals within that international.

BACKGROUND

Since 1934, collective bargaining agreements in the Pacific coast pulp and paper industry have been negotiated in joint conferences of employer and employee associations.[1] The Pacific Coast Association of Pulp and Paper Manufacturers acts as bargaining agent for the employers; and the Pacific Coast Pulp & Papermill Employees' Association constitutes the bargaining agent, legalized by the National Labor Relations Board, for a unit composed of thirty-eight local unions, which are affiliated with two international unions (AFL)—the International Brotherhood of Paper Makers and the International Brotherhood of Pulp, Sulphite and Paper Mill Workers.

The employers' Association normally holds its annual convention just prior to negotiations with the unions and there formulates its policy on labor relations and elects a negotiating committee of eight members, who meet directly with the negotiating committee of the unions. This employer committee is empowered to make the necessary commitments and concessions on behalf of the various employers, but the final draft of the tentative agreement must be referred to the Association, sitting as a body, for approval. A majority approval by the representatives of the various mills binds all the companies to an acceptance of the terms of the agreement.

[1] See Clark Kerr and Roger Randall, *Causes of Industrial Peace, Case Studies 1,* Washington, D.C., National Planning Association, 1948.

The Employees' Association is a regional co-ordinating body of the affiliated locals of the Pulp and Sulphite, and the Paper Makers' international unions on the West coast. The internal structure of the Association has been influenced by certain regional differences in the industry on the West coast and by the desire of local unions to exploit the differing wage-paying abilities of coast-wide employers. This led in 1938 to the formation of three state committees among the Pulp and Sulphite locals on the West coast, and to the formation of a Paper Makers' council embracing the Paper Makers' locals in the three coast states. Thus, the Association is actually a federation of the three Pulp and Sulphite state committees and the Pacific Coast Paper Makers' council rather than a federation directly of the affiliated locals.

The convention selects the important bargaining committee composed of eight members with equal representation from the two international unions. Each state committee selects one member; one member is elected at large by the Pulp and Sulphite delegates; and the Paper Makers' council elects the remaining four from among its delegates. This committee, along with officers and representatives of the two international unions, meets with the employers' committee and is empowered to present the workers' proposals and make the necessary compromises to arrive at an agreement. The international officers usually lead the negotiations, but they cannot commit the committee representing the local unions to any position without its agreement. However, the international officers exert considerable influence since they must approve and sign the agreement on behalf of the international unions.

The tentative agreement arrived at in negotiations is referred back to the employees' association convention for a vote of approval and then to the membership of each local for a referendum vote. Neither the employers' nor employees' association signs the resulting agreement as a principal; both serve merely as agents to facilitate the actual negotiations. The net result is a number of uniform local contracts simultaneously negotiated in a single bargaining conference—with each local union signing separately with its respective firm as employer.

STATEMENT OF FACTS

In the joint conference which took place in December, 1945, all the employers and a majority of the union locals (37 out of 38) agreed to a provision whereby paper machines would be operated on seven days per week in exchange for a 15 per cent increase in wages. During the course of the negotiations one of the union locals, Port Angeles Local 269, of the Paper Makers' Union, indicated its disapproval of the contract change and questioned its obligation to be bound by the agreement reached at the joint conference. The other locals indicated that Port Angeles would have to accept the majority decision. (See below for elaboration of this position.)

The proposals arrived at by the bargaining unit in December, 1945, were subsequently submitted to the local unions for their ratification through a referendum vote. All of the locals —with the exception of Local 269 at Port Angeles—voted for acceptance of the agreement. Local 269 rejected the proposals and refused to carry out the commitments made on its behalf by the collective bargaining unit.

POSITION OF LOCAL 269

Local 269 rejected the proposals on the ground that its constitutional rights were being set aside by the bargaining unit. The local union contended that the seven-day clause was contrary to both the letter and spirit of the union constitution and referred to the General Laws of the Constitution, Article I, Section 2, which reads as follows: "We endorse the 6-hour day and the 5-day week and whenever practicable shall endeavor to bring this change about."

This local further argued that it had a right to determine for itself under its own charter whether or not its members would operate the paper machines. It protested the attempt of any other agency to decide this issue.

POSITION OF THE OTHER LOCALS

The other locals held that Local 269 was bound by the union constitution to abide by the majority decision and to accept the terms of contract on which the majority had agreed. They stressed not only the constitutional obligation but also the moral obligation of each union to follow the established bargaining procedure in order to continue harmonious bargaining relations with the employer association. The provisions of the constitution relating to the signing of agreements read in part as follows:

"Section 1. In order to bring about understanding and to promote harmonious relations between the International Union, subordinate Unions and the employers in the paper industry, and to bring about a feeling of mutual responsibility in developing uniformity of wages, hours, and working conditions within the industry, and in all other matters concerning the interest of all parties, it is the policy of the International Union and the affiliated subordinate Unions to negotiate and sign agreements covering wages and working conditions under which our members will work. In carrying out these agreements it is the policy of the International Union, subordinate Unions, and members, to religiously abide by the rules and regulations set forth in the agreement, and it is the duty of all subordinate unions to exercise the necessary control over its members so that all agreements will be carried out in a spirit of mutual understanding and responsibility. . . . .

"Section 2a. No subordinate Union shall sign any agreement affecting the interests of the International Union, subordinate Unions or members of the subordinate Unions without first receiving the consent of the International President.

"Section 3. The International Union shall not have the power, through any of its officers or representatives, to sign with any employer, any agreement on labor contract relative to changing hours of labor, wages or conditions, or to renew existing contracts, without the consent of the subordinate Union affected; except where interlocking interests of subordinate Unions are involved, the majority of these shall decide under what terms the contract shall be signed."

REBUTTAL OF LOCAL 269

In reply to the argument of the other thirty-seven locals regarding the obligation to abide by a majority decision, Local 269 maintained that the provisions in the constitution relating to agreements applied only to agreements with an *individual employer* and did not apply where a *group of employers* were involved as in the present case. It called attention to the phrase in Section 3 (quoted in full above) "to sign with *any employer*" as validating its stand on the applicability of the provision only where individual employers are concerned.

FURTHER DEVELOPMENTS

Despite the disagreement, the contract was consummated and signed by all the local unions within the bargaining unit, including Local 269. The claim of Local 269 on its right to be bound was permitted by the signatory parties to remain in doubtful status during the period from December 22, 1945 to May 1, 1946, at which time the employer association served notice upon the President of the International Union that it reserved the right under Section 26 of the current contract to terminate the agreement at its expiration date unless this question was cleared up satisfactorily before June 1, 1946 (expiration date). The relevant part of Section 26 of the contract reads as follows: "In case negotiations . . . break down, either party may terminate this agreement upon the expiration of 10 days notice in writing, mailed by registered mail, to the other party."

In an attempt to arrive at a satisfactory settlement of the question, the local unions in the bargaining unit, including

Local 269, tried to negotiate between themselves and with the employers in their unit. There is some indication that settlement of the question was hampered by the influence of rival unionism and a secession movement within Local 269. This is implied in a statement made by the International President at a meeting of Local 269 on May 1, 1946. At that time, he indicated that if the members of Local 269 were to take any affirmative step by way of seceding from the over-all group, nothing in the contract could be so construed as to prevent them from exercising their individual rights. He called attention, however, to a 1943 NLRB decision wherein the AFL unions had defeated a CIO attempt to organize the Rayonies Corporation. The NLRB had then decided that a single employer unit was not an appropriate bargaining unit within the ranks of the association, and the President warned that the secession of Local 269 would make it, too, an inappropriate unit and place it in a "twilight zone" so far as collective bargaining was concerned.

Inasmuch as the question revolved around a provision in the constitution of the International Brotherhood of Paper Makers and inasmuch as Local 269 was unable to resolve the difficulty by itself, the issue was brought to the International President for his interpretation and ruling. The President had two alternatives: (1) either to require the new contract to be consummated and its commitments fulfilled, or (2) to permit Local 269 to steer an independent course and thus allow the existing multiple bargaining unit to go by the board.

DECISION

The President ruled that the Port Angeles Local 269 or any other local union in the International Brotherhood of Paper Makers within the bargaining unit was controlled and bound by the decision of the majority of the local unions comprising that bargaining unit. In making his decision, the President indicated that he was influenced by the following considerations:

1. Under the union setup as represented in the Pacific

Coast Employees Association, all participants were collectively responsible for the workings of the organization.

2. The Constitution of the International Brotherhood of Paper Makers provided for multiple local unions negotiating and consummating agreements with single employer units, the majority of local unions in the group deciding the issues or questions with respect to signing an agreement with that employer and/or, where the employer's interest was joined with competing employers, a majority of the members voting in each of the locals involved determining the position of the local union on all questions involving the agreement.

This statement indicates that the President interpreted the phrase in Section 3, "to sign with *any employer*," as signifying *any employer bargaining unit*, whether that unit includes one or more employers.

3. All questions on wages, hours, and conditions of employment would have to be decided by a majority of the local unions in the bargaining unit, else the purpose of collective bargaining would be defeated and confusion and deadlock would result.

4. The locals in joining their interests and in bargaining as a unit with the employers had increased their strength. To separate their interest would be to weaken their bargaining position.

5. It would be unfair to the local unions of the Pulp Workers for the International Brotherhood to exercise veto power over the bargaining unit because of the position of one local. According to the provision of the constitution, a majority of the locals, both Paper Makers and Pulp Workers together, could exercise the veto power at the expiration date of any contract in any year. This was felt to be a sufficient safeguard against any possible attempt to regiment the local unions and tie them to conditions which were not acceptable to them.

QUESTIONS

1. Would you agree with the President's decision in this case?

2. Is it in the interest of industrial democracy to permit a union to

be used to force on workers a bargain which they do not wish to accept? Is it desirable that the terms of bargains be adapted as far as possible to variations in conditions and to variations in the preferences of different groups of workers?

3. If Local 269 were successful in keeping out seven-day operations from its plant, would it be a competitive menace to the other locals? Or would the employer of Local 269 be placed at a handicap in competition with other employers? Should the President of the Paper Makers' Union take these questions into consideration in making his decision?

4. What advantages does the Union derive from bargaining simultaneously with all employers for uniform conditions? Could the regional bargaining unit be maintained if any local were permitted to withdraw whenever it so desired?

5. If Local 269 were to withdraw from the Paper Makers' Union, would it lose its bargaining rights? Would it be entitled to representation in the Pacific Coast Employees' Association even if it were not affiliated with the Paper Makers' Union? May a group of men required to be represented by a bargaining agency which denies them representation? May their right to be represented in a bargaining agency be predicated upon their willingness to affiliate with a certain union?

Index

INDEX